"With a clear and direct language, Marc Aixalà immerses us in ancient and modern psychedelic research, therapeutic practice, and their spiritual dimensions, opening new horizons in the field of 'skillful integration' and giving us an innovative vision anchored in therapeutic traditions and psychedelic lineages alike."

— Chris Timmermann, PhD, Centre for Psychedelic Research,
   Imperial College London

"*Psychedelic Integration* gives us efficient and replicable frameworks and structures aimed at helping people ground their exciting, intra-psychic, interpersonal, or transcendental insights into the less glamorous, mundane dimensions of ordinary life. This book is a wonderful, elaborate, and heart-based blueprint for those of us who are at the service of helping each other make sense and create meaning out of our non-ordinary journeys so we can induce long-lasting positive changes in our lives, our communities, and the world at large."

— Adam Aronovich, PhD Cand, Director of Therapy and Integration at Rē Precision
   Health, and Ayahuasca Community Committee at Chacruna

"*Psychedelic Integration* shows the importance of an integration process for facilitating the transition from the psychedelic experience to deep, long-term, and sustainable change. This book is an essential read for anyone who is, or aspires to become, a psychedelic therapist or integration provider."

— Ido Cohen, PsyD, Founder of The Integration Circle

"Marc Aixalà's dynamic model for psychedelic integration gathers insights from Indigenous and spiritual traditions and Western psychology alike, inspiring therapists from different schools, facilitators from multiple traditions, and anyone interested in psychedelic therapy, regardless of their background."

— Bia Labate, PhD, Executive Director of Chacruna Institute for Psychedelic
   Plant Medicines

"*Psychedelic Integration* is an important contribution in an evolving field of specialism that offers a necessary framework for supporting experiences in expanded states. This book will accompany many practitioners as they support people on their journey into the deep."

— Maria Papaspyrou, Co-founder, Institute of Psychedelic Therapy & Co-Author,
   Psychedelics & Psychotherapy: The Healing Potential of Expanded States

PSYCHEDELIC INTEGRATION

PSYCHEDELIC INTEGRATION

*PSYCHOTHERAPY FOR NON-ORDINARY
STATES OF CONSCIOUSNESS*

MARC B. AIXALÀ

FOREWORD BY JOSÉ CARLOS BOUSO, PHD

SYNERGETIC PRESS
SANTA FE • LONDON

Published by Synergetic Press | 1 Blue Bird Ct. Santa Fe, NM 87508
& 24 Old Gloucester St. London, WCIN 3AL, England

Library of Congress Control Number: 2022937350

ISBN 9780907791393 (paperback)
ISBN 9780907791584 (ebook)

Cover design by Amanda Müller
Book design by David Good
Managing Editor: Amanda Müller
Project Editor: Noelle Armstrong
Printed in the USA

To my parents, Carlos and Maria Isabel,
for their unconditional support.

And to my grandfather, Rafel Aixalà,
a man of integrity.

CONTENTS

FOREWORD

In the April 2010 issue of *Playboy*, the American adult entertainment magazine, Steven Kotler published an article titled: "The New Psychedelic Renaissance." The article began with the story of Mara, a 33-year-old woman who was diagnosed with terminal colon cancer a year earlier, a very unusual medical situation for someone so young. Mara was about to take 110 mg of MDMA in an underground session, hoping to work on the emotional situation she faced at the end of her life. The article echoed the therapeutic work with hallucinogens (we will discuss this term later) that had been done by underground therapists for the previous forty years, ever since these substances were classified as dangerous drugs and their use was banned. Likewise, the text also illustrated instances of LSD and psilocybin underground therapy, and no less importantly, it communicated to a general public how therapeutic research with these substances had returned, after forty years, to the domain of scientific research authorized by governments—in this case, in North America.

The studies carried out by MAPS (Multidisciplinary Association for Psychedelic Studies) with MDMA—the drug popularly known as "ecstasy"—for the treatment of post-traumatic stress disorder (PTSD) were already underway, as was the research with psilocybin studying its mysticomimetic potential, which could address the existential anguish suffered by people who were at the end of their lives. It could also serve people who wanted to abandon drug dependence, including alcohol and tobacco. After forty years of prohibition and being ostracized by the scientific establishment, even as they were still being used in recreational contexts or in underground therapies, these substances were coming back, with renewed interest, to the field of therapeutic research. The *Playboy* article spread like wildfire among the psychedelic community because it framed these substances outside of their countercultural label, restoring their epistemic dignity: the knowledge they offer to the initiate provides not only therapeutic transformation, but also ontological and therefore existential meaning. The "Psychedelic Renaissance" has since become a meme that has been used by numerous authors, whether they are writing informative articles, academic papers, or books (almost never citing the original source of the expression). In that same month, April of 2010, the first Psychedelic Science conference was organized by MAPS, the non-profit foundation with a public benefit orientation that was promoting the development of MDMA as a medicine. The conference was attended by the main psychedelic researchers of the moment and more than a thousand people from the general public—a true celebration that definitively inaugurated the era of the Psychedelic Renaissance. And if 2010 was the era of the Psychedelic Renaissance, the 2020s are the Cambrian era, as we will see later.

But getting there has not been easy. As Marc Aixalà masterfully narrates in the first chapter of this book, during the 1950s, 1960s, and the first half of the 1970s, hallucinogens were widely and profusely used, both in basic (pharmacological) research and applied (therapeutic) research in most North American, European, and South American universities. A mixture of political pressures and administrative complexities, the description of which is beyond the intention of this text[1], led to the discontinuation of this research for decades; it wasn't until the 1990s that research with these substances was resumed. Kotler's article omits most of these later investigations, probably for having occurred outside of the North American territory. But these investigations were the ones that laid the foundations for the renaissance to take place. Different research groups in the United States, Switzerland, Germany, and Spain conducted clinical pharmacological studies that guaranteed the safety of these substances when used in a controlled clinical context. Dr. Strassman at the University of New Mexico investigated the pharmacology of DMT (N, N-dimethyltryptamine), a hallucinogen that, when administered by inhalation or intravenously, elicited an experience of extreme intensity for a short duration of ten to twenty minutes. Dr. Charles Grob at UCLA restarted neuropharmacological research with MDMA and proposed a first protocol for its use in terminally ill patients, a protocol that he would never put into practice. Dr. Franz Vollenweider's group conducted the first studies using neuroimaging techniques with psilocybin, MDMA, and ketamine at the Zurich Psychiatric Hospital in Switzerland. The same was done by Dr. Euphrosyne Gouzoulis-Mayfrank at the University of Cologne, Germany with psilocybin, ketamine, DMT, and MDE (an analog of MDMA). At the Municipal Medical Research Institute in Barcelona, Spain, Dr. Magí Farré and his team characterized the pharmacology of MDMA, while at the Drug Research Center at Hospital de Sant Pau—also in Barcelona—Dr. Jordi Riba carried out the first pioneering studies on the neuropharmacology of ayahuasca. There were other groups, especially in the United States, such as those of Dr. Manuel Tancer at Wayne State University or Dr. John Mendelson at the University of California, San Francisco, who conducted less systematic research with MDMA. Before the end of the decade, in 1999, I launched the first therapeutic study using MDMA for the treatment of PTSD in female victims of sexual assault; political corruption, however, interrupted it prematurely, after only six of the twenty-nine women considered in the protocol had been treated.

With the safety foundations of the clinical use of these substances well established, the decade of the 2010s led to the clinical studies conducted by MAPS, focused on the treatment of PTSD with MDMA, led by the incombustible Dr. Rick Doblin and the beloved main investigator, Dr. Michael Mithoefer (along with his wife Ann, Marcela Ot'alora, Bruce Poulter, and others). This also led to the research at John Hopkins University, headed by Roland Griffiths with the captivating Bill Richards as lead therapist, which explored psilocybin's mysticomimetic potential and its application for people at the end of their lives, a research project that was joined by Stephen Ross's group from New York University. This decade also saw the beginnings of a line of research which was unthinkable just a few years earlier: research on the prosocial effects of MDMA, followed closely by LSD and psilocybin. Prosocial behavior includes positive social behaviors such as altruism, empathy, cooperation, or the ability to recognize emotions and intentions. A drug that until a few years ago was popularly —and fashionably— held responsible for destroying the values of young people who used it during endless parties dancing to electronic music (raves), suddenly served as a pharmacological model to study what makes humans unique in relation to other species. When this unique relation is disrupted, we could potentially find the explanation for numerous neurological diseases, such as autism or Parkinson's, and psychopathological disorders, such as schizophrenia or depression.[2]

During the second decade of the 21st century, psychedelic research finally exploded. New research groups emerged, some derived from the early researchers who belonged to the pioneering groups of the 1990s, giving continuity to the work through their own research programs. Moreover, psychedelic conferences continue to multiply, with growing audiences both in the United States and in Europe. For example, the third World Ayahuasca Conference, held in 2019 in the city of Girona, Spain and organized by the ICEERS foundation (International Center for Ethnobotanical Education, Research, and Service), brought together about 1,200 attendees, hosted an Indigenous representation of different Amazonian cultures and an artistic exhibition hall, all dealing monographically with ayahuasca. This explosion places MDMA and psilocybin as two substances of imminent medical regulation. Until that happens, the FDA—the agency that regulates the marketing of drugs in the United States—has classified MDMA and psilocybin as "breakthrough therapies," a qualification given to drugs that have substantial potential, beyond that of any existing medicines, to treat serious clinical conditions, such as PTSD for the former or treatment-resistant depression for the latter. Currently, MDMA and psilocybin are in Phase 3 clinical trials in the United States and psilocybin is in Phase 2 in Europe. Some of the small research laboratories are growing to become centers for psychedelic research, as is the case of the Imperial College group—which developed into the Center for Psychedelic Research—the Center for Psychedelic and Consciousness Research at John Hopkins, or the Yale Psychedelic Science Group, among many others. Psilocybin is being tested for the treatment of tobacco dependence or alcoholism, groups are emerging in Brazil that are investigating ayahuasca in the treatment of treatment-resistant depression, and the research is opening up to other molecules, such as salvinorin A (active component of *Salvia divinorum*) or 5-MeO-DMT. At ICEERS, in collaboration with the Sant Joan Hospital in Reus, Spain, the first clinical trial to treat opiate dependence with ibogaine has begun, and the University of São Paulo in Ribeirão Preto, Brazil, in collaboration with ICEERS, has approved the first clinical trial to treat alcohol dependence—the world's most problematic drug—with ibogaine. The psychological mechanisms underlying psychedelic-induced therapeutic change are being investigated (something that is discussed in depth in this book) and, not least of all, notable advances are being made in the molecular mechanisms of brain action for these drugs and using neuro-imaging technology to increase knowledge of neural networks and the brain areas that they modulate.

The enthusiasm that these substances arouse in the field of psychiatry is inversely correlated with a sad reality that even the most reactionary guilds within psychiatry struggle to admit: It is not only that our standard pharmacological treatments do not improve the patients' clinical conditions, but that in the medium and long term they are responsible for the perpetuation of the problems they intend to solve.[3] The pharmaceutical industry has stopped investing in psychiatric research, firstly because of the ineffectiveness and the long-term problems caused by these drugs and secondly because of the astronomical fines they are required to pay for fraudulent promotion and the subsequent loss of social prestige. Today, basic and applied research has been consolidated; results are being published in the most prestigious, specialized journals; and the media has stopped broadcasting reports about dangerous drugs, focusing instead on their potential to induce transformative spiritual experiences to treat depression and PTSD. Many people who suffer from these disorders—also consumers of the news—do not want to wait for these substances to be "authorized," choosing instead to put themselves in the hands of underground therapists while millionaire companies take advantage of this, investing in the development of these drugs to turn them into medicines as alternatives to classic psychiatric medications. Some research groups from prestigious European universities, such as Imperial College London or the Basel Psychiatric Hospital, are associated with these companies—COMPASS Pathways or MindMed—and clinical trials with MDMA, LSD, and psilocybin multiply by the day, focused on their therapeutic potential for all types of psychiatric and neurological disorders. Research today is so profuse that it is difficult to follow, and larger companies emerge that eat the small ones, such as ATAI. If Kotler first made the Psychedelic Renaissance visible in his *Playboy* article, it is the best-selling author Michael Pollan who—with his 2018 book, *How to Change Your Mind*—presented this new panorama to the general public. Like Kotler's article, Pollan's book is biased towards North American research, offering just a small taste of the European scene and mistaking the part for the whole. And so, with the arrival of the great corporate sharks, the old dream that psychedelics may one day be the birthright of humankind turns into a blur as they become the birthright of capital. The regulations of clinical trials ensure that only big industry can turn a drug into a medicine—in the hands of private millionaire companies— a restriction that has now caught-up with psychedelics. Except for MAPS, which is about to see MDMA turned into a drug, and Usona, which is doing the same with psilocybin—both non-profit organizations—the rest of the companies have already set a lucrative research and development agenda designed to perpetuate their profit through millionaire investments. All the research of these enterprises has been carried out with public money, through non-profit organizations or philanthropists. Do you remember the studies of Strassman, Grob, Vollenveider, Gouzoulis- Mayfrank, Farré and Riba, and those that came later, investigating prosocial behavior and positive psychology? The ones who laid the foundations for the advent of the new Psychedelic Renaissance? Psychedelic Big Pharma is exploiting all that knowledge to generate its patents, its clinical trials, and the development of its medicines. Will they give any of that social investment back to society?

In parallel (also during the 2010s, although its origin stretches back to the 1990s), a new and no less resurgent phenomenon has gradually established itself and grown: the interest in ancestral rituals involving the traditional uses of plants such as ayahuasca, iboga, or peyote, as well as the increasing recognition of the cultures that use these plants as models of integral health, community organization, and spirituality—associated with values such as ecology, decolonizing epistemologies, anti-extractivist ontologies, and the de-medicalization of life. If the development of psychedelic medicines entails the medicalization of hallucinogenic drugs, reducing their uses to fit into our biomedical paradigms, then the expansion, popularization and, to a certain extent, trivialization of ceremonies with traditional plants seeks to reintegrate them into the community and civil society, bringing these plants back to their original context—one that, on the other hand, they have never left: that of popular medicine. Although many try to discredit them by brushing them off as pseudo-therapies, far too many people are interested in them to immediately dismiss them. ICEERS arises from this context, aiming to reestablish the relationships that contemporary societies have with psychoactive plants and their traditional uses (again, we will return to the conceptual problem later). In animist Indigenous cultures, it is not the subject who becomes ill, nor is it the subject who must be cured. There is no tradition of health that considers diseases of the body, nor of the brain: the intrapsychic simply does not exist. There is not even such a thing as "health." What exists is harmony, which is nothing other than an alignment of the person, the community, the ecosystem, and the geographical territory. When any one of these levels of experience—and they are all levels of experience—is disturbed, disease sets in. The interest in psychedelic plant medicines, as they are now commonly called for lack of a better qualifier (something that, again, I will address later), is not an interest in a substance as it occurs in the field of biomedicine. It is an interest—and a quest—for health systems and knowledge systems that are not limited to the plants, but related to the ontological framework in which they are used. A search for well-being that has to do not so much with pleasure as with self-care, where the people who provide medicine are not the doctors, the psychiatrists, or the psychologists, but representatives whom the larger community has validated as experts, not because of their academic degrees or diplomas, but because of their expertise as technologists of the spiritual world. Furthermore, it cannot be ignored: We carry a long tradition, fostered by prohibitionism and even encouraged by it, of *psychonauts*, urban shamans, garage chemists, and the cosmically curious who have perfected ecstatic techniques outside of ritual and sourced from both natural and synthetic sources, making them available to anyone. The psychedelic experience has never been as democratized and accessible as it is now. And there are no signs that this will stop. Freedom of consciousness has become a universal human right that, beyond laws and legal prosecutions, is currently accessible to almost every citizen on the planet, if I can indulge this hyperbole, given that the objectives of the 2030 agenda for sustainable development are unfortunately becoming a matter of fiction rather than a reality.

In the 1980s and 1990s, the sociopolitical context forced the struggle for the social recognition of psychedelics to pass through validation as prescription medicines first, with MAPS initiatives aimed at making MDMA into a prescription drug and the Heffter Research Institute's parallel efforts with psilocybin. At the same time, a whole new generation trained in the analysis of drug policies was opening another front: the recognition of civil rights, framing drug policies within the framework of the human rights movement, which included, in its most contemporary version, the right to do science. The regulation of drugs in general, and that of psychedelics in particular, no longer constitutes the exclusive domain of biomedicine, but belongs to civil society, and its regulation does not have to be exclusively biomedical, but social and cultural. Recent movements such as Decriminalize Nature are achieving the de facto legalization of psychoactive plants, forcing the biomedical commercialization of psychedelic drugs to coexist with their cultural acceptance and the increased accessibility it entails for everybody.

This process has not been exempt from problems. Even before Peru declared traditional medical practices with ayahuasca to be part of the nation's cultural heritage, massive numbers of tourists in search of shamanic spiritual enlightenment were rushing to the Amazon in search of ayahuasca revelations, to Gabon for iboga or to Mexico for peyote, intertwined with all the intercultural problems that I will not describe here. This has also caused the turn of a paradigm that was believed to be hegemonic, and that is now plummeting towards an empty abyss: the paradigm of global mental health, which aims to export psychiatric models typical of the Global North to territories of the Global South. If pharmacological psychiatry has failed in its territories of origin, the pretense of exporting it to external territories is doomed to fail due to its own arrogance. Conversely, traditional health systems based on psychoactive plants are dazzling and blinding the Global North, but the political-medical managers of the Global North have not fully realized this yet. Similarly, they have not realized the extent to which psychedelics have taken root in contemporary societies. Therefore, the phenomena we have described so far are not at all innocuous. Hence the importance of this book. But, I will return to this subject later too. Before I do that, let me finally speak a little, and more technically, about what kinds of substances and practices we are referring to.

Sometimes dreams are wiser than waking. - Black Elk[4]

The truth is that these substances—chemical compounds, plants, secretions of animals, and fungi—escape any attempt at categorization.

Our president at ICEERS, Dr. Joan Obiols, has listed dozens of different names to refer to them. The most common are hallucinogens, psychedelics, and entheogens, but names such as entheodelics, cosmodelics, phantastica, delyrogens, psychotomimetics, psychodysleptics, eidetics, and disperceptinogens have also been proposed. The term entheogens refers to their purported ability to bring out inner divinity, something that those who proposed this term say they do. Psychedelic, a term coined by the psychiatrist Humphry Osmond, means that they reveal the content of the mind. "Hallucinogens" is the pharmacological classification that refers to the ability of these substances to induce experiences that do not come from the senses, that is, hallucinations.

Personally, I use the terms psychedelic and hallucinogenic interchangeably and the term entheogenic almost never, although I tend to use the term psychedelic more when I speak of its uses in psychotherapy and hallucinogenic when I speak of basic research, although, as I said, I do not always comply with this norm. I'm not uncomfortable with the term hallucinogenic: If anyone thinks that these substances do not cause hallucinations, either they have never taken the appropriate dose or they are deluding themselves. The term hallucinogenic has become discredited because it has served to stigmatize this group of substances, using that label to assume that they inherently produce psychopathological experiences. But I think the term hallucinogenic must be dignified. Hallucinations are not necessarily pathological, nor are they necessarily uniquely related to reality. On the contrary, the hallucinations that hallucinogens induce, when they occur in an appropriate context and with adequate preparation, connect the person with realities that are no less real because we do not have access to them through the ordinary senses. The spaces that these substances can open up for the person, provided that they are used properly (although it is neither a necessary nor a sufficient condition, and how this proper or good use is a priori developed is partly addressed in this book), are populated with realities that are just as real (or more) than ordinary reality. They may open a reality that, far from being alien to the subject, is atavistically attached to them, as are dreams, to use an example that can most accurately relate in nature and significance to these hallucinogen-induced hallucinations. And from these realities, the person usually returns renewed. Some call them mystical experiences, others spiritual experiences, some speak of autobiographical resolutions, others of deep ontological knowledge, and still others of incalculable and profound psychotherapeutic value. If this is so, after all, hallucinations may not be pathological manifestations of the psyche, but healing manifestations. The fact that hallucinations are a symptom of psychiatric disorders does not mean that they cannot also be a symptom of mental empowerment. The work with these substances consists precisely in taking advantage of the hallucinations in their healing sense. This is how countless cultures on this planet have used psychoactive plants in their traditional medicine systems: mainly, precisely, as medicine. And this is where we find another stumbling block. None of the terms proposed to refer to these substances identify or recognize any of the Indigenous cultures that use them. For the animistic psyche, the term hallucination is not a good fit, since reality is always real and Indigenous medicines, as I mentioned above, do not operate on the individual, but on the individual-community-ecosystem-territory alignment. So any term that we could propose from "this side" is doomed to be rejected by this view. Consequently, I will stop here, as far as this is concerned.

A scientific term that is recently gaining popularity is that of "serotonergic psychedelics," and this is because substances such as LSD, psilocybin, mescaline, or DMT, have a common principle of action, which is their effect on serotonin 5-HT2A receptors. Other hallucinogens exist, such as *Salvia divinorum* or the *daturas*, but their neurobiological mechanisms are different. When we talk about psychedelics, they will generally be serotonergic, because they are the ones being most systematically investigated. The activation of the 5-HT2A receptors produces a release of glutamate, which increases the rate of neuronal firing, hence the feeling of many initiates that they are receiving some type of unique information, which is real. Glutamate is responsible for the consolidation of memories and for neuronal plasticity, which is why the potential of these drugs as possible anti-dementia drugs is being researched. Functionally, serotonergic psychedelics modify the connection of neural networks, sending information through circuits which it does not normally travel which, in clinical terms, is proving useful in the treatment of psychopathological disorders such as depression. Anatomically, the prefrontal cortex is activated, which is where the most phylogenetically evolved functions of our brain reside: the organization of reality, abstract thinking, task planning, decision-making, and much of the repertoire of what has already been categorized as prosocial behavior. Not surprisingly, hallucinogens are part of the creation myths of many cultures on the planet.[5] I am not going to explain what these substances do on the psychological level, since Marc Aixalà does it marvelously in this book.

There is an exception to this effect, which is the case of ibogaine, an alkaloid present in the African plant *Tabernanthe iboga*. Although ibogaine also has an action on 5-HT2A receptors and its chemical molecule is similar to that of serotonergic psychedelics—which are all either tryptamines (similar in structure to serotonin) or phenylethylamines (similar in structure to dopamine, adrenaline and norepinephrine)—its effect is not like that of serotonergic psychedelics. Ibogaine acts on multiple neurotransmission systems, but it has a peculiar effect that other hallucinogens (or any other known compound) do not have: it eliminates the opiate withdrawal symptoms and the craving (or desire to consume) for psychostimulants and alcohol. You could say that ibogaine is an anti-drug. After ingesting it, it opens a therapeutic window in which the person is free of withdrawal symptoms and cravings (at least for a time, which can vary from a few days to several months), which allows for therapeutic work. Various reasons related to the politics of science, which I am not going to go into, make ibogaine unavailable today as a drug dependence treatment (perhaps because it was not a doctor who discovered its anti-addiction effects, but an addict). Every day, 200 people die from opioid overdoses in the United States alone. No treatment, no matter how toxic, will be so awful as to result in such a slaughter. Letting these people die, however, is standard practice. There is a whole medical subculture of ibogaine that offers underground treatments in countries like Mexico where there are hundreds of clinics that receive North American patients, especially because ibogaine is prohibited in the United States (it is not prohibited by international law nor in most countries, although it is illegal in a few —in Spain, it is not). As with everything, there are some honest treatment providers who take better care of their patients and there are some that are less so. Unlike the rest of the serotonergic psychedelics, which are unquestionably safe and not very toxic from an organic perspective—for most of them there is no known lethal overdose—ibogaine has a toxicity profile that must be monitored during treatment. Although the current interest in ibogaine is minor in comparison to that of classic psychedelics, the opioid crisis that we are experiencing across many wealthy countries is undoubtedly increasing the demand for treatments.

MDMA also has its own mechanism of action, different from serotonergic psychedelics. It inhibits serotonin reuptake (like drugstore antidepressants), while promoting serotonin release. Although MDMA is a synthetic drug, its neurobiological mechanism of action is paradoxically more "natural" than that of classic psychedelics. In the latter, it is their active principles that bind to the receptors. With MDMA, the effect is caused by the serotonin itself, released by the MDMA. Let us say that MDMA acts as a catalyst for endogenous processes. The release of serotonin that it produces causes the hormone oxytocin (vasopressin in men) to be released and, with it, all the associated psychological processes, including the display of prosocial characteristics.

To summarize, these substances are nowadays being investigated in universities and public and private research centers; in the former cases purely for social-scientific purposes and, in the latter, purely for commercial ones (with the inherent risk that the industry will commit the same outrages that it has historically committed in the development of other psychiatric drugs). Simultaneously, an incalculable number of people travel each year to the places where rituals with psychoactive plants are performed. These rituals have also traveled outside their places of origin, having been reinvented, and today it is easy to find ceremonies—mainly with ayahuasca—in almost every metropolitan European and American city, and many African and Asian cities. Likewise, the methods of extracting active ingredients from plants or the home cultivation of some of them (such as the extraction of DMT or the cultivation of psilocybin mushrooms, which contain psilocybin) have become popular and are cheap and accessible to almost anyone. On the other hand, in countries such as Spain or the Netherlands, where drug use is not criminalized, there is a proliferation of underground therapists who offer ceremonies with different products, and clandestine psychonautic chemists have perfected and made accessible compounds analogous to those which are prohibited but still legal, de facto disabling the prohibition. At the same time, the media echoes these advances, in alignment with scientific progress, managing to destigmatize the use of these substances for therapeutic purposes and moving legions of people to seek remedies for life's difficulties within them. In addition, psychedelic culture has reached digital audiovisual content platforms and mainstream culture in the form of books that have become bestsellers, while initiatives based on decriminalization proliferate. In this context of mass popularization, it is easy to fall into trivialization and the accidents that inevitably follow. The psychedelic experience includes a profound lived experience that touches the pillars of being and reality, confronting us with the most distilled essence of existence. That has its existential benefits, but also its risks, which I am not going to describe because that is why you have this book, a book that describes the risks in detail while inviting you to take advantage of them, benefitting from these risks instead of being harmed.

It is precisely in this current context, in which the psychedelic experience is readily available to anyone, that this book becomes essential and, above all, timely. It arrives exactly when it had to arrive, written by the person who had to write it: Marc Aixalà, a young psychologist and telecommunications engineer (curious, isn't it? psychedelics are, after all, and among other things, telecommunication systems) with unparalleled experience in the trenches of psychedelia, as he modestly recounts. However, those of us who have been nearby while he did his work (the rest of the fatigued ICEERS team) have witnessed how, based on tenacity, deep concern, and commitment to his training as a professional, coupled with high doses of self-learning and creativity, rigor, seriousness, and professionalism, he addressed with utmost humanity the most complicated cases imaginable: these challenging experiences—as they are now called in lieu of their correct term, that is, adverse experiences. More than ten years of experience grant him the authority to write this pioneering book, which inaugurates, I would say, a new bibliographic genre which will oscillate in the future from scientism on one hand to the purest esotericism on the other, and which will flood our libraries in the coming years, since integration is now in fashion.

To finish, I just want to make a comment about the discipline to which the book on integration that you are about to read now belongs— the genre in which a book that inaugurates such a discipline should be framed: psychology. As Aixalà explains in his book, there is tremendous confusion regarding what integration is, and there are integrators of all natures and conditions. While it is not clear that those responsible for administering hallucinogens to people must be psychologists or psychiatrists, they are definitely the most prepared to practice integration. Knowledge of hallucinogenic technology is known in depth only by the shaman, and the shaman is legitimized by their community, not by a title or an academy. Psychiatry and clinical psychology, which have traditionally dealt with pathologizing any type of altered state of consciousness and whose medicines and techniques consist precisely in eradicating them, cannot be the disciplines responsible for guiding psychedelic journeys. They become necessary, however, when things become difficult, not only to bring the person back to baseline, but to help them take advantage of the experience, making them psychologically stronger. For a practice to be considered psychological, other than being artful, it must be supported by theory. If not, it could be all sorts of things, but not psychology. And things that are not solidly supported by theory can easily slip into deception, self-idolization, and the "pseudo" prefix. Therefore, there is no alternative but to develop a psychological theory of psychedelic integration, although that psychological theory does not have to be rigidly reduced to a single theoretical model. Finally, those who study these disciplines recognize the value of integrating different models, each supported by its own theoretical basis. In the construction of his integrative psychological theoretical model, with a stroke of genius, Aixalà incorporates one of the most creative and fun models in psychology: the strategic, brief therapy of the Palo Alto school. But this is all I want to write about the theoretical model, since you will have the pleasure and the joy of reading it in the words of the author himself.

Finally, as much as an integration book should be a psychology book, since it deals with psychedelic substances, it cannot exclude a spiritual perspective. Aixalà goes another step further, writing a psychology manual on the integration of psychedelic experience, which also includes some models from spiritual traditions. Masterly. This book is therefore a true manual. As such, it should continue to be perfected and, ideally, improved and nurtured by ongoing research. Being a manual, not only can one learn the theory of how to carry out psychedelic integration, but it constitutes a whole research plan in itself, which should give rise to a whole new discipline—a field that will have an undeniable demand in the decade to come when the psychedelic experience will become ordinary and normal practice.

Those who are preparing to guide or conduct these experiences already have an unavoidable obligation: to read this book.

José Carlos Bouso
Scientific Director of ICEERS

PREFACE

"Blessed is he who thankfully remembers his ancestors, who joyfully speaks of their actions and their greatness and who serenely rejoices to see himself at the end of such a beautiful row."

GOETHE

"The man does not contain the boy, but the men who preceded him. The story began a long time ago."

PHILIP K. DICK

My interest in psychoactive substances and non-ordinary states of consciousness began in the basement of my mother's pharmacy, among the custom medications she compounded in her laboratory. As a child, I spent hours helping her weigh her powders, mixing them with her mortar, preparing and carefully cleaning the capsules to rid them of their bitter taste. In that room, I did my homework, and when the homework got too boring, I would get up and walk among shelves lined with containers full of active ingredients with unpronounceable names, imagining what they could be for. One afternoon I came across a book called *Plantas medicinales: el Dioscórides renovado*, by the Catalonian writer Pío Font Quer. In the book's introduction, I read the story of the meeting between Gordon Wasson and María Sabina and the first magic mushrooms experience as told by a white man. That story had a profound impact on me, and for the next several weeks I immersed myself in the *Dioscórides*, reading about plants that had amazing effects. It became my secret passion.

In the year 2000, I had my first personal contact with the worlds that I had read about in the *Dioscórides*, at a time when I was a student of Telecommunications Engineering. My first experience was one of sublime beauty, and it marked a before and after in my life. I was able to start overcoming some difficult personal circumstances that I was going through and I felt that my true vocation was in the study of non-ordinary states and their therapeutic application.

Throughout my time as a Telecommunications Engineering student, I continued to seek these experiences in different contexts and I began to learn from people who were dedicated to this type of work. In 2006, I went to Boom Festival for the first time (a psytrance music and psychedelic culture festival). This was another crucial experience in my life. I have attended ever since, mainly as a volunteer for the psychological emergency service called Kosmicare. In later years, I have been a team leader and the trainer/supervisor of the volunteer teams. Being a part of this service has been an enormously formative experience, since I have been able to observe and support the sort of difficult psychedelic experiences that can be the source of later problems.

Over the course of those years, I read the work of Stanislav Grof. I was completely baffled to see my most intimate experiences described in astonishing detail in his expanded cartography of the psyche. This encouraged me to learn more about his work and in 2005 I participated for the first time in a Holotropic Breathwork workshop. Grof's proposed format of working with our breath became the backbone that structured all my previous experiences. I was able to contextualize everything that I had experienced up to that point, which led me to develop the concept of process and, within it, the need for integration. From 2006 to 2012, I trained as a Holotropic Breathwork facilitator, later giving myself to offering workshops and training, also as a member of the Grof Transpersonal Training team.

In 2007, I spent a year in Peru, completing my degree's final project on telehealth in rural areas. For a little over a month, I was able to visit different communities along the Napo river basin, where I met Shipibo communities and had my first contact with ayahuasca and traditional medicine practices. Shamanism has never been my path, but from that moment on, I developed a deep respect for these Indigenous traditions and their ancestral knowledge.

After finishing my studies—and working as an engineer for a few years—I realized that I needed to pay attention to all the signs and experiences that I had come across in my path and follow my true vocation. I decided to completely change professions and dedicate myself to psychology, psychotherapy, and non-ordinary states of consciousness. So I went back to school to study psychology. I graduated in 2012, opened my private practice, and continued my training in integrative therapy, strategic brief therapy, and other disciplines.

In 2012, I also started collaborating with ICEERS (International Center for Ethnobotanical Education, Research and Service). My job was to provide support for the people who contacted us by email and phone. We received all kinds of questions about the use of psychoactive substances, as well as stories and reports of difficulties after complex experiences with ayahuasca and other substances. We created a support service that was then called the "Help Center" and later became the "Integration and Support Service." Over the years, I have served more than 700 people who needed some kind of support, whether in the preparation or the integration of their experiences, or both.

I was also fortunate when MAPS invited me to train as an MDMA-assisted psychotherapist in a seminar taught by Michael and Annie Mithoefer in 2015. And a few years later, I started working as a therapist at the Sant Joan de Déu Hospital in Barcelona, in a study that used psilocybin to treat major depression. I was thus able to gain a methodical and scientific vision of what research in this discipline implies.

I share this with the intention of illustrating, through my own story as an example, the progressive integration of my experiences over more than fifteen years. Only with time have I been able to materialize some of the realizations that happened during those singular hours.

Over the last decade, the need to integrate psychedelic experiences has become a matter of increasing interest. Without much forethought or planning, I began to specialize in this, gaining experience through my private practice, my work as a Holotropic Breathwork facilitator, and my work in the ICEERS integration service.

The field of integration is very young and still underdeveloped. Although we frequently use the concept of integration nowadays, each therapist has their own idea of what integration means and how it should be carried out. We use the same word for totally different concepts and practices. Furthermore, when I began writing this text, there were no books dealing specifically with integration and no schools that addressed this part of psychedelic therapy. *If one wants to learn about integration, where should one go?* This is a question that I had often been asked in my talks. Therefore, it seemed appropriate to try to summarize and systematize my understanding of integration in a book that could serve as an inspiration for other people to continue developing this field. I thought I had a lot of knowledge to bring to this field, with a head full of new and interesting ideas.

I took a few months off and went on a trip. One afternoon I was at Bodhi Zendo, a Zen monastery in Tamil Nadu, India. I was reading a text by Ramakrishna and came across the concept of *yoga-brashtas*, "the fallen ones of yoga." Surprisingly, his description was very similar to one of the problematic situations in integration that I had named "repeated experiences without integration." This was a moving experience for me: on the one hand, seeing my independent observations validated, but on the other hand, questioning the novelty of my contributions. That text made me rethink the whole book. Rather than simply recounting my reflections on integration, I first had to find out what had been written in the past about what we call "integration."

On the way back from my trip, I began documenting as exhaustively as possible. I consulted classic books on psychedelic therapy, as well as scientific articles from the 1950s and texts from different spiritual traditions. I was looking in these texts for specific references to integration practices and related knowledge. The psychedelic literature abounds with phenomenological descriptions of these experiences, methodological information on conducting sessions with substances, and descriptions of research methods and their results. However, the therapeutic practices carried out during preparation and integration sessions are much more cryptic and unclear—so my reading of the literature was mainly focused on understanding the conceptualization of integration and related practices to see if I could better understand what these pioneers did in their integration sessions.

The task of documenting left me with a mixed feeling of amazement and humility. Many of the ideas that I thought I had discovered in my years of practical work were described in texts from more than fifty years ago, and some were even formal aspects of different ancient spiritual traditions.

Therefore, rather than merely presenting my own thoughts on integration, I decided that this book should prioritize the many facets and interpretations of integration while honoring the work of the pioneers who came before me. In addition, I will also present my own version and the systematization of my therapeutic work in recent years.

This book contains a psychological and therapeutic perspective, as well as a spiritual perspective. There are also some historical threads, which I personally find exciting. I have tried to be descriptive and precise as well as entertaining, and I hope that the inconsistencies that may exist throughout this peculiar synthesis will be a source of curiosity and reflection rather than a nuisance.

In the first chapter, I present a historical review of the psychedelic and psycholytic schools, placing special emphasis on their particular vision of integration.

The second chapter reflects what integration is and what it requires, its dimensions and implications. With this, I intend to provide elements for a more complex and comprehensive conception of integration.

The third chapter contains useful theoretical concepts for understanding therapeutic intervention more broadly and is intended to synthesize the different schools of thought. Any inconsistencies in this chapter are not the responsibility of any of the described schools but solely my own. I am aware that the contents of this chapter may generate some controversy and resistance among those readers who are therapists. My theoretical model has been and continues to be in constant evolution, so what I describe is not intended to constitute a finalized vision but rather a sample of current reflections on which theoretical models we may use as we approach a therapeutic intervention.

The fourth chapter focuses on practices that maximize benefits and can be useful for both therapists and laypeople. I describe a few different tools that can be useful in the integration of experiences that have not been particularly difficult. I also describe some of the risks entailed by a non-integration.

In the fifth chapter, I have sought to review the adverse effects that can occur after psychedelic experiences. On the one hand, I present different visions of various pioneers who analyzed this phenomenon before me. On the other hand, I present my own classification based on recent clinical experience.

The sixth chapter, again quite technical, consists of a description of different therapeutic interventions I have found useful in the cases I have worked with. This chapter also contains a description of the evolution of my therapeutic method, which has developed over the years and is still evolving. Again, it is intended to be more of an inspiration than a fixed intervention manual.

Throughout the text, you can also find clinical cases, as well as drawings, mandalas, and other artistic expressions of patients, which I hope can help to illustrate the presentation of theoretical content.

Dear Reader: I want to express my sincere gratitude for your interest in this book. I hope you find it as exciting to read as the process of writing has been for me.

Marc Aixalà
Sitges, May 2020

ACKNOWLEDGMENTS

Looking back after months of arduous work, I want to express my gratitude to all the people who have contributed to this book, helping in some way or another to make it a reality.

My deepest gratitude goes to the ICEERS foundation and to my colleagues, with whom I am honored to work and share the experiences that life offers. They are all unique people, without exception, who continue to inspire me with their knowledge, their care, and the way they live in accordance with their values and principles. I am also especially grateful for the efforts and patience of Benjamin de Loenen and the entire team, allowing me the resources and time needed to give myself to this project fully. ICEERS is an example of a job well done and an example of human values, respect, and integrity, made possible by all the people who are part of the organization. I could have never imagined a better context than ICEERS to carry out my work, with flexibility, seriousness, and good humor. Further gratitude goes to Genís Oña, for his review and comments on the first chapter and Igor Domsac for his impeccable style corrections.

I want to express my admiration for José Carlos Bouso—friend, mentor and reference—whose knowledge, humility, and dedication are a constant source of inspiration. José Carlos is undoubtedly a pioneer in many fields and every minute spent with him is an honor for me. Without his support, many of the experiences that have allowed me to write this book would never have happened, and I wouldn't be the person or the professional I am today. José Carlos gave me access to the MDMA-assisted psychotherapy training organized by MAPS, and he was the one who allowed my participation as a therapist in a clinical trial of psilocybin for the treatment of depression. For these and many other reasons, including his meticulous revision of this manuscript, I am forever indebted and eternally grateful for the trust that he has always placed in me.

This book would never have happened without the generous donation from the Francisco Javier Crespo Royo Foundation. Thanks to his support, I have been able to work calmly, fully giving myself to this project. My special gratitude to Pat Escudero for her generosity and trust, as she was the one who proposed this collaboration. Without her, this book would never have become a reality.

My Holotropic Breathwork mentors and teachers have played a crucial role in my life. They have supported me in my personal process and have served as impeccable role models who taught me, with patience, the art of supporting people in non-ordinary states. Their teachings will always stay with me, and I hope that my work is aligned with the values and attitudes that they have transmitted to me and that my work can be a source of satisfaction for them. My heartfelt thanks to Tav Sparks, Jean Farrell, Diana Medina, Nienke Merbis, Juanjo Segura, Sitara Blasco, and Stan and Christina Grof.

Two persons who deserve a special mention are Juanjo Segura and Sitara Blasco who, in addition to being teachers, have been friends and mentors at different stages of my life and without whom I would not be where I am now. It is an honor to share space and learn by their side, always embodying an example to follow. Thanks to Sitara for her valuable hours of editing, proofreading, and commenting on the ideas in this book.

Thanks to Débora González who, in addition to being a good friend, is also a passionate researcher. Because of her, I have been able to work in contexts that I would never have imagined. Her tenacity and warmth allowed us to overcome the difficulties we encountered in the study we carried out for the treatment of complicated grief. Many of the insights from those months and the experiences we shared on our journey through the Brazilian Amazon have inspired parts of this book.

Toni Piera, Víctor Amat, Agustí Camino, and Maria José Pubill, have all aroused, each in their own way, my interest in unconventional forms of therapy and have taught me to embody an attitude of curiosity, respect, and passion in my work with people. I owe them a lot in terms in my clinical praxis and intellectual development.

Much of the knowledge reflected in this book has been passed down to me by therapists, psychologists, facilitators, and shamans that I have met over the years. Their work on the front lines in sessions with people and holding ceremonies for groups has allowed me to confront the theoretical aspects of my work with practical, lived realities. Thanks to this, I have been able to better understand the needs of the people who provide these services, and of those who receive them. My sincere gratitude to these people, who must remain anonymous in the present circumstances.

John Ablett and Katharina Wolter, as well as others whose names remain anonymous, have contributed their magnificent pieces of art to illustrate this book. My heartfelt gratitude for sharing these intimate testimonies of your personal process.

A special Thank You goes out to all those people with whom I have been able to share my work and whose suffering I hope I have helped ameliorate. To all the patients of the ICEERS integration and support service, all the participants in the Holotropic Breathwork sessions, the participants in the clinical studies and all those people who at some point have trusted that my work could bring them greater well-being. Of course, this book would not exist without each of them, and I am forever grateful for their trust and courage.

And to my beloved partner Marina, who has patiently been there throughout all the working hours, with a smile, a hot cup of tea on cold winter days, a stroll by the beach when we needed to clear our heads, and countless beautiful moments. You are the best company I could ask for.

Marc Aixalà
Sitges, October 2020

THE ORIGINS AND EVOLUTION
OF INTEGRATION

"*The future may teach us how to exercise a direct influence, by means of particular chemical substances, upon the amounts of energy and their distribution in the apparatus of the mind. It may be that there are other undreamt-of possibilities of therapy.*"

SIGMUND FREUD (1940)

"*We are the latest of generations of experimenters who, from before the dawn of history, in every part of the world, have sought for means by which a man could alter, explore, and control the workings of his own mind, thus enlarging his experience of the universe.*"

HUMPHRY OSMOND (1957)

THE ORIGINS OF INTEGRATION: PSYCHOLYTIC AND PSYCHEDELIC PSYCHOTHERAPY

The first experiments with psychoactive substances in modern Western culture were conducted by the French psychiatrist Moreau de Tours in his late 19th century studies of hashish, chloroform, ether, opium, and nightshades. He is thus regarded as one of the fathers of Psychopharmacology. These substances were used with the intention of inducing a hypnotic trance, just as barbiturates were used in the so-called "narcoanalysis" to treat repressed conflicts and especially "war neurosis" (Passie, 1997). This diagnostic category preceded post-traumatic stress disorder (PTSD).

Years later, during the 1920s, more experiments were carried out with psychedelic substances—known at the time as Phantastica (Lewin, 1924)—mainly using mescaline (Bentall, 1990; Passie, 1997; Carhart-Harris & Goodwin, 2017). The dramatic effects of mescaline sparked a tremendous initial interest in describing the specific effects and the phenomenology of the experience, even if the said experience was not yet understood as a manifestation of intrapsychic phenomena but as mere pharmacological effects. Soon afterwards, the first insights regarding the potential of these substances appeared in the clinical (Beringer, 1927) and psychoanalytic (Baroni, 1931) context.

Pharmacological and psychiatric research entered a new phase on the 19th of April, 1943, with the discovery of the psychological effects of LSD, when researchers and therapists[6] began exploring the various potential applications of LSD, trying to discover its useful and proper applications (Stoll, 1947). In 1950, the first publication stating that psychedelic substances may have useful applications as adjuncts in psychiatric treatment appeared (Busch & Johnson, 1950). From then on, publications followed at an increasing rate (Sandison, 1953; Frederking, 1955; Chandler & Hartman, 1960), reaching their peak in the 1960s with more than seven hundred publications on the therapeutic potential of psychedelic substances. During this golden age of psychedelic research, various researchers developed diverse therapeutic methods tied to different methodologies and multiple interpretations regarding the role of these substances in the global treatment framework. At one moment in time, up to eighteen different centers in Europe existed in which different psychedelic psychotherapies were developed.

Two major schools or approaches to the use of psychedelic substances for therapeutic purposes have traditionally been described: psycholytic therapy and psychedelic therapy.

Broadly speaking, psycholytic therapy was based on the repeated use of low and medium doses of psychedelic substances, mainly LSD. The intention behind psycholytic therapy is to facilitate the emergence of unconscious material, thus accelerating and deepening the therapeutic process. The model in which psycholytic sessions were framed was mainly psychoanalytic and the material that emerged from these sessions was analyzed accordingly. The intention was to restructure the patient's personality[7] through a maturation process that relied on analyzing the contents emerging from the ongoing experiences and the transference.

On the other hand, the psychedelic therapy model used high—or very high—doses of LSD on very specific occasions, usually spanning one to three sessions. The intention was to provide a peak experience that could help reorganize the psychic and personality structure of the patient in such a way that it would manifest in immediate behavioral changes. In this context, the material that emerged in the session was not analyzed with any particular emphasis, unlike the psycholytic therapy model. Instead, the focus was on accompanying the session in a way that was the most appropriate for the production of a peak experience, as well the suggested preparation—of a spiritual orientation—that favored the occurrence of mystical experiences.

Psycholytic therapy is usually referred to as the European school, while psychedelic therapy is known as the American school due to the reception that each modality had in the different continents and the respective paths they followed. However, there are fascinating examples of psycholytic oriented psychotherapy that have been used in the United States (Abramson, 1955, 1956, 1973) and which are more accessible to readers who do not speak German. This methodology is less discussed, as its publications have not been translated or disseminated widely. Similarly, there are examples of treatments in Europe in which psychedelic doses were used (up to 400 µg of LSD) and a small number of sessions were carried out with hardly any verbal exchange during the session (Sandison, 1954). In these sessions, the focus was on achieving a transcendent and spiritual experience. This mixed line of psycholytic-psychedelic approaches was proposed by several authors (Alnaes, 1964; Grof, 1970), and combined approaches were developed in which both high-dose and other low-dose treatments were provided (Baker, 1964).

The combined experience of these different schools allowed various aspects of psychedelic psychotherapy to be developed and refined. The American schools with a psychedelic approach (high-dose, few experiences, spiritual orientation) developed their specific preparatory methods. Their methodology of conducting psychedelic sessions to maximize positive results and spiritual experiences—developed mainly through the contributions of Al Hubbard and the Saskatchewan group, as well as Timothy Leary and Stanislav Grof—is of special interest. Psychological schools developed a larger body of theory about the psychodynamic aspects of psychedelic experiences and their interpretation from an analytical perspective. These aspects are quite well known today, while their integration practices, if there were any, are less well known. To this day, we find ourselves with the question of how to consolidate the perceived improvements after a successful psychedelic experience.

Integration in Psycholytic Therapy

At the theoretical level, integrating the use of psychedelic substances into a psycholytic therapy framework does not seem to present too many challenges. The paradigm in which the sessions are framed is psychoanalytic and, broadly speaking, psychedelic substances play the following roles: Firstly, they reduce psychological defenses. Secondly, they allow a greater production of unconscious material during psychoanalytic sessions. Thirdly, they facilitate the ability to relive experiences and produce catharsis, and lastly, they amplify the therapeutic relationship[8] (Eisner & Cohen, 1958).

In the course of psycholytic psychotherapy, analytical therapy sessions are interspersed with periodic sessions aided by substances. During the sessions with substances, the material is gathered and processed, after which an attempt is made to obtain a good understanding of what has emerged. During the psychoanalytic sessions, the material is still analyzed through the prism of the therapist's guidance, be it Freudian, Jungian, or similar (Fericgla, 2006). It makes sense then that specific integration techniques were not developed for this model since the treatment followed its usual course, with the difference of more intense and longer sessions, additional material to analyze, and the hope of a shorter treatment (Abramson,

1955). In this case, the integration consisted of regular analytical therapies. Similarly, although following a different theoretical paradigm, we often still work in the same way: we try to interpret and clarify the meaning of the experience.

The development of psycholytic psychotherapy contributed several important lessons for the evolution of psychedelic-assisted psychotherapy. On the one hand, it revealed the need for another type of intervention during psychedelic sessions: something beyond verbal support by the therapist and the usual tools provided by psychoanalysis, such as free association and interpretation. It also illuminated the needs in terms of the clinical staff required and the physical place where the treatment was to be carried out (Sandison, 1954)[9]. On the other hand, they experimented with the use of different substances as adjuvants for psychotherapy (mescaline, LSD, amphetamines, gas mixtures, barbiturates), and various therapists reached their own conclusions regarding their preferences for one substance or another. LSD turned out to be the one most widely used, although, for example, some authors reported that in its absence, methylphenidate (an amphetamine derivative) can be very useful for building a good therapeutic relationship and giving fluidity to sessions (Eisner, 2002). This is a surprising premonition of future MDMA therapy.

Furthermore, the development of psycholytic therapy showed the possibility that patients might need support after a session with substances.

Sandison (1954) makes perhaps the first implicit reference to integration, which he calls "rehabilitation," when he states that:

> It seems almost certain that a more or less prolonged period of mental rehabilitation will be required after the course of treatment by LSD has been concluded. The patient may be tempted to make major alterations in his environment and way of life during the more disturbing phase of treatment. It is wise to allow the patient to make at least some experiments in readjusting his life but any major alterations, particularly where these involve the question

of marriage, marital separation, or divorce, should be decided on only after the LSD phase of treatment has been concluded. We have found that about one-half of our cases required extensive rehabilitation involving the establishment of a new set of conditioned social responses.[10]

Sandison points out the need to discuss the experience, whether at the end of the session or in later sessions if necessary. Both individual and group psychotherapy were used in his therapeutic model for that purpose. Furthermore, Sandison (1959) found that, as in psychoanalytic practice, the catharsis and abreaction induced by LSD were not therapeutic by themselves if a re-evaluation of said abreaction was not conducted after the experience.

We find another good example of the need for support after a psychedelic session in the correspondence between Betty Eisner—researcher and therapist on Sidney Cohen's team—and Humphry Osmond. Eisner recounts the difficulties she experienced after her experiences with LSD and the little importance that Cohen gave to such events. Eisner discovers in her own flesh the need to do something with what happened to her during the experience, and the letters she exchanged with Humphry Osmond are an example of the first documented attempts to integrate an experience (Eisner, 2002).

After the second LSD I ended up, not in chaos and confusion but with the blackest depression that anyone could dream up. Depression had never been a symptom I suffered from. [...] In profound physical and psychological distress, I walked to the corner to a pay phone, forced myself to wait in line, and called, finally reaching Sid. He refused to take me seriously, saying to get a good night's sleep and all would be well in the morning. I clearly remember telling him that it wouldn't look good for the research if the psychologist who was the subject committed suicide. He was unimpressed.

Eisner eventually managed to overcome that period through a curious intervention for that era: reading the writings of St. John of the Cross in the *Dark Night of the Soul*.

Cohen, throughout his career, dedicates much of his research to the complications that occur after a psychedelic experience and shows that this type of therapy is not without risks (Cohen, 1960, 1962, 1963, 1966, 1985). Among the potential post-treatment risks, Cohen describes the inability to integrate the traumatic material that may emerge, the return to everyday life after a transcendent experience, and the depression that might follow if the insights acquired in the session are not properly applied in daily life (Eisner & Cohen, 1958). As we will see later, this is a good description of some of the problems that people might encounter after psychedelic experiences and for which they ask integration support. A good fictionalized example of early psychoanalytic LSD treatment, including a range of interpersonal and integrative difficulties, can be found in *Myself and I* (Newland, 1962), a book that describes the author's psychedelic treatment, depicting the issues of personal boundaries, projection, and other challenges that can appear in psychedelic therapy.

It is interesting to note that the words "integrate" and "integration" were already used in that context and at that time. We find references to integration in the publications of Eisner, Cohen, Alnaes (1964) and Abramson (1973). However, the practical meaning of the word corresponds to a different concept than the one we have today (and that we have yet to develop in a consistent and consensual way).

Some authors within the psychedelic stream understand two types of experiences that can occur during psychedelic therapy: "problem-solving experiences" and "integrative experiences." Problem-solving experiences happen when critical and problematic unconscious content is uncovered, often coupled with experiences of anxiety and varying degrees of discomfort. It is understood that the patient is moving through these conflicting areas of the psyche and that if the material is processed correctly, the ordeal can be resolved in a positive way.

The "integrative experience" is defined as one in which "the patient accepts himself as he is, and there is a massive reduction in conflict. There is a feeling of harmony with the environment and an increase in creativity. Sometimes this is experienced as a fusion between subject and object" (Eisner & Cohen, 1958). The presence of visions of light and beauty, sensations of relaxation, insights, and a sense of order and meaning are also commonly described. In that sense, it resembles the kind of mystical experience that Walter Pahnke (1969, 1966, 1967) speaks of, although with some differences contrasted to the general criteria and obtained in a different context and via low doses, thus the phenomenology was probably quite different from what we see today (Griffiths et al., 2006, 2008, 2011, 2017).

Psychoanalytic authors propose that this type of experience can be understood as a "massive integration of the id-ego-superego" (Bergman, in Eisner, 2002).

Abramson proposes the term "integrative function of the psyche" (Abramson, 1955). He points out that it is the subject's own psyche— under the effects of psychedelics—that directs and regulates the experience, as long as it is under the supervision of the therapist and embedded in the appropriate context. Abramson, in a way, points to the concept of "inner wisdom" that Van Dusen also mentions concerning psychedelic experiences (Van Dusen, 1961). It also resonates with the idea of "inner healing wisdom" that Stan Grof would develop decades later. For this author, it is during the peak moments of the LSD experience that the person can integrate different pieces of information. He points out that in classical non-drug therapy, such integration could take much longer. The mechanism by which this integration happens, according to Abramson, rests on the ability of low doses of LSD to produce a paradoxical effect. On the one hand, they cause a disturbance of the personality structure: an ego-depression (equivalent to the decrease in defenses and the greater ease with which unconscious material surfaces) while at the same time undergoing an ego-enhancement, a strengthening of the ego that allows for a better overall functioning and integration capacity. Whether this synergy between ego-depression and ego-enhancement occurs depends on various factors, but mainly on the dose. These old claims are fascinating to contemplate in the light of novel neuroimaging research on the effects of LSD on the default neural network, in which a neurophysiological correlation to Abramson's claims can somehow be intuited (Carhart Harris et al., 2008, 2014, 2017; Lebdev et al., 2015; Smigielski et al., 2019), as well as the paradoxical effect of LSD (Carhart-Harris et al., 2016).

Abramson's conception is similar to the typology of experiences that can occur according to the German psycholytic authors. Hanscarl Leuner distinguished between three different courses in a psychedelic experience: 1) the continuous-scenic course, 2) the stagnant-fragmented course, and 3) the extreme-psychotic course (Passie, 1996). In this model, positive results can only occur if the patient remains on the continuous-scenic course. Furthermore, the extreme-psychotic course could even be harmful. The determining factor, according to Leuner and similar to Abramson's assertion, is the dose.

As we have seen previously, a common practice in the various psycholytic treatments was the combination of different substances (Eisner, 2002; Abramson, 1966), in particular methylphenidate during the session with LSD. In addition, sedatives, barbiturates, and antipsychotics such as chlorpromazine were also commonly used to manage potential problems: ending the experiences, inducing sleep, or dealing with prolonged reactions and avoiding flashbacks (Baker, 1964; Sandison, 1957). Difficult experiences and subsequent adverse reactions were treated mainly pharmacologically, although there were occasional attempts to manage post-experience anxiety through telephone conversations with patients or personal interviews (Eisner & Cohen, 1958). However, the pharmacological approach allowed "treating a greater number of patients without having to admit them" (Sandison, 1957). The results from such an outlook did not seem so promising even then: "We have had experience with a small number of cases in which LSD was given at weekly intervals with the minimum of supervision by the therapist. Most of these patients produced a great deal of material which they wrote down but which they failed to integrate and the results were poor." In other cases, electro-convulsive therapy (what is commonly known as electroshocks) was used to end prolonged and psychotic-like reactions (Baker, 1964).

Seen through the prism of psycholytic therapy, integration consists of two interrelated processes. On one hand, it relies on a therapeutic relationship—whether analytical, Freudian, Jungian, or any other school of therapy—in order to process and make sense of the contents that appeared during the session. On the other hand, the second process is the unfolding of an "integrative experience," a kind of mystical experience that emerges from integrating the different layers of the psyche as described by Freud, or the assimilation of the contents of the unconscious as seen from Jung's perspective. The dose is a fundamental factor: progressively higher doses are usually used, allowing a conservation of the ego or even an ego-enhancement, with the intention that the patient can follow the course of the experience. Analysis by the therapist is also essential to allow insights to occur. Thus, the integration of the emergent material is considered one of the fundamental elements for the experience to be successful and useful (Abramson, 1966; Sandison, 1954).

During this period, the first specific integration practices appear, although they are not explicitly defined and vary depending on the analytic school followed by each therapist. For the first time, some anecdotal activities are developed that are still used in integration today, such as telling the story of the experience, group therapy, drawing, and working with clay sculptures. These methods were developed independently, primarily by Betty Eisner and Ronald Sandison.

Here we find a methodology based mainly on psychoanalytic psychotherapy and therefore the integration is carried out from the psychoanalytic perspective. The objective of psycholytic therapy coincides with that of psychoanalysis: to reveal the contents of the unconscious throughout the different stages of development and to understand the unconscious drives so that there can be a symptomatic reduction, a maturation, and a better adaptation to the context and society as the result of a profound change in personality (Abramson, 1973; Ling & Buckman, 1963; Alnaes, 1964). Or, according to Freud himself, the analysis ends when two conditions are met: "First, that the patient does not suffer from his symptoms and has overcome his anxiety and inhibitions, and second, that the analyst judges that so much repressed material has become conscious [...] that there is no need to fear a repetition of the pathological processes in question" (Freud, 1937, in 2001).

From the psycholytic perspective, psychedelic substances can shorten the duration of the therapeutic relationship by optimizing the sessions. This is achieved due to a decrease in defenses, a greater flow of unconscious material, and the possibility of integrative experiences, either during the psychoanalytic session or subsequent psychoanalytic sessions. Shortening therapy is considered desirable by many authors (Abramson, 1956; Sandison, 1954; Ling & Buckman, 1963) and even Freud, seeing the limitations of psychoanalysis in practical terms, debated how to shorten therapy and prophesied that perhaps this could be accomplished by chemicals:

Experience has taught us that psychoanalytic therapy—the release of some of the neurotic symptoms, inhibitions, and character abnormalities—is a time-consuming affair. Thus, from the beginning, attempts have been made to shorten the analysis. [...] There is no doubt that shortening the duration of psychoanalytic treatment is desirable, but we can only achieve our therapeutic purpose by increasing the power of analysis so that it can help the self. Hypnosis seemed to be an excellent instrument for this purpose, but the reasons for abandoning it are well known and a substitute for it has not yet been found (Freud, 1937, in Complete Works, 2001).[11]

But therapy concerns us here only to the extent that it works with psychological means; at the moment we have no others. Perhaps the future will teach us to influence directly, through specific chemical substances, the volumes of energy and its distribution within the mental apparatus. Other unsuspected possibilities may open up for therapy. (Freud, 1940, in Complete Works, 2001)

It seems, then, that psycholytic therapists did find this substitute and that, indeed, unsuspected possibilities for therapy were opened.

Integration in Psychedelic Psychotherapy

The development of the psychedelic therapy format and the evolution of the paradigm that led to its formulation are part of a gripping story. This story is closely linked to the treatment of alcoholism and includes famous names such as the Saskatchewan group (made up of Abram Hoffer and Humphry Osmond—the psychiatrist who administered mescaline for the first time to Aldous Huxley and who coined the term "psychedelic" in 1957), Bill Wilson (the creator of Alcoholics Anonymous, who had his experience with LSD at the hands of Sidney Cohen and Betty Eisner), and others who are less known but just as influential, such as Charles Savage and his team at the Mental Research Institute of Palo Alto and "captain" Al Hubbard.[12] Furthermore, the development of psychedelic psychotherapy implied, perhaps for the first time in recent history, a contact with traditional forms of medicine and spirituality (Terrill et al., 1962). In 1953, Osmond, Hoffer, and other researchers participated in a ritual officiated by the Native American Church, using peyote in a traditional way to combat the ravages of alcoholism and get in touch with God. The Red Pheasant Cree Nation invited them to participate in the ritual to build support for continued legal access to peyote for Native Americans

(Oram, 2018). Osmond, Hoffer, and the Saskatchewan team realized that the treatment they were devising had precedents among ancient cultures.

The history of the development of psychedelic therapy is beyond the scope of this book. The interested reader can visit various sources where it has been extensively documented and described (Mangini, 1998; Sessa, 2007, 2016; Eisner, 2002; Pollan, 2018; Oram, 2018).

Different research groups engaged in what could be understood as psychedelic therapy in the period between the 1950s to the 1970s, although their methodologies varied enormously. For example, in some cases the patients were not told anything about the substance they were to receive (a high or very high dose of LSD). After the administration of the substance, a three-hour interview was conducted, followed by intervals of intermittent observation, all while the patients were tied to a hospital bed, without any music playing (Smart et al., 1966). In other studies, there was no therapeutic intervention or preparation whatsoever. Instead, only high doses of LSD were administered and the results were measured (Hollister et al., 1969). At the other extreme, we find the studies of the Spring Grove team, in which an extensive preparation was done before the experience—up to twenty hours—designed to create a positive bond with the therapist. Furthermore, these experiences took place in a comfortable, well-equipped, and tastefully decorated room, paired with carefully selected classical music, supported by two therapists (a man and a woman), and the inclusion of multiple psychotherapy sessions after the session (Pahnke, 1970). The Spring Grove intervention model evolved over the years due to the influence of the therapists and researchers who made up the team. Grof contributed his knowledge of the psychoanalytic therapy he had practiced in Czechoslovakia and suggested that psychedelic substances could increase the effectiveness of other psychoanalytic therapeutic interventions. In the late Spring Grove days, before the psychedelic research program was canceled, they developed a mixed method that combined psycholytic sessions with psychedelic counseling sessions (Rhead et al., 1977).

Other researchers used a combination of hypnosis and LSD, which they called hypnodelic therapy (Levine and Ludwig, 1963, 1965, 1966). This technique was somewhat unusual, as the experimental sessions lasted for about three hours after the ingestion of the LSD (in doses of 125 to 200 µg). During these sessions, hypnotic inductions were made before the manifestation of the pharmacological effects, supported by a type of psychodynamic therapy based on insights and interpretations and directed towards the patient's trauma, finished with post-hypnotic suggestions. Eventually, the patient was left alone—under frequent supervision if necessary—for the remainder of the day and night. During this period, the patient was encouraged to continue reflecting and writing down the experience. The negative results of this study had a significant impact on the general academic opinion. However, they have helped highlight the importance of the therapeutic and extra-pharmacological factors inherent to psychedelic-assisted psychotherapy.[13]

The methodological requirements in those days differed substantially from the current ones. The therapeutic and research designs were diverse and varied, making it difficult to draw univocal conclusions from their results. For this reason, many of these studies have not been of great importance and have mostly been forgotten.[14] Some studies were methodologically stricter (Kurland et al., 1971; Krebs, 2012) and others had certain shortcomings (Bowen, 1970; Mangini, 1998; Krebs, 2012). However, what is perhaps most surprising is that, in almost all cases, the initial results were promising, with a general reduction in alcohol use after the LSD session and greater maintenance of abstinence compared to the control groups during the first months. Furthermore, this seems to be the case regardless of the setting and the therapeutic format used. However, over time, the improvements faded and some studies did not even find significant differences between the control group and the LSD group at twelve months (all had improved somewhat from baseline, thankfully). The control groups varied widely depending on the study, some even receiving low, psycholytic doses of

LSD, at doses of 25-50 µg (Bowen et al., 1970; Kurland et al., 1971). Similar things happened in the treatment of neurotic patients: the results at six months were very promising, but at twelve and eighteen months, no significant differences were observed between the high-dose, low-dose, and control groups (Savage et al., 1973). Therefore, it is difficult to draw conclusions about best practices and which factors played key roles in patients' improvement. Furthermore, it seems even more challenging to establish any pattern regarding the different integration practices carried out, when there were any at all.

Joyce Martin (1957, 1964) and McCririck used anaclitic therapy, also called fusion therapy, a method that does not quite fit with psychedelic therapy as it is commonly understood, although it does share some important similarities. In this model, the therapists administered doses of LSD and then facilitated the person during the experience through an intimate hug, in which they tried to repair early separation traumas. This type of practice highly influenced Grof's method of psychedelic psychotherapy and his later development of Holotropic Breathwork. However, psychoanalysis remained the general framework for the therapeutic process so that anaclitic therapy as a whole is closer to the usual psycholytic therapy, even if this particular intervention was developed to satisfy the needs of his patients in a state of regression.

In the context of the varieties of psychedelic therapy, Bowen, Soskin, and Chotlos (1970) ask a question that is still relevant today: "The question of whether the short term changes can be maintained is an intriguing one. There is something magical about expecting a single experience [...] to drastically change an individual's habitual lifestyle."

The therapeutic mechanism that was singled out from the multiple studies carried out under the psychedelic paradigm seems to be the mystical experience happening during the LSD session (Kurland et al., 1967, 1973; Savage, in Terrill et al., 1962). Although the different therapeutic methodologies seem to have little in common with each other (hypnosis, psychotherapy, internalized experience, etc.), it appears that the best results coincided with patients reporting a very particular type of experience called "the psychedelic experience of mystic consciousness" (Pahnke and Richards, 1966). According to these authors, the attributes of the mystical experience include: 1) a feeling of undifferentiated unity, 2) objectivity and reality (or noetic quality, in terms of William James), 3) transcendence of time and space, 4) the sensation of sacredness, 5) a profoundly positive mood, 6) paradoxical nature, 7) ineffability, 8) transience, and 9) positive changes in attitudes or behaviors (Pahnke, 1970; Pahnke & Richards, 1966).

These results seem to coincide with the conclusions of the studies that are currently being carried out as a continuation (Griffiths et al., 2008, 2011, 2016; Garcia-Romeu et al., 2015; Carhart-Harris (personal communication), MacLean et al., 2011), in which a correlation has been found between the occurrence of a mystical experience and clinical improvement.

Thus, a positive unfolding of psychedelic therapy, regardless of the method used, seems closely related to the occurrence of a mystical experience. Therefore, it is necessary to investigate how such an experience can be induced or facilitated to occur. Another question that arises is, "How do we maintain the positive effects produced by a mystical experience over time?"—since it has been observed that these experiences tend to dissipate quite often. As Pahnke describes: "Indications are, however, that what one does with a psychedelic experience may be more important than merely having it. Without integration [...] the experience may be only an irrelevant memory, no matter how beautiful" (Pahnke, 1967).

It is interesting to look at what clinicians and researchers have done outside of the pharmacological sessions. This information, as we have seen, seems rather scarce. However, there are a few examples in which more detailed practices are found.

It is with the Spring Grove team, at the Maryland Psychiatric Research Center, where the word "integration" became used more frequently within the treatment protocol. Albert Kurland, Charles Savage, Walter Pahnke, Bill Richards, Stan Grof and others start to systematize working with LSD, DPT (dipropyltryptamine), and other psychedelic substances. Here, they define and refine in much greater detail the way of working during the psychedelic session, they create lists of music specially selected for each phase of the experience, define the type of interventions that are carried out, and develop, improve, and systematize the method devised by Al Hubbard. This mysterious character had already influenced other researchers such as Osmond and Hoffer. Additionally, Hubbard served as inspiration for the first manuals detailing interventions during psychedelic experiences, which contained only a few indications for integration, such as the interview, the account of the experience, and "informal contact" among those who have participated in the experience, as well as referral to Alcoholics Anonymous groups.[15] Although scarce in integration methods, these manuals recognized the importance of the post-experience period: "The subject should be told in advance that the LSD experience does not constitute a cure for alcoholism. It offers an experience which can make the AA (Alcoholics Anonymous) program more acceptable and inspiring"(Blewett & Chwelos, 1959).

The Maryland Psychiatric Research team also places particular emphasis on the preparation phase, dedicating around twenty hours to it. They discover the importance and influence of this phase on the eventual outcome of psychedelic sessions, emphasizing the development of a good therapeutic relationship (Grof et al., 1973; Richards, 1979). In the words of Pahnke:

> Beneficial results observed are not due to either the psycho-pharmacological effects of LSD or the placebo effect (suggestion and preparation) alone, but rather a combination of set, setting, and drug. For the best results it seems essential that the placebo effect be utilized to the utmost in

conjunction with the psychedelic drug which is then seen to be a necessary, but not sufficient, condition.[16] *(Pahnke, 1971)*

The methods of preparation for the subject, as well as the methodical and warm intervention during the session, respect for the content emerging during the experience, the mapping of the nature of psychedelic experiences, and the need for prior personal experience on the side of the therapists, will forever remain a unique contribution from the Spring Grove team to the development of psychedelic-assisted psychotherapy. Proof of this is that its pioneers continue to practice. Bill Richards still collaborates with the recent studies at Johns Hopkins Hospital, while Grof's methods continue to be a benchmark in the studies of MAPS[17] with MDMA and constitute a blueprint for the training of future therapists.

The development of integration practices, however, was less explicit. An example is the following comment by Grof: "Immediately following the psychedelic session and during the subsequent days, the therapeutic effort focused upon working through, integrating, and consolidating the psychedelic experience. The patients were asked to write out or dictate a subjective account of the session in as much detail as possible." (Grof et al., 1973).

Proper integration practices, as we know them today, are outlined by Grof in some detail only in much later publications (1980). In his integration program, Grof proposes different activities for the subject after the experience: 1) rest; 2) to remain in a meditative state; 3) to be in contact with nature; 4) to listen to music (especially music that was used during the psychedelic session); 5) a "long interview" with the therapist, to share the experience and analyze "disconcerting aspects;" 6) a visualization of the recording of the psychedelic experience; 7) to write an account of the experience (as a basis for later therapeutic analysis); 8) artistic expression of the experience (drawing, poetry, music, etc.); and 9) to remain attentive to dreams.

Grof indicates that the integration process can take days or weeks and that the activities listed above are often sufficient for integration. However, sometimes the process is not completed spontaneously and requires further work by the therapists. In such cases, Grof used certain techniques to re-activate the experience, consisting of intense breathing exercises inspired by "rebirthing" (and which were the basis for the later development of Holotropic Breathing). And if that did not work, another LSD session was scheduled "as soon as possible," in the hope that the next session could resolve the situation.

The approach to integration is thus rendered in the following way: appropriate elements are provided so that the subject can make their own integration (rest, artistic expression, nature), as well as an interview to analyze the content of the session, hoping that it is enough. If not, another non-ordinary state of consciousness is induced and the first integration strategies are applied again until the situation is resolved.

We can see an integration process that is focused on the psychedelic experience and based on its good resolution, empowering the subject to achieve coherence with the experience by their own means. However, we do not know what happens in the interviews between the subject and the therapist, nor what therapeutic mechanisms the professionals use beyond providing the space, materials, time, and if necessary, another psychedelic session.

Grof left the field of psychotherapy and integration open by outlining his psychedelic therapy program:

"I have outlined the more general principles of a comprehensive LSD psychotherapy program. The therapeutic and tactical strategy for each individual case depends on many factors, and therapists have to develop it creatively based on their clinical experience and first-hand explorations in LSD training sessions. The practice of psychedelic therapy is based as much on intuition as it is on knowledge of therapeutic principles and probably always combines elements of art and science" (Grof, 2005).

The in-depth study of these factors, individual cases, strategies, and useful tactics—based on my clinical and personal experience—constitutes the main purpose of this volume and I humbly hope that I can further expand the knowledge contributed by the pioneers of psychedelic psychotherapy.

THE PSYCHEDELIC RENAISSANCE

Integration in Modern Psychedelic Research

Although the "psychedelic renaissance" is often time-stamped in the year 2000, it actually began earlier, during the 1990s. During this time, the first few studies with different psychedelic substances were published: studies with DMT (Strassman, 1994, 1996), with MDMA at the Institut de Recerca Biomèdica de Barcelona (Mas et al., 1999; de la Torre et al., 2000; Camí et al., 2000), as well as in Switzerland (Liechti et al., 2000)—where they were also studying psilocybin, D-amphetamine, and MDE (Vollenweider et al., 1998; Gouzoulis-Mayfrank et al., 1998, 1999). The subsequent explosion of studies around the turn of the millennium was the result of all the research carried out during the previous decade.

Perhaps one of the most important peculiarities of modern psychedelic research is their exclusive focus on some pathologies. This is in addition to a better methodology compared to previous research and an emphasis on the necessary studies about the safety and tolerability of different psychedelic substances (dos Santos et al., 2018). Psychedelic-assisted therapy has thus focused on specific sectors of the population and current patients must have been diagnosed with certain pathologies, in particular post-traumatic stress disorder (PTSD); treatment-resistant depression; addictive disorders (specifically alcohol and tobacco); anxiety and depression co-morbid with life-threatening diagnoses such as cancer or Parkinson's disease (dos Santos et al., 2018, 2019); and others such as complicated grief (González et al., 2019, 2020). Although addictions were also investigated in the 1950s and 1960s, the diagnoses at that time were less specific and psychedelic substances were used for "neurosis" and "psychosis," without many more specifications, particularly in combination with psychotherapy.

Broadly speaking, we currently find two distinct approaches to the use of psychedelic substances for the treatment of different pathologies. On the one hand, there is psychedelic substance-assisted psychotherapy with a non-directive (or "inner directive") and supportive approach, as used in the case of MDMA for the treatment of PTSD (Bouso et al., 2008; Mithoefer et al., 2011, 2013, 2018; Oehen et al., 2013) or psilocybin for the treatment of depression (Carhart-Harris, 2016, 2017). On the other hand, there are trials that use a specific psychotherapeutic method, independent of the use of psychedelic substances, and add a specific number of sessions using psychedelic substances as adjuncts to psychotherapy (Johnson et al., 2014; Bogenschutz et al., 2013, 2015; Wagner et al., 2019).

This allows us to understand more about the integration of experiences with these substances, in addition to their global integration into an already existing treatment designed to address a specific pathology. We can see how psychedelic therapy is combined with the usual psychotherapeutic approach for these pathologies.

Some interesting examples are the treatment of PTSD using a combination of MDMA-assisted psychotherapy and cognitive-behavioral psychotherapy (CBT) for couples' therapy (Wagner et al., 2019), in contrast to the more common non-directive and supportive approach to MDMA-assisted psychotherapy (Mithoefer et al., 2011, 2013, 2018). Another example is the treatment of tobacco addiction with the use of psilocybin, within the framework of a cognitive-behavioral treatment (Johnson et al., 2014), or for the treatment of alcoholism with psilocybin and Motivational Stimulation Therapy (MET) (Bogenschutz et al., 2015, 2016; Nielson et al., 2018). In general, there seems to be a renewed interest in the potential combination of psychedelic therapy with third generation cognitive-behavioral therapies, such as Acceptance and Commitment

Therapy (ACT), Dialectical Behavior Therapy (DBT), Mindfulness-Based Cognitive Therapy (MBCT), and the like (Walsh et al., 2018).

In these studies, psychedelic substances are used with the intention of boosting the effectiveness of a psychotherapeutic treatment. The treatment proposed by Wagner is particular in that the MDMA is given in joint sessions—to the patient diagnosed with PTSD and to their spouse. On one hand, the use of MDMA is intended to boost the couple's communication skills and on the other hand, to facilitate the processing of traumatic memories, helped by the marked reduction in anxiety and avoidance induced by the MDMA. The intention for using psilocybin in combination with psychotherapeutic treatment is less clear, beyond the aforementioned preliminary findings of the 1950s and 1970s, which pointed to the usefulness of peak psychedelic experiences in the treatment of different addictions and the reported reduction in anxiety and depression in terminally ill patients, as well as the neurophysiological effects of reducing the default neural network (DMN), which would correlate with a decrease in depressive symptoms.

The therapeutic methodology of these studies can be simplified as follows: there is a standardized treatment that is used for the different disorders (CBT for PTSD, CBT for smoking, and MET for alcoholism). The treatment is applied as established in the manual, but sessions with MDMA or psilocybin are interspersed, together with dedicated preparation, integration, and other debriefing sessions (Bogenschutz et al., 2015; Wagner et al., 2019).

Thus, we have two different aspects of integration. Firstly, we have integration within the framework of a standardized treatment, similar to the psycholytic uses of the early years in which psychedelic substances did not a priori modify the unfolding of the therapeutic model. Secondly, we have the so-called integration or debriefing sessions after each experience.

Although the theory behind an integration built into the therapeutic framework of a standardized treatment may be more or less coherent, justifiable, or intuitive, it seems that this solution does not carry too many issues. The subjects of the studies adhere to both standardized treatment and sessions with psychedelic substances, similarly to how the psycholytic therapy model—in relation to psychoanalysis—adheres to standardized treatment manuals that exist and can be consulted. This way, the treatments that are specific to the intervention can be easily known.

Regarding the "debriefing" or integration sessions that are carried out in these trials, we face the same problems that we met between the 1950s and the 1970s, with a lack of clarity about what is being done and the purpose of these sessions. For tobacco-addiction treatment, the interventions during integration sessions include the participant's re-telling of their psychedelic session (Johnson et al., 2014). In the case of MDMA for PTSD, integrated with CBT, a debriefing is performed and behavioral tasks are assigned for the next session. In the case of alcoholism, it is simply indicated that a debriefing session takes place after the experience. Thus, we see that the descriptions of the integration sessions are not very precise.

In other cases, however, the practices used during the integration sessions are more detailed. Perhaps the best example can be found in the integration method described for MDMA-assisted psychotherapy for PTSD in a non-directive and supportive context (Mithoefer et al., 2013).[18] In this method, Michael Mithoefer describes very clearly the type of interventions that may be necessary for the integration sessions after the administration of MDMA. Perhaps the most remarkable thing is that he defines integration as a process that may unfold according to different possible scenarios. Integration can be easy and require little intervention by the therapist or difficulties may appear after the MDMA experience, and the patient may need additional support as they deal with the difficult emotions or somatic manifestations that may arise.

For Mithoefer, "the ultimate goal of MDMA-assisted therapy is to eliminate symptoms and achieve a better level of well-being and functioning."[19] This can occur throughout a process that extends well beyond the MDMA sessions through the continued processing of emerging emotions, insights gained, and new perspectives on the problem itself. The role of the therapist is to help the person relate in a beneficial and fruitful way to the ongoing changes and to consolidate and ground them in their daily life, in relation to themselves, their environment, and their narrative about past traumatic events.

The attitude of the therapist during this phase is attuned to validate the person and the account of their experience, answer any questions that the person may have, and encourage them to continue processing the emotions as they appear. We work with the insights and the meaning of the memories or images that have emerged during the session, and some interpretations can be offered as minimally as possible, encouraging autonomy in the process of integration and understanding of the experience.

The standard tools for integration previously discussed (Eisner, 2002; Sandison, 1954; Grof, 1980), such as drawing, writing, artistic expression, or contact with nature, among others, are prescribed during this period as different activities that the clients can carry out on their own outside of the psychotherapeutic sessions.

During the integration sessions, different interventions are carried out. These include validation; the possibility of a detailed retelling of the experience; the exploration of the possible meanings attributed to the content of the session; psychoeducation regarding the continuous nature of the integration process and its potentially different manifestations; the processing of difficult emotions and stress; or working with existing cognitive dilemmas, among others. An interesting intervention is the use of "bodywork," focused on supporting the processing of somatic or emotional discomfort that resists verbal approaches. Thus, the Mithoefer method explains which approaches are followed in the integration sessions, although how the interventions are carried out is less explicit. In this case, however, it does seem that a method exists which could be taught and learned.

We then see that the method proposed by Mithoefer[20] is detailed, comprehensive, and encompasses a wide range of interventions. It is based on Grof's proposals and draws from the influence of the Holotropic Breathwork training that both Michael and Annie Mithoefer underwent to become certified facilitators in the Grof Transpersonal Training (GTT). The elements of validation (as opposed to interpretation), the provision of tools for artistic expression, and in particular the use of bodywork with the intention presented by the Mithoefers, are all essential elements in the work of Grof and his Holotropic Breathwork framework.

Another relevant methodology for the integration of psychedelic experiences is currently being tested. Although it is not yet well-known, Method Of Levels (MOL) is a type of interview based on the theory of perceptual control (PCT). This technique consists of a semi-structured interview using specific types of questions intended to keep the participant in the present moment, attentive to what is happening to them while they talk about a relevant aspect of their psychedelic experience. It is an a priori non-directive technique, although it does require a lot of intervention on behalf of the therapist. It is intended to provide the patient with a "felt sense" of what is happening to them while they process the content of what they share, and at the same time capture and make them aware of the thoughts in the background (background thoughts) that are produced during the process. Through a focused dialogue, the goal is for the person to become aware of the different levels involved in a given situation or experience, become aware of the conflicts that may appear at each level, and to climb to higher levels that encompass these conflicts. It is a primarily cognitive technique, although it provides a remarkable subjective experience for the patient who participates in this structured questioning by the therapist.

The principles of MOL intervention are simple, although their implementation by the therapist is much more complex. An interesting aspect of this technique is that it can be taught and learned relatively quickly and can be standardized, so its implementation can be quite independent of the therapist who applies it. A perhaps complicated aspect for most therapists is that this method requires a complete abandonment of the usual therapeutic frames of reference, maps, and cartographies of psychedelic experience or therapeutic progress. In addition, it is necessary to abstain from the majority of classical interventions (paraphrases, interpretations, suggestions, etc.), so it can be difficult for some therapists to absorb. For more details about this method, see Timothy A. Carey's *Method of Levels: How to Do Psychotherapy Without Getting in the Way* (Carey, 2006).

MORE FRAMEWORKS FOR INTEGRATION

Although the concept and practice of integration occur within the clinical and research context, its rise and popularization have emerged mainly among non-professional circles. Following the globalization of the use of psychedelics, many users and facilitators have realized the need for the implementation of safer practices—primarily focused on better preparation and sound integration—to reduce or palliate inherent risks, address potential damage from occasional accidents, and support and facilitate the long term maintenance of psychological improvements. As a result, various contexts for the use of "integration" have emerged, although its meaning and implementation vary enormously.

Integration Circles

Meetings of people who have had psychedelic experiences and want to share their personal processes are becoming increasingly common. There are different ways of implementing these integration circles or groups, depending on the orientation and intention of the person organizing them. Sometimes, the therapist or psychedelic experience facilitator organizes these meetings a few days after the session for the participants of that particular experience. At other times, they are independent groups that do not organize psychedelic sessions but provide a periodic space to which anyone can go.

How one facilitates these encounters also varies greatly. In some groups, a therapist directs the dynamic and intervenes in a more or less active way, making interpretations, giving feedback, or proposing certain exchanges (be they songs, prayers, interpersonal dynamics, etc.). Other groups have a more horizontal approach, and the organizer only provides the space and structure, but no therapeutic interventions are carried out. In some groups, dialogue between participants is allowed, and in other groups they are encouraged to listen actively while refraining from making any comments.

Integration circles are thus an increasingly common format, although the practices carried out in them are disparate and not very specific. Furthermore, the integration circle can represent only the beginning of other activities and group integration formats.

Holotropic Breathwork

Holotropic Breathwork (HB) is a consciousness modification technique created by Stanislav and Christina Grof in the 1980s (Grof & Grof, 2010). Through a specific breathing technique, the use of evocative music, a focused bodywork model, and the creation of a particular context, a non-ordinary state of consciousness with therapeutic and heuristic potential is induced.

HB work is grounded in the concept of the psyche's own ability to promote healing, or as the Grofs call it, "inner healing wisdom." Therefore, it is a non-directive form of experiential work, in which support for the participant's experience, whatever it may be, becomes the primary factor. Fundamental importance is given to good preparation and support during the experience, proper completion of the experience for each participant, and adequate integration. All interventions aim to create a safe context where each participant can fully surrender to their internal experience.

HB sessions do not just involve the practice of a specific breathing technique. The contextual elements—the set and the setting—are as important as the breathing technique itself. Each HB experience lasts around three hours, with participants alternating between "breather" and "caregiver" roles throughout the workshop. Facilitators provide support to participants who need it, both during the experience and after. Once the session is over, certain techniques are offered to promote the beginning of integration through artistic expression and the sharing of the experience. These techniques—and others—are described in the fourth chapter.

For some people, HB is a complementary path to their experiences with psychedelic substances or with master plants since it serves as both preparation and integration of their psychedelic experiences. For others, HB is a path in itself, given the power and safety of the technique.

The HB format provides a broad and inclusive context, since both the technique and the context created are based on solid theoretical foundations and contain multiple useful elements for integration. These include a secure personal and interpersonal context; the possibility of accessing an emotionally significant experience that helps to process incomplete content; attention to the preparation and integration of said experience through artistic expression and sharing groups; a non-directive, non-denominational, and respectful format adequate to the plurality of participants and experiences; and a setting that promotes healthy interpersonal relationships.

Gestalt

Another school in which the use of psychedelics has long been incorporated is Gestalt psychotherapy, particularly the lineage initiating with Claudio Naranjo. In this therapeutic approach, both psychotherapy (or different types of psychotherapies) and the collective use of substances that modify consciousness have been used within the framework of a long-term therapeutic process. This model is quite far removed from other more exclusively transpersonal or psychedelic approaches since it emphasizes the preparation process (Naranjo, 2016). During preparation, one works on one's character—the knowledge of neurotic patterns and identification of the main features—which is carried out under the prism of the Enneagram of Personality. The way of conducting the sessions is also quite different from what is usually understood when we speak of psychedelic therapy since there is generally more interpersonal interaction between patients and between therapist and patient (Naranjo, 1974).

In most cases, integration is carried out from a Gestalt therapy perspective, both individually and in a group. However, it is not easy to define what specific practices are carried out during these sessions. Therapists experienced in this type of process have argued that what is done during integration is "pure Gestalt therapy," so there does not seem to be a specific integration methodology. Instead, it is a method more similar to psycholytic psychotherapy, but with the study of character and its transcendence as a background paradigm, in which psychedelic sessions act as instruments in a continuous Gestalt therapy process. Gestalt therapy, in turn, encompasses diverse practices and unfolds differently depending on each therapist and their understanding of psychotherapy, making it impossible to systematically define psychedelic integration from the Gestalt perspective.

ABOUT
INTEGRATION

2

"Psychedelics awakened in people not just a thirst, but a sense of the possibilities for exploring the mind and body—that they could live in a different way. Then they began to develop those sensitivities and those visions without repeatedly taking psychedelics by undertaking some spiritual discipline, yoga, or meditation. Finally, many people began to see that even their meditative practices wouldn't stabilize when the rest of their life wasn't included. They found it was necessary to take care with their actions in a way that was non-harming and compassionate. So we have gone on to discover that the root of fundamental change must be grounded in our ethical behavior and compassion, followed by a systematic inner training. Those are the supports for long lasting and integrated access to these transformative experiences."

JACK KORNFIELD (2015)

WHAT IS INTEGRATION?

In the psychedelic community, the word "integration" is frequently used, and references are made to the enormous importance of this concept in the different frameworks of psychedelic substance use, whether in research contexts, neo-shamanic contexts, or settings of self-experimentation. Although the use of the word "integration" is common, and there seems to be an agreement about its meaning across contexts, integration practices have varied significantly since the beginnings of psychedelic therapy. Similarly, the understanding of what integration implies is very diverse, both in its theoretical approaches and in its practical implementation.

The concept of integration is usually one aspect of a broader conceptual chain. The usual scheme is typically as follows: 1) preparation, 2) session, 3) integration, and it is crucial that we understand these phases as interrelated elements belonging to a continuous chain of events—to a process, rather than seen merely as isolated events. Thinking in terms of process is crucial in developing any type of therapy, particularly psychedelic therapy. More than conceiving specific interventions at different times, it is convenient to understand everything that happens as a necessary step for the development of the whole. Each phase has an important influence on the direction, the course, and the results of therapy. Thus, work done during the preparation period will have a decisive influence on what happens in the session.

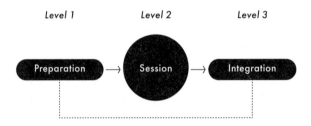

Preparation and Screening

"Preparation" is understood as everything that happens before the psychedelic experience, both on a personal and intra-psychic level, as well as the interventions carried out by the therapist, facilitator, or shaman prior to the session. The purpose of the preparation is manifold. Firstly, it includes the entire process of screening, or the selection process of the candidates who will have the experience (in which physical and psychological health, as well as the social context, must be explored). Secondly, it also includes the specific preparation of the participants: their expectations, their knowledge about potential reactions, the context in which the experience will unfold, and the general dynamics of the session in its specific setup. Lastly, it factors in the preparation of the physical space in which the session will take place, as well as arranging the necessary equipment, material, and emergency plans.

One of the first references regarding the need for preparation before an LSD session is found in Abramson (1955), in which the author argues that the anxiety of the future patient can be reduced when informed about the treatment two weeks in advance and when allowed to ask questions about the procedure.

In his 1980 work *LSD Psychotherapy*, Stanislav Grof lists a few different factors that may influence the development of a psychedelic session. These factors include the substance used, the personality of the therapist, the personality of the patient, the preparation and the integration of the experience, the mental state (or the "Set"), and finally, the context (the "Setting"). The preparation of the experience is an explicitly listed factor, and we could also argue that some more of these factors relate to the preparation, such as the patient's personality and the personality (which could include the training and experience) of the therapist.

Most of the motivation for having a screening process revolves around the need to assess the patient's personality. It is a common assumption that certain people cannot engage with psychedelics safely—people for whom these experiences are not recommended because they could be harmful due to certain physical or psychological factors. It is traditionally understood that there are different psychological factors that could predispose participants to adverse reactions (for example, Fischer et al., 1968). These reactions can be understood in different ways. Their severity can be highly variable, ranging from episodes of acute anxiety or panic attacks to the so-called "bad trips" or negative experiences, flashbacks, or even, at the deeper end, transitory psychotic reactions of greater or lesser duration, suicidal or homicidal ideation, and acute or prolonged paranoid states (Smart & Bateman, 1967; Malleson, 1971; Cohen, 1966; Kleber, 1967). The factors that may predispose a person to these reactions have become a matter of discussion, controversy, and discrepancy, both in clinical and academic settings and, more recently, in neo-shamanic, self-exploration, and underground therapeutic contexts.

Traditionally, it has been understood that the use of psychedelic substances is not indicated for people diagnosed with disorders within the psychotic spectrum (schizophrenia, previous psychotic episodes, etc.), nor for people with mood disorders (particularly bipolar disorder, which often includes psychotic symptoms), due to the possibility that existing symptoms would be exacerbated by the psychedelic experience, inducing a new psychotic or manic episode or producing a symptomatic decompensation (Vangaard, 1964).

People with personality disorders are also often excluded from clinical trials (for example, in Bouso et al., 2008; Wolfson et al., 2014; Mithoefer et al., 2011), in particular people with borderline personality disorder, dissociative personality disorder, and other disorders that the clinician considers may interfere with the development of the study. The exclusion of people with personality disorders is not usually due to fear of their symptoms worsening but rather because of the difficulty in establishing a good therapeutic relationship between the clinician and the patient. The lack of good rapport and trust between the patient and the therapist is probably the clearest indicator of a poor prognosis in therapy. Certain therapists have, in the past, ventured into treating people with psychotic disorders using psychedelic substances in clinical settings, although the results were variable, as will be described in the following pages.

In the absence of psychopathological diagnoses, the question remains as to which people are more likely to have a difficult experience during a psychedelic session, failing to improve and suffering adverse reactions. The use of MDMA, psilocybin, ayahuasca, LSD, and other substances has been shown to be safe in controlled clinical settings when screening factors are taken into account (Johnson et al., 2008; Mithoefer et al., 2010; Dyck, 2006; Gasser et al., 2014; Kaelen et al., 2015; Kreb et al., 2012; Schmid et al., 2018; Barret et al., 2017; Bogenschuts et al., 2015; Carhart-Harris et al., 2017; Carhart-Harris et al., 2016; Carhart-Harris et al., 2018). Even so, some studies have tried to find the factors that can predispose some people to a difficult experience with adverse reactions, including the precipitation of a transitory psychotic episode in extreme cases (Lienert et al., 1996; Carrillo et al., 2018; Haijen et al., 2018; Studerus et al., 2011).

Predictors of the outcome of psychedelic experiences appear to be multifactorial and associated with dose, personality, mood at the time of the experience, previous psychopathology, previous psychedelic experiences, and the context of the experience (Studerus et al., 2012; Haijen et al., 2018). Positive expectations and the state of mind prior to the experience (presence or absence of anxiety, among others) represent the most determining factors according to various authors and clinicians (Metzner et al., 1965; Haijen et al., 2018). Cohen (1985) indicated that people at risk were those with unstable, immature, or rigid personalities; those who presented excessive paranoid content; people suffering from acute depression; individuals with schizoid features; and those with a family history of schizophrenia.

The occurrence of difficult psychedelic experiences in the past appears to be a significant predictor of their repetition (Hemsley & Ward, 1985). Therefore, it seems important to explore whether a person has had bad experiences with psychedelic substances before, in addition to exploring their relevant life experiences. Not surprisingly, people who present psychological difficulties after one or more psychedelic experiences report having "bad trips" during their first years of experimentation with psychedelic substances, or a difficult experience that involved a period of more or less serious psychological destabilization.

These early episodes can leave an imprint that tends to reappear in similar contexts and situations, such as new psychedelic experiences or shifts in states of consciousness, even if no apparent consequences related to this episode are obviously apparent in daily life. These states can be understood as state-dependent memories: experiences and memories that are activated and regain their emotional charge when we are in a certain state of consciousness, but which remain inactive for the rest of the time. In Grof's paradigm, it is considered that the material that we access during non-ordinary states of consciousness, if not adequately resolved during a session, has a tendency to appear on future occasions to be processed again and resolved. Thus, from this perspective, it is not a pathological phenomenon, but rather an attempt by the psyche to resolve an unfinished gestalt (Grof, 1980).

Another factor that is commonly discussed due to its influence on adverse reactions is "neuroticism." In the Big Five model, this personality trait is associated with a greater propensity for negative emotions and a lower ability to cope with stress (John et al., 2008), as well as greater vulnerability to psychopathology, particularly when associated with difficult interactions with environmental stressors (Widiger & Smith, 2008), a category that can include psychedelic experiences (Barret et al., 2017). Neuroticism is related to a greater occurrence of difficult psychedelic experiences (Lienert & Netter, 1996) and a greater difficulty in letting go when experiencing an ego dissolution (Ditrich, 1994; Barret et al., 2017). It has been traditionally understood that people who score high in neuroticism could not benefit from the psychedelic experience (Vangaard, 1964; Savage et al., 1973). Therefore, it seems prudent to evaluate this character trait in potential candidates for psychedelic experiences.

From a non-academic perspective, neuroticism relates to rigidity of character, that is, the difficulty in producing a broad spectrum of behavioral responses to stressful situations. It can also be understood as a tendency towards negative emotions and nervousness, anxiety, irritability, insecurity, tension, and irrational perfectionism. It also implies difficulties in handling stressful situations and having few coping strategies. For example, people who present much difficulty in adapting to a certain context or environmental conditions, whether labor-related or interpersonal, have more difficulty navigating disease or job changes (John et al., 2008). In the context of a group workshop, neuroticism could manifest itself in difficulty adapting to new routines, meal times and activities, exaggerated reactions to unforeseen situations (problems with food, conditions, accommodation, etc.), or difficulty in relation to the rest of the group. This trait manifests both in interpersonal relationships and intrapsychic dynamics due to the same inflexibility in dealing constructively with difficult internal states or when a feeling of threat or lack of control is perceived. A psychedelic experience can be, by its very nature, a difficult situation for people with high levels of neuroticism.

Considering all of the above, we must be aware that people who score high on neuroticism and emotional instability tend to experience suffering from these same reasons, therefore seeking help via different therapeutic modalities, including psychedelic therapy. Substances such as MDMA can be of great help in these cases, allowing greater cognitive flexibility and helping reduce neuroticism. Therefore, as psychologists we must be able to work with these people, taking into account that they may require more focused attention than people without these characteristics.

Another factor commonly studied when predicting potential difficulties during or after the experience has been schizotypy. This character trait, also present in all people to a greater or lesser degree, relates to the manifestation of psychotic-like behaviors or thought patterns while not falling within the diagnostic rubric of schizophrenia. Schizotypy instead refers to certain peculiarities in one's character that, while sharing commonalities with certain psychotic manifestations, will only rarely devolve to a full-blown psychosis or schizophrenia (Chapman et al., 1994; Mohr & Claridge, 2015; Fonseca-Pedrero et al., 2011), although a schizotypal personality has been considered a predictor of schizophrenia in past times.

Claridge described schizotypy as a cluster of symptoms grouped around four main axes: 1) Unusual Experiences, 2) Cognitive Disorganization, 3) Introverted Anhedonia, and 4) Non-Compliant Impulsivity (Bental et al., 1989; Claridge et al., 1996). Raine et al. (1994) described three differentiated dimensions of symptoms belonging to the schizotypal personality. The first is positive schizotypy, which consists mainly of symptomatology related to magical thinking, unusual experiences, and spiritual and religious beliefs. The second dimension corresponds to negative schizotypy, related to apathy, social isolation, and physical and social anhedonia (the inability to enjoy food, social and physical contact, sex, and general contact with other human beings). The third dimension corresponds to cognitive disorganization, related to difficulties in producing coherent and consistent thought sequences, unusual behavior, disorganized speech, and general eccentricity.

Chapman et al. (1994) investigated predictors for psychotic experiences, finding that the constructs of magical thinking and perceptual aberration (set of symptoms related to positive schizotypy) seemed good indicators to predict the appearance of eventual psychotic symptoms, although they did not anticipate the onset of schizophrenia. However, those with a combination of magical thinking and social anhedonia were the most likely to develop a psychotic disorder, including schizophrenia.

These findings are consistent with those of other authors, who describe how positive schizotypy does not seem to be a predictor of psychosis, even when these people engage in shamanic or paranormal experiences (Rock et al., 2008; Mohr & Claridge , 2015; Schofield et al., 2007). However, cognitive disorganization and anhedonia are the factors that determine whether a person is capable of sustaining and integrating a paranormal or "strange" experience. McCreery and Claridge (2002) described this type of positive schizotypy as healthy schizotypy and attributed adaptive functions in terms of increased subjective well-being and openness to different experiences, even hypothesizing about the function and potential evolutionary advantages of schizotypy (Mohr & Claridge, 2015; Schoefield & Claridge, 2007).

Although these studies almost certainly did not have the psychedelic experience in mind (even if they did include experiences of shamanic trance, as in Rock et al., 2008), their conclusions are still very useful in the context of psychedelic therapy.

Thus, it seems that people with positive schizotypy, combined with good levels of cognitive organization and low levels of anhedonia (a set of factors known to facilitate positive social contact, a good support network, and a well-established therapeutic alliance) are not at greater risk of having an unpleasant or difficult experience than people without these traits. The cognitive organization factor seems especially important in our discussion; good cognitive functioning enables strange and unusual ideas and experiences, however peculiar, to be incorporated into a belief system, which in turn allows one to draw more benefit from an unusual experience, including its integration in the case of a difficult experience.

However, other studies do not align with these statements, having found different results such as higher rates of neuroticism, mood disorders, and substance abuse in people with high levels of positive schizotypy (Chabrol & Raynal, 2018). These same authors attribute the perception of well-being in people who score high in positive schizotypy (these people perceive a high level of quality in their social relationships and a level of well-being comparable to people without schizotypal traits, for example) to a cognitive bias, the use of magical thinking, denial, or to narcissistic character traits. Be that as it may, it seems that these people can construct an adaptive and positive story about their life experiences and symptoms, even if these are unusual and even if the story does not conform to the social norm. This can be a protective factor when faced with difficult psychedelic experiences, since the experience can be assigned meaning.

Negative schizotypy, especially if cognitive disorganization is present, can be a factor in the occurrence of difficult experiences. Social anhedonia is an element present in negative schizotypy and, as we have seen, a predictor of the occurrence of psychosis. Thus it seems that the evaluation of negative symptoms (isolation, contact avoidance, schizoid withdrawal, among others) constitutes an important factor in assessing possible adverse reactions in a psychedelic experience. As a result, people with these characteristics may have smaller social circles, few meaningful relationships, and a poor support network. These elements are vital for the integration period since they can increase the capacity to sustain difficult emotional states and are therefore factors that must be taken into account, especially during the screening period. At the risk of being repetitive, little consideration is often given to contextual and social factors in relation to screening. However, their importance is paramount, and they should always be taken into account.

Difficult psychedelic experiences can be more difficult to integrate than pleasant experiences (Roseman et al., 2018; Carbonaro et al., 2016), hence we are interested in knowing who may present these difficulties. However, it should not follow that people who have difficult experiences, or are prone to having them, cannot benefit from psychedelic therapy or non-ordinary states of consciousness under proper supervision. Difficult experiences of catharsis, abreaction, and other psychological processes; experiences of death and rebirth; or of ego dissolution, even if experienced together with anxiety and other difficulties, can have therapeutic effects (Grof, 1980; Haijen et al., 2018). However, a more intensive therapeutic program and an ongoing psychotherapeutic process may be required, or it may require a restructuring of said abreaction in relation to the patient's present emotional attitudes (Sandison, 1959).

Taking all of this into account, we must remember that serious adverse reactions and psychotic experiences are very rare in controlled contexts, and even in recreational and ritual contexts (dos Santos et al., 2017; Jiménez-Garrido et al., 2020). In the early decades of psychedelic research, concern about long-lasting psychotic reactions animated research in this area (Cohen, 1960, 1966; Cohen & Ditman, 1962; Smart & Bateman, 1967; Malleson, 1971; Strassman, 1984; Johnson et al., 2008). It was found that these phenomena were rare, both in healthy volunteers and in psychiatric patients (dos Santos et al., 2016, 2017), of the order of 0.8 out of every thousand and 1.8 out of every thousand, respectively (Cohen, 1960). Recent research has found that the occurrence of psychosis in members of the Ayahuasca church of the *União do Vegetal* is even lower than among the general population (Gable, 2007).

We have tried to understand better which people are more likely to have difficult psychedelic experiences through this analysis. This analysis is neither exhaustive nor decisive; although this may have some statistical validity, dealing with people at the individual level renders the variability of responses somewhat unpredictable.

In a 1958 letter to Humphry Osmond, Betty Eisner wondered what made someone benefit or not from the insights received during an LSD experience, and she speculated that perhaps there was one key aspect: maturity.

A Broader View of Screening: The Holotropic Attitude

As we have seen previously, a multitude of complex factors need to be taken into account before deciding whether a psychedelic experience can be safe and therapeutic for someone. This debate tends to get complicated and often turns into a polarized diagnostic discussion. We usually hear phrases such as, "ayahuasca is for everyone, but not everyone is for ayahuasca," with similar sayings for different substances.

There are multiple interpretations of these assertions, yet research does not always align with these tropes. Psychedelic substances and master plants are being used nowadays to treat different pathologies such as post-traumatic stress, resistant depression, and alcoholism. All the participants in these studies belong to clinical populations with a defined diagnosis who have usually undergone, without success, various pharmacological and psychotherapeutic treatments. Therefore, these are people with complex and resistant symptoms: a priori, they do not seem like good candidates for psychedelic experiences. And yet they can participate in clinical trials and benefit from them. In the 1950s, 1960s, and 1970s, much psychiatric research was conducted with LSD and other psychedelic substances, and among the patients and subjects were also clinical populations: people with alcoholism (Abramson, 1966, 1967; Grof, 1973; Rhead et al., 1977; Savage, 1973; Ludwig et al., 1969; Hoffer, 1966, 1967, 1970; Soskin et al., 1973), psychotic patients (Busch & Johnson, 1950; Martin, 1964; Johnsen, 1964; Grof, 1970; Rojas-Bermúdez, 1960; Rhead, 1977; Sandison, 1954; Sandison & Whitelaw, 1957; MacLean,

1961), and people diagnosed with different types of what was labeled neurosis, such as obsessive compulsive disorder.

The results obtained from this population group vary across the different trials due to differences in ongoing support or follow-up and the type of therapy used in each case. While Grof (1970) and Martin (1964) reported improvements in a small number of patients with psychosis, Vangaard (1964) observed a worsening in various patients at Powick hospital in England. In 1997, more than one hundred former patients decided to go to court to seek compensation for the adverse effects derived from those LSD sessions (Dyer, 2002). Many of the patients who suffered long-term adverse reactions did not have any type of underlying psychotic pathology. Instead, it seems that malpractice in the administration, accompaniment, and supervision is what led to unfortunate situations (Kelso, 1999).

Thus, patients without any apparent contraindication felt harmed after poorly executed LSD therapy while, in other instances, psychotic patients—who would be considered high risk—benefited from psychedelic therapy and good emotional support. Therefore, the question is not so much who should or should not have a psychedelic experience. Rather we could ask, "What resources are necessary to support a certain person?" and, "Considering the patient's needs, can I support them as their therapist, with the staff and resources available to me?"

It is likely that, the more someone deviates from ideal physical and psychological health, the more support they will need, whether before, during, or after a session. It is also likely that, the greater this deviation, the greater the need for psychological and psychotherapeutic care. Therefore, it is not a matter of merely assessing the suitability of a specific therapy for a particular person but also their compatibility with the therapist and the material, along with the temporal and personal resources available to support them. With unlimited resources, we could probably support almost anyone, regardless of diagnosis, through psychedelic-assisted therapy.

Every therapist should be honest with her patients and with herself about this issue.

As a Conclusion

We have studied the theoretical aspects of preparation and screening in some detail, given that many patients tend to ask for support in the integration phase following a difficult experience during their session. This is often related to the factors previously described, both in relation to personality, temperament, biographical aspects, and personal coping mechanisms, as well as those aspects that the therapist, shaman, or facilitator has neglected during the preparatory phase and their subsequent impact on the development of the session, leading to difficulties during integration.

Every therapist facilitating the integration of difficult psychedelic experiences thus needs to consider their clients' personality profiles and unique needs and track the variety of different factors involved in the unfolding of the difficult experience that prompted the clients to seek professional help. Considering only the phenomenology of the experience would be reductive, limiting the establishment of a good therapeutic relationship and, therefore, a good prognosis.

In Appendix 1, you can find a model medical record based on the Grof Transpersonal Training model and Holotropic Breathwork, adapted for the psychedelic context, which may be useful as a preliminary screening tool.

PSYCHEDELIC SESSION

It is not the main objective of this volume to discuss the proper ways to conduct psychedelic therapy, nor to describe the various existing methods and schools. Perhaps Grof's *LSD Psychotherapy* (2002) is the best work to understand this practice, continuing to influence new generations of psychedelic researchers and therapists. No other work to date contains as much useful information about the theoretical and practical aspects of psychedelic therapy. Other classic texts are Myron Stolaroff's *The Secret Chief: Conversations with Leo Zeff* (2022) and Claudio Naranjo's *The Healing Journey* (1974) or a more recent book, *Psychedelic Explorations* (2016).

Other modern works useful for understanding the essential aspects of psychedelic-assisted psychotherapy sessions are: the manuals for the use of MDMA for the treatment of post-traumatic stress (Mithoefer et al., 2013), the manuals for the use of MDMA for the treatment of anxiety in people with serious illnesses (Ruse et al., 2014), the manuals and publications of the Johns Hopkins University team (Garcia-Romeu & Richards, 2018; Johnson & Griffiths, 2017; Johnson et al., 2008), and William Richards's book *Sacred Knowledge* (2015). The recent publication, *Psychedelic Psychotherapy: A User Friendly Guide to Psychedelic Drug Assisted Psychotherapy* (Coleman, 2020), summarizes with simplicity and depth many crucial aspects for providing support for people during their psychedelic experiences.

There are multiple training options for people interested in learning to support and facilitate non-ordinary states of consciousness. Perhaps the most extensive, on a practical and experiential level, is the Grof Transpersonal Training. Here, the foundations of transpersonal psychology, as well as the Stan and Christina Grof model, are taught and intense practical training is carried out, including experiential training in non-ordinary states of consciousness through Holotropic Breathing, a non-pharmacological method capable of inducing intense non-ordinary states with therapeutic and educational potential.

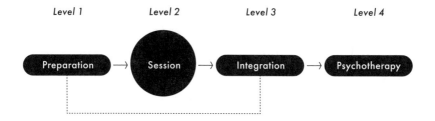

INTEGRATION

The different definitions and meanings of the phrase, "to integrate," all have to do with the formation of a whole from its parts or the joining together of the missing parts in order to make it complete. Another meaning is: something or someone becoming part of a whole or a larger structure. Integrating thus entails understanding what parts or elements a certain set should contain in order to be whole. Integrating also refers to the act of bringing together concepts, ideas, currents, or schools of thought which, although they may seem different or divergent, can nonetheless be articulated and synthesized in a single, broader current or school. Thus, integration has to do with the creation and construction of structures at a higher logical level; more inclusive and flexible structures with the capacity to contain multiple elements which, at a certain moment, may have been strange or alien to this structure, or may even have come into conflict with it.

In the context of psychedelic therapy and the psychonautical or neo-shamanic use of drugs, integration is usually understood as the higher level understanding of the experience and the proper application of the insights and lessons derived from it in our daily lives.

The definition of integration in this context is neither formal nor specific, and there is very little agreement on which practices must be carried out for this elusive "integration" to happen. Integration is a complex concept that includes many different situations and events which may or may not be causally related. An added difficulty in understanding what integration is relates to disparities in the understanding of the psychedelic experience—its usefulness and value among the different schools of thought and practice that work with non-ordinary states of consciousness. What is understood as integration from a neo-shamanic vision is very different from the concept of integration proposed by the Ayahuasca churches, the psychotherapeutic uses in clinical trials, or the idiosyncratic visions of the different and varied underground therapists.

It is thus of limited use to impose a univocal definition of integration. Instead, I think it may be more productive to illustrate different aspects of what integration can be. One way to approach the understanding of the subtleties of integration is through metaphor, evoking different dimensions of integration, which we will see in the following sections.

Distinguishing Integration from Psychotherapy

It is useful, for didactic purposes, for the implementation of specific and effective integration interventions, and for bringing greater clarity to the process, to include in this chain a fourth element: psychotherapy. Thus, the schema would be as follows: Although integration often takes place in psychotherapeutic contexts and professional interventions can be understood as psychotherapeutic practices, integration and psychotherapy are not the same.

The objective of integration is limited and restricted to solving the problems that have led the person to seek the help of a professional, instead of continuing with the integration of the experience on their own. Therefore, the mission of integrative psychotherapeutic intervention is for the client to regain the feeling of control over what is happening to him due to the psychedelic experience and to be able to continue on his way without the help of a therapist. When the content of the integration sessions no longer deals with the problems derived from the psychedelic experience, the integration intervention should end. Ideally, the client and therapist would agree upon the termination of therapy when the original problems have seen resolution. The intervention could also end when the client no longer feels the need to continue the therapeutic process, even if the situation hasn't been fully resolved.

A clear example of the practical implementation of integration practices is the one carried out during the same workshop or retreat, designed to maximize the benefits of the experience. Although artistic expression, sharing circles, and the retelling of the experience can be therapeutic practices in themselves, we would not think of calling this psychotherapy. These integration practices have a clear beginning and end, their contents and intent are clearly defined, and the person can continue to carry out these practices on their own later if they wish.

Psychotherapy, on the contrary, at least in many schools of thought, is usually an open-ended process in which there is no time limit or a pre-defined number of sessions. Frequently, the objectives are not clearly established or are modified as needed along the process. On the other hand, the integration process has a time limit and a clearly established objective: to process the experience that has originated the demand. After a process of integration, the client may decide to start an open-ended therapeutic process, and if that is the case, it will be easier for both the therapist and the client if this transition is made clearly, consciously, and explicitly.

Although this separation may feel somewhat surprising or artificial for some therapists, we do find examples of these different modes of intervention in psychedelic psychotherapy. If we look at the schools already described in the first chapter (the psycholytic and the psychedelic), we can spot the differences, in format and purpose, of the way in which integration is carried out. In psychedelic psychotherapy, the integration sessions were meant to achieve an understanding of the experience, using drawing, writing, and the therapeutic sessions as the vehicle. A professional therapist helped to interpret and clarify the meaning of the experience. This is the model that is currently followed in many of the presently ongoing clinical trials, in which the main focus is on the potential of the psychedelic experience and the effects of the substance on the healing of a certain pathology. No specific therapeutic interventions are mentioned in this model, beyond helping to understand the experience and, if necessary, facilitate its resolution.

As previously observed, there is no distinction between integration and psychotherapy in psycholytic therapy since the psychedelic experience is an addition to an ongoing therapeutic process, an additional tool meant to facilitate the emergence of more material to work on during the sessions. In this sense, integration is simply an extension of the usual therapy, and we could even say that there is no integration phase as such, but after the psychedelic experience, therapy simply continues.

The intention in making this distinction between psychotherapy and integration is to gain a better understanding of a very particular phase of a therapeutic or self-exploration process and to help develop the specific practices that may be most useful during this phase of psychedelic therapy.

USEFUL METAPHORS TO UNDERSTAND INTEGRATION

Since it is not easy to give a precise definition of integration, metaphors help to understand some of its different aspects. Metaphors are useful tools in any type of psychotherapy and useful for understanding complex phenomena. The power of metaphor lies in its inclusive capacity and creative potential that allows personalized understandings of complex phenomena, which can be approached from multiple directions. In addition, metaphors allow numerous interpretations and enrich our perception of a given phenomenon. They expand rather than reduce and are holographic in nature, containing the entire phenomenon in an apparently simple example. Different metaphors can help illuminate the concept of integration.

Metaphor 1: The Piece of the Puzzle

A common metaphor for integration relates to the pieces of a puzzle. We can understand a psychedelic experience as a puzzle piece that needs to be incorporated into the previously existing mental schema. After an experience in modified states of consciousness, many people wonder how they are to understand and interpret what they just experienced, how to accommodate that knowledge, and how and where they can actualize it in their daily lives. As if it were a previously unseen piece, the psychedelic experience must be integrated into a larger structure. To do this, we have to work with this piece and shape it to fit; this is what we see in the image. The lines on the edges of the piece indicate that the piece must be polished, modified, and filed to fit within the previous map. But it is the same with the previous structure of the puzzle: this one also requires work, modification, and polishing. Thus, we have to work with the new piece to fit it into the previous set, but we must also elaborate the structure and adapt it so that the new piece can have a place.

On many occasions, a psychedelic experience not only forces us to delve into its meanings and symbols but also prompts us to reconsider our starting points, our underlying worldview, our set of values and the principles that, until that moment, perhaps we considered unalterable.

Metaphor 2: The Non-Existent Ball and Cube

Another visual metaphor is the one that appears in this figure. When asked what we see in this image, most of us will answer without any doubt that it is the depiction of a soccer ball. While the answer is true, that is not what is depicted in the image. What appears in the image are six black spots shaped as irregular pentagons. However, we see a soccer ball, and without a doubt, the soccer ball is also there.

On the one hand, this image shows us that our brain has integrated the six pentagonal spots into a larger set, a larger whole, both at a structural and semantic level. Our brain automatically attributes the meaning of "soccer ball" to these spots, defining the shape and contour of the image; it happens without any effort on our part. This is also one of the aspects of integration: it can happen spontaneously and effortlessly. Intellectual work with symbols, or emotional or cognitive processing, is not always necessary to carry out the integration. We saw how Abramson (1955, 1956, 1973) spoke of the integrative functions of the psyche, which are activated during a psychedelic experience. This would serve as an example of this spontaneous functioning on a small scale.

Another aspect of integration derived from this image is that we can see a soccer ball because a soccer ball already exists in our experience.

We have seen balls in different ways throughout our lives; hence our brain can recognize this generic pattern in the image and understand it as a soccer ball. If we had never seen a ball, this spontaneous integration would very likely not happen, and we would have seen something else entirely.

In the following image we have another similar example. While we perceive a cube, the image consists of eight black circles with certain white stripes. In this case, our brain is taking a further leap, integrating what is not there. The black spots are not part of what is evoked, but we recognize the cube in what is not drawn. Thus, we are integrating a non-apparent part of what is presented, something not manifest. Something unconscious, we could say. Another interesting phenomenon occurs in this image. If we observe it for a while, we will see that the arrangement of the cube allows for two different interpretations: outwards or inwards, that is, with the lower left vertex being the closest to the observer, or being the furthest. Thus, in the face of what is perceived and integrated, we can hold different interpretations and sensations. Furthermore, both cannot occur simultaneously; we can only perceive one at a time. Here we see another paradox of the integration process: the multiplicity of interpretation that the same phenomenon or experience can have. The paradoxical nature is inherent in the psychedelic experience and the mystical and transcendent dimensions of the psyche. The integration of paradoxical experiences is only possible through the process of finding higher logical levels, such as metaphors or the "Koan" of the Zen tradition, since they contain all possibilities: the background, the form, and the various possible manifestations and interpretations.

$$\int_{a}^{b} f(x)dx$$

Metaphor 3: The Mathematical Integral

In the language of mathematics, integration refers to an operation by which we try to find the origin of the function presented to us (that which derives from the original function we intend to find). If we recall our years of mandatory formal education, we will remember that the procedure is relatively simple. One simply had to learn a series of rules and protocols and proceed in the established order, arriving at the result without much effort. However, the integration process was a different matter altogether. Solving the integrals used to require a lot more effort and, above all, creativity. The function we were looking for was unknown, the methods for arriving there could be diverse, and in most situations we did not have a clear, straightforward path to success. Integrating was more difficult than deriving because in the second case, we start from something known and break it down, while in the first, we start from the derivative and work our way back to its origin, to something we have never seen before. Even if we succeeded in reaching the integral, there was always a degree of uncertainty: the famous term + C, which indicated that there were infinite possibilities for that integral function. During the derivation process, we lost a level of information and, when trying to go back, that level was impossible to recover. This example shows the complexity of integration and the infinite possibilities and results, all of which are potentially correct and satisfactory if we accept that our capacity for understanding and precision is inevitably limited. It also illustrates our limitations in relation to reaching definitive and conclusive results, mirrored in our inability to unequivocally access the spiritual and transcendental dimensions of existence: the fact that the afterlife is ultimately inaccessible and essentially mysterious.

$$Life = \int_{birth}^{death} \frac{happiness}{time} \, \Delta time$$

Metaphor 4: The Everyday Integral

The following representation is a humorous example of the applications of mathematical integration to everyday life. The image shows that life equates to moments of happiness in relation to the passing of time, beginning at the moment of birth and leading up to our death. In this example, we understand the need for integration to have practical and useful implications for our everyday lives. We do not work on integrating a psychedelic experience for the fun of it, but to make our life better.

Metaphor 5: The Tree with its Branches and Roots

The integration process is also reflected in the tree that grows tall towards the sky while its roots sink deep into the earth. "Feet on the ground and eyes on the stars," goes one saying. In the Hermetic tradition, it is stated that "as above, so below." A well-integrated psychedelic experience implies an ingrained and ongoing contact with everyday reality, as well as an evolution and elevation towards transcendental realms. One aspect that should be taken into account in an intervention intended for integration is that the knowledge acquired during the experiences can be incorporated (*in corpore*, to integrate into the body) so it does not remain volatile and ethereal. In cases where this deep rooting is not achieved, we can observe some of the unwanted effects of the psychedelic search, such as ego inflation and spiritual bypass. In addition, some pathological manifestations that result in dedicated requests for integration are also related to this lack of rooting and will be detailed in more depth in the chapter dedicated to the adverse effects.

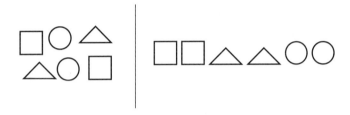

Metaphor 6: Chaos and Order

In this image we see multiple shapes, organized in two ways. We could say that the content of the images is the same; nevertheless, the second image conveys a greater sense of order and coherence. Sometimes integration does not necessarily imply a discovery of new meanings, but simply assigns a specific meaning to what is already manifest, creating meaning from the elements already in our possession. In the second image, the distribution could have been different in any other way; there are a number of possible configurations that would also give the feeling of coherence and meaning. Interpretations and constructions of meaning are not unique, quite the contrary: they are multiple and, most importantly, variable over time. When it comes to integration, the important thing is that the construction is meaningful for the person, not for the therapist. The therapist may have particular maps or preferences, but should never try to adjust the construction of meaning to his personal preconceptions; he should merely empower the clients to create meanings that are maximally useful for them.

Metaphor 7: Planting Seeds

The process of a sprouting seed can reflect various aspects of integration. Often we can refer to the psychedelic experience as "planting a seed," something new, a change, a new beginning (Jackson, 1960). The psychedelic experience shakes us from our slumber and inspires us to transform and walk a new path or go on exciting new life adventures. Sometimes we can discover unknown or neglected emotional spaces and decide to live life in a way that honors and nurtures them. For a seed to grow, one has to take care of it, plant it in the right soil, give it enough water and sunlight, perhaps compost, and attend to it, ensuring it grows protected from threats. However, none of these things will accelerate the natural rhythm of that seed's growth cycle. Moreover, overwatering, changing the soil over and over again, abusing the use of fertilizers, or even digging it up to see if the roots are growing under the soil can become counterproductive to the desired result. Similarly, a psychedelic experience must be nurtured, ideally without obsessing over it while maintaining a good balance in our attention to it. We do not plant a tree just to observe its growth constantly. We take care of the tree and promote its well-being so that later we can enjoy the shade that it provides for us or the fruits that we obtain from it. It would not be wise to dig up the seed again or to focus obsessively on the seed once we are enjoying the shade of the tree. In turn, the fruits of a tree contain new seeds that, although identical in shape, are different seeds from the original one. Similarly, we can continue to see the original experience in the results and fruits of integration.

Metaphor 8: Weathering the Storm

A simile that can help us understand a different dimension of integration is that of a drogue. Drogues are devices used in navigation to help maintain position. Unlike a standard anchor, the drogue does not reach the ocean floor but floats a few meters from the surface. It provides greater stability by helping the boat face the incoming wind and waves. In rough sea conditions, in which navigation becomes impossible due to the crew's exhaustion, seasickness, structural damage, or accidents, the drogue allows the boat to remain stable and the crew to rest, overcome seasickness, or fix the damage, maximizing safety and maintaining the position. The drogue minimizes the risk of boat drift and tipping while providing safety for the crew and the boat. In Spanish, we have the expression *capear el temporal,* literally translated to "weathering the storm." This expression refers to the act of moving through the storm while experiencing difficulties with considerable hold-ups, simply adapting to the conditions. In more severe situations, the role of integration psychotherapy is like this drogue, providing security and relief while keeping us afloat in the middle of the storm, facing the waves and the wind ahead of us, albeit slowly, calmly, and as safely as possible.

Metaphor 9: Decompression

Another situation that reflects different dimensions of integration includes the hyperbaric chamber used by a deep-sea diver, which regulates pressure and decompression before returning to land. Similarly, spaceships have hatches in which the astronauts regulate after their spacewalks, restoring air pressure and temperature before the suits can be removed. In this in-between space, normal conditions are reestablished, safety is checked and maximized, and a successful return is made. Here, conditions are regularized and communication between external and internal environments is made possible without the risk of sudden changes in pressure or oxygen losses. It is a space that guarantees safety. This image reflects the importance of immediate integration after the experience, which we will see in more detail once we discuss the different dimensions of integration.

As a curiosity, the "overview effect" is the name given to the transcendental experience that some astronauts have when observing the Earth from space. Sometimes, after this overwhelming experience, astronauts report a greater global, ecological awareness and an intuitive knowing that we are all part of the same organism.

Metaphor 10: Developing a Photo

Another metaphor that can illustrate some aspects of integration is the development of a photograph. In the days before digital cameras, people were accustomed to the uncertainty involved in taking a photograph without seeing its result immediately. The image was taken at a certain time and printed on a negative, containing all the information, albeit in a way that could not yet be fully appreciated. Only once the negatives were developed could we intuit what was in them. It was necessary to wait for the development and printing of the actual photograph to appreciate its full detail. The negative image contained many aspects that were not immediately accessible to our understanding. But above all, the final result depended on the type of development chosen. Determining factors include the exposure time on the photo paper, the kind of paper, whether we chose a glossy or matte finish, and even the print size, which did not necessarily always match the entire negative.

The development process entailed the creation of a specific interpretation of that negative. We do something similar with the psychedelic experience; the way we reveal and process its content will lead us toward a certain understanding of what was experienced.

Metaphor 11: Weaving a Web

Psychedelic experiences can be understood as distinct nodes, each containing a large amount of information yet disconnected from each other and our daily reality. Building bridges, creating connections, and establishing patterns across these nodes allows us to weave a richer web of knowledge than the sum of its isolated nodes. The exercise of relating different experiences and concepts, even if they are apparently disconnected or unrelated, gives greater solidity and strength to the integration of these experiences. It is no longer an experience that is interpreted on the basis of its own contents but in relation to external and relational aspects, increasing its validity and sustaining it with greater complexity and coherence.

Ultimately, integration, knowledge, and transformation do not lie so much in individual experiences—not even in their symbolic content—but in those bridges and connections that weave them together with other significant experiences. That is how we weave the canvas on which our conception of reality is drawn.

Ontological Integration vs. Therapeutic Integration

This book is primarily about therapeutic interventions contextualized within the therapeutic use of psychedelic substances. This statement sounds redundant, however, it is crucial to make clear distinctions regarding the intentionality of the interventions that are carried out, both in psychotherapy and in the use of psychedelic substances.

Psychedelic substances are used in different contexts and with different intentions. They are used as therapeutic tools to treat certain diagnostic categories such as post-traumatic stress disorder, treatment-resistant major depression, alcoholism, the anxiety that often occurs alongside serious illnesses, tobacco addiction, and many others (dos Santos et al., 2018). Psychedelics are also used for their potential to induce mystical and spiritual experiences; they have religious applications (Griffiths et al., 2006, 2016, 2017; Barret et al., 2015); and they are potential tools useful in social conflict resolution (Ginsberg, 2019; Roseman et al., 2019). In addition, psychedelics are being researched for their potential to increase creativity (Janiger, 1989) and the possibility that they can help us solve technical and technological problems.

Psychedelics are also used with mixed intentions by experience seekers who might find some relief from the anguish of everyday life and gain access to spiritual experiences, as well as enjoying them for recreational purposes.

The intentionality behind each use is different. Although the intervention during the different experiences may sometimes be similar, the interventions carried out during the integration phase will undoubtedly vary depending on the context in which the experience occurred. Thus, in the context of an ayahuasca workshop aimed at spiritual growth, the integration sessions will be different from those carried out in the context of a clinical trial for major depression.

When we speak of therapeutic interventions or therapeutic uses of psychoactive substances, we are referring to a particular use, with a specific intention and context. The word "therapy" comes from the Greek θεραπεία, whose meaning refers to "healing, of a service performed for the sick, treating medically, caring for someone." Therapy is equal to healing. Therefore it is aimed at achieving pragmatic objectives, that is, curing the patient of their ailment. Doing therapy implies that there is a problem to be solved, a pathological condition to cure. If there is no problem, there can be no therapy—maybe there is something else, but it is no longer therapy by definition. Thus, when we work within the paradigm of psychedelic therapy, we must assume that we are working at this level, pragmatically looking for certain results. That is precisely why clinical research can be done with psychedelic substances—because we assume that they can have a positive and measurable impact on the different pathologies that we have indicated above.

Now, not everything is therapy. Psychotherapy is one of the many branches of psychology. Thus, we can have psychological uses of psychedelic substances that are not therapeutic: as in the case of studies on creativity and technical problem solving, the use of microdoses of LSD or psilocybin as nootropics, and even the infamous politico-military uses of the MK-ULTRA project, in which psychedelics were explored as potential chemical weapons, proposed as a truth serum among other ethically reprehensible uses. None of those applications is therapeutic, although they relate to psychology.

And we can even go beyond psychological uses. From Leary, Metzner, and Alpert in their research with psilocybin, or Aldous Huxley with *The Doors of Perception* (Huxley, 2014) or his *moksha medicine* in *Island* (Huxley, 2007), all the way to modern and current research on the spiritual and mystical potential of psilocybin, the ontological dimension of the psychedelic experience has been primary and prominent since Western society came into contact with these experiences. This ontological dimension is also primary in the use of intoxicating plants that are part of the rites of passage of many Indigenous traditions. In these instances, a significant experience elicits and marks an important transformation in the evolutionary state of the individual in relation to their society.

The psychedelic experience is a highly complex phenomenon that defies simple and univocal definitions. This renders the implementation of wide regulatory frameworks a challenging enterprise, as it is hard to systematically understand and interpret the phenomenology that unfolds during the acute effects. We do not quite know whether they are drugs of abuse, medicines, chemical substances useful for understanding our neuropsychological processes, tools for personal evolution, sacraments that grant us access to spiritual realms of experience, or a simple oddity of nature. We often try to classify them without much success based on a clearly limited and limiting perspective. Even so, adopting a didactic mindset and with a clear understanding of the limitations of this classification, we can safely speak about two general and main scenarios related to the integration of psychedelic experiences: on the one hand, we have the ontological integration and, on the other hand, the therapeutic integration.

Ontological integration refers to content pertaining to the spheres of metaphysical, spiritual, and philosophical conceptions about existence and our relationship to it. At the ontological level, psychedelics can help us refine our understanding of our own intra-psychic processes, the structure of our character, and how our inner world affects our particular perception of the universe. They can also be useful in sharpening our knowledge and experience of reality and its spiritual dimensions. At the ontological level, we are not addressing a specific mental pathology. We are not looking for immediate pragmatic results; instead, we are trying to broaden our understanding of ourselves and the world around us. We could compare this dimension to what is commonly known as "personal growth," although there is a great deal of confusion regarding what "personal growth" truly entails, often conflated with practices that have therapeutic intent. The so-called personal growth workshops are usually packed with people who are looking for relief from their suffering. Furthermore, these workshops often promise a wide range of therapeutic and healing results. This is where the confusion begins.

Therapeutic integration is the practice aimed at resolving a certain symptomatology or problem through a combination of psychedelic experiences and "integration psychotherapy" sessions. The problem in such cases may be pre-existing (a person who suffers from depression, trying to heal with psilocybin, as an example), or it may be a result of the psychedelic experience itself. Sometimes, an experience may be so overwhelming that it destabilizes the mental state of the person experiencing it. Past traumas, intense fears and anxieties, or challenging emotions might surface during the psychedelic session with the potential to significantly interfere with the person's life if not fully processed. In such cases, we speak of therapeutic integration since what we want is not to obtain new philosophical knowledge but to restore psychic stability, even if both can emerge over the course of therapy.

Whether we choose to focus more on the ontological or therapeutic realms will depend on the unfolding of the participant's experience rather than on the intention of the therapist or facilitator. A participant in a clinical study may have a transcendental experience, brimming with new insights about life and existence while increasing well-being and helping reduce their psychopathological symptoms. For such an individual, an ontological approach might be a better choice. Conversely, imagine a previously undiagnosed person attending an ayahuasca retreat whose mental state is severely altered following some difficult experiences, to the point of greatly impacting their daily life. This person will need a therapeutic approach rather than an ontological one.

That said, certain people will a priori be predisposed towards a particular scenario. Grounded people with long years of structured personal work behind them, who are socially well adjusted with a relatively trauma-free biography and psychic stability are more likely and able to benefit from integration work at the ontological levels. People with difficult biographies, or people who are new to personal growth, people with anxious or depressive symptoms, interpersonal relationship problems, and less mental stability, may perhaps benefit more from an integration plan focused on therapeutic support.

We are still in the early stages of defining what psychedelic integration is and how it can best be accomplished. However, it is important that we begin distinguishing between different scenarios in order to develop better integration practices, adapting to the needs and situation of each individual. These distinctions have existed in various spiritual and psychotherapeutic schools. For example, Viktor Frankl writes: "It is not possible to calm a realistic fear, such as the fear of death, by way of its psychodynamic interpretation; on the other hand, a neurotic fear, such as agoraphobia, cannot be cured through philosophical knowledge" (Frankl, 1991, 68). Here, Frankl distinguishes between *psychogenic* neurosis and *noogenic* neurosis. Psychogenic neurosis is a neurosis in the strict and habitual sense, born from conflicts between impulses and instincts. Noogenic neurosis, on the other hand, emerges from moral and spiritual conflicts, a product of existential frustration and the longing for a meaningful existence. While psychogenic neurosis was considered a mental illness, noogenic neurosis was not, even when both imply real suffering. The treatment was also different: "It is obvious that in noogenic cases, the appropriate and ideal therapy is not general psychotherapy, but logotherapy: a therapy that dares to penetrate the spiritual dimension of human existence" (Frankl, 1991, 58). In Frankl's theory, we observe a clear distinction between the two dimensions described in this section.

Of course, these two scenarios are not disconnected or mutually exclusive. It is not unusual that the person continues into a phase of ontological, philosophical, and spiritual search after an initial therapeutic stage. The therapeutic integration practices are meant to help the person regain the psychic stability required to continue (or start) their own process of spiritual inquiry. Alejandro Jodorowsky (2004) defines it as follows: "If I have a nail in my shoe, my whole world, my sensitivity, will be affected. Before trying to go further, prior to sharpening my vision, I have to get rid of the nail. Similarly, when we suffer from a trauma, our entire existence suffers. It is therefore important to heal this trauma" (112).

Similarly, Grof, while talking about LSD psychotherapy, shares about his own experiences as a psychedelic therapist and researcher: "With an open-ended approach, the process that initially began as 'therapy' will often automatically shift into a spiritual and philosophical quest" (Grof, in "Ken Wilber's Spectrum Psychology").

Purposes of Integration

If we ask ourselves the questions, "What is integration for?" or, "What motivates an individual to carry out integrative practices?" two large categories emerge from the participant's perspective. On the one hand, integrating a psychedelic experience can serve to maximize the potential benefits derived from it. On the other hand, integration may be needed due to possible adverse effects or difficult reactions lingering after the experience. Maximizing potential benefits and dealing with adverse reactions are different arenas of action that present specific needs and involve different practices. Furthermore, in most cases, the professionals who can carry out these interventions are usually different for one case or the other.

The most common situation after a psychedelic experience is when integration practices are aimed at maximizing benefits. Most people tend to go through the experience without much difficulty. Once the effects have worn off and they have adequately rested, they are able to rejoin ordinary reality without major difficulties. Most of the time, we feel that a meaningful experience has opened up new possibilities which have yet to be realized. Integrative practices might be useful for that, and many of these practices can be carried out by the facilitators or guides themselves. We find some practices intended to help integrate the experience in almost every workshop or ceremony. These usually occur at the end of the workshop and can include the drawing of mandalas; journaling and writing; verbally sharing the experience in a group context; and sometimes the interpretation or further processing of the material by the facilitator or guide. However, some of the more sophisticated and pioneering techniques require a trained and experienced professional to carry them out. In the next chapter, we will explore more detailed analysis of different techniques, interventions, and tools.

It is essential to mention that we should not perceive any adverse effects when a psychedelic experience has been correctly integrated—whether it was pleasant, smooth, or complicated. With the proper integration, we should be left with emotional stability, regardless of the predominant emotion, and an absence of anxiety and physical symptoms.

However, the opposite is not necessarily true. The absence of adverse effects or reactions does not always indicate the successful integration of an experience. In many cases, even transcendental experiences fade over time, and their positive impact on our well-being completely dissipates. In other words, although we may not face any difficulties after an experience, we may still have failed to integrate it properly. An anthropologist I met once said that "entheogens take back everything that they give you" if a good integration does not occur.

At the other end of the spectrum, there are situations where adverse effects appear after the psychedelic experience. This scenario is more common when the experience has been particularly difficult or daunting, when the content has been disruptive or when harmful interactions have occurred within the group. These adverse reactions can also occur after seemingly complete experiences that weren't experienced as too overwhelming but which present complications further down the road. This can happen due to the unfolding of new insights and memories over time or due to the perceived benefits suddenly fading away and experiencing a painful return to the initial situation of suffering. A detailed description of the different situations that may contribute to adverse reactions and the relevant interventions for each of these situations will be presented in Chapter 5.

These situations are characterized by the perception that the emotional state following the experience has worsened in relation to the emotional state before the experience. The person thus interprets that the experience has been harmful. In such a case, the person will often seek professional support to resolve an unpleasant and uncomfortable situation.

In situations like these, practices designed to maximize benefits are of limited utility, often failing to address the suffering experienced by the person. This is particularly true for the most common techniques (creating mandalas or sharing the experience, for example). However, certain techniques involving structured interviews can also be useful in these circumstances, as we will see in the corresponding chapter. This suggests that these interventions are closer to formal psychotherapy than to the integrative practices carried out in workshops, retreats, and ceremonies by facilitators. A professional trained in psychotherapy, who has an excellent personal understanding of the psychedelic experience and its possible complications, is often required for these interventions. This is a fundamental factor that differentiates the two categories that we are describing.

The poetic words of Rabbi Abraham J. Heschel (1976) describe this situation using a powerful image:

> When a vessel sails into a typhoon and the maw of the boiling maelstrom opens to engulf the tottering prey, it is not the pious man, engrossed in supplication, but the helmsman who intervenes in the proper sphere with proper means, fighting with physical tools against physical powers. What sense is there in imploring the mercy of God? Words do not stem the flood, nor does meditation banish the storm (239).

SEVEN DIMENSIONS OF INTEGRATION

Psychedelic experiences are often complex, both in content and the ways in which they are lived. They often include an important cognitive aspect, related to the visual or narrative content, coupled with an intense amplification of emotion. Furthermore, these experiences usually include a marked somatic or bodily dimension. Sometimes these effects are directly related to the substance (nausea and vomiting in the case of ayahuasca, or an increase in body temperature when under the influence of MDMA), but other physical experiences related exclusively to the psychic content of the experience may also emerge. The psychedelic experience is, in turn, inseparable from the spiritual experience, and it is common for people to experience a sense of wonder, revelation, and contact with the sacred.

Integration must be observed at different levels, according to the two categories described in the previous section (maximizing benefits or dealing with adverse effects). Integration is commonly understood according to the school or tradition to which one belongs. While some might emphasize the cognitive and psychological aspects of the psychedelic experience, others might consider the spiritual aspect more relevant. A comprehensive approach must thus consider the multiple dimensions of integration.

The seven dimensions of integration are as follows:

- Cognitive
- Emotional
- Physical
- Spiritual
- Behavioral
- Social
- Temporal

The Cognitive Dimension

On a cognitive level, the psychedelic experience tends to be rich, opening up our capacity to access different levels of consciousness and immense amounts of information. It is common for people to feel overwhelmed by the amount of information and by the intensity and the speed at which the content appears: a lot happens in a relatively short time. Likewise, there is usually the feeling of being unable to remember all the events, coupled with the difficulty of fully understanding the cognitive content. Sometimes people speak of the psychedelic experience as "downloading information."

The cognitive dimension of integration is the one most often taken into account. For Westerners, it seems particularly important that we understand the meaning of our visionary experiences and that we manage to decipher and interpret the symbols we encounter. In most shamanic contexts, this is not necessarily true; the content of the visions is not always as relevant, and its interpretations are often less complex than the ones we would expect from a Western psychologist. A literary example is found in the books of Carlos Castaneda. In these stories, the protagonist keeps trying to understand his visionary journeys, while Don Juan seems to have little to no interest in delving into the content of the symbols and visions, to the frustration and despair of the sorcerer's apprentice.

However, the Western context tends to prioritize assigning meaning to our lived experiences. From a constructivist perspective, it is essential that we are able to produce a coherent narrative about the experience in order for it to be properly processed. Furthermore, it is especially important that this narrative has continuity with the ongoing narrative of our life thus far.

In cases where the experience is perceived as a disruption of our life history, we face difficulties in its integration. This can be observed particularly in experiences that clash with our worldview or the underlying operating paradigm. For example, consider the experience of a deeply religious person who comes into contact with an existential void in which the ultimate reality is one of nothingness, where there is no God. This experience will have to be incorporated into the previously existing narrative in a way that gives continuity to the story, to the meaning that this person attributes to the experience in the ongoing unfolding of their life.

Whether the story fits any particular paradigm or school is not essential. The story does not need to ring true for the therapist; the story does not even need to be coherent with the therapist's worldview. The important thing is that the person achieves internal coherence between their experience and their life, having assigned proper meaning to the experience—any meaning, as long as it is constructive and functional. The assigned meaning does not have to be permanent either, it can—and probably will—change over time as new experiences and reflections enrich our inner world.

In cognitive terms, a "good integration" allows our story to continue to unfold and expand, to evolve with the person as they evolve. A "good integration" allows for new meanings and more sophisticated understandings to take place over time. Like all good stories, there has to be both an exoteric and an esoteric dimension. The exoteric is the part that is shared and understood on a rational level, while the esoteric part is that which is derived from experience, subject to multiple interpretations and deeper understandings.

Among the Indigenous Australian cultures we find creation myths—called Dreamtime—often in the form of songs. These myths describe archetypal animals of titanic dimensions who journeyed through the country, across the land, creating the landscape, the mountains, rivers, and forests. The literal versions of these songs are meant for the *dgi-dgi*, for the children, since they only describe the literary and exoteric aspect of the story of creation. However, as the children grow, they gain the wisdom to understand the subtler dimensions of the story. True initiation does not consist of the revelation of new songs or specific knowledge, but in deepening their connection with the esoteric and hidden dimensions of the same songs they have sung since childhood.

The same is true in Judaism. The Torah describes the Jewish creation story and the relationship of the people of Israel to God. Beyond the literary story, there are subtler levels of knowledge. Through a careful and critical reading of the text, we can discover wisdom emergent from a subtler interpretation. This is where the inner spiritual dimension found in the sacred texts begins. The development of the Mishnah, the Gemara, and the Talmud as a whole are good examples of this, culminating in the mystical and cryptic interpretations of the Zohar. Four levels of reading and interpretation or exegesis exist in the Jewish tradition: *Peshat* (פשט), the literal reading; *Remez* (רמז), symbolic or allegorical readings; *Drash* (שרד) the comparative or midrashic sense (the rabbinic interpretation and extension of the original meaning); and *Sod* (סוֹד), the reading of the mystical or esoteric sense. Similarly, a psychedelic experience can be read and interpreted from multiple levels.

Working on the cognitive dimension of integration implies the ability to produce a narrative without gaps in experience. This can be difficult to achieve and becomes a significant concern. The human mind tends to fill in the gaps of what it does not know: it does not leave blank holes in an experience, instead filling them in with anxiety and fear. This does not mean that our story has to contain all the exact details of an event from the perspective of an outside observer. It simply means that the person's internal story has to be continuous and coherent, even if that means leaving out certain things that happened during the session.

We often find this tendency—to fill in the gaps or leave details behind, in order to create a coherent narrative—in experiences where the person comes into contact with energies that could be understood as "demonic." In many of these situations, what may be clear for an external observer is not so for the person with the lived experience. Sometimes, after coming into contact with the "demonic," they might only describe encountering intense energies and anger. At other times, they may experience amnesia, an inability to recall what happened during those moments, even if a certain memory of intense catharsis remains accessible. It is not important for the person to recall the experience in full detail. In fact, on many occasions, we will not be able to recover those details unless we have a video recording of the experience. The important thing is that the person can reconstruct a coherent version, any version, of the lived experience.

Meaning-making after a psychedelic experience can be done individually, although the help of a therapist, skilled in the use of "amplification"—as Jung understood it—can be very valuable, contributing to the creation of a richer and more complex narrative. Therapists from different schools will approach this work differently, consistent with their unique understanding of the human psyche. However, from a constructivist perspective, it is important to honor each person's individuality by not forcing our own maps on the patient. It is not the patient's experience that has to adapt to the worldview and school of the therapist, but the therapist who must adapt their approach to the worldview and reality of the client.

It is essential for the therapist to develop a curious and respectful attitude towards the client, as it is necessary that they hold a broad and inclusive map charting a vast range of experiences. Grof's "enlarged cartography of the psyche" is perhaps one of the best general maps for this job. It describes three major experiential realms: the biographical, the perinatal (relating to experiences of biological birth, intrauterine life, and themes of death and rebirth), and the transpersonal (experiences that transcend the usual limitations of the ego and spacetime). The reader interested in delving into this cartography can find detailed descriptions in Grof's books (1975, 1980, 2019).

It will be useful to dive deeper into these three general realms. Classical psychoanalysis offers some good metaphors and explanations of child development and the structures of the psyche. Many of Freud's theories can be observed during psychedelic experiences when we are presented with clusters of symptoms and curious symbols (Oedipus complex, castration complex, etc.). Evolutionary models such as Ken Wilber's or Erik Erikson's Stages of Development can also be quite useful, giving a temporal, social, and environmental context to the experience. Jung's analytical psychology can be helpful for understanding and explaining certain phenomena that touch on both biographical and transpersonal aspects (such as shadow work or the influences of the anima/animus archetypes) (Shulgin, 1995; Lammers, 2007). Knowledge of Eastern schools of thought and spirituality such as Buddhism or Hinduism can provide context for certain types of transpersonal experiences; the chakra system and the theories of the different subtle bodies can serve as useful maps to locate specific experiences.

Another useful concept worth mentioning is COEX, coined by Grof and previously mentioned (albeit by different names) by other authors such as Freud and Jung.

A COEX system is a system of COndensed EXperience, and can be defined as "a specific constellation of memories—and associated fantasies—related to a certain period in the life of the individual. A COEX system can help us articulate a more comprehensive meaning of psychedelic experiences since memories belonging to a particular COEX system have a similar basic theme and contain similar elements, including similar emotional charges" (Grof, 2005).

Identifying COEX systems simplifies the understanding of certain experiences and facilitates their integration, affording a broader perspective in relation to the narrower and more specific phenomenology emergent during the session. COEX systems may integrate different—and sometimes seemingly unrelated—elements of a psychedelic experience; they allow for a reduction in the number of concepts needing to be integrated, as they group different aspects of the experience under a common heading.

For example, during a psychedelic experience someone could begin experiencing intense emotions of grief regarding the loss of a loved one, move on to scenes from childhood when they got lost in a mall and could not find their parents, and eventually encounter images of genocides, concentration camps, and evictions. On some other level, there could be feelings of utter cosmic meaninglessness or connection with scenes from Greek mythology concerning Persephone's kidnapping and imprisonment in the underworld. These sequences may seem unrelated and confusing, but if looked at through the lens of a COEX, all of these experiences share a common thread: grief, loss, separation. Therefore, what has become activated during this experience is a separation COEX, and that is what the person has been working through in its multiple manifestations.

The concept of integration as a whole is often identified with the cognitive dimension of integration; it would be a mistake, however, to understand integration from this perspective alone. It is essential that we also consider the following dimensions as well.

The Emotional Dimension

One of the most commonly experienced aspects of a non-ordinary state is an increased accessibility to a wide spectrum of potentially intense emotional states. During a psychedelic experience, it is common for people to experience emotional states with great depth and intensity. It is not uncommon for an individual to access an emotionally charged space that, up until now, has remained inaccessible to them. For example, experiences of "a great well of sadness," atrocious fears or a deep and primitive fury are not uncommon, as well as states of ecstatic joy or a sense of peace, love, and general well-being of ineffable proportions.

In the emotional sphere, the good integration of an experience is characterized not by the presence of positive emotions, but rather by the presence of an open attitude while exploring the emotions that emerge in the process, as long as its intensity is manageable and it does not interfere with the daily life of the person. An integration process does not entail that we must override or replace sadness, fear, or anger with "positive" emotions, nor that we justify or resign ourselves to those emotions. In integration, we must work to properly process our emotions, whatever they may be, striving to regain healthy control over them, without repressing them, rejecting them, or over-identifying with them.

If we do not process our experiences properly, we can get stuck in certain emotional states. For example, someone diving deep into the "well of sadness" may face lingering difficulties if the experience ends without them fully processing and resolving that content, which remains activated and easily accessible in their day-to-day life. The experience of this ongoing deep sadness becomes traumatic as we lose control over it, leaving us vulnerable and restless, unable to regulate our emotions in a healthy way.

Because a scenario like this is relatively common, it is essential for the therapist to have useful and relevant resources. One of the main challenges for inexperienced therapists is the discomfort involved in witnessing the intensity and depth of the emotions that emerge during the integration process. Sessions of integrative verbal psychotherapy can include very intense emotional manifestations, sometimes just as much as during the psychedelic experience itself. This may frighten some therapists since it may seem like the person is still under the influence of the substance or that some irreversible pathological process has been unleashed. On many occasions, however, these dramatic manifestations are a necessary step on the integration journey, required to process the unfinished contents of the session thoroughly. These manifestations should not be understood as pathological or exaggerated but as healthy attempts to resolve ongoing internal emotional conflicts.

We must have the capacity to contain and witness these episodes while remaining calm and adequately supporting these situations and our own emotional resolution. Intensely emotional episodes can occur in face-to-face sessions or in the patient's own environment, so integration therapists should be able to provide support and containment during face-to-face meetings, as well as provide effective tools for the patient to use at home without the immediate support of a professional.

The Physical Dimension

Experiences in non-ordinary states often include a wide range of physical sensations and somatic manifestations, regardless of the method used to induce these states. This is mostly true for ayahuasca, a substance that tends to induce copious vomiting and diarrhea, coupled with general physical discomfort. In various Amazonian and neo-shamanic worldviews, these are not side-effects but essential aspects of the experience, understood as aspects of purging and healing. Intense somatic and physical manifestations also occur during Holotropic Breathing, a technique where the body constitutes an essential part of the experience; it is often through the physical body that repressed emotions and unconscious contents are accessed, including experiences of abreaction and catharsis. Synthetic phenylethylamines and various research chemicals are known for their body-load; 2C-B stands out for its markedly somatic effects and the fact that part of the psychedelic experience occurs through the body. In general, any psychedelic substance or consciousness modification technique such as Holotropic Breathing, rebirthing, the different types of meditation (Vajrayana, Vipassana, Zen, and others) include important physical manifestations in their experiential range.

Grof (2019) formulated a theoretical approach to this phenomenon by integrating Wilhelm Reich's ideas into his LSD psychotherapy model. Reich was an Austrian psychoanalyst known for his controversial ideas which led to his expulsion from the psychoanalytic circle.

Although Reich followed Freud's thesis regarding the centrality of sexual energies in psychological health, he introduced the idea that emotional traumas and sexual energies were repressed through patterns of muscular tension, becoming trapped in the body. Reich called this pattern of tensions the "character armor," whose function is to protect us from potentially terrifying encounters with our repressed sexual traumas and energies. Reich's theories and therapeutic approaches were systematized by Alexander Lowen, the creator of bioenergetics. We can observe how physical tensions intensify during modified states of consciousness: these tensions can be understood as the aforementioned "character armor." Working with these tensions during a psychedelic session can lead to intense energetic discharges, not only of sexual energies but of other energetic buildups accumulated through previous exposures to intense, painful, traumatic, stressful, or frightening situations.

In some therapeutic models or cultural contexts in which psychedelic substances are used, limited attention is paid to the somatic dimensions, despite abundant evidence that they constitute an essential part of the process of self-discovery and healing (Grof, 1980, 2019; Mithoefer, 2013). The same occurs in certain models and schools of traditional (non-psychedelic) psychotherapy, in which the emphasis is placed on the emotional and cognitive aspects but not on the physical sensations that go hand in hand with them. Considering a broad vision of what integration is, it is essential to include the physical sensations and other somatic manifestations that the client experiences during the integration sessions.

The human body and our physical sensations are excellent tools for integration, and there are situations in which it is imperative to be well-attuned to our bodies. On the one hand, while we are focused on maximizing the long-term benefits of a positive and well-resolved experience, the body provides us with an immediate and useful way of recovering sensations and content from the session. It also allows us to engage in "anchoring"—the fixation of positive states within our bodies. The body thus becomes a resource through which we gain access to the cognitive and emotional contents that may have remained inaccessible until that point.

An example here can perhaps better illustrate this situation: It is relatively common, after experiences with Holotropic Breathing or MDMA, to experience states of deep peace, relaxation, well-being, and mental clarity, together with a marked reduction or disappearance of previously perceived problems. These states have profound healing potential and, while under the influence, they seem natural, clear (even obvious), and easy to reach without effort. However, once the experience wears off, these blissful states tend to dissipate and fade, whether they linger on for a few hours, a few days, or a few weeks. In such cases, it can be useful to work from the physical level upwards, first recovering some of the sensations experienced during those blissful moments. This can be done through various methods. Some people can relive these sensations just by thinking about and remembering the experience, listening to the music from their session, seeking pleasurable physical experiences like massages or warm baths, and even through experiential therapy in regular talk-therapy integration sessions. Our capacity to recover the bodily sensations we experienced during non-ordinary states can allow us to access them again. The physical dimension of the experience becomes a fundamental aspect that helps us embody or incorporate the experience while rooting abstract or ethereal contents that otherwise tend to blur or disappear if they remain exclusively within the cognitive or emotional realms.

Another type of situation in which we must keep the physical dimensions of integration in mind is when the experience remains unresolved, and we are focused on harm reduction. In such cases, it is common for people to report bodily tensions, pains, and physical discomfort, often unrelated to explicit psychological or emotional content. While physical discomfort is present, there is no conscious awareness of its relationship to the unresolved aspects of the experience. Even when there is an awareness that the discomfort has appeared following the experience—and it is therefore likely related to it—the person may be concerned that the nervous system has been damaged or that they have sustained some irreversible brain damage. In such cases, working directly with these physical manifestations may be a straightforward way to access the unresolved emotional contents of the experience, using the body as a way of accessing the unconscious contents so they can be amplified and resolved.

In addition to the psychological and therapeutic aspects, there are plenty of everyday aspects to the physical dimension of integration. A proper, healthy integration process requires an appropriate physical context in terms of rest, hygiene, and food. It also requires an appropriate physical space to process the remnants of the experience in the following hours and days. Without these basics, it is challenging to integrate properly. In fact, difficulties in integration are often attributable to suboptimal physical and environmental factors rather than experiential or psychological issues.

Without the proper context, without the necessary rest and minimum buffer between the experience and our return to ordinary reality, unexpected difficulties can appear. It is not ideal to have an overly full work schedule following the experience. Going back to work too soon or lacking an appropriate context—in terms of personal interactions and access to basic needs—can be important factors that create difficulties for the integration of the experience. Examples of this are often seen in the recreational and psychonautical context—say, psychedelic festivals like Boom Festival—in which adverse reactions might follow a failure to meet basic needs such as adequate sleep, hydration, thermal regulation, and nutrition. On many occasions, simply by ensuring that these basic needs are addressed, the person can find balance again and continue their process on their own.

The Spiritual Dimension

Spirituality and the psychedelic experience are inseparable. Western culture has given a good account of this, from the appearance of Aldous Huxley's *The Doors of Perception and Heaven and Hell* in 1959 to the psychedelic therapy treatises of Humphry Osmond and Abram Hoffer (in which the therapeutic mechanism was the induction of a mystical experience through the use of high doses of LSD), as well as Walter Pahnke's seminal Good Friday experiment (1967). Modern reconstructions of this experiment (Doblin, 1991), research on the use of psilocybin to induce mystical experiences (Griffiths et al., 2006, 2011), and various positive therapeutic results in treatment following a mystical experience (Johnson et al., 2014; Garcia-Romeu et al., 2015) are current examples of the importance of the spiritual dimension, from the perspectives of their central place in the phenomenology of psychedelic experiences and in their therapeutic potential. Thus, it makes sense that any integrative psychotherapy should pay attention to the spiritual and transcendental dimensions.

In the psychedelic context, mystical experiences are commonly understood according to the definitions given by Pahnke and Richards (1966, 2015), in turn based on the works of William James and others. The characteristics of a mystical experience include: 1) a sense of unity; 2) transcendence of space and time; 3) a deeply positive mood; 4) a sense of sacredness; 5) a noetic quality (an insight felt at an intuitive level and perceived as true and real); 6) a paradoxical quality; and 7) ineffability. Another type of non-unitive spiritual experience has been described recently by Strassman (2014), who took into account the prophetic states represented in the Hebrew Bible, common in various monotheistic religions.

It may be surprising that the spiritual aspects of integration can present serious integration challenges. However, on many occasions we indeed find the spiritual dimension at the root of potential problems and possible solutions.

Firstly, we may find ourselves within a context where there is limited understanding of the spiritual implications that psychedelic experiences can bring. For example, both the therapist and the experimenter may subscribe to a materialistic and mechanistic worldview, in which spiritual dimensions are not taken into account. In such cases, the conceptual framework will be severely limited in its capacity to understand states of mystical consciousness, experiences of non-duality, contact with archetypes, oceanic experiences, death and rebirth sequences, or a wide variety of states of consciousness and levels of absorption that have been described in multiple spiritual traditions. Without the proper context for them, and with a limited capacity to interpret or understand a mystical or spiritual experience, many of their potentially long-lasting therapeutic effects might be discarded or ignored.

Secondly, we might face the reverse situation: too much emphasis on the spiritual. Psychedelic experiences tend to be multidimensional; they include a spiritual aspect, yet in many cases the content can be heavily biographical, personal, or interpersonal. Furthermore, it is common for these different dimensions to coexist in the same experience, often being related to each other; biographical content might be intertwined with transpersonal or perinatal content. These experiences contain different octaves, the phenomena unfolding in different levels pertaining to the same content. Considering the spiritual or transpersonal aspects as being more important than the biographical ones can lead to biased and incomplete interpretations of an experience. Moreover, this can lead to harmful experiences such as spiritual bypass, a loss of contact with consensus reality, and a neglect of other ordinary dimensions of life such as family, work, and intimate relationships. This can create an imbalance in the life of the individual, who might be able to access a multitude of spiritual or transpersonal content yet be relatively immature in other important areas. Sometimes, a "false" spirituality can manifest, in which transpersonal experiences become a mechanism for avoidance of certain painful aspects of psychic life. While this may be a benign compensation for a difficult and complex life situation, sometimes it can be a factor that perpetuates a problem that needs to be addressed.

Thirdly, in some contexts, we might come across the imposition of a specific spiritual framework forced on the participants by the therapist or guide. This can lead to a wide range of conflicts. On the one hand, it may provoke a clash of spiritual paradigms or even whole worldviews, resulting in confusion and the inability to relate to the contents of the experience in a personally meaningful and constructive way. On the other hand, it may involve a conflict of values or beliefs if the person identifies with another tradition. Furthermore, the leader, shaman, or therapist may embody a messianic or authoritarian attitude, imposing certain interpretations, judgments, or prescriptions on the participants.

Such a paradigm clash is quite common, given that psychedelic experiences tend to transcend any previous expectations, bringing out contents that may be completely alien and strange. This is a situation that should be familiar to any integration therapist. A couple of examples I came across while conducting international workshops were provided by a facilitator of ayahuasca ceremonies and a therapist working in harm reduction, both Israelis. Although many Israelis are secular and do not observe religion, they are familiar with Jewish tradition and are aware of frowned upon behaviors. Whether it is an ayahuasca ceremony or a rave with trance music, they may have difficulty integrating their experiences if they believe they are doing something wrong or sinful, such as consuming mind-altering substances or doing activities prohibited on holidays. Cultural aspects are important factors when trying to make sense of the difficulties that somebody is going through after coming into contact with foreign practices that evoke unpredictable experiences, particularly when they contain elements and imagery of other spiritual traditions.

The terms "spiritual," "mystical," "religious," and "sacred" can have complex connotations depending on context; different people understand them differently. Some people may feel resistance to them for cultural or intellectual reasons. In the psychedelic context, we often talk about "numinosity," coined by the German theologian Rudolf Otto and popularized by C.G. Jung. This term is more neutral and often more appropriate for describing the transcendental aspects of the psychedelic experience. Any psychedelic therapist or guide should be able to accept this term and the experiences to which it refers, drawing from their own understanding of psychedelic phenomenology, safeguarding their own worldview, and preventing the imposition of any particular worldview on their patients.

The modern psychonaut Christopher Bache speaks about the integration of the spiritual: "How do you integrate being One when you are one out of many. [...] I don't think you can integrate the infinite into the finite, the only thing you can do is integrate your finite existence into infinity, become a servant of infinity, surrender to it."[21]

The Behavioral Dimension

Talking about behavior in the context of transpersonal psychology and psychedelic therapy often raises suspicions about a reductionist behavioral or cognitive-behavioral perspective. The behavioral dimension has thus been somewhat neglected in the humanistic and transpersonal fields, especially in some therapeutic approaches that emphasize the supposedly spiritual aspects.

However, an authentic spirituality will always take into account behavioral aspects, which we could also consider ethical. When we talk about behavior, we include the ethical dimensions inherent in our behavior. Some ancient spiritual traditions, Buddhism and Judaism for example, particularly emphasize the ethical and behavioral dimensions, beyond the internal beliefs, prayers, and rituals that they prescribe.

In Theravada Buddhism, the measure for evaluating a practitioner's spiritual evolution is the development of increased compassion. Spiritual evolution is not measured by the ability to access states of concentration or *samadhi*, nor by whether multiple levels of consciousness have been reached, or by knowledge of various spiritual realms; evolution is a function of the development of compassion, as reflected in our relationship with other living beings, as we assume the precepts of the Noble Eightfold Path.

The Jewish tradition emphasizes the fulfillment of the 613 *mitzvot*, the precepts given by God to the people of Israel in the covenant of Mount Sinai. It may be surprising to discover different levels of fulfillment. One can fulfill a certain *mitzva* (precept) because they find it reasonable and are in agreement with it; the action comes from within one's own heart. The precepts can also be fulfilled simply because God said so, even if one does not personally understand the precept, nor perhaps even agree with it, and the action does not happen naturally. For certain schools of the Talmudic tradition, there is greater merit in carrying out the commandment out of respect for the divine will without having to agree with it. This could be understood through the lens of devotion, as in Bakhti Yoga, where one pays devotion to the guru, because this is the path to enlightenment. By following precepts—behavioral impositions and limitations—we do not experience a restriction of our free will. On the contrary, they are tools of liberation.

Another aspect of the behavioral dimension of integration is its practical implementation, how the lessons and insights obtained in higher states of consciousness become realized and actualized in our daily lives. An *ayahuasquero* friend of mine rightly said, "It is easy to forgive your father during an ayahuasca experience. The difficult part is to return home and act accordingly, with real forgiveness." This is one of the real dangers of using psychedelic substances or any technique that induces non-ordinary experiences. As previously mentioned, "psychedelics can take back everything they give you;" if we do not make an effort to ground those realizations in a tangible plane, they tend to disappear after a while, becoming merely a memory. Many people enter into a fruitless spiral, chasing experience after experience while deluding themselves that they are doing great inner work. From the outside, however, the self-absorption, stagnation, and neglect of other areas of life become apparent. Excessive attention to our internal worlds can become counterproductive when we are out of balance with the rest.

The signs of a good integration—other than stability in the cognitive and emotional dimensions—must thus include successful, positive changes at a behavioral and ethical level. Following a successful therapeutic process, people often make changes in important aspects of their lives. These are signs of the good integration of a multi-layered psychedelic experience, as the spiritual levels have manifested upon the physical plane, empowering us to have a greater positive influence on the world and our loved ones.

After a difficult experience, certain maladaptive behaviors may appear: coping mechanisms such as trying to deal with uncomfortable emotions through the use of drugs or engaging in risky behaviors that may endanger the integrity of the person or the people involved. All of these aspects must be taken into account by the therapist.

Furthermore, it is also important to consider the opposite scenario. After a particularly joyful and positive experience, a person might feel the need to act impulsively and make a major change in their lives, such as moving to another city, ending a romantic relationship (or starting a new one), making important financial decisions, changing jobs, or initiating risky conversations with people who are close to them. While these decisions may be correct and appropriate, they should always be given their proper space. If a decision is appropriate right after an experience, it will remain appropriate for the following month. The psyche speaks in metaphor and symbols, and we often need time to elucidate and shape the final form of that initial intuition. Perhaps a change has to take place, but it may not be exactly what we envisioned during our psychedelic experience. It is about finding the balance between impulsivity on the one hand and inertia and lack of action on the other hand.

Integration-oriented therapy should never neglect the behavioral dimensions or unpleasant symptomatic manifestations that may occur after a psychedelic experience. Although the symptoms often relate to the outermost layers of a pattern—or a COEX—they are still part of it, and depending on their intensity, they can interfere in significant ways with daily life. When a person is overwhelmed by a poorly resolved experience, it is very difficult for a fluid integration process to take place. The integration process stagnates, and the person may become reluctant to deepen their exploration of their own psyche in order to resolve the situation. Behavioral aspects must thus be integral to a comprehensive therapy, and a broad-minded therapist must know their way around behavioral prescriptions to address the symptomatic level. A purely behavioral approach would be limited in its capacity to address something as complex as a psychedelic experience. By including an appropriate management of behavioral symptoms, however, we can regain the stability needed to continue the integration process at deeper, subtler levels.

The Social Dimension

The social dimension of integration is perhaps the least recognized; its therapeutic impact, however, can be enormous.

In shamanic societies, the concept of integration does not exist. This includes Indigenous groups from the Amazon basin such as the Shipibo-Conibo, the Shuar, or the Asháninka, as well as the Cofán from the Colombian Putumayo, who use ayahuasca or *yagé* in their religious and cultural practices. This also includes the members of the Bwiti religions and their use of *Tabernanthe iboga* in Gabon, as well as other cultural groups that regularly engage in non-ordinary states of consciousness during their social interactions, such as the Brazilian ayahuasca churches of Santo Daime, União do Vegetal, and Barquinha.

Of course, local and autochthonous practices exist that fulfill the same Western integration practices. However, these groups do not refer to integration as such, nor have they elaborated this concept specifically related to the positive processing of the internal states and experiences that occur under the influence of visionary plants.

In the *vegetalista* tradition of the Shipibo people from the Peruvian Amazon basin, there is extensive knowledge of the use of a variety of medicinal plants besides ayahuasca. The *vegetalista* tradition holds ayahuasca in high esteem, and it includes a rich worldview based on its use and preparation. A large number of plants are part of a wide pharmacopoeia that is used for shamanic purposes, that is, to cure ailments, acquire power and knowledge, solve personal and social conflicts, prevent and counteract the spells and magic darts of enemy shamans, and so on. This tradition posits that a diet is necessary for the proper use of ayahuasca and other plants. This diet involves certain restrictions, which vary depending on the area and tradition (most commonly refraining from spicy food, onion, garlic, toothed fish, pork, alcohol, sugar, salt, and a relatively long list of variables). A diet also involves the restriction of certain behaviors, such as prolonged periods of isolation and silence or abstinence from sexual relationships. These restrictions usually apply before the plant is taken and can carry on for days, weeks, or even months after, depending on the particular practice.

In addition to this sort of diet and the restrictions that it carries for before and after, there is also the concept of dieting a plant; this consists of a period of similar restrictions, including isolation, in which we ingest a plant or tree prescribed by the traditional doctor on a daily basis. The goal is to become intimately familiar with the peculiarities of this plant and turn it into our ally. During this process, which can last days, weeks, or months, the participant takes the plant and enters an introspective space, exclusively interacting with the healer. The learning happens during dreams, daydreams, or deep states of absorption; not much psychological work is done with these contents. Once the process is finished, this diet is cut. However, the dieter must continue with the restrictions of certain foods and behaviors for the time prescribed, in order to allow the spirit of the plant to continue working. In some traditions, a failure to comply with the restrictions is considered dangerous, and there is a strong encouragement to remain disciplined. Failure to do so may result in the loss of some or all of the benefits gained from dieting with that plant or even incur potential harm due to risky energetic interactions such as prematurely engaging in a sexual relationship.

From this example, we can see that complex and specific practices exist for integrating experiences and diets. However, we do not refer to the "diet" as an example of integration since the complete experience is a continuum that involves the period of ingestion of the plant itself and the subsequent period of dietary and behavioral restrictions.

In shamanic societies, the concept of integration is not necessary; the use of psychoactive plants that grant access to non-ordinary states or the spiritual dimensions of existence is already integrated into their worldview. There is nothing to integrate because that is already part of their way of life—it is already integrated. In a shamanic society, it is not necessary to explain to anyone, including the children, the implications of attending an ayahuasca ceremony. If, after an experience with a healer or shaman, someone is somewhat disoriented or needs a period of recovery, no one is surprised or requires further explanation. Both the use of ayahuasca and the experiences that ayahuasca induces are nothing out of the ordinary.

When I was deciding whether or not to visit a healer in the jungle, a friend who was familiar with the Amazon and the ayahuasca traditions recommended: "Ask the children, they will tell you if the healer is trustworthy or not." I did so, and I was surprised by the children's precise explanations of why they recommended one and not another: "That one has more experience and does better work. Besides, his house is cleaner."

A similar situation in any Western society today is unimaginable. Imagine someone who, after a difficult experience on a Saturday night, has to return to the office on Monday morning. This person will likely make every effort to ensure that nothing unusual or strange is noticed and that her bosses and colleagues do not suspect that something out of the ordinary had occurred over the weekend. Even if her bosses and colleagues were open-minded, it is unlikely that they would be able to offer much understanding. Furthermore, they might even be somewhat judgmental or try to warn her about the danger of these practices. In another situation, we might encounter people who hold an infantile, detached fascination towards these experiences.

In Western paradigms, we lack a well-established common language to truly understand these experiences for ourselves, let alone talk about them with other people. In many integration circles, you can hear phrases such as, "I have no words to share what I have experienced," or "I still cannot make sense of what happened in my experience." Furthermore, we lack culturally established methods to access non-ordinary states, so we must travel to places and rely on techniques that might feel special, exotic, unusual, and even illegal. Likewise, we lack the proper structures that can integrate these practices into a functioning society, and we lack the spaces (physical and temporal) to properly interact with each other around these experiences. Grof argues that some of his work has provided "language, method, and structure" for experiences in non-ordinary states of consciousness. Although this has materialized in Holotropic Breathing and psychedelic therapy, it has not expanded to more social sectors. There is still quite some distance between many of these practices and the mind of an average Westerner.

David L. Rosenhan states: "What is considered normal in one culture can be seen as completely abnormal in another. The differentiation between normality and abnormality, which in psychiatry is traditionally based on the apparently objective criterion of an individual's 'adaptation to reality,' may therefore not be as exact as is generally considered"(Rosenhan in Watzlawick et al., 2015). This becomes even more relevant when dealing with phenomena experienced in non-ordinary realities induced by unusual techniques or little-known substances.

As Westerners, in order to process these experiences, we need liminal zones, intermediate spaces between the non-ordinary and the ordinary, both at the individual and the intra-psychic level. We also need spaces in the social and interpersonal spheres, such as the consultation of a psychologist or attending an integration circle. We need practices that allow us to receive something profound from the experience, to translate from the spiritual or transcendental worlds back to our daily, rational lives. We need a translation sourced from the experiential domains back to our everyday reality and Western modalities of thought.

Ideally, in the future we will not need integration as discussed in this book. The future of integration, if we get it right, is that there is no need for integration. If the day comes when these experiences and practices are part of our customs and ways of life, and we develop the language and the spaces needed for this phenomenon to be adequately understood, then integration as such will likely be unnecessary.

We could follow the lead from our use of other substances. Alcohol is so well integrated within Mediterranean societies that it is considered an expression of these cultures. Infrastructures are created around grape production and wine processing. We have perfected cultures and methods of fermentation, aging, and bottling of wine. We have a rich vocabulary to describe its flavors and textures. We even have an ancient tradition of wine production and consumption from which to draw. Without having to study much, we know which wines are best suited for which meals. No one would dream of serving a warm sparkling wine next to a veal steak. We have also created rituals around the use of wine: uncorking the bottle, the initial tasting, the toast, etc. There is a significant social dimension in the use of wine, in which the pharmacological effects are used to facilitate social interactions and entertain an evening with friends. We also know the risks and implications of drinking excessively, and we know it best to limit consumption to certain times of the day and in certain situations. We know what a hangover is and the discomfort that it causes. Parents of teenage children are able to understand when their child is terribly hungover and cannot eat a bite of the cannelloni or the roast on New Year's. It is not necessary to explain any of these things; we do not have to do anything particular to integrate the use of wine in our society since it is already integrated. Knowledge exists even if we are not aware of it. Of course, no one would buy a book called *The Integration of the Drunken Experience*.

Another relevant aspect of the social dimension of integration lies in the role that society and our environment play in one's individual experience. In tribal communities like the Bwiti—or any other group where initiation rites exist—it is of utmost importance for the person to go through the initiatory experience. The person faces all the tribulations and challenges and confronts their own psychological difficulties while the rest of the community bears witness to it. The act of witnessing has important implications. The experience becomes something undeniable, etched in the collective memory even if the individual were to forget about it. The identity or role of that individual is thus changed, and the rest of society recognizes it. He is no longer a child but a man—for example—and that has implications for future interactions, his rights and duties, and for the individual's own identity. In 1966, Sarett, Cheek, and Osmond published a paper evaluating the efficacy of LSD therapy amongst a cohort of people struggling with alcoholism. For the paper, they interviewed the patients' wives to gain their perspective on their observed changes. The authors found mostly positive changes in both the patients and their wives, thus supporting the view that psychedelics can have a bi-directional social influence.

In Western cultures, our identities are largely determined by what Jung calls the "persona." This archetype refers to the mask we use to navigate the world and interact with it. Attached to these masks are certain behaviors and social expectations (Jung, 1990). According to Jung, one of the problems we might face during our individuation process is becoming overly identified with a particular mask, hindering the process of self-knowledge that leads towards our true essence. This same situation can also have the opposite effect. Following a psychedelic experience, the persona may get in contact with the Self or with some transcendental dimensions that loosen the grip of our identification with the ego and the "persona." However, our social group has not necessarily shared our experience, and from their perspective, we are still the same person. The social image of the "persona" has not changed, so even if one decouples from that identity and changes that mask internally, part of our perceived identity is still coupled to the identity attributed to us by others. This is more complex today than back in Jung's days since now the construct of the "persona" is further influenced by our social media identities and online relationships. Jack Kornfield tells of the great shock he experienced upon returning to New York for a reunion with his family after years of intense meditation while training as a monk in Burma. He recounts how, having reached blissful heightened states, he watched all his spiritual achievements collapse when he got back in touch with his family and close friends (Kornfield, 1997, 2001).

The social dimension of integration, as we can see, is complex and important. This area of integration is currently underdeveloped, and hopefully in the future we will further emphasize the social factors of integration (Carhart-Harris et al., 2018; Kaelen et al., 2018), in addition to other extra-pharmacological factors that influence the outcome of psychedelic therapy such as set and setting, music, or the modality of intervention. For example, a remarkable phenomenon occurs in this regard during Holotropic Breathwork workshops. Holotropic Breathing is a non-pharmacological technique that can induce intense non-ordinary states in which we access biographical, perinatal, and transpersonal content. However, these experiences may not always be as intense as some seasoned psychonauts would expect. We could debate whether the intensity and the therapeutic potential of an experience are directly proportional; in either case, most people expect to have intense experiences and become disappointed or underwhelmed when that is not the case. Regardless of what kind of experiences each participant had, we consistently observe a valuable and therapeutic effect based solely on the relationships that were crafted among them. The social aspect can sometimes be more therapeutic and valuable than the Holotropic Breathwork in itself. One of the most powerful aspects of this technique is the social container that is created, which allows us to deepen our own internal exploration surrounded by people with the same intention, who act as respectful and kind witnesses to each other's individual process. This social container, once set in motion, precedes the experience itself and continues after it. Weaving a specific social network to support this type of work is invaluable, allowing us to work within a community and process or overcome difficult experiences more easily.

The same phenomenon can be observed in many other communities that are structured around experiential psychotherapies, be they ayahuasca circles, Claudio Naranjo's Seekers After Truth (SAT) process, or any other group that is conducted in an ethical, professional, and responsible manner.

An excellent example of how important the social dimension can be in integration is found in the story of Christopher Bache. Bache spent twenty years systematically using high doses of LSD (400-500 µg) for introspective purposes, listening to classical music in his headphones and wearing an eye mask. He carried out seventy-three clandestine experiences with high doses of LSD while teaching philosophy at the university as his day job and managed to keep his psychonautical experiments a secret from his colleagues. His experiences led him to visit various spaces from Grof's expanded cartography, both biographical and perinatal as well as transpersonal. Bache recounts having experienced a great distance between his public life and his private life, partly due to the lack of safe spaces to process the multiple experiences throughout the years. Bache also reflects on the different levels of integration of his experience, including his perception of a deeper integration once he began to share his experiences. By talking about them, his relationship to the experiences changed and kept evolving and unfolding (Bache, 2019). In his own words:

> There was a split between my public life and private life. I didn't have a place to process. A level of integration could take place privately, psychologically before I started to speak. When I began to give the talks and share with people what I had done, I could also take in what they had experienced. I found that the integration of those experiences began to deepen, they began to live in me differently than before I started to talk about them. It began a process that is continuing to evolve. Somehow the transcendent divine and the immanent divine seem to be reaching a deeper merging, synthesis, in my life now that I have shared and opened the conversation.[22]

The Temporal Dimension

The temporal dimension underlies and permeates all the other dimensions of integration; the integration of an experience evolves, in all its dimensions, over time. We can clearly distinguish two main periods in integration. One is the period immediately following the experience and, the second, integration in the long-term.

Integration immediately after the experience relates mainly to the physical and emotional domains. After an experience, it is convenient to rest and recover our physiological and psychological baselines. In the case of experiences catalyzed by substances, this means allowing the effect of the substance to completely dissipate through rest, hydration, and nutrition until we are back at "normal." This in itself does not guarantee the proper integration of the contents and lessons that emerged during the experience, but it does imply that it is an indispensable condition for integration. In the fifth chapter, we will cover some cases where adverse reactions can occur; in many of these cases, this immediate integration did not take place, leaving the person in a state of hyperarousal, lacking sleep and physiological regulation. This can go on for days and even weeks after the experience, particularly when the experience has been traumatic, stressful, or evoked panic states. This phase of integration also happens in time. It is necessary to allow for the necessary time and the right space for a proper physiological deactivation to take place. Thus, to carry out this type of integration, there must be a period of doing nothing, where nothing happens, not even the integration of the experience. Another aspect related to this phase consists of working with the pain, tension, blockage, or other somatic symptoms that may have appeared after the experience. These manifestations are especially common in experiences induced by Holotropic Breathwork, although they can also happen in substance-induced experiences, particularly LSD, MDMA, and long-lasting psychedelic amphetamines such as DOC and DOB, among others. Somatic manifestations can be approached in different ways depending on the context. In Holotropic Breathwork, we address this immediately after the session has ended but before formally closing the experience. In the case of psychedelic substances, proper rest and hydration will usually dissipate any lingering bodily effects. In any case, the same principles can be followed if there are clear indications that the manifestations have a somatic origin.

In addition to the somatic, the emotional content must also be addressed immediately after the experience. Fully processed emotions during this stage are of vital importance later on. This means fully exploring and experiencing the emergent emotions until their intensity is extinguished. For a good integration, the emotional intensity must be stable and manageable, regardless of the emotions themselves. If these emotions are just bottled up, or we rely on distractions to avoid confronting them, there is the possibility that they will burst out of control hours or even days after the session, with the added shock and complication that this entails. Once the intensity has become manageable, processing and confronting emotions may require a cathartic experience by the end of the session. It may be necessary to reactivate the material to induce catharsis. This can be done via rapid breathing or simply by paying conscious attention to the breath while internalizing the experience—immersing oneself in the inner experience, with the eyes closed—and surrendering to the process. The help of the facilitator is usually necessary to reach this point of catharsis since the natural tendency will be to move away from the experience by trying to control and suppress the emotions, usually through distractions (opening eyes, talking a lot, starting to do things).

When this immediate integration has taken place, we can say that we have reached "closure." The concept of closure belongs to the tradition of Holotropic Breathwork and is taught in great detail during their facilitator training course. This immediate integration, or this closure, usually takes place in the same context as the workshop—if the interventions have been done professionally and appropriately. This is easier in the context of Holotropic Breathwork, both because of the format and paradigm of this type of work and the nature of the breathing experience.

In the case of substance use, we may not have access to such an ideal situation, either due to the physiological process related to the substance used, which might be quite taxing on the body and require a longer recovery time, or due to the format of the work ("sharing circles" and other non-individualized closing experiences are more common in psychedelic or shamanic group work). In the context of clinical trials, closure would be more similar to the Holotropic case due to the individual format and the demands of the clinical context.

From this perspective, when an integration therapist has to work with someone after a psychedelic experience who is experiencing relatively severe adverse effects, immediate closure was not properly achieved. Therefore, we will be working "out of time," trying to close something that ideally should have happened on the same day of the session. The goal then, and the overall goal of integration psychotherapy, is to provide the closing point that allows the person to focus on long-term integration. Chapters Three and Five focus on laying down the principles of this type of work, which is what I personally understand as psychotherapeutic integration work.

When we talk about integration in the long term, we refer to everything that follows after this immediate stage; here, we begin to work on the different dimensions as a whole. For the most part, we usually find ourselves in interventions that are not clinically significant, so we focus on maximizing the potential benefits of the experience. This part of integration has no time limit and is an open process. Insights and interpretations of the experience can change and shift over time. Sometimes, the fruits may be reaped many years later, when something reminds us of certain aspects of an experience that we believed were integrated and forgotten, surprising us with new and useful material to inform our development. I do not consider this to be a psychotherapeutic intervention per se, as it can be done in non-clinical settings. This is mostly referred to in Chapter Four when we explore the various techniques we can use to maximize benefits.

A dramatic example of a long-term integration process is found in *Shivitti: A Vision*, written by Auschwitz survivor Ka-Tzetnik 135633. After his release, he underwent LSD treatment with Dr. Bastiaans, during which he relived the atrocities he suffered in the extermination camp. Against the opinion of the doctor, he decided to abandon the treatment before finishing due to the harshness of the sessions. Only a decade later was he able to accept and integrate the content of those sessions and begin to deal with his memories and experiences. We must keep a broad perspective on the temporal dimension of integration, remembering that meaningful experiences can continue to provide new insights and interpretations over the years.

THEORETICAL FOUNDATIONS OF THE CLINICAL INTERVENTION

3

"From another distant land, from the desert, came another voice, the voice of a doctor that spoke of what disturbed people told him. These stories were so different from the orthodox ones that scientists said they were tales of a sorcerer, a shaman, and were therefore completely unscientific."

STEVE DE SHAZER, ABOUT MILTON ERICKSON (2010)

"Professor Bastiaans, [...] before we proceed, I would appreciate if you understood that I didn't come here as a patient, but because I have heard that you have the key for a door that I have been trying to go through. So please, open that door for me, but once inside, be so kind of leaving me there alone."

KA-TZETNIK 125633 - SHIVITTI, A VISION.

THE NEED FOR A THEORETICAL PARADIGM FOR INTEGRATION WORK

The practice of integration in relation to psychedelic experiences is a very young discipline. In the first few chapters of this book, we have explored how—from the early days of psychedelic research—certain practices are carried out both before and after the experience for their added value. The same has been true for traditional societies. Most of these practices have been developed in a specific context and carried out by the doctors, facilitators, or shamans themselves—that is, the people who directly attended or facilitated the psychedelic experience.

For the most part, this is still the case today: Workshop and ceremony facilitators often include dynamics specific for integration, and researchers include psychotherapy sessions in their clinical trials. In both cases, the person leading the psychedelic experience usually facilitates the integration sessions. Although in each of these contexts, specific practices are carried out in coherence with the theoretical paradigm or the tradition embodied by the person facilitating the experience, we find a common denominator in all of them: they either focus on benefit maximization or on ontological integration. Intentionality, as we have seen, can be therapeutic in itself, thus creating some confusion regarding the logical levels of work.

Recently, a new phenomenon has emerged from the landscapes of underground psychedelic therapy and neo-shamanic retreats. People undergo these experiences under the care of a specific facilitator or shaman; however, quite often (and particularly when they face difficulties after the experience), they might look for an external professional who can help them integrate that experience. This professional has not been present at the session or ceremony and may not even know or even agree with the approach, theoretical paradigm, or worldview of the facilitators or shamans. It is this professional, nonetheless, who must attend to the person who is going through difficulties.

As an example, after a difficult experience in which relatively severe anxious or depressive symptoms manifest or, less commonly, symptoms that could be conflated with what traditional psychiatry calls "psychotic," the person might seek help from their physician or even end up at the psychiatric ER. In such cases, it is likely that the professional who is caring for this person knows little about what their patient is going through. Guided by his best intentions, the professional will most likely choose a treatment determined by the psychiatric paradigm, based on a diagnosis and subsequent pharmacological treatment meant to suppress symptoms. Of course, this might not be what the patient needs. In a reversed situation, that same person goes to a shamanic practitioner to treat this poorly resolved psychedelic experience; the diagnosis and the interventions will be different, perhaps of an energetic or spiritual nature, but equally rooted in the tradition and worldview of that particular shaman. The shaman would then diagnose and prescribe a treatment based on their particular school of knowledge, regardless of the specific needs of the patient.

Since we all belong to some cultural system, this bias is unavoidable and difficult to overcome. It is worth being aware of these biases, particularly when diverse shamanic practices have become global, and the use of psychedelic substances is widespread. It has become transcultural and more accessible to segments of the population who are not usually interested in these matters, as we saw in the introduction to this book.

Nowadays, a therapist might receive requests for integration from people who have participated in shamanic retreats in the Amazon involving ayahuasca or after "dieting" with a plant or tree according to some Indigenous lineage. Integration services are sought by people who participate in neo-shamanic retreats, where they may consume a diverse combination of substances such as ayahuasca, *Bufo alvarius, yopo,* or *changa*, among others, or by people who took part in therapeutic sessions using MDMA, psilocybin, or another substance. Today, we encounter an infinite variety of contexts, constantly changing and expanding.

Faced with this multitude of practices, each one enveloped by a specific paradigm and worldview, imbued with determined theoretical models and offering concrete interpretations of the meaning of the psychedelic experience, it is necessary for the integration therapist to have a theoretical model of intervention that allows them to navigate these unpredictable situations with relative success. We must remember that the integration therapist, in most cases, has not been present in that original session and is often unaware of the specific context and worldview. Furthermore, the therapist may even disagree or dislike that particular way of working.

In other words, it is impossible for an integrative therapist to adopt (or even know) the worldview of all the different patients he treats, and it is equally impossible (and undesirable) for patients to adopt the worldview of the therapist or his school of therapy. Therefore, it is necessary to establish a theoretical intervention paradigm that can be adapted to these complex realities and allows effective communication between patient and therapist.

Common Paradigms

At the present moment, we do have some good models on different aspects of the psychedelic experience, in particular descriptive models of the phenomenology and evolution of experience, either from a therapeutic or spiritual perspective (Grof, 1975, 2002), a cognitive perspective (Shannon, 2003), or an evolutionary psychology perspective (Wilber, 2008), as well as mixed schools between psychiatry and spirituality (Nelson, 2008). Recently, more therapeutic-oriented schools focused on trauma and its treatment have gained popularity: for example, the model of Dr. Gabor Maté (2008) or the paradigms for treating post-traumatic stress with MDMA. Other schools are those provided by the "shamanic" traditions of Indigenous peoples, who have their own models for understanding both the phenomenology and the therapeutic aspects of the experience.

If we focus on the psychotherapeutic aspects, and especially on the concept of integration in the main Western models, we can see that a strong emphasis is placed on understanding and interpreting experience. Regular integration psychotherapy implies working with the phenomenology of the experience in order to, on the one hand, map the experience somewhere within the existing cartography and, on the other hand, to provide interpretation for the phenomena in alignment with the psychotherapeutic school of choice. For example, the first psychotherapeutic uses of LSD happened within the framework of a more or less classical psychoanalytic treatment, as we saw in the first chapter (Newland, 1962). We find a similar dynamic in Jungian-style psychotherapies that work with the contents of the psychedelic experiences in the same way that they work with dreams or fantasies. The same dynamic happens with Grof's transpersonal perspective, where experiences are interpreted and located within the expanded cartography of the psyche, emphasizing the particular aspects of the different basic perinatal matrices.[23]

This aspect of integration work consists of categorizing the different experiences and giving them a certain meaning within a broader process. In the case of psychoanalysis, we would speak of early traumatic events, psychosexual development, and the Oedipus complex. Appropriate interventions in this case would be free association, interpretations, and transference analysis. In Jungian analytical psychology, we would interpret similar events as emergences of the personal and collective unconscious and work with unconscious archetypes such as the shadow and the anima within the broader framework of the individuation process. The interventions would be those used by Jungian analysts (Zweig and Abrams, 1993). In Grof's transpersonal paradigm, we would talk about the different phases of the process: the biographical review, the process of birth, the experience of the ego death, and the access to the transpersonal domains. Through our interventions, we would aim to understand the different phases of the process and allow its adequate resolution, usually by facilitating additional experiences in expanded states. In Wilber's cartography, we would classify the types of psychedelic experience according to the "fulcrum" or stage of development to which they belong, and each stage would correspond to a specific practice, from pharmacological therapy to the meditation of non-dual schools (Wilber, 1990).

The previous analysis is clearly limited and superficial, but it leaves us with the understanding that each school of thought believes that its own interpretations best explain the psychedelic experience, even though they exist alongside many other maps and interpretations. Therefore, the main interventions are simply meant to locate this experience within the larger context of each school's map of the psyche and move towards the analysis.

Most of these schools propose an integration methodology based on the same therapeutic method, which is ontologically shared by all of them: the continuous deepening of the analysis. The usual practices are related to what we have called "benefit maximization" or ontological integration, although, in situations where the person is going through an acute crisis, these approaches are not optimally desirable. All these schools suffer thus from the confusion mentioned in the second chapter, regarding the two great categories of integration: the ontological and the therapeutic.

The maps they propose are useful and valid, both for understanding experiences and for making them meaningful. A deep knowledge of psychoanalysis can probably be extremely useful for the understanding of psychedelic experiences based on biographical content. Grof's model can describe in minute detail the experiences of the perinatal domains and help us make sense of the symbology reflected in the dimensions of an internal process. In addition, Grof's cartography labels a wide variety of transpersonal phenomena, similar to Jungian analytical psychology.

Any integration therapist would benefit from knowing these cartographies in detail, in addition to any others that offer a deep and detailed understanding of the contents of the psyche and the relationships between our conscious and unconscious minds. All this can be enriching in integration therapy, but it does not in itself constitute a theoretical intervention paradigm that allows us to combine ontological and therapeutic aspects. Furthermore, although they propose an interpretive model, these schools do not offer pragmatic therapeutic interventions to effectively solve the crisis situations that may appear and, above all, they do not distinguish between the two major integration modalities of which we have spoken.[24]

An Integrative Paradigm

Taking into account the complexity of the psychedelic experience, the multiplicity of approaches, interpretations, and the infinite range of possible experiences, our theoretical framework cannot be exclusively therapeutic. We need a paradigm that can be applied to both the ontological and therapeutic dimensions of the experience. Therefore, it must have theoretical solidity and validity to explain the multiple phenomena. At the same time, it must provide us with practical applications so that we can develop useful intervention methods in the different integration scenarios. Furthermore, it has to be a theoretical paradigm in which spiritual phenomena and experiences can coexist with biographical events, traumatic memories, and ordinary, daily life. We are looking, then, for a meta-paradigm, a stream of thought or a philosophical school able to accommodate everything that has been done before, giving it internal coherence.

Complex problems often have simple solutions. The theoretical paradigm that adapts to these particular demands exists and has been widely developed by some philosophers and therapists. Furthermore, this meta-paradigm has quietly influenced multiple authors over the past decades. This paradigm is called constructivism, and it is, in my opinion, the most suitable for working in integration, due to its ability to adapt to the multiple realities that coexist in the different formats of psychedelic and shamanic work.

Constructivism is a philosophical current that springs from the assumption that all knowledge is built by humans. All the natural sciences—and all their theories—are therefore mental constructs created from the interpretation of our observations. Somehow, constructivism asks itself, as stated by Watzlawick, "How do we know what we think we know and whether reality is really real?" (Watzlawick, 2015, 2019).

Constructivism is not a new trend. Rather, it has been present in multiple traditions, even if its formulation in psychological terms and its application to psychotherapy appeared during the 1970s. Even so, in many traditions, we find ideas equivalent to those of constructivism, particularly in those traditions that understand psychological phenomena and the perception of reality as something illusory. Examples of such traditions are Buddhism, Hinduism, Taoism, or Jewish Hasidism. We even find constructivist aspects in the development of psychedelic psychotherapy and its conception over the past fifty years, given that the effects of psychedelic substances themselves are influenced (and we could even say determined) by extra-pharmacological factors, such as those which create a personal and social reality. Hartogsohn's studies (2016, 2017) demonstrate how the subjective effects are dependent on the context, and the social reality of the particular historical moment constitutes a key factor in this context. Mortimer Hartman, a psychiatrist who worked with LSD in the United States and administered this substance to Hollywood star Cary Grant, realized how important the paradigm of the therapist was in the subsequent phenomenology unfolding during a psychedelic session. According to Hartman, the therapist's "orientation inevitably altered the content of the patient's" experience, such that Freudian-oriented therapists elicited more childhood memories while Jungian-oriented therapists encountered more transcendental experiences (Oram, 2018). As Don Juan says in *Journey to Ixtlan*: "Things are only real after one has learned to agree on their realness" (Castaneda, 2018).

The constructivist perspective that I share here is based on the school of the Mental Research Institute of Palo Alto, which integrates aspects of different disciplines, such as Bateson's Cybernetics (1967), General Systems Theory, Human Communication Theory (Watzlawick et al., 1981), and the further development of Brief Strategic Therapy (Watzlawick & Nardone, 2003). However, we do find glimpses of the constructivist perspective even in psychoanalysis. In "Constructions in Analysis" (Freud, 1938), Freud argues that the analyst's task is to "follow the clues" leftover by the repressed facts, with the explicit intent to "construct" those facts. The analyst constructs some facts and gives them to the patient, only in this case the construction is based on the paradigm of the therapist and it is the patient who has to adapt to it. For Freud, the word "construction" better represents the analyst's work than the term "interpretation."

The interested reader can find the most relevant aspects of psychological constructivism and the principles of intervention presented in their purest version in the writings of Watzlawick et al. (1976, 1981, 2002, 2003, 2015, 2019) and in those of Fisch, Segal, and Weakland (1984).

These types of psychology and psychotherapy have been considered superficial by the schools of deep psychology—including the psychedelic and transpersonal lenses—because they focus on the management of symptoms but fail to reveal the roots of the symptomatic manifestations. It is thus believed that they fail to catalyze profound changes in personality and the perception of the relationship with oneself, the world, and reality.

Short and strategic psychotherapies have been dismissed for lacking depth. This criticism is not without value if we only contemplate the application of these psychotherapies without considering the theoretical and epistemological formulations that underlie the practice. However, if we go to the sources, we will see that the people who formulated the principles of constructivism (as applied to psychotherapy) were people of deep knowledge and concern. Gregory Bateson greatly influenced the development of the methods at the Mental Research Institute of Palo Alto. Moreover, (and a less known fact) he was also one of the participants in "The Use of LSD in Psychotherapy," a congress that took place in 1959. He was also a close friend of Grof and influenced some of his ideas. Paul Watzlawick was a Jungian analyst before becoming interested in other therapeutic methods. His books are replete with references to broader disciplines, including different spiritual schools, and there are even references to psychedelic experiences and the difficulty of their integration: "Hallucinogenic drugs seem to produce a similar effect [in relation to the access to the right brain, through the blocking of the left, rational hemisphere], but it is always striking that it is difficult, if not impossible, to bring something 'from there' that is useful for daily life" (Watzlawick, 1976, 83). Even if not explicitly stated, one suspects that perhaps the author knew of the "there" he wrote. Not surprisingly, Watzlawick had a relationship with Milton Erickson, an enigmatic character from the American Midwest. In fact, he harbored a suspicion that "the figure of Don Juan in Castaneda's books was actually Erickson" (ibid., 152).

In the closing lines of his masterful work *Change: Principles of Problem Formation and Problem Resolution*, he writes:

> *This book could have been written from the apparently very different context of what is vaguely defined as mystical experiences, that is, from the sudden and unpredictable passage from the usual and everyday field of reference to a totally new perception of reality, which, however brief the experience itself may be, will never allow us to forget that reality, as such, can be totally different (Watzlawick et al., 1976).*

The intention of this book is summarized in Watzlawick's quote. This book does not intend to provide an exhaustive exposition of the principles of constructivism applied to psychotherapy but rather to interpret them from the perspective of psychedelic integration. Constructivism and its application encompass an extensive field that includes abundant literature, solidly developed by outstanding authors. I lack the depth of knowledge needed to even pretend I can contribute something to this discipline or even fully communicate its uses. However, I have tried to present the basic principles relevant to psychedelic integrative psychotherapy. At the same time, I have tried to broaden or reformulate those aspects of constructivist practice already developed with specific contributions to the field of the psychedelic experience by including references to other non-specifically constructivist systems, such as a variety of spiritual traditions, psychedelic cartographies, and widely established psychological schools that have not based their a priori assumptions on a constructivist view of reality. Of course, any inconsistencies in this synthesis are solely my responsibility.

Psychedelic Experiences and Psychotherapy:
Two Conflicting Logics

Perhaps the main difficulties in creating a methodology that is useful for the integration of psychedelic experiences are the distance and separation between two different realities: the reality in which the experience occurs and that in which the integration takes place.

The psychedelic experience takes place in a non-ordinary reality, or in a non-ordinary state of consciousness. So what happens during these experiences is, by definition, out of the ordinary, something different from what happens in our waking state of consciousness, ineffable. However, integrative psychotherapy takes place under our day-to-day, ordinary state of consciousness. Moreover, the therapeutic effects and long-lasting changes following a successful psychedelic therapy have to manifest in this ordinary reality as well.

Therefore, the first difficulty lies in integrating something non-ordinary, and even extraordinary, into the ordinary; this might turn out to be an impossible task. And indeed, Bache has previously reflected on how to integrate the infinite into the finite.[25] In the Hasidic tradition, this is a subject of passionate study. For the Hasids, these poles are integrated into a non-dual conception through different qualities of the divinity or the absolute: one with a tendency to manifest (*Chesed*) and the other to hide (*Gevurah*) (Steinsaltz, 1989).

Another difficulty derived from the above is that the logics that are in place during a non- ordinary state of consciousness are different from the prevailing logics of ordinary reality. It is practically impossible to change the logic by which we operate voluntarily. External intervention is often required, be it a psychedelic experience, a fortuitous event, the transmission of *shaktipat* by a guru, or a skillful therapeutic intervention. For the most part, the logics underlying non-ordinary and ordinary experiences stand in opposition to each other.

In our ordinary logic, we usually understand processes in a linear way, according to causal and individual dynamics. Meanwhile, in non-ordinary states of consciousness it becomes easier to perceive the circular, interdependent, and interactional nature of all dynamics.

One of the challenges when it comes to finding a suitable intervention model for integration psychotherapy then lies in solving this conflict or, in other words, reaching a therapeutic logic that is consistent with the non-ordinary logic of psychedelic experiences.

Paradoxes: Fear of the Symptom

The logical conflict between psychedelic psychotherapy and traditional psychotherapy, in relation to integration, can be summarized as follows:

In psychedelic psychotherapy, we encourage the person to come into contact with any content that appears during the experience. We encourage the person to fully experience any emotion and sensation that comes up in their session, regardless of its nature, be it positive, negative, or neutral. We also ask that, as far as possible, judgment be suspended and the analysis be left for the following days. We encourage participants to confront their symptoms and allow themselves to feel their fear or sadness as intensely as they are able to. The guidelines suggest getting deeper into the experience, fully accepting and experiencing whatever happens.

After the experience, however, our attitude as therapists changes and we become frightened if the person continues to show intense emotions or has lingering emotional or somatic symptoms. We often wish that it was not happening, and we look for ways to get rid of it. It is surprising that facilitators, *ayahuasqueros*, shamans, and other professionals, who are greatly skilled at managing the intense expression of emotions and other symptoms during the actual session, cannot deal with the same manifestations when they linger or manifest after the experience. Most providers seem to have very few resources to deal with these situations beyond reassuring words, distraction maneuvers, the up-selling of additional psychedelic sessions, or asking the person to "be patient and trust the process." They often deal with these situations by trying to get the person out of their experience, by trying to control, and discouraging indulgence in these intense internal states.

While intense manifestations or symptoms are quite normal during a non-ordinary experience, we tend to be afraid of them when they happen in ordinary reality. This is true even among therapists, who feel anxious when their patients exhibit severe symptoms. The integrative therapist should not fear the symptoms but learn to love them, to be fascinated by them.

Viktor Frankl (1991) said: "I consider it a false and dangerous concept for mental hygiene to assume that what man needs first of all is balance or, as it is called in biology, 'homeostasis;' that is to say, a state without tension. What man really needs is not to live without tension, but to strive and fight for a worthwhile goal." The symptoms are the expression of that internal struggle. As such, they must be respected and honored as the organism's attempt to reach a state of greater fullness and greater meaning.

In this sense, the purpose of integrative psychotherapy is not to eliminate symptoms (from a merely functional perspective) but to make use of the symptoms to resolve the unfinished conflict.

We must then use non-ordinary logic, what Frankl called "paradoxical intent," or what Watzlawick and other authors referred to as the blocking of dysfunctional "attempted solutions." We will see practical examples and further elaboration of these principles in Chapter Five and Chapter Six.

Another relevant aspect of the logical conflicts underlying most integration practices has to do with the directivity of the process. The intervention during the sessions of modified states of consciousness is usually done from a non-directive perspective, merely providing support to the natural unfolding of the experience; it is generally understood that the person's own psyche is capable of resolving any conflicts that might arise during the experience through its "integrative function" (Abramson,

1955), the "wisdom of internal healing" (Grof, 2002), or any other conception of the operating mechanisms of the psyche in non-ordinary states. Bill Richards says that a psychedelic experience is like a boomerang: "No matter how far the boomerang seems from you, it is the same force that drives it away that makes it return." Psychedelic therapists can thus comfortably assume a supportive, non-directive role.

However, when it comes to integration, therapists assume a different role and get rid of the non-directivity. For understandable reasons, they adopt the interpretive lens of their own school of training, be it Freudian, Jungian, Gestalt, Grofian, etc. Then, they try to fit the experience that the person has had within the conceptual framework of their theoretical school, which implies both a specific purpose for the intervention and a specific interpretation and management of symptoms. Thus, even with the best intentions, the therapist often becomes directive without even being aware of it, or worse still, while pretending not to be directive. Here we meet the first maxim of Human Communication Theory: "It is impossible not to communicate" (Watzlawick et al., 1981). In any interaction, not just a therapeutic interaction, all our interventions will be communicating something. Therefore, we must be aware that, whether we want to or not, we will be directive. Thus, the important thing is not whether or not one is being directive, but rather where it is that we are going. In many cases, the therapist's intended direction may be confusing and arbitrary, and we run the risk of not being aligned with the patient's intended direction.

The paradox that plagues many psychedelic and other humanistic therapists is that one actually has to learn to be consciously directive, decide in which direction one is going and then do it without complexes. In the psychedelic-constructivist perspective, the direction is clear and non-negotiable. The direction is set by the patient themselves, guided by their own process (it is internally-directed).

Sometimes, we will doubt the adequacy of our procedures in light of the symptoms and external manifestations of the patient's inner process following his psychedelic experiences; as integration therapists, we might lose our direction. When a person seems anxious during their session, and the anxiety lingers in the following days or new symptoms appear, we may be tempted to turn to distraction maneuvers or to encourage the patient to "hang in there," hoping that the situation will eventually resolve. This is when we proceed with the seemingly paradoxical interventions used by Frankl, Watzlawick, Erikson, Haley, and others. In the words of Frankl (1991): "If architects want to strengthen a decrepit arch, they increase the load which is laid upon it, for thereby the parts are joined more firmly together. So if therapists wish to foster their patients' mental health, they should not be afraid to increase that load through a reorientation toward the meaning of one's life."

Therefore, the apparent paradox turns out not to be a paradox at all, since it is the same strategy carried out in psychedelic therapy, according to the understanding that if a session has not been resolved well, one way to resolve it is through another session (Grof, 1980). We are not trying to distract ourselves from the process but to delve into it.

We must follow the same logic, both when we are working in non-ordinary states and when we are in our city office conducting integrative psychotherapy.

The apparent paradox, then, is not a paradox at all.

APPLYING A CONSTRUCTIVIST PERSPECTIVE

In this section, I interpret some important aspects of the psychedelic experience and their integration from a constructivist perspective. I also describe some concepts belonging to psychotherapeutic constructivism that are either already present in psychedelic therapy (mostly implicitly), or that could be helpful for understanding some other factors of the therapeutic applications of visionary experiences.

First and Second Order Realities

Alan Watts once wrote that, "Life is a game whose first rule is: this is not a game, it is something fatally serious."

Unlike solipsism, which posits that everything we experience is real—including the external world—as an emanation of our mind, constructivism does not deny the existence of a real natural world "out there," but it does deny the possibility of knowing this world in an "objective" way. Therefore, what we call reality is a concept needing a more precise definition.

On the one hand, there is the consensual reality that we perceive with our senses, measurable and defined by its physical properties. It is the reality of facts, which are somehow repeatable and verifiable by different observers. This reality is known as a first-order reality.

On the other hand, there is another reality related to the meaning and value that we assign to the facts of first-order reality. This aspect of reality is called second-order reality (Watzlawick et al., 2015, 2019; Nardone & Watzlawick, 2003).

Some examples can illustrate the difference between both aspects of reality. The physical properties of diamonds have been described in minute detail: We know their chemical composition, the covalent bonds of their atoms, their hardness and connectivity, and their optical characteristics. However, all these characteristics have nothing to do with the value and meaning we assign to diamonds. An engagement ring with a beautiful diamond does not become a splendid gift because of the physical properties of the diamond, not because of its price (first-order reality), but for complex reasons related to meaning and value. The color white has the same wavelength everywhere, and all human beings, presumably, perceive it in the same way, or at least there is a consensus about it. However, a bride dressed in white at a wedding in India would be inappropriate, as white is associated with mourning in India. It would also be inappropriate for a guest to wear a white dress at a Western wedding, as she would be perceived as taking the spotlight from the bride.[26]

Epictetus and Shakespeare remind us of the distinction between both aspects of reality. Epictetus says, "We are not disturbed by what happens to us, but by our thoughts about what happens to us," while Shakespeare writes, "Nothing is good or bad, but thinking makes it so" (Watzlawick, 2015). Rabbi Ibn Ezra affirms that: "The human soul conceives everything according to its own capacity, elevating what is below and lowering what is above" (Steinsaltz, 1989). However, confusion between first and second-order realities is common in our conceptions of reality. We tend to forget that we are always immersed in some context and we cannot escape interpretation, mistaking our perception for reality. Unfortunately, this confusion is frequent in psychiatry: When faced with our perception of symptoms—be they thoughts, emotions, or behaviors—we tend to mistake human psychological constructs with reality, in this case the so-called "mental illnesses." The psychiatrist or psychologist diagnoses a mental illness as if it were something that really exists, effectively creating a second-order reality that can have devastating effects for the person being diagnosed. Once the construct is accepted by the patient and by his social and family circles, it can turn into a self-fulfilling prophecy.

David L. Rosenhan writes about the pernicious effects of psychiatric diagnosis, demonstrated by "healthy" people who faked their symptoms with the intention of being admitted to a psychiatric hospital, only to behave normally once admitted. His work is fascinating for a few reasons including that the "patients" (in reality healthy people) were not detected by the medical professionals (Rosenhan in Watzlawick, 2015). Subsequently, the opposite experiment was also carried out: The researchers released a (false) warning that a number of "false patients" would try to get themselves admitted to different psychiatric hospitals over the course of a few months. Trained psychologists and psychiatrists identified, out of a total of 193 incoming patients, 19 people deemed "suspicious" by at least two clinical staff members. In reality, there were no "false patients." A second-order reality inevitably influences the people immersed in it, even if it has been artificially created.

Ernst von Glasersfeld writes: "Constructivism is radical, since it breaks with conventions and creates a theory of knowledge which no longer refers to an ontological, 'objective' reality, but refers exclusively to the ordering and organizing of a world made up of our experiences" (von Glasersfeld in Watzlawick, 2015).

This theoretical position is useful when trying to understand psychedelic experiences, particularly when creating a psychotherapeutic approach that includes the use of these substances. Psychedelic substances are used for various purposes, including spiritual development, healing from disease, and overcoming suffering in many systems and traditions. However, each tradition attributes a certain role to these substances or plants within the process. For example, the conceptual role of the different master plants in a shamanic context is completely different from the conceptual role of MDMA in the Western treatment of post-traumatic stress disorder.

In the shamanic worldview, there is no such thing as "PTSD," although a somewhat similar concept called "*susto*" may be found (Hahn, 1978; Andritzky, 1989; De Feo, 2002). Although "*susto*" can be understood as being similar to "PTSD," in no way does it refer to the same set of symptoms nor does it belong to the same explanatory model. The understanding of the therapeutic mechanisms underlying these experiences also differs in each of these systems. While some rely on spiritualistic or spiritual explanations, others provide metaphysical or energetic explanations. In our most immediate context, the underlying explanatory model is often psychological.

But even in a purely Western context, where a relative consensus positions psychedelic experiences exclusively within the psychological sphere, the interpretations of the therapeutic mechanisms and the purposes of these experiences can vary immensely. As we have seen in the first chapter, psychedelics have been used in the framework of psychoanalytic, Jungian, or behavioral therapies, as well as humanistic, transpersonal, and Gestalt psychology, amongst others. Each school has its particular understanding of the role of these substances, and each school interprets the contents of the experience according to a certain worldview, which is not usually shared by other approaches, to the extent of often being incompatible across different schools. Is there, then, an appropriate lens through which we can construct the correct interpretation in a psycho-therapeutic context? What perspective should we adopt in the face of a probable conflict of worldviews between the patient and the therapist? Must the therapist always believe the objective reality of the patient's psychedelic account? Should the patient learn and conform to the therapist's language and model?

According to Watzlawick (2015):

> [C]onstructivism does not create or 'explain' any exterior 'reality,' but rather reveals that there is neither an interior nor an exterior, a world of objects that is in front of a subject. Constructivism, rather, shows that there is no separation between subject and object (an assumption upon which an infinity of 'realities' are built), that the division of the world into opposites is set by the living subject and that paradoxes open the way that leads to autonomy.

When read in a psychedelic context, this quote perfectly matches the worldview of many who have had a mystical experience. In non-ordinary states, we can come to experience a transcendent reality of a paradoxical nature (Pahnke, 1967; Richards, 2015), which somehow contains and includes all other realities. Good and evil can coexist in a coherent balance, death and life can be parts of a whole—included and transcended, our problems can be real and painful and at the same time, relative and insignificant. All these realities constitute emanations of a reality that is transcendental, paradoxical, ineffable, and rich in significance (Pahnke and Richards, 1966), where multiple valid meanings can be evoked. Constructivism, therefore, allows us to assume this transcendental reality without having to experience it at all times. It allows us to distance ourselves from the patient's interpretations and our own, binding all these interpretations into a higher, more functional, respectful, and adaptive framework. At the same time, assuming a constructivist stance implies radical respect for the reality and idiosyncrasy of each individual patient. In psychotherapy, we deal mainly with second-order realities and therefore realize that no interpretation is more "true" than another. Simply, some are more effective than others in our interaction with the world, each other, and ourselves.

Watzlawick (2019, 150) writes, "What is truly illusory is to suppose that there is a 'real' second order reality, known by 'normal' people but not by the 'mentally disturbed." We could also add that this "real" reality is thought to be known by the therapists, not by their patients. In turn, the famous Terence McKenna said: "Who is to say what is real and what is not? 'Real' is a distinction of a naïve mind."

Thus, for the integrative therapist, it is vital to realize that we are working exclusively within second-order realities.

Mechanisms of Change:
Type 1 Change and Type 2 Change

Watzlawick, Weakland, and Fisch (1976) coined these names to denote two types of changes that can be employed as strategies to solve a problematic situation, be it a mathematical puzzle or a personal or interpersonal conflict. In their seminal work, *Change*, the authors drew on two mathematical theories—Evariste Galois's Group Theory and Whitehead and Russell's Theory of Logical Types. On the one hand, the Group Theory of the impetuous Evariste Galois explains the concept of the group, composed of different elements who interact through a series of properties. This is studied in school, when we are taught about the commutative properties of addition or multiplication in mathematics class—the neutral element and the opposite or absorbing element. The most interesting characteristic of a group of elements is that the combination of its members results in an element that is still a member of the same group (for example, the sum of any natural numbers, the result of which is still a natural number).

The Theory of Logical Types also refers to sets of elements united by a certain common characteristic; however, in this theory these sets are called "classes." The differential characteristic of a class is that the comprised elements of a class must not be a member of the class. For example, humanity is the collection of all human beings, but humanity is not a human being, nor is the overall behavior of humanity comparable to the behavior of an individual human being. A common mistake is to confuse individual members with the class and make attributions based on this error; for example, Catalans, Jews, Scots, shamans, or therapists. The "therapist" class is not a therapist. A logical error happens when we refer to a class by a member, or vice versa, as in the stylistic device of metonymy.

In this context, a type 1 change is a change that happens within the same set or class and through the same operational logic. For example, when faced with an episode of insomnia or anxiety, an attempted solution could consist of trying to calm down, breathe deeply, relax, and promote sleep or decrease anxiety. If deep breathing doesn't work, other solutions can be tried, such as counting sheep, self-hypnosis, playing relaxing music in the background, or structured breathwork techniques that time the inhales and exhales. Although these actions seem different, they are all part of the same class and follow the same logic: the class of "actions to relax and fall asleep." Any change in action from this same set—such as taking a hypnotic pill or inducing an orgasm—is understood as type 1 change since they belong to the same class and to the same operational logic: "actions to relax and fall asleep."

The type 2 change, however, is one that implies a change of class, that is, one that follows a different logic. Type 2 change is understood as a "change of change" (Watzlawick et al., 1976). Following the same example of insomnia or anxiety, a type 2 change could be getting up to read that book that we have pending or taking advantage of our insomnia to tidy up the kitchen. The logic used here is no longer inducing sleep or relaxation but staying awake and engaging in another activity.

That is, when applying a type 1 change to an element of one group, it remains a member of the same group (the addition of two natural numbers is a natural number). In contrast, a type 2 change means that the changed element ceases to be part of the previous group (a division of two natural numbers may not be a natural number). There have been changes in the operative logic and in the rules that govern the group.

Watzlawick proposes a very clear example: In a persecution nightmare, type 1 changes would be changes within the dream, such as running, hiding, or getting into a car to escape. All these changes do not alter the reality of having a nightmare. Awakening, on the other hand, would be a type 2 change. We change to a higher logical level, to a different reality.

In *The Matrix* (1999) film, we find a contemporary example that aligns with the theme of this book. In the film, Neo is dissatisfied with life within the Matrix and tries to find answers and solve his predicament by any means. However, all of his attempts are unsuccessful: His attempts to escape the system through the most marginal and hidden parts of society fail, and he always ends up where he started. These are type 1 changes. It is not until Morpheus appears that things change. He offers a real alternative: the red pill or the blue pill (the type 1 change or the type 2 change). By choosing a type 2 change, the red pill, Neo acquires a higher level of logic, realizing the existence of the Matrix.

There is an unsettling element in that scene, which makes perfect sense from the perspective of psychedelic therapy. Faced with the choice of the red or the blue pill, Morpheus tells Neo: "Remember, all I am offering you is the truth—nothing more."

It is not that a type 2 change is inherently better than a type 1 change. It is simply about being aware that in certain situations, we must apply one logic or another in order to reach a satisfactory solution. Watzlawick, Weakland, and Fisch (1976) distinguish between different difficulties: undesirable situations that can be solved with common sense, unresolvable situations that we must learn to cope with, and seemingly unresolvable problems that unleash crises (the kind that appear when we fail to properly address our problems). According to these authors, there are three ways to improperly approach problems (Watzlawick et al., 1976):

1. We attempt to solve a problem by denying its existence. Although some action must be taken, no action is taken.

2. We attempt to resolve a problem that does not exist, or cannot be practically solved. An action is taken when it should not be taken.

3. We make a logical mistake and create an "endless game" by attempting a type 1 change in a situation that can only be changed from a higher level of logic, or we attempt a type 2 change when a type 1 change is appropriate.

The distinction between these types of change is relevant in the psychotherapeutic context since many of us have tried all kinds of methods and therapies to solve our problems without much success. However, most of these attempts have drawn from the same logic as our prior solutions and were therefore ineffective.

Solutions and Problems

By distinguishing between a difficulty and a problem, we can see that a problem only appears by addressing a difficulty improperly. That is, the problem only becomes such if we apply a solution that does not work. Otherwise, we simply experience facing a difficulty or challenge, and we do something to fix it, so it never becomes a problem.

In other words, the problem is not defined by its difficulty, but by the way we try to solve it. The problem, then, is the inappropriate attempt to solve that difficulty. This is the concept of ineffective or dysfunctional "attempted solutions,"[27] which underscores the therapeutic approach of the Palo Alto school. According to this model, constructivist psychotherapy aims to block dysfunctional attempted solutions by understanding that they are the factor that maintains the existing problem. Many of the difficulties that people encounter in the different phases of the integration of their psychedelic experiences can also be attributed to these types of dynamics, especially when they try to avoid or resist their ongoing internal processes, as Watzlawick argues that they keep trying to force an outcome that can only happen spontaneously.

The formation and establishment of dysfunctional attempted solutions can happen due to multiple factors. On many occasions, the dysfunctional solution was an adequate solution in the past, but it is no longer an adequate solution in the present moment. For example, in the past, whenever I had anxiety at work, I would take a few deep breaths and manage to calm down. However, after my difficult experience with ayahuasca, I experience anxiety but cannot calm myself solely with my breath. Furthermore, the more I try, the more anxious I get because I keep failing to calm down. One way to conceptualize this dynamic from a perspective that integrates both the transpersonal and the Palo Alto views is that the dysfunctional attempted solutions are rooted in the COEX systems (Grof, 1980) and can be understood as their visible and behavioral layers. COEX can "selectively influence the subject's perception of himself and the world, his thoughts and feelings and even his somatic processes" (Grof, 2002). We might further add that they can even influence his behavior, in a vicious circle that leads to a self-fulfilling prophecy and the perpetuation of such a system. The late Tav Sparks used to call this an "honest mistake" that our psyches make.

For example, some people who have suffered physical and sexual abuse in their childhood have difficulty establishing healthy emotional and sexual boundaries in their adult intimate relationships. These people often accumulate abusive events throughout their biography, a fact that may seem surprising to a non-expert outside observer. However, due to that child's lack of security and love, the adult person has not learned to establish those boundaries. Of course, the person tries to do so by creating new situations where they can receive that love and protection as a way to correct those initial abuses. These attempts to create restorative situations (attempted solutions) become new sources of suffering. Thus, the problem is not so much "what" the person does, but rather the "how."

Behaviors that are harmful and problematic in appearance, like substance abuse, obesity, or toxic relationships, amongst others, may actually be attempts to solve or deal with past traumatic events, and they still play, in a way, a positive function to keep certain stability or prevent worse problems (van der Kolk, 2020).

In most situations where people request support in the integration of their psychedelic experiences, we find great difficulties, such as intense emotional states, conflicts of values, doubts, ambivalence, and difficulties in accepting certain painful aspects of the experiences. However, these only become a problem when we oppose or resist such emotional states, or because of how we try to deal with these situations, usually through avoidance, irrationally trying to control, obsessively ruminating hoping to elucidate the solution, or through the eternal search for the hidden cause of such symptomatic manifestations.

Human beings do not fall into these dynamics for a lack of intelligence or common sense. In fact, our common sense and intelligence often mislead us to believe that our attempted solutions are adequate and that, if they do not work, we just need to keep trying and do more of the same. However, it is the excess of that attempted solution that aggravates the original difficulty and turns it into a problem. In this sense, anything—even a therapeutic process—can become a dysfunctional solution that aggravates our situation.

From another perspective, but following the same logic, Alejandro Jodorowsky says, "A labyrinth is but a tangle of straight lines. I ask myself if analysis and therapy do not sometimes have the tendency to introduce curves into the straight lines" (2010).

Viktor Frankl gives an example of this dynamic: "The meaning of life is to be discovered in the world rather than within man or his own psyche, as though it were a closed system. What is called self-actualization is not an attainable aim at all, for the simple reason that the more one would strive for it, the more he would miss it"(Frankl, 1991). Frankl's underlying logic can be found in many seekers of psychedelic experiences;

faced with a difficulty that is poorly defined and addressed, our solutions may only perpetuate and further complicate that problem. Psychedelics can become a dysfunctional attempted solution and are the main cause of one of the cases requiring integration, which we will discuss in detail in Chapter Four and Chapter Five.

Therapeutic Mechanisms in Psychedelic and Integration Therapy

The therapeutic potential of psychedelic substances has been the subject of much discussion and research since Western culture "discovered" these substances. If we ask ourselves, "Why are these substances therapeutic?" or "What are the mechanisms through which psychedelic substances can be therapeutic?" we will find multiple and diverse answers.

On one side, we find pharmacological and biochemical explanations: how the neurophysiological effects of psychedelic substances can improve certain conditions by rebalancing brain biochemistry, catalyzing structural changes (Bouso et al., 2015), inducing neurogenesis (Ly et al., 2018), or eliminating the tolerance of certain narcotic drugs, as in the case of Iboga. Or from the neurophysiological point of view (Carhart-Harris et al., 2014, 2017): By studying the neurons affected by these substances, we learn that they decrease the activity of the default neural network (DMN), allowing a kind of psychic reset (Speth et al., 2016; Palhano et al., 2015; Tagliazucchi et al., 2016).

On the other hand, we can find purely psychological explanations, which attribute the therapeutic effects to the subjective experiences caused by these substances. The experience itself, with all its complex mental and emotional phenomenology, would be the cause of this therapeutic quality (Wagner et al., 2017; Carhart-Harris et al., 2017; Stolaroff, 1993), as well as the effects on personality (Aixalà et al., 2018; Bouso et al., 2018), in addition to the context and other variables (Franquesa et al., 2018; González et al., 2019). Even within these explanatory models, however, there is no absolute consensus on which experiences are therapeutic and which are not or why some experiences are more therapeutic than others. This depends mainly on the psychological and therapeutic school to which one belongs and the optics through which we understand these phenomena. In a general sense, however, it is accepted that it is the subjective experience, more or less independently of the pharmacological and biochemical effects, that is responsible for the therapeutic qualities of psychedelics.

Furthermore, we also have explanatory frameworks of a spiritual nature in which the plants themselves, or the plant spirits, or other spirits and entities, are responsible for the healing, often offering mixed psychological/spiritual mechanisms (Adamson & Metzner, 1988).

Without disregarding spiritual and biochemical theories, in this work we will focus on the psychological view from a constructivist perspective, as we seek to understand the psychological mechanisms responsible for the therapeutic properties of the psychedelic experiences (and their potential risks). This, of course, does not exclude the possibility that biochemical and spiritual aspects also constitute relevant factors in the therapeutic process.

Grof (2005) describes the therapeutic mechanisms of an LSD session from a transpersonal perspective. Psychedelic substances can intensify common therapeutic mechanisms (catharsis, transference analysis, insight, corrective emotional experiences), in addition to promoting transpersonal mechanisms.

The same mechanisms that are therapeutic during the psychedelic experience are the ones that we should try to implement in integrative psychotherapy: either by allowing them to happen after an unresolved psychedelic experience or by promoting practices, tasks, and exercises that can help them continue to develop and consolidate throughout the process.

Corrective Emotional Experiences

Virtually all schools of psychotherapy agree that a corrective emotional experience is the best way to promote therapeutic change. In the psychoanalytic context, the concept of corrective emotional experience was

125

introduced by Alexander and French (1946) by observing that patients who had a significant emotional experience improved, even without much depth in the understanding of their problem or, in psychoanalytic terms, without having completed their analysis. The authors realized that it was not necessary to relive all the significant events in the patient's biography for them to improve (this turns out to be impossible most of the time anyway). Furthermore, they realized that improvement occurred even in cases where such memories were never recovered.

Such a corrective emotional experience could happen, according to the authors, because of the transference with the psychoanalyst (for example, they received from the therapist the parental love they were denied in their childhood), or because of the "new life experiences" experienced by the patient, or both at once.

Psychedelic substances have a unique profile when it comes to inducing these corrective emotional experiences. Mystical experiences are probably the greatest example of this. We have seen how, in the psychedelic therapy settings of the 1950s, alcoholic patients improved dramatically after a mystical experience—without, we might add, really having gone to the source of their problems, or having undergone any kind of therapeutic process (Chwelos et al., 1959; Hoffer, 1966; Krebs, 2012). The same happens in modern clinical studies, in which mystical experiences are correlated with a highly significant improvement (Roseman et al., 2018; Garcia-Romeu et al., 2015; Johnson et al., 2016, 2018). The psychedelic-induced mystical experience is probably the best corrective emotional experience that can occur. The reasons might be related to verified changes in the personality trait of "openness to experience" following a mystical experience (MacLean et al., 2011) and psychedelic experiences in general (Bouso et al., 2012, 2015, 2018; Erritzoe et al., 2018, 2019; Aixalà et al., 2018, 2019).

There are other kinds of corrective emotional experiences that are not mystical experiences. MDMA has the ability to provide an experience that, without meeting the criteria for a mystical experience, induces in the person a feeling of wholeness, coherence, and well-being. The magic of this MDMA-induced state is not the disappearance of our problems but the possibility of being and feeling well despite those problems. Again, this paradoxical nature is one of the great therapeutic mechanisms of psychedelics, which allow us to rise to higher levels of perception and observe problems from another perspective. Not only that, but they also provide a direct personal and emotional experience of what it feels like to transcend those layers of suffering.

In some ways, it resembles the resolution of the biblical Book of Job; after suffering countless tragedies, Job asks God the reason for all of it. God's response is transcendental and places Job in front of the greatness of the universe and creation, highlighting the insignificantly significant role that Job occupies in all that drama. Thus, psychedelics often give us the same response God gave to Job.

Corrective emotional experiences, as Alexander and French pointed out, can also happen in the interpersonal domain. The relationships established between therapist and patient in psychedelic psychotherapy are often highly significant and of a very different nature than the usual therapeutic relationships. This is the reason why the therapist's intervention is so important during sessions involving non-ordinary states. Such a relationship can provide new interpersonal experiences of respect, support, acceptance, compassion, and love that the patient may not have experienced before. The fact that this happens while in an expanded state of consciousness makes this experience more powerful.

Perhaps one of the most remarkable characteristics that psychedelic substances have is that they can induce a complete experience without the need for much action. We can experience a huge and intense range of emotions, sensations, thoughts, sensory experiences, and visions without ever having to move from a couch. This presents a unique possibility for achieving these corrective emotional experiences while at the same time being one of the factors that make the proper integration of these experiences necessary. Since the person has not had to do much in the real world or carry out any particular action to have that experience, sometimes the memory of it can fade quickly unless they explicitly anchor it or learn to induce it again by their own means. Hence, many people just jump from experience to experience trying to permanently grasp the fleeting state of grace that has been granted to them during the experience. Seeking methods to arrive at certain aspects of this corrective emotional experience without the need for a new psychedelic experience is the basis of integration techniques focused on maximizing benefits.

Thus, the therapeutic mechanisms of psychedelics are often related to the induction of an emotional experience, rather than pure insight.

Induction of a Type 2 Change

One of the therapeutic mechanisms of psychedelic experiences is the ability to arrive at a correct logical framework for a problem and the possibility of devising creative solutions. During a psychedelic experience, we can access higher and more global levels of logic when addressing the problematic situation at hand. In terms of the Palo Alto MRI, the psychedelic experience can induce a type 2 change.

Thus, psychedelic substances have been attributed with the ability to help us think outside the established frameworks, and references are often made to the red pill that Morpheus offers Neo in the Matrix. Distancing ourselves from the problem—transcending it and our own ego—and detaching ourselves from our habitual way of thinking are ways in which we can access and contemplate new potential solutions. During the 1960s, this line of research was carried out by Harman, McKim, Mogar, Fadiman, and Stolaroff. They experimented with the potential of an LSD experience to inspire creative solutions for problems of various kinds, from technical issues to everyday situations. They documented this preliminary essay in their book *LSD, The Problem Solving Psychedelic* (1967), where they offer many examples of innovative solutions found through psychedelic experiences.[28]

These experiences, in which insights are produced and new solutions to certain problems are found, may or may not include corrective emotional experiences that lead to a restructuring of the situation, depending on the general intensity of the overall experience.

Catharsis, Abreaction, and Elaboration

Another common therapeutic mechanism, perhaps the one most frequently contemplated in therapeutic paradigms, is the potential of psychedelics to induce emotional catharsis and help rework past traumatic experiences through confrontation and experimentation in a safe and supportive context.

The confrontation with repressed emotions and their subsequent release can have therapeutic effects (Grof, 1980; Naranjo, 1974; Haijen et al., 2018), although an adequate processing of said catharsis is needed so that the effects are long lasting. Otherwise, improvements tend to fade over time (Freud, 2001; Sandison, 1959).

Sometimes, catharsis does not involve emotional outbursts but rather heartfelt re-experiencing of the traumatic situations, as is often the case when people who are recovering from abuse work with MDMA. Uncovering and experimenting with repressed emotions can lead to a greater understanding of the conflict that ensued after this traumatic event.

Jenny's case

During her experience with MDMA, a war veteran described a surprising traumatic situation. In the situation, she found herself at a roadblock, fearing an enemy ambush. A few children began to get into the truck she was driving, and her anxiety intensified rapidly as she waited for an explosion or an attack to happen at any moment. In the end, nothing happened, and after a few eternal minutes, she was able to continue her journey. However, the true trauma of that event was revealed during the therapeutic experience. In those intense minutes, the idea of aiming her weapon at the children crossed her mind since she perceived them to be potential terrorists. Jenny was about to shoot them, and that was the specifically traumatic experience of the entire event. An important part of the healing process was her acceptance of those emotions, as was being able to share them with the therapist without being judged.

Brian's case

Brian was a man who had been sexually abused by various teachers in his childhood. He had suffered from symptoms of depression, anxiety, and existential confusion for several years, and had undertaken a multitude of psychotherapies with relative success. During his MDMA psychotherapy, he re-experienced abusive situations from a distance, as if he was observing them from a corner up on the ceiling. He was able to accept the familiar emotions: anger towards his perpetrators, the disgust they produced in him, fear, and sadness. However, he also realized that during those abuses, his body reacted automatically, and he experienced a certain degree of pleasure. This was unacceptable to him, a source of the shame that he had experienced throughout his life. Getting in touch with that shame and experiencing all the ambivalences of those situations—and others that occurred later—were the key to advancing his therapeutic process.

In the context of a purely verbal psychotherapy, it is very difficult to access such complex and paradoxical experiences. Several contradictory emotions can be experienced simultaneously, and which make sense on a higher level of logic. However, psychedelic substances and non-ordinary states of consciousness have the capacity to elicit these types of global experiences, in which a real experimentation of what happened and its subsequent elaboration can take place. Without proper elaboration during the integration period, the therapeutic potential of a cathartic experience is often limited in duration. Therefore, it is important to root the therapeutic results, promoting significant life changes that can contribute to the development of a more adaptive life situation and greater well-being. In this way, we make sure that the experience does not become just another pleasant memory.

Cognitive and Emotional Reframing

Another potentially therapeutic mechanism of the psychedelic experience lies in its propensity to induce experiences that facilitate the cognitive or emotional reframing of past traumatic experiences and of present conflict situations.

In the context of research, "Hexaflex" is a model that is currently being used to better understand the psychological mechanisms involved in psychedelic experiences. This model describes six factors related to how we process mental experiences and psychic content: 1) values, 2) committed action, 3) self as context, 4) cognitive defusion, 5) acceptance, and 6) contact with the present moment. All these factors lead to greater or lesser psychological flexibility. This model is part of the therapies known as ACT (acceptance and commitment therapy).

In most psychological and therapeutic schools, it is understood that psychological rigidity is the basis for the development of pathologies. When our reactions (both internal and external) to stressful situations and challenges are rigidly determined, our capacity to adapt decreases, which entails a greater risk of suffering from the feeling that we are victims of an inescapable situation. Extreme examples are people who suffer from obsessive-compulsive disorder, who cannot stop reacting in certain ways even when fully aware that such reactions are unhelpful. Similarly, people who suffer from depression are often less able to make objective judgments of complex situations and tend to see things in black and white. We have previously described rigidity as an aspect of neuroticism, a predictive factor for difficult psychedelic experiences.[29]

The psychedelic experience can positively influence certain factors of the Hexaflex model, probably by "cognitive defusion," that is, by improving our ability to disidentify with our own thoughts and emotions. It can also play a role in the acceptance of different emotional and cognitive states, contrasted with the tendency to avoid uncomfortable experiences (Franquesa et al., 2018; González et al., 2019).

These terminologies point to something that we intuitively know: that psychedelic experiences can open up new ways of observing and understanding ourselves and the world around us, making us more psychologically flexible. Psychological flexibility helps us restructure our lived experience and potentially create a better framework through which to assess our own situation (Lyons et al., 2018).

Therefore, one of the main therapeutic mechanisms of these visionary substances may be that they promote greater psychological flexibility, potentially offering complex and rich cognitive and emotional restructuring and favoring the development of better psychological coping mechanisms for future situations. That is, they increase our capacity to accept our experience and strengthen our ability to disidentify with our internal states.

Oscar's case

Oscar was participating in a pilot study on the treatment of complicated grief. The death of his father, with whom he had a very conflicted relationship since childhood, had caused a profound destabilization in his emotions, which manifested through outbursts of crying and intense emotions. He alternated between periods of deep sadness with ambivalent feelings of anger and rage towards his father. In his Holotropic Breathwork experience, he felt that the suffering and frustration he was experiencing in his work, concerning his family and other personal situations, was the same suffering and frustration that his father must have experienced. He saw his father as an emotionally unsophisticated man who had very few coping mechanisms. This identification with his father allowed him to see his entire biography, including his relationship with his father, in a new light. Oscar realized that while his father's actions were often reprehensible, he understood some of the underlying causes and felt compassion for him.

In the image above we see the "Portrait of Sonja Knips," which Klimt painted in 1889. On the bottom left we see a photograph of Sonja Knips at the age of 24, taken in the same year. In the bottom right image we see a photograph of Knips ten years later, in 1908. Its resemblance to the portrait is much greater than when it was taken.

MAXIMIZING BENEFITS

4

"Of course the 'cure' isn't permanent. But at least one can see where the sun rises and sets and the horizons and the galaxies and know the infinite peace of liberation. And since the air is purified by truth, it gains something for use in everyday living. And one can never be content to live always in the valley at sea level when one has experienced the rarefied ozone of the higher altitude. So it serves as a map left in the intellect, as a warmth or remembered radiance in the emotions, and as a still small voice or an agonizing goad in the conscience and a longing in the heart."

LETTER FROM BETTY EISNER TO HUMPHRY OSMOND, AUGUST 3, 1957 (EISNER 2002)

THE NEED FOR INTEGRATION AFTER A POSITIVE EXPERIENCE

The therapeutic potential of psychedelic medicines is beyond question. These substances have the ability to induce mystical experiences and a spiritual openness that can radically change our perception of the fundamental truths of consciousness and existence. They can also induce cathartic experiences, releasing us from the burden of our repressed emotions. They can allow us to safely experience past trauma so that we can restructure these experiences and move toward overcoming them. Sometimes, they can even rid us of annoying symptoms like anxiety or depression. So why do we talk about integrating these positive experiences?

As we see in the quotation that begins this chapter, perhaps the main setback that has been observed since Westerners began to use psychedelics with therapeutic intentions is the impermanence of the positive changes induced after a significant experience. Sooner or later, the person returns to their previous state of being. In the words of Grof and Halifax (1978):

These transformations are usually very pronounced for several days or weeks after a profound and well-resolved LSD session involving the death-rebirth experience. Changes are frequently so striking that LSD therapists refer to them in their clinical jargon as "psychedelic afterglow." Sooner or later they tend to decrease in intensity; under the influence of the demands and pressures of the social environment, many subjects more or less lose touch with their cosmic feelings. However the new philosophical and spiritual insights into the nature of reality that the experiencer discovered tend to persist indefinitely. With discipline it is possible to use the profound knowledge acquired in the death-rebirth process as a guideline for restructuring one's entire life.

We see that, although the immediate positive effects—symptomatic relief—tend to fade over time, an imprint of the experience does remain, potentially inspiring a longer-lasting subtle and gradual transformation. In most cases, this positive imprint gives us some confidence in our own internal processes and helps us develop an optimistic attitude towards life. Even knowing that ups and downs are inevitable, the indelible awareness that states of greater openness, connection, and well-being are possible remains in our psyche. In the 1960s, some people were drawn to the exploration of traditional Eastern practices and a spiritual life after having their first few psychedelic experiences. Some of them even became spiritual teachers. Ram Dass is a well-known example, who gave LSD to his teacher Maharaji in 1967, while on his own journey to India—Maharaji felt no effects. Another example is the quote by Jack Kornfield at the beginning of Chapter Two. A good illustration of the relationship between psychedelics and spiritual paths can be found in Badiner and Gray's (2015) book, *Zig Zag Zen*. The role of psychedelics as catalysts for a subsequent spiritual quest cannot be underestimated while confronting the fact that psychedelics did not provide the permanent states of being desired by these young seekers and spiritual teachers.

These statements in themselves are not extraordinary: It is perfectly reasonable for the results of an intervention to be temporary in nature.

In other fields of medicine, this impermanence is naturally understood: If we have a headache, we can treat it effectively with a pain reliever, but that does not mean that we will never have a headache again. Suppose we suffer spinal compression due to long hours of work in front of the computer and we go to the chiropractor. In that case, we may get some relief from the pain, but if we do not modify the environmental factors, it is illogical to expect that we will never experience the pain again. However, in psychiatry and psychology, we do not approach the problem in the same way. We try to find therapeutic tools and treatments that are permanently effective. This is the case with psychiatry and its reliance on prescription medication—even when the results are unfortunately not permanent or particularly optimistic (Oña & Bouso, 2018, 2020)— and also with psychology, all the way back to its origins when Freud (1937) hoped that a successfully completed psychoanalytic process would be an antidote for future neurosis.

Similarly, we hope that psychedelic therapy, or the mere use of a psychedelic substance, will be the panacea that will cure our suffering once and for all. We know, both qualitatively and quantitatively, that this is not usually the case. After the passionate optimism of the first investigations in psychedelic therapy, we find critical voices that are rising to counterbalance this narrative, pointing out important biases in psychedelic medicine and its complex search for the definitive solution to suffering (Oña, 2018; Carhart-Harris et al., 2016; Hendrie and Pickles, 2016).

By the end of the analysis, Jung hoped that the person would have developed effective mechanisms for relating to his personal and collective unconscious that would result in a definitive cure for the neurosis. But he already warned us that "there are no magic cures for neurosis," and he continued by saying, "Neither the doctor nor the patient should give in to the illusion that analysis is enough in itself to undo a neurosis. Ultimately, it is infallibly the moral factor that decides between health and illness" (Jung, 2019, 308). We could very well substitute "analysis" with "having a psychedelic experience" to get an updated version of the same dilemma.

We have seen that psychedelics can be catalysts for spirituality. They can play a similar role from a therapeutic perspective. Psychedelics can provide a deeply significant experience, but ultimately healing is the result of greater psychological and cognitive flexibility and the capacity to adapt constructively to life situations as they happen, rather than the result of a life free of emotions or symptoms, as we discussed in the previous chapter. This chapter thus deals with the question, "How does one fully take advantage of a meaningful experience to maximally benefit from this increased flexibility?"

This is not a minor issue either. For many people who have felt trapped in a life marked by distressing symptoms, the relief encountered after an ecstatic experience can be as intense as the pain of familiar suffering re-surfacing again after a few months. Living in hell is terrible, but crashing down again after experiencing the heavenly dimensions is unbearable and hopeless. While it may seem natural to aspire to live in the heavenly spheres permanently, the solution lies not in heaven but by inhabiting the earth, with all its worldly complications and everyday pleasures.

The practices aimed at maximizing the benefits after a psychedelic experience can vary significantly. There is no recipe for this integration. The personalized application of these techniques will depend on each person's situation and context. For a participant in a clinical study, the first phases of integration will probably be done through an interview with their psychotherapist. In contrast, integration will probably be based on a group sharing circle for a participant in an ayahuasca retreat. Integration will happen in different contexts: There are instances of individual integration that happen in solitude; there are contexts of integration among equals (sharing circles, discussion groups, etc.); and contexts where integration happens with a professional. One of the few books published that delves into this type of specific integration practices is *Epopteia, avanzar sin olvidar,* available only in Spanish at the present moment

(Fericgla, 2004). After a positive and uneventful experience, no integration method is inherently better than another. The goal should be that one is able to take responsibility for their own integration process and find the necessary resources, becoming agents of their own integration rather than a patient or the recipient of an expected miraculous healing.

From a western perspective, Jack Kornfield has approached the intricacies of the therapeutic and spiritual paths with respect, wisdom, and an eminently practical approach. He warns us of the dangers and promises we may find along these roads, as well as a practical, wise, and simple way to work with the different states of being we encounter along the way (Kornfield, 1997, 2001). Kornfield warns seekers that "all experiences are side effects."

THE RISKS OF NON-INTEGRATION

Skipping the integration phase or not paying enough attention to it can have some negative effects, even in cases where the experience has been positive and spiritually significant. These risks are not very serious for the most part and do not involve significant suffering or discomfort, unlike what can happen after a difficult experience. These risks, however, can be a serious obstacle to our personal and spiritual evolution. Therefore, although they usually do not involve any type of clinical complication, they must be taken into account by psychonauts and all people who seek access to non-ordinary states of consciousness as part of their spiritual and healing path.

These are the situations described below:

- Not taking full advantage of the experience.
- Ego Inflation.
- Spiritual bypass.
- Attachment and addiction to experiences.

Not Taking Full Advantage of the Experience

Perhaps the most common of the "risks" we face when we ignore the integration phase is the risk of not taking full advantage of the experience. Even after positive and enlightening experiences, the positive effects that we experience during and immediately after the experience often fade over the course of a few days or weeks.

Humphry Osmond put it this way: "I am sure that [...] LSD 25 properly used by those who are prepared gives immense self-understanding. But as the mystics insist, this is never absolute or permanent, but then in life nothing is. It has to be used and good habits built on the new foundation[...]" (Osmond, in Eisner, 2002).

As an example, we have the image of a mandala drawn by an individual after his experience with magic mushrooms. The experience was rich in visions and symbols and was perceived as highly significant in psychological and psychodynamic terms. The course of the session was placid and without setbacks. The client decided to create a "mandala" of his experience, taking special care to capture, in a meticulously detailed and orderly way, certain color patterns that were apparently highly significant. After dedicating some time to the task, he decided to take a break and never got back to it (or any other task). The mandala remains unfinished, and, to this day, this individual cannot remember any aspect of the experience, the contents, the general theme, or even the predominant emotional tone of the session. Thus, an apparently significant experience has vanished from his memory, serving as little other than a didactic example of the problems derived from ignoring integration (which remains a nice paradox).

As we can see, this situation is not serious in psychological terms. Nevertheless, it implies wasting an opportunity for growth and is, in a way, a waste of time if one aspires to experience a genuinely transformative or therapeutic experience. Probably—for some people—not all psychedelic experiences must be meaningful and transformative, in the same way that, for a classical music fan, not all concerts are memorable.

However, the important thing here is the honesty that each one has with their own practice. The use of psychedelic substances with the intention to have an aesthetically pleasing experience or to increase the sensory enjoyment of certain events or situations seems (to me) absolutely valid. I am not against the recreational use of any substance if the person does it responsibly and consciously. It is important, however, to be sincere with oneself about the intention that one places in these experiences. As I have written elsewhere (Aixalà, 2018), psychedelic substances are used in many different ways, most of them respectable. It is simply a matter of knowing why and how we are using them, being aware of the results that such a use can entail. If one indulges in the psychedelic experience for sheer recreational pleasures or for *psychonautical* exploration, perhaps one does not have to expect a therapeutic or transformative result. The way I see it, there is value in seeking an experience for the sake of the experience itself. In some cases, it can even have positive consequences on both a psychological and spiritual level; however, these aims are different from those discussed in this book.

Many of the pioneers of psychedelic therapy have described the risk of not taking full advantage of experiences. Leo Zeff recounts how people with hundreds of psychedelic experiences under their belt felt that none of those trips had contributed anything compared to those experiences carried out under his tutelage and within the context proposed by Zeff. "It's those who have tripped a lot—well they will all say that the trip they do with me is very different, very different" (Stolaroff, 2004). Similarly, Grof speaks of people who have had hundreds of experiences with LSD but have not yet begun the process of introspection and transformation through the contents of what he calls the expanded cartography of the psyche (the biographical, perinatal, and transpersonal domains): "I have also met a number of people who had taken LSD on their own in an unsupervised, externalized way and in a social context, and had not really even begun this process in spite of hundreds of exposures to the drug" (Grof, 1985).

As we saw in a previous quote from Betty Eisner (2002), one of the factors that seemed to be related to whether the experience was put to good use or not is the maturity of the person. Thus, even transcendent experiences may have little positive impact in psychologically immature people.

If repeated frequently and over time, this failure to take full advantage of our psychedelic experiences can lead to other more complex situations. Clinically, the least relevant aspect is ego inflation, which we will see below. In more pathological situations, we find what I have called "repeated experiences without integration," which we will address in the next chapter.

Ego Inflation

Psychedelic substances can allow us access to transcendental experiences with relative ease. It is not uncommon for people without any previous training in spiritual disciplines or previous knowledge about the numinous dimensions of the psyche to have experiences that can be described as spiritual. The inner worlds that we can access and the ecstatic experiences that often occur under the influence of psychedelic substances can be fascinating to the neophyte. This can lead to a feeling of having lived an exceptional experience, therefore identifying ourselves as exceptional people. It is not unusual that after a few psychedelic experiences, people feel that they must initiate others into these worlds or that, having had some experiences with ayahuasca, they feel the call to become shamans. There is usually a stage of psychedelic infatuation, in which everything related to the experiences is fascinating and causes an almost excessive euphoria. Thus, ego inflation amongst beginners is quite common. However, it is usually only a temporal phase that tends to pass, whether by abandoning the path of inner exploration or continuing in it.

Ego inflation, however, is not exclusively a risk for the neophyte. After a more or less lengthy personal process in which we successfully confront and experience some of the darker, painful aspects of our being, we might feel like we have freed ourselves from a great burden. The feeling of having done lots of personal work appears after overcoming some of the difficulties that up to now have caused our suffering. This can sometimes happen after our first experience of "ego death," as it is known in Grof's cartography. If this experience is completed in a satisfactory way, the resulting expansion of consciousness can lead toward a new and wider identification with our being, a reconciliation with some aspects of the shadow, or a greater understanding of the mysteries of consciousness. A well-integrated ego death process often goes hand in hand with a sense of humility in the face of the greatness of the psyche, creation, the universe, or the mystery. Often, however, the processes of death and rebirth can remain half-finished. In such cases, the ego has experienced an opening towards the spiritual dimensions, and while greater degrees of freedom have been glimpsed, the process has not been completed. In Grof's model, this is known as an incomplete transition between the third and fourth perinatal wombs. In such cases, it is not unusual for the person to feel euphoric and complete, even with manic overtones. This can be under-stood as momentary ego inflation, which can be adequately resolved if the process is followed through and completed.

But the situation may be even more complex. Beyond specific experi-ences, even in the case of a well-resolved process and after having success-fully completed a death and rebirth experience, an ego inflation can still occur. These are perhaps the cases that require most of our attention here. In *The Teachings of Don Juan*, Don Juan speaks of the enemies of a man of knowledge. The first of these enemies is fear. We fight to overcome our fear, eventually getting there. "When this joyful moment comes, the man can say without hesitation that he has defeated his first natural enemy. [...] he is free from it for the rest of his life because, instead of fear, he has acquired clarity—a clarity of mind which erases fear. By then a man knows his desires; he knows how to satisfy those desires. He can antici-pate the new steps of learning and a sharp clarity surrounds everything. The man feels that nothing is concealed. And thus he has encountered his second enemy: Clarity! That clarity of mind, which is so hard to obtain, dispels fear, but also blinds" (Castaneda, 2017).

Before defining ego inflation, it may be necessary to limit what we mean by "ego." It is not the intention of this book to go into detail about the psychology of the ego, nor do I have the knowledge to do so, so this subject will be approached with simplicity and the knowledge that the descriptions that follow are limited. Broadly speaking, we can say that there are two common definitions or conceptions of the ego that differ from each other and can create confusion in our understanding, particularly when we talk about ego death or ego inflation.

On the one hand, we find the Freudian concept of "ego," understood as one of the three main aspects of the psyche according to Freud's structural vision. For Freud, the psyche is divided into the id (it), ego (I), and superego (over-I). The Freudian ego is in charge of mediating between the instinctual impulses of the id and the moral and social demands of the superego. The ego is the metaphorical battlefield in which this confrontation happens. It is also the place where communication between the id and the superego and between the conscious and the unconscious happens. The ego is in charge of dealing with reality, keeping us functioning properly. If we stick to Freud's original conception, this is not the kind of ego that one wants to kill; this ego is adequate and necessary for our functioning, and the concept of inflation gets more confusing in this case. In fact, it seems much more appropriate to strengthen this ego, to better manage both our internal life and our interaction with others and society.

On the other hand, the Jungian concept of ego is understood as the false self or a false conception of oneself. This ego is a construct self-created by each one of us, a specific self-image that reflects our conception of who we are at a given moment. This ego includes beliefs about different aspects of our identity, such as gender, profession, personal characteristics, strengths, weaknesses and fears, personal history, and so on. When we ask ourselves the question, "Who am I?" we usually answer with our notion of ego. It is evident that this ego is something variable, that it evolves with time and changes according to our life experiences. In Jungian theory, the ego is presented in opposition to the self, the latter being understood as the archetype of the whole and which, of course, transcends the ego (Blasco, 2018). So when we talk about ego inflation or ego death, we are talking about the Jungian concept of the ego, not the Freudian one.

Jung describes in detail the mechanisms of psychic or ego inflation, understood as the dilation of the personality beyond individual boundaries that happens when we appropriate unconscious contents that do not belong to us, such as those of the collective unconscious and the subsequent identification with these contents. Thus, psychic inflation takes place when we are unable to discriminate between what content is personal and what is collective. Although it may seem that this inflation somehow propels us forward in our path of growth and individuation, it is rather the opposite. According to Jungian theory, when our personal identity disappears among the influx of collective psychic contents, the conscious personality is left adrift at the mercy of these controlling impulses (Jung, 2009). Jung himself warns us that this phenomenon can trigger pathological processes, as we pointed out when we talked about the relationship between repeated experiences without integration (also understood as frequent exposures to collective psychic contents), ego inflation, and the more dramatic manifestations described in the next chapter. Jung sees in this dynamic something akin to the concept of "spiritual emergency," coined much later by Stanislav and Christina Grof (Grof & Grof, 2001).

In the process of traversing the different stages of a therapeutic or spiritual path, particularly when this path includes non-ordinary states of consciousness that may grant access to transcendental dimensions, our ego structure may change. For example, if we have identified with the role of the victim for most of our lives due to difficult childhood circumstances, and at some point in our process we manage to overcome these traumatic events, our self-image, our ego, acquires a new identity. We may no longer be a victim, but someone with enough strength to overcome great difficulties and grow from them. When we have experiences of contact with the Self or with the transcendental dimensions, or when we have a mystical experience during non-ordinary states of consciousness, our ego can absorb those insights inappropriately. For example, Ram Dass used to tell a story about his brother, who was admitted to a mental hospital because he believed he was Christ. Ram Dass tells him, "I too am Christ." Then, the brother asks him, "Why am I the one who is locked up here and you are not?" Ram Dass replies, "Because you think you are the only one."

Having made contact with the numinous dimensions of the experience, the ego may be susceptible to appropriating that experience, fostering a self-absorbed and competitive spirituality—a comparison with others in which one always wins—while experiencing a simultaneous, egosyntonic increase in neurotic traits (meaning, in a manner that does not entail suffering). The transcendental experience can thus become a hindrance to spiritual development. Jung describes it as follows: "I also showed that to annex the deeper layers of the unconscious, which I have called the collective unconscious, produces an extension of the personality leading to the state of inflation" (Jung, 1953 in Hopkins, 2008).

Every seeker has to constantly deal with ego inflation. A single experience of ego death does not imply that one has transcended their ego. Even when we experience it in various depths and levels, the mere experience does not guarantee immunity from future ego inflations.

Abraham Joshua Heschel describes it this way: "It is a useless endeavor to fight the ego with intellectual arguments, since like a wounded hydra it produces two heads for every one cut off" (Heschel, 1951). Elsewhere the rabbi warns us:

Religious thinking, believing, feeling are among the most deceptive activities of the human spirit. We often assume it is God we believe in, but in reality it may be a symbol of personal interests

that we dwell upon. We may assume that we feel drawn to God,
but in reality it may be a power within the world that is the object
of our adoration. We may assume it is God we care for, but it
may be our own ego we are concerned with. To examine our reli-
gious existence is, therefore, a task to be performed constantly
(Heschel, 1955).

Spiritual Bypass

Another possible outcome of a therapeutic process or a spiritual practice that includes non-ordinary states of consciousness is the widely described spiritual bypass.

The term "spiritual bypass" was coined in the 1980s by John Welwood, a Buddhist psychotherapist and practitioner. The term refers to the tendency to use spirituality and spiritual experiences as avoidance mechanisms. We might try to avoid the suffering derived from living in the world through pseudo-spirituality. We may nurture the tendency to minimize our circumstantial suffering by alluding to spiritual ideas such as transcendence, the unreality and impermanence of all things, the existence of a greater plan or a cosmic game of which we are all part, or the supposed disidentification from the ego and what is a clearly inadequate detachment from our experience. Our spiritual practice and experiences can thus turn into an escape route from reality.

Frequently, these people may have had genuine spiritual experiences that led to a childish and unproductive form of spirituality due to poor integration. A spiritual bypass becomes an obstacle to true introspection and the development of a mature spirituality.

Masters (2010) writes that, "Genuine contact with the ultimate reality does not guarantee a genuine spirituality." Among the possible manifestations of a spiritual bypass, he includes:

An exaggerated detachment, emotional flattening, repression,
an exaggerated emphasis on the positive, fear of anger, blind or

exaggerated compassion, weak or porous boundaries, an unbal-anced development (cognitive intelligence is much more devel-oped than emotional and moral intelligence), poor judgment in relation to one's negativity or shadow, a devaluation of the per-sonal in relation to the spiritual, and delusions of having achieved a higher way of being.

Masters also differentiates between gross and subtle forms of spiritual bypass, reflected in the degrees of sophistication that these mechanisms may have for different people.

The current context of rapid globalization, the popularization of sha-manic practices, and the increased interest in the psychedelic experience, whether as a therapeutic tool or a spiritual practice—all in the context of a global market—do not quite help us deal with this phenomenon. While it is true that spiritual consumerism has always existed, it is perhaps more present today than ever. We find an extreme abundance of retreat centers that offer diverse and novel therapies, sometimes marketed as "miracle treatments" that combine, often in an excessively eclectic way, a range of different substances and multiple methodologies and paradigms. In order to survive in the spiritual market, each of these products must stand out from the others, hence the tendency to promise miraculous healings and express illuminations, guaranteeing immediate and infallible results. These offerings, however, very often promote spiritual bypass. Furthermore, the growing paradigm of positive psychology boosted by an increasing tendency to blame individuals for their own suffering, seeing people as responsible for their own illnesses, coupled with the aforemen-tioned mercantilism, all contribute to the creation of a paradigm defined by its superficiality. Our Western capitalist mentality favors an under-standing of spirituality as a linear endeavor with a tangible goal that, once achieved, guarantees us a happy and trouble-free life. We are often sold this idea instead of a real understanding of the subtleties of spiritual maturity, with all the nuances and contradictions that life implies. Jack

Kornfield teaches that even after reaching enlightenment—after experiencing ecstasy—we are still confronted with the daily task of translating that freedom into our imperfect lives. We face the fact that we need to do our laundry (Kornfield, 2001).

Heschel, in yet another stroke of visionary inspiration, writes: "God would be beyond our reach if we were to search for Him within the maze in the light of our mental fireworks" (Heschel, 1951). Assigning transcendence or sacredness to the internal fireworks of psychedelia can become an obstacle to true transcendence. Our inner visions can trick us into thinking that we have spiritually matured beyond our actual level of development, fostering both spiritual bypass and ego inflation.

While most of the implications of spiritual bypass hinder the development of a mature spirituality and can impair our ability to cope responsibly with our pending tasks, this phenomenon can also have positive aspects in some situations. People who are going through difficult moments of life, such as painful loss, or people whose lives have been filled with traumatic events and suffering, may experience states of freedom, joy, and happiness or encounter spiritual dimensions through their psychedelic experiences. To an outside observer, the enjoyment of these states may seem like an attempt to avoid confronting painful and unprocessed unconscious material. And the outside observer may very well be correct. However, this period of spiritual bypass can also be understood as a necessary step in the journey towards deeper levels of the psyche. Although these positive experiences and the temporary transcendence of pain may not be quite "real," they can leave a tremendously valuable imprint that allows the person to become confident in their own worth and internal process, perhaps for the first time. These states of bypass and inflation can be an oxygen tank for someone in a vulnerable state. Therefore, a spiritual bypass should not be immediately confronted without considering the situation of the person as a whole. Suppose someone is immersed in a therapeutic process or on a path of personal development and has the support of a skilled therapist or an understanding teacher. In that case, they will eventually be able to transcend those experiences of immature spirituality, understanding them as important pieces of their subsequent development.

Attachment and Addiction to Experience

One of the arguments typically employed to justify the therapeutic use of psychedelic substances is their low potential for abuse and the fact that they do not create addiction or dependence. This is undoubtedly true from a pharmacological point of view, and little can be argued against it. All psychedelics, with the exception of ketamine, lack the potential to cause addiction.

This is not to say that people never abuse these substances. Human beings can develop unhealthy or dependent relationships with almost anything: sex, games, food, intimate relationships, extreme sports, etc., and psychedelic experiences are no exception. Because of the astonishing nature of non-ordinary states and the myriad spaces and possibilities they may open up, some people can develop an attachment to these experiences. In such cases, these individuals might venture too frequently into the non-ordinary realities that these tools provide, whether through the use of psychedelic substances, breathing techniques, or by attending workshops where certain psycho-spiritual techniques are taught.

Although not risk-free, the consequences of such an addiction are not as severe as other types of addictions. On the one hand, our consciousness might be obscured rather than developed further, getting stuck in the illusion that the progress of our therapeutic or spiritual process requires constant access to these states and these experiences. A fleeting state is confused with a more stable and developed awareness. We focus on the phenomenological aspect of the experience, such as the visions or ecstatic emotions, thinking that they constitute the true spiritual experience in themselves. However, in many Eastern and Western traditions, such experiences and phenomena are considered only byproducts of the broader spiritual process. In Zen, they speak of *makyo*; in Hinduism, *maya* or *lila*; in transpersonal psychology, experiences in the astral dimensions; and in non-dual schools like Advaita Vedanta, they recognize the appearance of visions or *siddhis*. All these schools teach that these experiences must be eventually transcended.

Psychedelic therapy—as it stands today—seeks a lasting influence on the well-being and development of the person based on either a single or a small number of experiences. The psychedelic experience thus becomes a catalyst, an experience that can unleash a deeper personal process of better adapting to their own personal reality while taking care of some of the symptoms. In the psychotherapeutic model, psychedelics are not meant to become the patient's spiritual path, nor even a long-term "treatment" to be administered indefinitely.

For many psychotherapists, teachers, and spiritual practitioners, psychedelic experiences can be useful at specific moments, opening worlds of possibilities that otherwise could not have been accessed. However, most of them also argue that it is unnecessary for these experiences to be repeated over and over again. Alan Watts is well known for saying, "When you get the message, hang up the phone." Jack Kornfield reminds us that, "The most dangerous risk of all is the myth that these experiences will transform us, that a moment of 'enlightenment' or transcendence will completely change our lives for the better. This is rarely true and attachment to these experiences can easily lead to condescension, infatuation, and self-deception" (Kornfield, 2001, 119).

Spiritual teachers whose inner search was kickstarted and catalyzed by psychedelic experiences often acknowledge having had to eventually transcend the idea that enlightenment could be achieved through a specific experience (Badiner & Gray, 2015). Some used their initial experiences as the motivation needed to undertake a spiritual practice in a particular tradition and never used these substances again. Others, however, consider that specific psychedelic experiences at the right time can be useful on their spiritual path, whose backbone is built upon a particular discipline, be it Zen, Vipassana, or any other.

We thus make the useful distinction between "techniques of awakening" and "paths of awakening," and in later sections we will explore some immanent practices that can be helpful in spiritual integration. Most people experienced in non-ordinary states approach them as techniques for awakening and, therefore, they must be understood as such. For some others, however, non-ordinary states of consciousness can become part of a path, although they never constitute a whole path on their own, to the best of my understanding. These psychonauts, the navigators of the soul, use non-ordinary states as a tool to know internal and external reality and create their conception of the world. Psychonautics could be understood as a path, a spiritual practice, as is the case for some groups such as the psychedelic festival community or some neo-shamanic communities that routinely organize psychedelic ceremonies. However, I think it is important to distinguish between two types of people that we can meet in these contexts: those who organize or work in these events to make them possible and those who participate in these events as consumers and clients. For the organizers, the non-ordinary states of consciousness have probably become a path; furthermore, they have the will to be of service to the rest of their community. It is thus not simply about seeking individual experiences but about following a path of service that ensures that others can also access these "techniques of awakening." A shaman has made shamanism his spiritual path, but it is not an individual path. The shaman gives themself in service to their community, helping others with their knowledge. The shaman's path is a commitment to themself and the well-being of others; it is not only about an inner spiritual or philosophical quest. Non-ordinary states of consciousness as a path, in my understanding, cannot be separated from the path of being of service to others. Perhaps following a path of service is the only way to prevent the potential dangers we addressed earlier: ego inflation, spiritual bypass, and dependence on the non-ordinary states.

This prior paragraph is not intended as a blanket endorsement of the shamanic way; it is instead meant to illustrate that seeking non-ordinary states is not a path in itself, not even in paths in which they are seen as an essential practice. Shamans, therapists, and facilitators can also suffer from the risks associated with non-integration. Ego inflation and spiritual bypass can perhaps be most dangerous and detrimental when experienced by the leader of a session, often without being aware of it.[30]

IMMANENCE AND TRANSCENDENCE

Levels of Consciousness

As we have seen, an enlightening psychedelic experience is often followed by a period of peace and well-being, free of symptoms, free of anxiety or depression (for example, Grof and Halifax, 1978; Carhart-Harris et al., 2016; Mithoefer et al., 2019). Similarly, in some cases, these positive effects tend to fade, disappear, and be replaced again by the previous circumstances (Grof and Halifax, 1978; Eisner, 2002; Mangini, 2012; Carhart-Harris et al., 2017; Coleman, 2020). This is the reason why we are increasingly paying attention to integration and writing volumes like the one you have in your hands.

In my opinion, one of the key aspects of understanding this phenomenon is the differentiation between a state and a stage. Psychedelic substances can be useful tools for reaching non-ordinary states of consciousness, often with spiritual and transpersonal qualities. However, these states of consciousness are temporal, as is often the acquired wisdom. There is an old joke where a person asks a friend who has experimented with LSD, "Can you describe what the psychedelic experience is like?" To which the friend replies, "I took LSD last night. I understood the meaning of life and the secrets of existence. When I woke up this morning, however, I had already forgotten."

Most people who have had positive encounters with MDMA have experienced something similar. While the acute effects last, it is relatively common to approach problematic situations or traumatic memories through a perspectival prism that allows those memories and situations to be experienced without much pain. The insights and solutions seem natural and simple, even obvious or common sense, and we may feel that these insights will stay with us forever. However, as the effects fade, that security and confidence begin to collapse and we might begin to doubt the clarity which we experienced just moments ago. In later experiences, we may access this state of clarity, feeling that what we are experiencing is simple and obvious, perhaps even something that we already knew. These are called "state-dependent memories," that is, memories that we can only access when we are in a particular state of consciousness.

Another example is the type of experience produced by the plant *Salvia divinorum*, in which different worlds or planes of reality are perceived at once. Yet somehow they are not all completely compatible or capable of coexisting. Upon returning from an intense experience with *Salvia divinorum*, we may realize that we are returning to a known reality (our ordinary reality). The salvinorin universe begins to fade, and we might find it challenging to recall the details of the experience. In later encounters, we may return to those spaces and realize that we already knew what it was like to be there—the feeling of déjà vu occurs, and we find ourselves surprised to have forgotten the feeling of that particular state and experience.

These liberating psychedelic experiences can thus give us a few hours, days, or weeks of relief. They may allow us to contemplate the reality of our lives from a different perspective. We may feel like we have risen toward more equanimous states of being, devoid of suffering and conflict, and we may feel like we have been cured of all our illnesses, traumas, and neuroses. We might even feel like we have reached a higher state of consciousness. However, this feeling only reflects a temporal state of consciousness. That is, a specific experience limited by time. States of consciousness are only temporary modifications of our day-to-day consciousness. However, the subjective experiences can very well resemble state-dependent memories, imprinted experiences we can access while in that same state.

Now the stages of consciousness are something different altogether. Authors such as Piaget, Kohlberg, Villegas, Maslow, Naranjo, Erickson, Wilber, Nelson, and even Freud have spoken of phases or stages in the evolution of consciousness: from birth to the establishment of an autonomous personality and its subsequent transcendence as we continue our spiritual and moral development. These phases or stages are structures that develop over time and have a tendency to evolve, becoming more complex and integrated. One of the characteristics of these structures is that we fully identify with them as we go through them; that is, our self-perception is defined by the structure or level that we inhabit, which also defines our level of consciousness and perception of reality. This perception is only transcended once we evolve towards another higher structure. We disidentify from the lower structure to identify with the next one. The successive structures are thus superimposed—they do not disappear, yet something new is built on the previous foundations.

Although these stages evolve, all of them are permanent. Once a particular structure or level is reached, it solidifies and serves as the basis for higher structures. Our perception of existence and the possibilities of our immediate experience depend on the structure we inhabit in that particular moment. Transcending these structures can take time for an adult who has already achieved a degree of personal autonomy.

Perhaps Ken Wilber has described in most detail the different levels of the evolution of consciousness through his psychological, spiritual, and philosophical gaze. In his multiple works, Wilber (1989, 1990, 1994) describes the different levels of consciousness and the experiences attached to each one of them. He also defines which psychological and spiritual schools have addressed each of these levels. His model is complex and constantly evolving, but his theories prove extremely useful for guiding us with clarity through a process of psychological and spiritual development. I recommend the aforementioned works for a deeper understanding of Wilber's ideas.

Perhaps the most relevant aspect of the psychedelic experience is that it grants us access to encounters that belong to a higher state than the one we normally inhabit. The psychedelic experience also allows us to revisit lower states of consciousness—this is easier to assume at a theoretical level. Although the quality of our daily experience depends on our present level of consciousness, non-ordinary states of consciousness—hence their name—grant us access to experiences belonging to different levels of consciousness. It is precisely due to this dissonance between levels of consciousness that integration is necessary. We need to integrate something that cannot be automatically integrated since it does not belong to our baseline level or state.

Perceived from this vantage point, it becomes easier to understand why enlightening and liberating psychedelic experiences are temporary. Those feelings of spiritual openness dissipate over time, after which we return to our corresponding level of consciousness. Because the non-ordinary experience belonged to a higher state, it was simply a temporary state of consciousness and not the creation of a whole new structure.

Therefore, we can understand integration from another point of view. The integration of an experience implies a successful translation between states of consciousness: we must translate a higher-state experience to our current state. Hence the common difficulty we face in finding the right words to talk about and retain the feelings or insights we have experienced. If we follow the same logic, integration can also be understood as the gradual ascent from our present level of consciousness towards the stage to which the lived experience belongs. Of course, both procedures take time and are not mutually exclusive: We translate that experience, bringing it down to our level, while at the same time aiming to evolve into that higher stage.

Wilber, and other authors, speak not only of the basic stages of consciousness (the clearly differentiated main, discontinuous, and discrete structures) but also refer to transitional structures: temporary states that we inhabit when a higher structure is being built but has not yet replaced the present one. A good integration, focused on maximizing the benefits of a psychedelic experience, entails using those experiences to hasten our ascension to higher structures by taking advantage of these transitional structures precipitated by a non-ordinary experience.

The Transcendental and the Immanent Schools

In this evolutionary journey, we can distinguish between transcendent and immanent schools and practices. In the transcendent schools, we aspire to climb the mountain of enlightenment and reach powerful non-ordinary states of consciousness that allow us to open ourselves to realities beyond ordinary experience. In Rinzai Zen, we seek the experiences of *satori* or *kensho*; in the shamanic path, we seek the powerful visions and initiations in the spiritual worlds; in our use of entheogens, we seek the experiences of death and rebirth and the mystical experiences of unity; and practitioners of kundalini yoga aim to awaken the *Shakti* energy, allowing it to ascend the chakras, unleashing intense physical and visionary experiences.

On the other hand, the immanent schools have no particular interest in non-ordinary states of consciousness or the psychic phenomenology that takes place during practice. For Soto Zen Buddhism, all phenomena are nothing but *makyo* (illusion). The same is true in vipassana meditation, in which any manifestation beyond physical sensations is disregarded, and we are encouraged to remain present and detached from our internal experience. In some Hindu yoga schools, such as the Sivananda ashrams, the main focus is a physical practice, devotional rituals, and a simple lifestyle. In the so-called mystical schools of the Jewish tradition, we find a phenomenon analogous to what we find in Zen. While "in earlier days the Kabbalah tried to bring man to heaven, the main idea of Hasidism is to bring heaven to man" (Kaplan, 1989). Thus, Hasidism can be understood as the immanent school, while the Kabbalah would be transcendental (Mishor, 2019). Integrative approaches which seek to reconcile these two dimensions also exist. For example, they refer to the transcendental and unattainable reality of God as "higher unity" and the immanent reality that imbues each atom of creation as "lower unity" (Steinsaltz, 1989).

Psychedelics can and have been used to induce experiences of the divine in both its immanent and transcendent forms (Grof, 1972, 2019). Psychedelic therapy can be understood as a transcendental school and psycholytic psychotherapy as an immanent school. However, this theoretical distinction becomes more complex once we move on to the actual practice, as we saw in the first chapter when we reviewed the evolution of psycholytic therapy in the United States. We could consider that most people who approach the visionary experience do so, largely, from a transcendental perspective.

In this context, it has been repeated that psychedelics allow us to achieve, in just a few hours, the same states that we could reach after several years of meditation. It has also been said that the enlightenment provided by psychedelics is not true enlightenment, as it has been achieved effortlessly. This dynamic is usually illustrated with the metaphor of a man reaching the top of the mountain by helicopter, rather than climbing it by foot. This is an eternal debate in many Buddhist and meditation communities; it was widely in vogue among the early psychedelic explorers of the 1960s, including those belonging to the Beat generation and the hippies. If Zen meditation, Tibetan Buddhism, and Eastern philosophies became so popular, it was precisely because of the temporary nature of the psychedelic experience and the desire of many of these seekers to reach the more permanent stages of a higher spiritual development (Badiner & Gray, 2015; Kornfield, 1997, 2001).

The image of the mountain and the helicopter is not gratuitous, although it is missing some important nuances. Of course, the merit of climbing a mountain by our own means is a sign of greater mountaineering capacity than reaching the summit by helicopter, as the latter relies on relatively random factors such as the pilot, the weather, and whether one can afford that trip. The risks of a helicopter accident can indeed be greater than the risks of climbing on foot, although not necessarily. It is also true that many people would not even try to climb mountains without knowing what to expect at the top; in this case, the helicopter trip can be a good start.

Therefore, whether in psychedelic therapy or simply on a path of personal growth—aided by non-ordinary states of consciousness—the experiences themselves constitute a transcendental practice. The integration of these experiences and the associated practices would be the immanent aspect of this path.

USEFUL TECHNIQUES AND TOOLS FOR INTEGRATION

Many techniques are useful for integrating an uncomplicated experience that has been resolved with a favorable closure. Some of these techniques are general and can be implemented freely. In fact, most psychedelic retreats and ceremonies often include one or more of these techniques as a way to promote integration.

Psychedelic experiences are often positively integrated without the need for professional help; most integration practices are thus usually limited to those offered in the workshop. However, this does not mean that the integration is complete or that there is no more material to process. In fact, after an experience, most people tend to share that they have not yet been able to process and understand whatever happened during the session fully. The following days and weeks are a very fertile time for integration. New insights and understandings are produced, memories of the experience continue to appear, and the content can be allowed to settle.

The common principle shared by all the integration techniques described here is that they allow the experience to further unfold and evolve. These techniques are not intended to "turn off" or reduce the impact of the session, but rather the opposite: They aim to amplify and ground the experience by providing space, time, and attention.

Below I describe some of the techniques that may be useful for integration, commonly used during retreats, after ceremonies, and as part of protocols for sessions with modified states of consciousness. These techniques target one or more dimensions of integration previously described: the physical, emotional, cognitive, behavioral, spiritual, social, and temporal dimensions. Each person can use these techniques once they are back home after the experience and it is useful to spend some time engaged with them in the following days. Many of these techniques seem obvious and follow common sense: the intention in listing them is not to reinvent the wheel. Instead, it is to provide a broad and panoramic view of the various elements to consider when aiming to maximize the potential benefits of an experience in modified states of awareness and offer different integration alternatives for workshop organizers and participants.

These are the techniques and tools that are described in the following sections:

Techniques that attend to our physiological and physical needs:

- Rest
- Hydration and nutrition
- Ritual use of water

Techniques for cognitive / emotional processing and sense-making:

- Working with mandalas
- Collages
- Narrative account of the experience
- Working with stories and movies
- Tarot cards
- Sculpture
- Sand boxes
- Dreamwork

Techniques for processing and expressing emotions:

- Dance
- Singing and creating music
- Listening to music
- Meditation

Social techniques:

- Sharing circles
- Sharing in pairs

Techniques to promote spiritual integration

- Altars
- Contact with nature
- Immanent practices
- Taking action: following up on spiritual insights
- Rituals

Therapeutic interventions at the ontological level

TECHNIQUES THAT ATTEND TO OUR PHYSIOLOGICAL AND PHYSICAL NEEDS

Many traditions, such as Theravada Buddhism, Yoga, and Taoism, speak of the importance of the body as a vehicle of transcendence. In this idea, the body is the temple in which the spirit can dwell and through which we achieve enlightenment. After an experience in non-ordinary states of consciousness, the body is a territory to return to and ground, somewhere we can land after having navigated across the more subtle dimensions of our psyche. The body is both a tool that allows us to enter the psychedelic dimensions and the anchor that ensures our safe return to the physical dimensions. The body is also like a canvas on which the imprint of the experience can be fixed, so that it can be easily recovered later.

Rest

After an experience, having enough time to rest, recover adequately, and attend to our physiological needs is essential for good integration. Usually, experiences in non-ordinary states, whether through visionary substances or plants or non-pharmacological techniques such as Holotropic Breathwork, can be very taxing on the body. Many ceremonies take place at night and last for many hours, causing physical exhaustion, due to fatigue and lack of sleep, and in many cases due to dehydration and prolonged fasting.

Therefore, the first needs that must be taken care of are rest, hydration, and food. It is often difficult to get a good night's sleep after an experience, and sometimes the format of the retreat does not leave much room for rest. Therefore, it is crucial to sleep, at least the day after the experience, without any restrictions. Moreover, the psyche continues to work while we rest, and our dreams can help integrate the experience. After a successfully resolved experience, we may not dream as much. However, one might experience intense dreams if leftover material remains and needs to be processed (Grof, 1980). Dreams can be an essential integration tool since they allow the unconscious to express content freely and in a somewhat analagous format to the psychedelic experience. Analyzing or understanding the content of our dreams, however, is not yet so important at this point.

Hydration and Nutrition

Hydration and nutrition represent fundamental aspects of integration. After a long ceremony, we often experience uncomfortable physical symptoms, such as headaches, dizziness, general exhaustion, and bodily pain. Although these symptoms can sometimes be related to unresolved emotional issues, in many cases they are simply the somatic manifestations of dehydration, low glucose levels, and even coffee withdrawals. On another level, food makes us focus on the physical dimension and bring our attention to the body, which begins the process of digestion. Somehow, the message is conveyed that the time has come to return to the *hilotropic* dimensions (from the Greek *hylos*, matter), as opposed to the *holotropic* dimensions. Traditionally, fasting has been a widely used technique to induce non-ordinary states of consciousness and greater sensitivity. Food restriction can thus help maintain and prolong the non-ordinary state and make it difficult to return to ordinary consciousness. A sudden change in diet is one of the techniques used in situations of spiritual emergency, often incorporating red meat, cheeses, cereals, sweets, and honey (Grof and Grof, 2001), and breaking the strict vegetarian diet prescribed in some meditation retreats (Kornfield, 1997). In South American shamanic traditions where ayahuasca is used, particularly among the Amazonian people such as the Shuar and the Shipibo, diet is essential to prepare and integrate an experience. Certain foods are eaten after the experience or retreat to "close the diet." At this point, foods that had been temporarily restricted are gradually reintroduced into the diet.

Ritual Use of Water

The ritual use of water is another aspect related to the above. Since a long psychedelic experience can be challenging for the body, we might feel the need to tend to its hygiene. This aspect is perhaps more relevant for people who participate in traditional ceremonies with sacred plants, particularly when they take place in rural settings with little comforts and fewer amenities. Either way, after a prolonged, grueling experience, we often feel the need to wash. It is a good idea, therefore, to be able to come into contact with water. Taking a hot bath or shower can be a pleasant practice that provides both pleasure and comfort after an intense and long experience.

In some ayahuasca traditions, people are encouraged to bathe in the river or to receive fresh bucket showers (sometimes prepared with aromatic and medicinal plants) to help ground the experience. According to some traditional healers, "plants like fresh water."

There is an additional symbolic dimension to being in contact with water, which goes beyond the pleasant physical sensations. Water dissolves and carries away what we no longer need: In the same way that it dissolves and washes away sweat or sand from our body, contact with water is a symbolic and ritual form of cleaning and purification. In many traditions, water is used for these purposes. Whether in the aforementioned Amazonian cultures, the Jewish tradition and their use of the *mikveh*, the Japanese tradition of *onsen* (thermal baths), or the Nordic cultures that combine saunas with cold water immersions, many cultures have developed and engaged in ritual ablutions. On another level (that we will describe later), being in contact with large bodies of water, such as rivers, lakes, or seas, can be an experience of connection with the elements of nature and their intrinsic strength and harmony. Furthermore, floating in warm water can play a symbolic role of fusion and bonding with the environment or an intrauterine or cosmic fusion experience as described by Grof in his perinatal matrices (Grof, 1975). The act of simulating a pleasant feeling of fusion in the hours after an experience, when we are in a state of heightened sensitivity, can leave a positive imprint to close the session.

TECHNIQUES FOR COGNITIVE AND EMOTIONAL PROCESSING AND SENSE-MAKING

These techniques all favor emotional expression and processing and aid in the construction of meaning, which helps reinforce the experience. These techniques are based on the externalization of experience. They seek to translate experience into an external, objective, and observable *object*, and they create a tangible testimony of what happened, a reminder of the experience that exists beyond our internal memory. The creative arts appear as a common element not only in many integration practices but also in many spiritual traditions, from the ancient cave paintings that left testimony of their creation myths and other significant mundane or oneiric scenes to the elaborate mandalas of the Buddhist and Hindu traditions, the construction of mosques and cathedrals with their multi-colored glass paintings, and many other artistic and architectural marvels. The creative arts encourage us to surrender to our internal worlds, come into contact with them, and suspend judgment while we explore their multiple dimensions. Likewise, art validates our inner experience, allowing us to create our own testimony that can nonetheless be shared and reinterpreted by others.

Working with Mandalas

Drawing is one of the tools most commonly used during workshops, retreats, and similar experiences. Oftentimes, these drawings take the form of what is known in Sanskrit as a *mandala*.

Mandalas originate in Hindu and Buddhist traditions. They are complex and symbolic representations of the process of psychological and spiritual evolution undertaken by each individual psyche—the journey from the spheres of *maya* and *samsara* towards liberation, or *nirvana*. Mandalas also map out the process of involution—the opposite journey from the non-dual dimensions to individual incarnations and the world of illusion. Therefore, mandalas are reintegration tools between different ontological realities (Tucci, 1974). We also find creations analogous to mandalas, albeit less ornate than the Buddhist ones, in some Mesoamerican and other Native American traditions, some Christian traditions, and—spontaneously—in a whole range of artistic and architectural manifestations.

It is perhaps C.G. Jung who provides the best example of Western interest in these mandalas and their usefulness in the process of integrating the emerging contents of the unconscious. In *Man and His Symbols*, Jung describes the multiple mandalic representations that we find in different traditions, as well as an analysis of their meaning. Jung attributes the circular shape of the mandala to the archetype of the Self, the totality of the psyche, and its parts. The mandala is a representation of wholeness.

Jung used mandalas throughout his own personal process as a tool for psychological integration, particularly during the times when unconscious material was emerging with full force, threatening his own sanity. This series of mandalas can be found in *The Red Book*, which Jung created between 1914 and 1930, before studying in any depth the Eastern traditions from which mandalas originate.

Another example is Ram Dass' (1978) book *Remember: Be Here Now*, which is composed of writing and images of mandalas. After his psychedelic travels and his visit to India, the former Harvard psychologist wrote this book as a synthesis and legacy of his insights and teachings.

Drawing after a journey in an expanded state can be a good way to begin to integrate the experience. On the one hand, it is a technique that does not require verbal or cognitive processing: We can capture anything in the drawing, be it symbols loaded with meaning or simply colored spots. Therefore, it is a tool particularly appropriate for the initial stages of integration, when our cognitive understanding of the experience may still be very limited. On the other hand, it does not require any special knowledge or particular skills; the methodology is simple.

During Holotropic Breathwork workshops, people are encouraged to draw freely and without restrictions in creativity, using whatever materials they desire. Having diverse painting materials is important to provide people with different avenues of expression: pencils, watercolors, crayons, markers and pens, acrylic paint, finger paint, glitter, and any other available material. Some people choose to make detailed drawings that narrate certain aspects of the experience, and others decide to finger paint to create a more visceral and abstract composition. The final result of the mandala does not matter. The important thing is that a drawing is generated: something external, tangible, and observable, even if it is a blank page. Mandalas contain a lot of information about our experience, perhaps more than what we can communicate verbally. In addition, they hold this information in a quasi-holographic way. Even years later, we might be able to access vivid memories and sensations from that experience, simply by observing the mandala.

The mandala thus becomes a witness, a token that reminds us of our experience. It can be useful to leave the mandala somewhere visible during the days or weeks after the experience. If we strategically place the mandala in a visible part of our house, it can be a subtle but clear reminder of our experience, allowing us to stay in contact with it. Moreover, our perception and interpretation of the mandala may change, and we can find new details or new aspects that we have not discovered yet. The mandala lives on and evolves together with the integration of that experience.

In addition to being valuable tools for the integration of a particular experience, mandalas also serve as links in the ongoing chain of our personal process. It can be a moving experience to arrange and display our entire collection of mandalas, perhaps years after we made them, and to contemplate the implicit order or the evolution of the content and style of the mandalas. Regarded in this way, mandalas can help us understand our personal process beyond individual experiences. Perhaps this represents a higher level of integration when we transcend specific experiences and turn our eyes toward the whole traveled path. A similar technique that I have sometimes used in the context of a psychotherapeutic process aided by experiences in non-ordinary states is the rosebush technique. The person is asked to draw a rosebush and its surroundings, without additional instructions or restrictions. During the next session, we turn our attention to the rosebush, analyzing the different elements in the plant (presence or absence of thorns, number of flowers, leaves, size or position), as well as the elements of the environment (animals, people, buildings, clouds, or rain). Together, we interpret these elements to draw insights related to certain significant aspects of the experience. The rosebush is a projective drawing then, in which certain parts of the person or their present situation are represented. When using the rosebush in a therapeutic context, I ask for a drawing at the beginning of the therapeutic process (in the first session) and at the end of it. Comparing both drawings can provide a surprising testament to the changes that took place during the therapeutic process. This technique requires a therapist who poses questions throughout the session, so its application is different from that of the traditional mandala.

Collages

Working with collages can be an excellent alternative to mandalas for those who have difficulty drawing or feel that their representational abilities are not adequate to produce the desired mandala. Although there are different ways of working with collages, the original method designed by Seena Frost is called SoulCollage (Frost, 2001), which involves a specific way of creating, interpreting, and reading the artwork. In this model, we make a collage sheet in which the main image is combined with a background. We browse magazines for evocative images that represent a certain element of our experience or powerfully draw our attention. Each image is chosen and placed on a sheet with a background to create a desired mood or atmosphere. A single idea, concept, aspect, or particular energy should be represented on each sheet, with as many sheets as necessary to represent all the important elements of an experience. The meanings of the different sheets can be reinterpreted, combined, or elaborated upon afterwards. For more information about this method, you can refer to Seena Frost's book or to one of the many existing professional workshops that teach this technique.

A more straightforward way to use a collage is to find evocative images representing essential aspects of our experience and combine them on a sheet of paper as if it were a mandala made of photographs and clippings. Drawing and painting can also be combined with photographs to create the desired effect.

Narrative Account of the Experience

Writing an account of the experience can be an effective integration technique that contains different elements from the other techniques in this section, since it involves both verbal and cognitive aspects. It is simply a matter of writing an account of what happened during the experience. Although this can be done in different ways, a particularly effective way is to write a first-person, present-tense chronological account of the experience, as if the experience was unfolding while we were writing it. As a complement, the same music played during the session can be used in the background to facilitate the emergence of memories. Whether or not music is used, it is common for new memories to emerge as the account is being written. The act of writing can help us retain many more details of the experience, details that might otherwise disappear, just as the details of our dreams fade when they are not immediately written down.

The intention behind writing a story is to capture the content of the experience and weave it together to create a meaningful narrative, which is particularly important in the integration period. The meaning of the story does not have to be definitive; it can be modified over time and reinterpreted. The creation of meaning, of a narrative thread, allows us to remember the experience in more depth and detail while also connecting it directly with our life and our present situation.

There are other ways in which writing can be used as a tool; one of them is by creating a continuous story, accomplished by writing for a certain amount of time with no pauses, allowing the text to flow and the ideas to connect without restriction. This kind of automatic writing can allow undisclosed elements to be revealed, producing associations that would not have appeared simply through an organized and rational narrative. Giving a title to the story—as a manner of synthesis—can often be useful.

Working with Stories and Movies

Although each psychedelic experience is personal and its content is specific to each individual in that particular moment of their lives, some greater universal human themes often manifest in one way or another. Issues such as life and death; coming face to face with insanity and the fear of losing control; intense emotions of anger, fear, or sadness; and spiritual revelations and ecstatic experiences are all elements that frequently appear in psychedelic experiences. In our personal process, we often go through phases that are similar to other people's personal processes, although we each have our particular and individual phenomenological manifestations; the individual process and the collective processes run in parallel. Therefore, coming into contact with these overarching human themes can prove useful, as they have been previously experienced and expressed by many people at different historical times and in different ways.

Children's stories usually contain symbolic elements that transcend the princes, princesses, dragons, and treasures. The tales of the Brothers Grimm are evocative of unconscious material, hence their timeless quality. H.P. Lovecraft was a master at describing and inducing psychological dread of the unknown and an expert illustrator of the most grotesque dimensions of the human psyche, which can appear in their more extreme forms in a psychedelic experience. Gurdjieff wrote dozens of tales and metaphorical accounts in *Beelzebub's Tales to His Grandson*, inspired perhaps by Nietzsche's *Zarathustra*. *The Little Prince*, by Antoine de Saint-Exupéry, to this day captivates the young and old alike, evoking timeless aspects of the human experience. Dante Alighieri's *The Divine Comedy* describes a multitude of both hellish and heavenly symbolic scenes that reflect internal experiences available during non-ordinary states. Contemporary authors like Jorge Bucay have created sweeter versions of stories with spiritual and allegorical undertones. Italo Calvino has written precious books, like *The Invisible Cities* or *Difficult Loves*, abundant in metaphors that illustrate psychic realities of quasi-psychedelic complexity and address simple situations with vast implications. Novels such as Frank Herbert's *Dune* have inspired dozens of artists from different disciplines, including HR Giger, Alejandro Jodorowsky, Klaus Schulze, David Lynch, and others who have developed particular aspects of the novel's themes in their own paintings, films, documentaries, and musical compositions. By the same token, J.R.R. Tolkien's *The Lord of the Rings* or George Lucas's *Star Wars* sagas have spawned whole universes and worldviews beyond the originals created by their authors.

One of the greatest exponents of the symbolic and transforming power of stories is the Jungian analyst Clarissa Pinkola Estés, author of *Faithful Gardener*, *Women Who Run with the Wolves*, and a multitude of other stories. Her works are replete with complex tales and archetypal stories from diverse cultures.

After a psychedelic experience, it can be useful to approach quality literary and artistic sources that deal with topics similar to those we have encountered during the session. Many great human minds have accessed archetypal content, whether consciously or unconsciously, and have created art that manifests different aspects of these archetypes. Reading or contemplating a work of art related to the content of our session can therefore play an invaluable role in continuing to elucidate the emergent unconscious material, which would perhaps remain obscure or inaccessible otherwise. This is also true of films that illustrate collective themes. Watching films related to the content that emerged in the session or associated with the content of our integration work can be a way for us to broaden our perspective, enriching its content and meaning.

A selection of books, films, and music that may be useful during the integration process can be found in Appendix II.

Tarot Cards

In between the expressive and projective techniques, tarot cards can be a useful tool for interpreting different aspects of the experience and the subsequent states. There are many different decks that can be used, from the classic Marseille tarot to modern reinterpretations, such as the Osho Zen tarot or cards that represent certain archetypes, deities, or power animals. Each deck can be used in simple or complex ways, although sometimes it is enough to simply draw one card and read the interpretation proposed by the authors of the deck. Beyond esoteric interpretations, the act of picking a card and reading its meaning can catalyze an entirely new viewpoint of the experience or reveal aspects that until now we had not considered. The tarot is a tool that allows us to expand the meaning and possible interpretations of our experience. Surprisingly, unlikely situations often happen, such as drawing the same card several times in a row, or perceiving patterns and associations in seemingly disparate elements that cannot be explained by a relation of cause and effect, yet we perceive as having a symbolic or psychological relation. These synchronicities, in Jungian terminology, imply a non-causal connection that, according to some authors, shows how mind and matter can be connected (Jung, 2001; Grof, 2006). This can be helpful for integration, moving us a little closer to the physical dimensions and away from the purely psychological realm of our internal experience.

Sculptures

Less common, yet just as useful as the previous techniques, is modeling sculptures with putty or clay. There are different ways of working with sculptures. Some facilitators give detailed instructions about which elements should be molded and in what sequence; others suggest working with closed eyes, focusing on sculpting simply by following the tactile sensations and forming an object that evokes aspects of the experience. Other facilitators may prefer to make the sculpting materials available, with no instructions whatsoever. Touch is a sense rarely used in integration techniques, and incorporating it can have surprising and unexpected effects on participants.

Sandboxes

Jungian therapists use a technique that can be helpful during integration: working with figurines and sand trays. The original technique is called sandplay, created by a Jungian therapist named Dora Kalff (1980). During sandplay, the patient recreates his psyche's dynamics in a sand tray using many figures representing animals, plants, human beings, and even pyramids and other mythological elements. The bottom of the tray is usually blue: By displacing the sand, the person reveals the blue underneath, creating lakes, seas, and rivers. Similar to an altar, the representation of psychological dynamics can shift as time goes by, presenting new stories and plot threads that are symbolically resolved in the sand tray. The sandbox is thus a representation of our whole psyche, a microcosm that reflects our inner lives.

The sand trays allow us to work dynamically with the integration of our experience and the creation of its meaning while supporting the inward resolution of our psychological gestalts, as we will see in the next chapters, when we approach therapeutic intervention.

Dreamwork

We have seen that dreams can fulfill an integrative function through the mere fact of dreaming, allowing the psyche to express itself, further revealing unconscious material. Further work with the contents of our dreams can therefore be a valuable integration tool. The interpretation of dreams was considered by Freud to be the "royal road to the unconscious," as dreams contain an inexhaustible source of psychic material manifesting itself in our consciousness, albeit in a cryptic way. The psychedelic experience could be considered an even "better" royal road since it can be induced at will and allows a better recollection of the experience. As we saw in the first chapter, Freud hypothesized in 1940 that if we were ever to discover "specific chemical substances" that influenced the "psychic apparatus," this would result in unsuspected possibilities for therapy. Today, these substances are at our disposal and we can apply analytical techniques—whether Freudian, Jungian, Gestalt, or any other school—to the content of psychedelic experiences as we try to retrieve the underlying ideas.

The analysis of dreams and their individual and social significance does not belong exclusively to Western psychological culture. Since ancient times, humankind has attached great importance to the content of dreams. As mentioned previously, Indigenous Australian cultures have based much of their knowledge on dreams, and many of their oral stories retell how mythical animals created the universe in the "Dreamtime." The songs that describe the creation myths are reminders of those times, allowing us to understand their worldviews better. In ancient Greece, dreams represented expressions of divine will, symptoms of pathologies, premonitions, or divinations. Pythagoreans, Stoics, and Neoplatonists all held dreams in high regard. Native Amazonian peoples such as the Shuar have developed a worldview around visionary dreams; they use the same terms to refer to dreaming and the ayahuasca visionary state (Fericgla, 2017).

Since the early days of psychedelic therapy, people have approached the surprising contents of the psychedelic experience in a way analogous to how we approach dreams. Jung's analytical psychology is perhaps one of the most useful schools for the analysis of psychedelic content, given its spiritual nature and its ability to produce interpretations that expand and amplify the content, rather than reduce it, as can sometimes be the case with Freudian interpretations. Using a broad framework such as the one proposed in this text, interpretations from different schools can add richness to the integration process. Psychedelic experiences tend to cover multiple levels: the contents are manifested in different octaves simultaneously, so we can derive good interpretations from Freudian psychoanalysis, analytical psychology, or any other school of analysis and interpretation. It is perhaps interesting to consider how each of the different schools analyzes and interprets one level or octave, and not necessarily the whole dream or experience. A Freudian interpretation of a visionary experience can therefore produce profound insights at the biographical and psychodynamic level, while a Jungian interpretation of the same experience can shed light on the transpersonal and the dynamic aspects.

TECHNIQUES FOR PROCESSING AND EXPRESSING EMOTIONS

Dance

There are many techniques that use body movement as a tool for introspection or transcendence: Gabrielle Roth's 5Rhythms (1989), trance dance, ecstatic dance, the Sufi dances of the dervishes, or the dances of Gurdjieff, among others. Dancing can be a useful tool for emotional expression through movement and the body, combining the immediate experience of listening to music with the physical dimension of body movement and the social contact that dancing sometimes involves. Dancing can be a cathartic technique, favoring the release and processing of intense emotion; in the right context, it can also provide a socially acceptable container for the manifestation of intense emotions within a group. After the experience, many workshop facilitators like to provide a space for dancing, perhaps combined with drums and other percussion instruments. Other people choose to dance in solitude in their own homes as a useful way to integrate the emotions that might linger or appear in the days following an experience.

Singing and Creating Music

Another way to encourage creative, emotional expression is by singing and creating music. These more immediate forms of artistic expression can be applied both individually and in groups. Playing percussion instruments is usually an emotionally liberating experience, which can be combined with group dancing and the open expression of emotions through screams and sounds, which promote catharsis.

Rather sophisticated ways of using song and musical composition are found in traditions such as in the ayahuasca church of the *Santo Daime*, in which some participants "receive" songs—or hymns—during their sessions and later compile them into a "hymnal," which then becomes part of the doctrine. Those experiences may thus be integrated not only in the psyche of the individual who experienced them, but in the social context of the church as a whole. In other shamanic traditions, something similar happens: participants may "receive" *icaros*, or ritual songs, with specific therapeutic purposes. Neo-shamanic traditions have incorporated these practices and many Westerners have developed what is known as "medicine song," songs inspired by experiences with master plants and composed to be sung during the same sessions. The message is incorporated into a song, which is then transmitted to other participants in successive sessions, creating a kind of oral musical tradition.

Listening to Music

Listening to music can also be a useful integration tool, particularly if you listen to the music that was played during the experience (Grof, 2005). This may help bring forgotten parts of the experience back to the surface and, at the same time, support the processing of emotions. Music is evocative, and while listening to it, we may get in touch with emotions that might not be so accessible to us otherwise. Being present to music is also a way of allowing ourselves to do nothing else, simply connecting with ourselves, allowing whatever emotional states are present to flow and resolve.

If the music played during the original session is not available, any carefully chosen playlist can be useful for this purpose. Some authors have compiled music that they consider useful for periods of integration (Fericgla, 2004; Naranjo, 2016). Music that I often use when leading integration dynamics includes *Nanas de sol* by Luis Paniagua; *Music for Airports* by Brian Eno; the *Canyon Trilogy* by R. Carlos Nakai; *Moffou* by Salif Keita; some songs by Karam; compositions of classical music by Brahms, Chopin, Beethoven, and Bach; and compositions by contemporary musicians such as Ólafur Arnalds, Estas Tonne, and others.

Meditation

There is a particular synergy between meditation in all its different variants and the integration of non-ordinary experiences that makes their combination especially useful. Those with prior meditation experience often find their meditative practice is more effortless and more profound after an experience in non-ordinary states of consciousness. It seems that it becomes easier, after a visionary experience, to remain in states of concentration, mindfulness, and equanimity. In turn, people experienced in non-ordinary states of consciousness often feel that meditation allows them to ground the contents of the experience and remain connected to the higher states they have encountered in their psychedelic experiences.

I have participated in many retreats that mix both meditation and techniques of consciousness modification, both as a facilitator and as a participant. The results of a coherent and well-structured combination, led by experienced instructors in each of the techniques, are often much more satisfactory than each of the techniques on their own. This type of work often includes, on the one hand, the transcendental perspective of non-ordinary experiences and, on the other, the immanent perspective of the meditative schools.

SOCIAL TECHNIQUES

Sharing our experience with other people can be a particularly useful tool for integration. Sharing circles are an integral part of most retreats and ceremonies and are often the only integration technique used in a whole workshop. The way these circles are facilitated or guided usually varies depending on the school and the facilitators. Since the first psychedelic studies, the importance and natural necessity of sharing in a group have been well established. Sandison (1959) writes: "In a community where some of its members are taking LSD, there is an immediate tendency for the subjects to get together and to discuss its effects." Sharing circles are perhaps one of the oldest integration techniques for which we have evidence. In reference to the mushroom ceremonies he witnessed in 16th century Mexico, Bernardino de Sahagún writes that, "When the intoxication of the small mushrooms has passed, the Indians discuss their visions among themselves." If that is what the Franciscan friars witnessed after colonization, one may wonder how many centuries Indigenous people had been gathering in circles to share their visions.

For the sharing of these experiences to become useful and therapeutic, some preconditions must be guaranteed. The confidentiality of the experiences, for example, must be ensured by a collective agreement. Every participant must agree to keep the names of the participants and their experiences confidential. Thus the sharing can take place in a safe, quasi-sacred space, where people can freely speak their minds, knowing that whatever they share will stay within that space. Another essential condition for beneficial sharing is the implementation and maintenance of healthy and clear dynamics, ensuring that no harmful interference could turn a potentially therapeutic and useful experience into a source of additional conflict down the road.

After a psychedelic experience, people are often emotionally sensitive and vulnerable, so any feedback from the therapist or facilitator can have a strong impact with long-lasting consequences. Thus, sharing group facilitators and therapists should be particularly aware of their role at such times and carry out their interventions carefully.

Sharing Circles

One of the most useful ways to do a sharing circle is the model proposed in the Holotropic Breathing workshops, in which participants are encouraged to share content with "heart and meaning"[31] with the rest of the group. The goal is not to list a chronological account of everything that happened during the ceremony but rather to express the feelings we want to share with the rest of the group, witnessed by our fellow participants. In such groups, the dynamic is non-directive: there is no feedback, no interpretations, no questions, and no cross-talk during the sharing process. Each person shares while the group listens in silence. When the person sharing has finished, they are simply thanked for sharing, and the word is passed on to the next person. It is a simple and elegant sharing group dynamic that focuses on the participants and their experiences rather than on the workshop or the facilitator.

Oftentimes, sharing your own experience can be just as fruitful as listening to the experiences of others. We recognize ourselves in the experiences of others, and we discover that some are mutually shared. Through this shared experience, the feeling of community is reinforced, and the experiences themselves are put into context and perspective, often realizing that our experiences are not as unique as we might have imagined. We are able to contemplate, in others, some aspects of our own experience, witnessing each person's particularities in the way they process. Other people's stories can clarify confusing aspects of our own experience for which we perhaps haven't found an adequate expression.

When we share our experience in public, we must carry out a double exercise. On the one hand, we have to come up with a story that can be comprehended by others, so first we have to create that story within ourselves. This may be the first time we try to make sense of our experience as we try to weave a coherent story. Secondly, we often encounter a paradox: When recounting our lived experiences, they tend to lose some of their intensity, becoming easier to digest. While it may have sounded very dramatic in our own minds, our thoughts become clearer and more manageable by virtue of articulating and externalizing our account.

In many instances, immediately after an experience people are still at a loss for words and unable to produce a story: it is too early for them to share. This fact is completely normal and does not invalidate the usefulness of the sharing group. It is possible to simply share how we are feeling in that moment, focusing on our emotional state without revealing any details about the experience itself. Feeling supported and acknowledged by the group are important elements that favor the acceptance and subsequent integration of the experience.

It is essential that, after a workshop or ceremony, the participant has the opportunity to continue sharing the experience if they wish to do so. In such cases, the context and the rest of the group must follow the principles presented here: that is, room for an open sharing to take place without interruptions, interpretations, or analysis. It is crucial to avoid anything that can generate a defensive reaction. It is also important to take care of the experience and treat it with respect. A saying goes: The difference between a madman and a wise man is that the wise man knows who he can talk to about certain things and with whom he cannot. In periods of integration, it is imperative to be mindful of this and share the experience only in respectful contexts where there is support and trust.

The creation of groups, sharing circles, and finding spaces in which this type of interaction can take place are important aspects of integration, as we mentioned earlier in the section dedicated to the social dimensions.

Sharing in Pairs

Beyond sharing circles, dynamics can be created to share the experience with a more concrete objective in mind, facilitated by directive structures. As an example, this is one technique that I have used in the past: First, workshop participants are paired up and asked to choose who is going to share first. The other person simply listens throughout the exercise, and then they switch roles. The person is asked to relay their experience in seven minutes, sharing their interpretations and whatever else they consider relevant. Once finished, the same person is asked to retell their experience, this time in three minutes. Next, the person is asked to retell their experience in just one minute. After the three exercises, the partner who was in the listening role is asked to summarize in one minute what they understood from what they have been told, narrating their partner's experience back to them. Once this exercise is finished, the person is asked to title their experience by condensing it into a headline. Then they swap roles and do it all over again. This way of sharing helps synthesize and summarize the most relevant aspects of our experience, creating a backbone.

Different sharing dynamics can be created or implemented, depending on the orientation and intention of the facilitator and the context of the experience.

TECHNIQUES TO PROMOTE SPIRITUAL INTEGRATION

Although the spiritual dimensions of the psychedelic experience are perhaps the best known or at least the most historically emphasized, they are often the most difficult to truly integrate. Due to the very nature of these dimensions, the spiritual aspects escape rationalization and understanding most of the time. They can hardly be explained or their essence transmitted, and it is difficult to share them with people who have not experienced similar states. Although sometimes a spiritual experience manifests so clearly and overwhelmingly that it leaves an indelible mark, it can prove quite difficult to reconcile these states with our baseline physical reality and all its contradictions and painful situations. However, these dimensions hold perhaps the most tremendous therapeutic and evolutionary potential, with the power to help humanity as a whole, beyond our individual intra-psychic conflicts.

Altars

Working with an altar is a less common technique that involves a rich combination of elements that contribute to various dimensions of integration. Interestingly, many people use altars without being aware that they are doing something potentially useful for their integration and growth. For many people, this comes naturally, and practically all the world's traditions have used some type of altar, using everything from candles and bonfires to totems and representations of various gods, as well as tables (*mesas*) with flowers and power objects, to name a few.

Integration work with this technique consists of the creation of an altar, in which meaningful elements such as objects, photographs, beautiful fabrics, jewels, flowers, and other natural elements are purposely placed. Mandalas, sculptures, drawings, collages, and other elements that we have created related to our experience can also be placed on our altar.

The altar becomes a tangible and observable testimony of our experience. It contains elements related to the transcendental dimensions of the experience, reflecting our personal connection with the spiritual dimensions. Therefore, although it can be understood as a creative and expressive technique, it encompasses the spiritual aspects of integration through the physical and tangible representation of the numinous. An altar is something dynamic that can evolve over time: elements can be moved, new ones can be added, and older ones that are no longer considered necessary can be removed. The altar can be expanded or made simpler and smaller. For some people, the altar is considered sacred during their integration processes, and it can become a permanent fixture in our homes, dedicated to our relationship with spirituality.

The altar thus becomes an anchor between us, the experience, and our relationship with the divine and the transcendental, that which has no name or form but is intuited. It is a place where we relate to our own growth process; the altar is the fertile ground on which we can cultivate this relationship.

The altar can also be a place to go in times of need. A place to regroup, meditate, and connect with the echoes of experience, a place to let go and get in touch with the tides of our internal process.

Contact with Nature

Being in contact with nature is one of the best ways to promote integration. Going for long walks in the open air, crossing forest trails, watching the sun at dawn and dusk, being swayed by the wind, or coming into contact with the ocean can all be beneficial experiences after an inward journey. Modern science is just beginning to realize the benefits of contact with nature for our mental health (Bratman et al., 2012). The Japanese tradition of *shinrin-yoku*, or forest baths, has already reached the West, and its positive effects on the immune system and psychological health are being studied. Modern psychedelic research has also highlighted that the use of psychedelic substances is correlated with a greater connection with nature (Kettner et al., 2019), so being in contact with nature in the period immediately after the experience seems particularly useful.

Many traditions express reverence for particular places in nature: Bodh Gaya, the Kaaba, hermitages, caves, waterfalls, mountains, the Ganges River, Uluru, and Kata Tjuta are some examples. Nature has an ability to awaken our reverence and can double as a boundless and timeless altar of which we are anonymous but meaningful components. Contact with nature puts us in touch with the beauty of creation, without ornaments or embellishments, in all its raw splendor.

Nature connects us with the intrinsic harmony of creation. The various natural elements act effortlessly. Trees do not have to strive to be trees; a sunset is perfect every day; animals do not have to fight to be who they are. Nature functions on its own and despite us. It functioned before humans existed, and it will continue to do so after we have disappeared, following her own inexorable rhythm that, while rooted in time, seems to be beyond it. Contact with nature connects us with this timelessness, with this dimension of existence framed outside of time. As Rabbi Abraham J. Heschel (1989) says, "The ultimate goal of spiritual life is not to accumulate large amounts of information, but to face sacred moments [...] A moment of inner vision is a joy that transports us beyond the confines of time [...] Our spiritual life begins to decline when we lose that sense of what is eternal in time." Nature provides us with this combination of space and time, the basic needs for integration. A finite but unlimited space and eternal time flow ceaselessly and in harmony.

Immanent Practices

As we have seen in the previous section, each school approaches spirituality differently, even within the same tradition. The integration of psychedelic experiences, which are commonly understood as transcendental experiences, can be facilitated by the practice of the immanent schools both before and after the experience.

A well-known Zen story tells of a peasant who needed water for his field, so he began to dig a well. When he had dug half a meter, having found no water, he said to himself, "There is no water here," and he decided to start digging another well a few meters further. After digging half a meter, he found no water and concluded that there was no water to find there either. In response, he started a new hole a few meters away with the same result. And so on and so on. He ended up with many half-meter deep wells, finding no water in any of them, and concluded that water was not to be found. Similarly, those of us who seek healing and spirituality may spend our lives dabbling in a multitude of different techniques without developing real depth, providing us with rich experiences but without giving us the results that we seek.

Immanent practice is centered and focused on the visible physical world and its relationship to the spiritual. Therefore, it somehow forces us to remain grounded instead of focusing only on non-ordinary states of consciousness and temporary mood alterations.

A Zen master and friend told me:

> *My first teacher, Taisen Deshimaru, used to say that Zen is not a spiritualistic response to a materialistic world, but a way of life that transcends and includes both the spiritual and the material. That is what I have always liked about Zen, its practical spirituality, the fact that it flies just above ground. [...] When it comes to inner development, I feel that it is important to discern between "techniques" of growth or awakening and the "path" of awakening. Techniques are at the service of the path, but they cannot replace it. One of the modern problems is that many people experiment with many techniques, but they do not follow one path. The path is the backbone and the common thread that allows us to adequately integrate what we experience through the techniques. Zen is a way of life (Dokushô Villalba, 2019. Personal communication).*

Taking Action: Following Up on Spiritual Insights

During a non-ordinary experience, we can experience clear revelations, and suddenly all the conflicts inherent in our daily lives can seem irrelevant through the gaze of the expanded state. While having a good experience with MDMA, the problems that plague us seem to be much simpler and easier to solve. We might even think that all our problems have been solved in those moments of openness and acceptance. However, as the experience ends, that simplicity disappears and our doubts creep up again. That beatific state disappears, and we find ourselves back in ordinary reality with the same problems we had before. Other times, we might get a clear insight during our experience regarding how to resolve a certain conflict, but at the end of the experience, we realize that is not as easy to carry out, and often that insight remains simply that—an insight we had during the experience and nothing more.

The opposite case can also be true. During an experience, we may become aware of the changes we need to implement in our lives, and when we return home after the retreat or ceremony, we act impulsively. After a psychedelic experience, some people decide to end a committed relationship or make an important decision such as leaving a job, moving to another city, or making a major financial investment. This type of proactive energy is common after an intense and revealing experience, and finding the motivation and determination to take action can indeed be very important. However, one of the golden rules in these situations is that, "If this decision is right today, it will remain right in a month." The psyche often communicates through metaphors and symbolic language, and although it is probably true that we must make an important change in our lives, perhaps we are not quite ready yet to envision its final form. A reasonable amount of time must be allowed for the experience to mature, settle, ground, and take full shape before taking action. This phenomenon had already been observed in the first psychedelic studies during the 1950s, when Sandison spoke of the "rehabilitation period" (Sandison et al., 1954).

If, after a certain time, we still feel determined to implement that change or something else that has emerged during that period, then it is time to take action. We have to find the right balance between rushing into action on the one hand and avoiding the responsibility of making choices on the other hand. When we described the behavioral dimensions of integration, we argued that ethical behaviors manifest in tangible actions, as do all the insights and lessons we learned in these non-ordinary realities. Responsibility for our own decisions and actions is a sign of spiritual maturity. Kornfield tells us: "The root of fundamental change must be grounded in our ethical behavior and compassion, followed by a systematic inner training. Those are the supports for long lasting and integrated access to these transformative experiences" (Kornfield, in Badiner & Gray, 2015).

Rituals

We have seen the importance of turning insight into actions, including the ethical and behavioral dimension of integration and the materialization of the lessons learned from the psychedelic experience as a way to bring completion to the integration process. However, there are different ways to take this step into action. On the one hand, as we saw in the previous section, it can take the form of a decision-making process that culminates in action. In this case, the person defines the manner and the right moment to take action. On the other hand, someone else might give us some direction about how to proceed forward, even prescribing a certain ritual for us.

A ritual is nothing more than an intentionally designed sequence of acts (behaviors), rich in symbolic elements. Because of these elements, the performance of a ritual has both intra-psychic and external consequences. If we think about some of the rituals that are more familiar to us, such as baptism, circumcision, the first communion, a bar mitzvah, a marriage, or the oaths sworn on the Bible, all these acts seem to be meaningful and can have consequences not only for the psychic, inner life of the person but also on a social level. We know the importance of rites of passage in pre-industrial cultures, as well as the complexity of their design and execution.

Rituals focused on healing have been used in practically all traditions, from shamanic cultures—such as the Andean people—all the way to Christianity, which still carries out exorcisms. Some schools of psychotherapy prescribe ritualized behavioral sequences with therapeutic intentions (see, for example, Haley, 2006; Watzlawick et al., 1976). Perhaps Alejandro Jodorowsky has come the closest to a new psychological shamanism, articulating and describing his psychomagic (*psicomagia*) practices—clearly another form of the ritual. Jodorowsky writes, referring to his tarot readings:

> *After a two-hour consultation, many have exclaimed: 'I had not discovered so many things about myself even in two years of psychoanalysis!' This used to provide me with great satisfaction, and I was convinced that becoming aware of a problematic situation was all that was needed to solve it. However, this was not true. To overcome a difficulty it is not enough to identify it. An awareness that is not followed by an action is completely sterile (Jodorowsky, 2004).*

This is a reflection that applies quite literally to psychedelic psychotherapy.

The prescription of rituals in the way we have outlined here requires a skilled and creative therapist who is honest, humble, and sensitive. It is an exciting practice and a highly complex one; one must think of a ritual that can condense the many elements that could be useful for integration—as therapists, most of us will probably never be particularly skilled at it. However, considered through this lens, these often criticized behavioral prescriptions may gain a new dimension, allowing clinicians to prescribe more precise, meaningful, and individualized activities for each patient, rendering therapy a little more authentic and humane.

THERAPEUTIC INTERVENTIONS AT THE ONTOLOGICAL LEVEL

There are some schools of psychotherapy and personal growth, mainly based on cognitive methods, whose main aim is to influence the ontological perception of the client. They thus work on a more metaphysical level than the classic schools, be they psychodynamic, Freudian, Jungian, Gestalt, or cognitive-behavioral.

These methods seek to open pathways across the different levels of logic operating in the client, helping us become conscious of our underlying beliefs, a priori assumptions, prejudices, and the unconscious programming that conditions our general perception of the world. These schools address the person's second-order reality almost exclusively. In fact, it is often not even necessary to make explicit the phenomenology of our biographical events or the content of a psychedelic experience. This work is focused on the relationship between oneself and these contents, regardless of what they are.

One of these methods is based on the theory of perceptual control. The particular technique is called Method of Levels (MOL), and it consists of a therapeutic interview. The therapist's questions are intended to reveal the different levels of logic involved in the issue being discussed to illuminate underlying basic beliefs, motivations, and values. From this perspective, conflict arises not from whatever took place but based on how the person relates to their interpretation. Therefore, the problem—the suffering—is derived from a conflict between the person's beliefs and values. The goal of the interview is to show that this conflict is rooted in a certain level of logic and, given the possibility of accessing and contemplating a higher level of logic that is inclusive of all the conflicting beliefs and values, the conflict can dissolve and disappear (Carey, 2006).

An additional intention of this intervention is to allow the person to achieve a greater sense of control over their own cognitive and emotional processes, which helps better manage the conflict, now perceived from a higher and more inclusive logical perspective. The attribution of control over the entire process is a key factor in this type of intervention, to the point where the patient is the one who decides the duration of the sessions, their frequency, and when to end the therapy. The goal is for the entire therapeutic experience to become an example of how one takes control over their own process.

This technique is surprisingly simple and elegant but its successful application requires practice and skill. Furthermore, as it lacks the support of a complex theoretical corpus, it can be very useful in interventions focused on the integration of psychedelic experiences. This technique can prove tremendously useful and effective for a therapist who is able to offer only one—or a few—integration sessions. There is no complicated theoretical paradigm or specialized language that has to be learned by the patient and the therapist. Therefore, we can work with anyone, whatever their cultural background and beliefs. Based on the above, we avoid using classical therapeutic interventions such as paraphrases and interpretations, allowing the client to reach their own conclusions. This is often a difficult task for therapists; however, this often means that the client's resistance is minimized, their own belief systems are respected, and the whole therapeutic process follows at their own pace.

I have been able to test this method successfully in the form of integration interviews following Holotropic Breathwork sessions and experiences with MDMA and psilocybin. When faced with the request for an integration session from a stranger or from someone with whom there is no long-term therapeutic relationship (for example, people who only attend specific integration sessions and are not engaged in an ongoing process), I find this method to be simple, safe, and effective, even if it is somewhat difficult to implement since it requires some training and supervision.

Other schools apply more sophisticated methods based on multi-day workshops structured around ontological exploration group sessions led by specially trained facilitators. This style can be more confrontational, depending on the facilitator's preferences. Therefore, it is only indicated for people with stable ego structures who were not going through a crisis situation either before or after the psychedelic experience.

These types of therapeutic interventions at the ontological level are still minor in the context of psychedelic integration. However, it is an exciting field that is likely to flourish in the upcoming years.

CARTOGRAPHY OF
ADVERSE EFFECTS

5

"Do not decode
these cries of mine.
They are the road,
and not the sign.

Nor deconstruct
my drugless high—
I'm sober but
I like to fly.

Then quickened with
my open talk,
you need not pick
the ancient lock."

"ALL MY NEWS" - LEONARD COHEN (2006)

ADVERSE EFFECTS FOLLOWING A
PSYCHEDELIC EXPERIENCE

Experiencing adverse effects following a psychedelic experience is one of
the issues that has most concerned both users and researchers, historically
shaping public perception through its portrayal in the media. Following
the psychedelic revolution of the 1960s, it became quite impossible to
decouple psychedelic substances from terms such as madness, flashbacks,
"bad trips," "going off the deep end," or "losing one's mind," and an
endless array of other negative consequences of psychedelic use. Even
today, these concepts and idioms retain a certain halo of mystery, per-
petuating many of these misinformed rumors. Psychedelics were quickly

stigmatized by political authorities, their use publicly demonized and any sort of research discouraged.

In recent decades, this trend has reversed and the potential therapeutic effects of these substances has been increasingly emphasized. Even so, concerns still linger regarding the potential risks that these substances may entail, whether for the users, the therapists, or the researchers.

While it is true that the use of psychedelic substances entails certain risks, and that even when done in a controlled environment we might occasionally face emergency situations, these events are quite rare and can be resolved quite easily through pharmacological or therapeutic interventions (Cohen et al., 1985, 1963; Strassman, 1984; dos Santos et al., 2017; Grof, 2005).

When we talk about adverse effects, we are not talking about a homogeneous group of symptoms. There are multiple situations and experiences that could be cataloged as adverse even if, from a different perspective, they would not necessarily be considered as such. The approach presented here is based on the adverse effects most commonly found through my work with the ICEERS Integration and Support Center, during Holotropic Breathwork sessions and training, on the Kosmicare support service for psychological emergencies at Boom Festival and, lastly, the cases that I have seen in my private practice. Similar to those described by Strassman (1984), our working definition of adverse effects thus encompasses all those diverse situations that motivate a person to seek help from a professional, specifically to treat disturbances following a psychedelic experience.

The main questions that have motivated my work in the last few years have been: "Why does this person feel they need help following a psychedelic experience?" "Why does this person feel like they cannot deal with it on their own?" and, lastly, "What happened in this person's process that resulted in a problematic situation?"

My work has since been unfolding in this direction: on the one hand, trying to understand the sorts of problematic situations that arise and which factors have contributed and, on the other hand, developing therapeutic approaches that can be useful in these situations, while fostering a culture of integration capable of preventing some of these events from happening.

CARTOGRAPHY OF ADVERSE EFFECTS: A REVIEW

Throughout many years working for the Integration and Support Service of ICEERS, we have received a multitude of inquiries related to the use of traditional psychoactive plants and substances. Many of these inquiries concern the preparation and integration of these experiences, as well as the adverse effects and problems arising from these experiences. Since 2013, I have been in charge of addressing these inquiries personally. Throughout this period, I have provided attention to more than 700 people, facilitating many hours of integration psychotherapy in addition to the work I do in my private practice. This has allowed me a privileged perspective on the different cases and situations that require the intervention of one or several health professionals. After years of doing this work, I later focused on the revision of sessions and notes, along with the analysis of the collected data, attempting to draw useful conclusions for the general practice of integration psychotherapy.

One of the most relevant aspects of my job has consisted of finding and identifying common problems and profiles found among the multiple integration requests. Back in 2012, when I started working in this field, I was completely unaware of the wide range of difficulties that people could experience after experimenting with master plants and psychedelic substances, beyond the theoretical concepts acquired in my training as a transpersonal psychologist. During the first few years, most of my interventions happened "in the dark," so to speak, lacking useful maps that could guide the psychotherapeutic process. In 2015, after doing this work for a few years, I began to recognize common patterns, noticing that certain requests for support repeated more frequently; progressively,

I became more interested in the underlying reasons that caused people to contact me.

There are always different ways of approaching the same phenomenon and, in psychiatry and psychology, "symptomatic description" is one of the most common. The different diagnostic manuals—the various versions of the DSM or the CIE, among others—establish diagnoses based on groups of symptoms; that is, they evaluate the presence or absence of different symptoms and a diagnosis is determined based on a statistical model.

There are multiple problems with symptomatic descriptions focused on the establishment of a diagnosis. On the one hand, they do not explain the causes of the problem, obscuring the comprehension of the appearance and maintenance of symptoms by favoring a purported explanation for their occurrence. On the other hand, these diagnostic manuals seek to define a specific treatment for each diagnosis, oftentimes failing to do so. This tendency to seek specific treatments for specific diagnoses is likely to continue, however, at the expense of seeking treatments for specific and particular people.

This tendency is still prevalent within the psychedelic paradigm in its current medicalized expression. For example, we talk today about the best treatment for PTSD or resistant depression, giving ontological validity to the diagnoses themselves, as if they represent real entities that exist beyond a particular person and their context (Martínez-Hernáez, 2018). In this sense, psychology and psychiatry have raised the diagnosis to the realm of the archetype.

Sidney Cohen has investigated the adverse effects of psychedelic therapy perhaps more than any other author (Eisner & Cohen, 1958; Cohen, 1960; Cohen & Ditman, 1962; Cohen, 1963; Cohen, 1966; Cohen, 1985). Working as a psychedelic therapist over the years, Cohen became quite interested in the adverse reactions, devising a model of description and classification that evolved over the years.

Cohen describes the adverse symptomatology following the use of LSD and classifies it in two main groups: 1) acute reactions and 2) prolonged reactions. However, he does not make such a distinction in all his publications, and some confusion remains regarding the types of adverse events he catalogs. We know (and it will be addressed in the corresponding chapter) that difficult experiences can arise during the acute effects of any psychedelic experience, regardless of the substance or the context. A thorough discussion regarding how to best deal with these acute episodes well surpasses the objectives of this book. Therefore, we will focus on the prolonged reactions that occur and linger after the experience, as they are the ones more closely related to integration. Within this category, Cohen (1963) distinguishes four different groups of adverse effects: 1) prolonged psychotic decompensation (schizophrenia, intermittent reactions, or psychotic flashbacks); 2) depressive and anxious reactions (the most frequent complication, according to Cohen); 3) the activation of psychopathic or anti-social tendencies, anti-social behavior, and letting go of social responsibilities; and 4) paranoid reactions or the confirmation of delusions of greatness in relation to the transcendental aspects of the experience.

While the phenomenological description of the symptoms is extensive, the classification seems to change as his model evolves, with the different categories eventually including many overlapping elements. Cohen affirms that these episodes are infrequent, and most of them may be resolved in the course of a few days or weeks by means of psychiatric medication, but he also reports cases in which the adverse effects persisted for months or years (Cohen, 1963, 1966). In this regard, Cohen's approach to the integration and comprehension of these phenomena follows the aforementioned diagnostic line, quite confusing and impractical when trying to prescribe appropriate courses of treatment.

Perhaps more interestingly, Cohen (1985) further discusses the causes of prolonged psychotic reactions in some subjects. These include: 1) the character structure of the subject; 2) the context; 3) the insecurity and vulnerability entailed by a psychedelic experience; 4) the set and the contagious nature of the group experiences; 5) panic inducing negative experiences; 6) difficulties in "landing" while approaching the end of the experience; 7) dosage; 8) frequent use; 9) previous state of mind and stress levels; and 10) insufficient preparation.

Smart and Bateman (1967) characterized the most frequent complications caused by the use of LSD as such: prolonged psychotic reactions, non-psychotic disorders, and recurrent re-experimentations (flashbacks). In an extensive review of studies focused on adverse effects, Strassman (1984) classifies the different adverse effects within a temporal continuum, ranging from acute to chronic. In this continuum, we find the most common manifestations—the reactions of panic or "bad trips"—followed by the terribly labeled "LSD psychosis," which clumps together some functional psychoses and transient affective disorders with chronic and intermittent adverse effects such as the "flashback." Strassman (1984) concludes that the characterization of adverse effects over decades of psychedelic research is not homogeneous and hence challenging to systematize, involves multiple factors, lacks specific descriptions, and contains abundant personal interpretations and biases provided by each individual researcher, further hindered by the absence of any data about the patients' situation prior to their adverse reactions.

One of the adverse effects that has penetrated deeply into the scientific literature and popular culture is the phenomenon called "flashback." Although descriptions of it have not been consistent throughout the years, a flashback is generally understood as the transient re-experiencing of the effects of LSD (or any other psychedelic) in the days, weeks, or months after having taken the substance. These flashback cases were first documented by Leuner (1965), as well as Cohen and Ditman (1963), focusing mainly on the re-experiencing of the perceptual effects elicited by the substance (the visions or hallucinations) and the anxiety that followed these manifestations. There was a subsequent increase in the number of flashback complaints, particularly among the recreational users of the

Haight-Ashbury scene during the "Summer of Love" of 1968 (Shick & Smith, 1970). Rosenthal (1964) describes the symptoms of flashback as "persistent hallucinosis," focusing on the perceptual aspects.

The authors who best described the flashback were Fred Shick and David Smith (1970), who differentiated three distinct categories within the same phenomenon: 1) perceptual flashbacks (transient and non-problematic visual changes that do not require much therapeutic support); 2) somatic flashbacks (experiences of physical sensations similar to those of a previous psychedelic journey); and 3) emotional flashbacks (intensely re-experiencing unpleasant emotions such as anxiety, fear, or sadness). The first category of flashback received a lot of media attention and gave rise to the diagnosis of PHPD (Post Hallucinogen Perceptual Disorder). This diagnostic category remains controversial, and its prevalence is hard to estimate (Halpern et al., 2018).

Somatic and emotional flashbacks are relatively frequent phenomena and have been amply described as results of unsuccessfully processed difficult experiences. The way I see it, the re-experiencing is not related so much to a substance but rather to an experience that has not been fully resolved. Therefore, they could be considered prolonged non-psychotic reactions, following the terminologies of Cohen, Smart, and Bateman. Based on our current terminology, this can manifest in some of the specific problems that we will see below, in particular the "unresolved difficult experiences" that involve experiences of fear, the "dissociative traumatic experiences," and in some cases of emergent traumatic memories, that is, in profiles[32] that have a common phobic/anxious denominator.

These manifestations can be understood in the transpersonal paradigm as spontaneous attempts by the internal process to resolve itself, becoming overwhelming due to the intensity or the context in which the manifestations take place and prompting the person to resist or fight against them, establishing a dynamic that perpetuates the situation, exacerbated by the resulting anxiety.

Typically, these situations are experienced with varying degrees of intensity over time. There is usually a background of anxiety and a persistent sense that something is not going quite well, with crises happening at specific moments or in specific situations (for example, at night before going to bed, when consuming cannabis, or under much stress). These intense situations can be understood either as panic attacks or as flashbacks, therefore eliciting some confusion among researchers who have tried to categorize these types of adverse effects.

At the same time that the authors cited above were conducting research on LSD, Ungerleider and Fisher (1967) were describing adverse effects from a different perspective. Perhaps not surprisingly, they labeled as an adverse effect the fact that some people were no longer interested in working or participating in established social dynamics after their psychedelic experiences. They also spoke, a bit more successfully, of the proselytizing attitude that some psychedelic users adopted, something that continues to happen today by all means, although the tendencies have shifted towards traditionally used intoxicating plants. Perhaps they were the first to realize these less severe adverse effects related to the risks of non-integration (ego inflation, etc.) that we have seen in Chapter Four. Other adverse effects described are hallucinations, anxiety, depression, and confusion (Ungerleider et al., 1966 and 1968). Again, the criteria are mainly diagnostic, so they do not contribute much to our understanding of the phenomenology of the cases. We see that, in general, the diagnosis of "psychosis" in any of its aspects is usually nonspecific, inaccurate, and tends to add confusion rather than help the clinician.

In my work, I have independently reached some conclusions similar to Cohen's and an understanding of flashback similar to Shick and Smith's. I have described the different profiles and problems using etiological and causal criteria but with an eminently practical orientation that guides the psychotherapeutic treatment. The etiology and causality refer to the appearance and maintenance of the problem, not to the patient's previous intra-psychic or psychodynamic causes. My interest has focused on understanding what situation or experience has caused the present problem and the factors that are maintaining this problem in the present day.

In fact, the classification of these profiles took place after I designed the therapeutic intervention. Initially, my psychotherapeutic interventions were basically the same for all situations and, therefore, sometimes successful and sometimes clearly ineffective. The modification and particularization of the therapeutic strategy to increase its effectiveness has allowed me to better understand the problems involved in the different situations and, through this, typify the different profiles. This section provides a description of these situations, and the specific psychotherapeutic interventions proposed for the integration of each particular situation will be described later.

More simply put, Hoffer and Osmond (1967) write that there are three types of complications that follow an LSD session. The first two types correspond to reactions that are too long and reactions that are too intense. The third includes those complications ascribable "only to the inexperience, carelessness, or incompetence of the therapist and responsibility must be attributed to him, not to the LSD."

The truth is that crisis situations can be drastically reduced in most cases with good preparation, screening, and proper training in handling psychedelic sessions. In addition, with adequate intervention at the time of crisis—if it happens—these can be resolved favorably, so psychedelic therapists, shamans, and facilitators should be prepared to face these apparently "too long and too intense" situations with sufficient resources, training, and skill, so that they are not overwhelmed.

COMMON PROBLEMS IN INTEGRATION: A NEW CARTOGRAPHY BASED ON CLINICAL EXPERIENCE

This section describes the most common problems found among patients who request integration psychotherapy. This classification comes from the experience accumulated over the years in my clinical practice, both in the ICEERS support service, in my private practice, and in my role as a facilitator of experiences in non-ordinary states of consciousness.

After several years being of service to hundreds of people, I realized that while their underlying motivations were diverse, the problems they presented could be readily classified into a few categories. The classification criteria are both etiological (based on the situation that has generated the problem) and symptomatic (descriptive of the specific problems that arise in each case). Furthermore, this classification is intended to be useful in choosing and guiding the most effective therapeutic intervention.

The cartography of adverse effects that I present here has evolved over the years and will likely continue to evolve: it is not a closed model. Here I merely describe my current understanding of this phenomenon.

The categories of integration problems are the following:

Lack of preparation or context
Unresolved difficult experience
Emergence of a previously unknown traumatic memory
Abuse by the facilitator/shaman and interpersonal difficulties
Traumatic dissociative experiences
Seeking out repeated experiences without proper integration
Previously existing mental disorder

Lack of Preparation or Context

As we have seen before, preparation is an essential aspect of the psychedelic experience, which includes, but is not limited to, the screening of the potential participant. Lack of preparation, as many authors have observed (Blewett & Chwelos, 1959; Cohen, 1985; Grof, 1980, among others), is a factor that can cause problems during the experience and afterward. Many of the cases that I have worked with were cases where the preparation had been insufficient or inadequate. In some cases, this was the main determining factor in the unraveling of later difficulties, and in such cases, the prognosis was more favorable and the integration intervention was usually simpler and shorter. In other cases, the lack of preparation was one factor in addition to other problems, resulting in a more complex intervention with unpredictable results.

Ideally, either the therapist or the facilitator should prepare the participants properly so that they can adequately approach the experience. There are several important aspects regarding a non-ordinary experience that every participant or patient should be aware of:

1) The substance being used and its possible effects. This includes the expected duration of the experience, the likely time frames for the appearance and disappearance of the effects, the nature of the effects elicited by that particular substance (both psychological and physical), and any possible residual effects the substance may have. Some therapists or facilitators may overlook some effects they dismiss as being obvious, but these can be crucial factors if the neophyte is unaware that these experiences are quite normal. Examples include the possibility of experiencing some anxiety during the initial come-up of the effects of MDMA or the purgative effects of ayahuasca.

2) The possible and expected range of experiences. Depending on the context in which a substance is used, certain effects may be more emphasized than others. For example, ayahuasca is often offered as a "medicine," priming the neophyte to hope that it will have the usual effect of a medicine, that is, make them feel better. However, we know that the healing mechanisms of ayahuasca often involve vomiting, different ways of purging, and a confrontation with unpleasant or difficult subjective experiences. For someone who is not aware that these experiences can be therapeutic, the appearance of these effects can be challenging and negatively alter the course of the session. Sometimes, there is a certain tendency to present only a limited range of possible experiences: either those of a spiritual, transcendental, and healing nature or quite the opposite, those that prioritize a deep search for hidden trauma, a confrontation with our demons, and experiences of deep catharsis. Both approaches are

biased; the healing facilitated by psychedelic therapy most likely contains elements of both categories.

Beyond these digressions regarding the possible therapeutic mechanisms, the truth is that the phenomenology of a psychedelic experience varies greatly, making it necessary to provide the neophyte with a map so that they can orient themselves, even if it is in a simple and basic way.

The map or cartography of the experience used will depend on the theoretical paradigm of each tradition. In any case, it should be presented for what it is: a map, never to be confused with the territory. It is a guide that provides context for the experiences that can take place under the influence of a psychedelic substance. Ideally, the cartography should be presented in a neutral way, without making value judgments about which experiences are better than others, but simply describing the different possible experiential realms.

An example of a useful cartography is what Grof calls the "expanded cartography of the psyche," in which he includes four large groups of experiences (Grof, 1975, 1980): 1) the abstract or sensory ones, 2) biographical experiences, 3) perinatal experiences, and 4) transpersonal experiences. In the Holotropic Breathwork workshops, a brief introduction is made to these large groups of experiences, indicating that the nature of the psychedelic experience is usually multilevel and elements of more than one of these groups are usually present in the same experience. Furthermore, two additional aspects are emphasized: the non-linearity of the experience and the fact that no experiences are better than others. The non-linearity of the experience refers to the fact that there is not necessarily a temporally linear development in terms of the appearance of the contents belonging to the different groups. A neophyte may have a purely transpersonal session while someone with many experiences under their belt may get to grapple with unresolved biographical questions. The type of experience does not imply anything about the spiritual or developmental level of the person or the potential usefulness or therapeutic value of said experience, with the exception perhaps of mystical experiences, which seem to be associated with greater therapeutic outcomes in relation to the different conditions that have been investigated (Griffiths et al., 2006, 2008, 2011, 2016, 2017; Garcia-Romeu et al., 2015). In terms of whether some experiences are more desirable than others, it is important to avoid bias during preparation since setting expectations about what is desirable to happen, or about the success markers of a session, can backfire. This situation can unfold differently depending on the particular bias introduced during our setup. Sometimes we find that people reject and dismiss "useless" pleasant and peaceful experiences, where no confrontation with any difficult or traumatic material takes place, and when the person is attached to the idea that healing happens exclusively that way. The opposite case is also common.

3) Creating a good bond with the facilitators or guides. In the words of Grof (2005), "Probably the single most important factor that determines the nature of an LSD experience is the sense of trust and security of the person having the experience. This depends critically on the presence or absence of a guide, his personal characteristics, and the nature of the relationship between the subject and this person." When a good bond is not established between the person who is having the experience and the person who facilitates it, multiple problematic situations can ensue. The key factor is that there is no sense of safety, so the person enters the experience with fear and mistrust. This can leave the person feeling like they are unable to ask for help during the session, therefore not receiving the necessary support or becoming suspicious about the context and unable to fully surrender to the experience, risking a bad resolution.

In my work over the years, I have observed that when people have had a difficult psychedelic session and require help in integration, they often turn to someone other than the person who led the session. This phenomenon is relevant as the lack of trust in the facilitator or leader of the session can be inferred. On one level, they may not want to worry or offend the facilitator, while assuming that if that person was not able to help during the session, they will not be able to support later either.

Establishing a good therapeutic bond should perhaps be the main screening factor that defines whether psychedelic psychotherapy with a particular person is a good idea or not. This question is bi-directional: Can the potential patient trust the psychotherapist or facilitator? At the same time, can the psychotherapist or facilitator trust the potential patient? If this trust-based bond exists, even the most complicated sessions can be solved successfully.

4) Knowledge of the context and the working paradigm. In addition to establishing a good therapeutic relationship and describing the cartography of the experience and the effects of the substance, it is vitally important to define the context and the methodology that will be used during the session. There are many ways to conduct sessions in non-ordinary states of consciousness: for example, psycholytic psychotherapy, psychedelic psychotherapy, the psychosynthesis of Salvador Roquet (1981), the Gestalt use of psychedelic substances, the traditions of the Ayahuasca churches, the shamanic ceremonies of different traditions, and seemingly infinite specific methods created by different therapists. These forms can differ extremely from each other, ranging from the internalized individual experience—with masks, headphones, and minimal interaction with the psychotherapist as is typical of traditional psychedelic therapy—to group sessions in which the participants use different substances (sometimes unknown to them), interacting between them and even forming family constellations or participating in other group dynamics facilitated during the experience.

Those who participate in a session must be informed beforehand of the dynamics and types of interactions that will take place between participants or facilitators, whether any specific practices will be carried out during the session, and the proposed boundaries. Taking these issues for granted can lead to very complicated and potentially harmful situations when participants discover, once they have already taken the substance, that nudity or sexual intercourse are allowed or encouraged during the session or that the therapeutic methodology consists of getting a high dose and staying alone in an abandoned building. As outlandish as they may sound, these are real cases that have actually happened.

The most important thing about having prior knowledge of the context and the dynamics that will take place during the session is that one can make a choice and freely accept it, becoming better able to make sense of whatever follows. Going into an experience without knowing how it will unfold may elicit additional problems if a participant ends up in a sub-optimal and undesired environment under the effects of a psychedelic substance. The feeling of helplessness, vulnerability, and lack of control in these cases can be quite traumatic.

On the other hand, there is also the preparation that each person does individually before stepping into a journey. This has to do with the specific motivations, study, reading, physical practices, and dietary preparations that the person has made before deciding to participate, also taking into account any personal work they have done previously. A participant's level of maturity is one key factor that determines whether or not they will take full advantage of the experience. According to Eisner (2002), a lower level of maturity makes it difficult for the person to take advantage of the experience and to make transformative life changes afterward. Thus, any preparatory psychotherapy should pay attention to fostering a certain maturity in relation to the psychedelic experience. While not much can be done in a short period of preparation, it is possible to promote greater cognitive flexibility that reduces expectations regarding specific outcomes. Oftentimes, people who suffer from a disorder that makes their day-to-day life particularly difficult have a tendency to see situations as either "black or white" or as "bad or good." Such rigidity can become a factor limiting the potential benefits of an experience as complex and rich in nuance as a psychedelic journey.

Unresolved Difficult Experience

This situation can derive from experiences in which psychological material with a high emotional intensity emerges and, for whatever reason, it cannot be fully resolved or processed during the session. In these sessions, people might find it difficult to trust their own experience and the overall process. There may be a certain resistance to opening up to the immediacy of what is happening or it may be complicated for various reasons (whether psychological, psychodynamic, or contextual), in spite of a willingness to open up.

In these cases, the experience may not fully resolve over the course of the session as we fail to get appropriate closure. We feel stuck in a difficult emotional space that interferes significantly with our daily life, even if we can still function. This can take the form of frequent uncomfortable and unpleasant emotional states, intrusive thoughts, rumination, or obsessions, the activation of defense mechanisms such as avoidance behaviors, or the activation of harmful behavior patterns.

In my experience, this type of situation can occur both in supervised psychedelic sessions and in self-experimentation, with substances of medium to long duration, such as ayahuasca, MDMA, psilocybin, and particularly LSD, given its specific effects and long "comedown." Although these difficulties can also occur with short-lived substances such as DMT or 5-MeO-DMT, in such cases the intensity is usually more significant, with subsequent panic attacks and more dramatic manifestations. These situations tend to more closely resemble the "traumatic dissociative experience" profile.

The mechanisms of action in these phenomena are flawlessly described by Grof (2005) in his description of COEX[33] transmodulations. According to Grof, the outcome of a psychedelic session and the clinical manifestation of the person does not depend so much on the amount or the nature of the unconscious material that has been processed, but on the COEX that remains active "at the end of the session." Despite a positive session, a negative transmodulation can occur if a negative COEX system is activated towards the end, resulting in a negative outcome followed by the corresponding clinical manifestations. This concept is similar to what Cohen (1963) and Shick and Smith (1970) have written regarding paying particular attention to the closing part of the sessions in relation to the likelihood of the manifestation of prolonged adverse effects.

Therefore, the closing part of the session is a critical moment, and special efforts should be aimed at providing the best conditions for a positive resolution to take place. This can only be done individually and by giving the person the time, space, and support necessary to process the emergent material and close the experience in touch with a positive COEX or, at least, with the largest amount of properly processed material.

In cases where the session is not appropriately closed, people often report feelings of "being stuck" in relation to the experience for days, weeks, and even months afterward. It may feel as if the experience has not ended yet, since the contents are still very present, even reappearing spontaneously or motivated by thematically or contextually related external stimuli. Although they are not particularly common in these cases, flashbacks may happen, that is, the re-experiencing of some episodes from the session. In these situations, however, a more constant yet less intense re-experiencing is more common, as if the interpretation of that person's external reality had been tinted by a colored lens.

It is helpful to introduce the concept of "closure" to better understand these dynamics, as well as to move forward towards a more adequate therapeutic intervention in the integration of these situations. In the tradition of Holotropic Breathwork, "closure" is understood as the period towards the end of the session. At this point, specific interventions are implemented to help the person process all the material that has emerged during the session, allowing them to return to a state of ordinary consciousness. Thus, closure occurs in the liminal spaces between the non-ordinary and the ordinary states.

In the case of psychedelic therapy, the effects of the substance may subside or even fade after a few hours, but this does not imply that the unconscious material that has emerged has been processed properly. Sometimes we may find ourselves in a situation where the effects have practically disappeared, and the person wants to go home, yet a feeling of discomfort remains. The desire to end the session sometimes involves an external attempt to change or escape an unpleasant internal situation, which may consist of difficult emotions such as fear or sadness, painful memories, states of confusion, psychosomatic pain, or uncomfortable thoughts, leaving us feeling like we would like the experience to end, by escaping or avoiding what is present.

We consider it good closure or a properly "closed process" when we recognize emotional stability, the material of the session has been sufficiently processed, there is no pain or physical tension, and the person does not want to "flee" the session. Regarding emotional stability, a wide and complex range of emotions may linger at the end of the session, even if they are not "positive" emotions. These emotions are a good place for closure not because they have transformed into positive emotions, but because their intensity has become manageable, and the person can accept them as part of their life experience for what they are.

Closing the session is often one of the most complicated interventions for most psychedelic therapists aware of its importance. Many therapists or groups that organize sessions with psychedelic substances or master plants do not even consider the closure as a particularly sensitive moment. They end sessions rather informally without paying much attention to what is going on, or they simply perform a closing of the energetic space and a collective closing of the session for the group. However, the closure that we refer to in this context is an individual and particularized closure for each participant. In the clinical trials with psilocybin for the treatment of depression in which I participate, the closing is understood as a crucial moment in the session. Both the therapist and the psychiatrist have to verify that the person is in a position to end the experience. During mentoring and supervised sessions, therapists report encountering the greatest difficulties towards the end of the sessions. In the context of Holotropic Breathwork workshops, the closing is carried out individually whenever each person feels ready, even though the sessions are done in a group setting. In group psychedelic sessions, an individualized closing should ideally occur, even if it is just an individual check-up with each participant.

In psychedelic therapy, the final moments of a session are extremely critical. Although the closing lasts longer than might seem necessary, those additional moments can make a big difference in the outcome of the experience, as they allow the person to start integrating the experience. At the same time, it is a unique opportunity to create a positive impression that can elicit greater well-being after the session. Even for therapists who factor in the importance of proper closure, this intervention is often complex since there are as many different cases as there are people and psychedelic sessions, and it is difficult to define a standardized practice to carry out the closing. Therefore, supervised experience and participation in sessions with more experienced psychedelic therapists is the best way to develop a good closing practice.

Lilly's case

Lilly had a panic attack towards the end of a poorly planned experience with a high dose of smoked DMT. The anxiety and fear of death persisted for months afterward, so she decided to go to an integration group and began taking psychiatric medication. Her anxiety lessened, but she was unable to think about the experience without becoming very nervous, and intrusive thoughts often assailed her, particularly thoughts of death. Lilly, a young woman with extensive knowledge of psychedelic substances, contacted me because she wanted to "make peace with the experience."

Because of the context of her work and her social environment, Lilly constantly talked about her emotional state and the problems she had integrating that experience. Her partner and her friends are all very experienced in the use of psychedelic substances, and they frequently asked her how she was doing. Given her signs of suffering, Lilly's friends recommended various calming practices, but nothing seemed to work. Alternatively, Lilly avoided thinking about the experience and only focused on the present discomfort and the "adverse effects." Thus, Lilly's attempted solutions were to avoid the experiential confrontation with the DMT trip and rely on the calming effects of social support as she spoke about her state with her peers. Neither of these strategies proved suitable for her.

Lilly was functioning on a high level, and she did not experience disabling anxiety. Her social environment was supportive, and she had not experienced psychological problems before. However, the experience was still very much present in her daily life, manifesting as intrusive thoughts, anxiety, and unhelpful avoidance behaviors.

Lorena's case

Lorena participated in an ayahuasca retreat in Peru, where the concoction was consumed about ten times over the course of two weeks. Our first session took place a year and a half after the retreat; she did not share anything about the specific content of the experiences. The issue was that, upon Lorena's return from Peru, she experienced what she called a "spiritual emergency" that lasted four months. Upon returning home, she had started behaving unusually, feeling euphoric and making decisions based on her dreams regardless of their consequences. She began an affair with another man, onto whom she projected many characteristics of what she then understood to be "masculinity." The story culminated when Lorena decided to leave her husband to continue the relationship with her new lover. The new relationship ended traumatically after a few months, and Lorena eventually "woke up" from her spiritual emergency, recognizing that what took place was a confrontation with her shadow, which left her with feelings of tremendous guilt and anxiety.

As we spoke, Lorena shared that she started having transitory anxiety attacks after she retired. During these attacks, she felt like she was going crazy and losing control of herself; she also experienced feelings of sadness and uncontrollable crying. She defined them as flashbacks from the ayahuasca experiences. These states were improved by physical exercise and yoga, psychiatric medication for anxiety management, and breathing techniques. Lorena also tried meditation but then gave up, since she felt the practice worsened her condition. However, these anxiety attacks have returned in the last two months and are now more intense and frequent than ever.

Emergence of a Previously Unknown Traumatic Memory

A situation that can generate difficulties during integration is when we "discover" a previously unknown memory during a psychedelic experience. These memories can include various different traumatic situations, although the most problematic ones tend to be the ones related to physical and sexual abuse, which are also the ones that most commonly emerge during integration psychotherapy. Other types of memories can be related to perinatal trauma, such as abortion attempts during pregnancy, traumatic experiences suffered by the mother, or the increasingly common experience of losing a supposed twin brother while in the womb.

The issue of recovering repressed memories dates back to the birth of psychoanalysis. Freud (1895, 1896) registered these phenomena while treating what was then known as hysteria. Through hypnosis, dream analysis, and free association, Freud discovered the supposed sexual origins of every hysterical condition. In order for the healing process to be completed, the person needed to gain access to this primary generating event, the repressed and inaccessible sexual trauma. In Freud's theories, even when the original trauma has been forgotten, it still continues to cause pathological manifestations (Freud, 1895, 1896, 1905). All later theories somehow comprise an evolution of these early Freudian theories and can be collectively called "repression theories." A hitherto unknown memory is recovered, which had been repressed from consciousness due to the psychological risk involved in coming into contact with it (Brown et al., 1998). In these theories, the therapeutic context provides the psychological security needed to lift the repression and allow these memories to surface (Briere & Conte, 1993). It is important to note that for Freud, the concept of repression was not related to "forgetting" or some other unconscious mechanism for the disposal of memories but to an intentional effort to eliminate something from consciousness (Freud, 1905).

At the other end of the theoretical spectrum, we find theories that argue that recovered memories are not real, but rather "false memories." According to these theories, these remembrances of early abuses and traumas do not correspond to objective events that happened in child-hood. According to these authors, traumatic memories and abuse are often so intense that the greatest difficulty lies in forgetting them, not in remembering them. Therefore, memories "recovered" in a therapeutic process, whether through hypnosis, regressions, guided imagery, or other memory retrieval methods are questioned and not taken very seriously (Ceci &Loftus, 1994; Ofshe & Watters, 1994). These theories can also be called "false memory theories."

The conflict seems to be deciding if the memories recovered in non-or-dinary states of consciousness are objectively real or not, if they occurred as the person tells them or if they are a fantasy. It seems that we have to decide on the interpretation of repression or the interpretation of false memories. The controversy that has accompanied this fact has caused harsh confrontations between different therapeutic schools (Crews, 1995; McNally & Geraerts, 2016), and even legal litigation between relatives, therapists, and authorities, with devastating results for all par-ties (Geraerts et al., 2008; Ofshe & Watters, 1994; Otgaar et al., 2017; Gudjonsson, 1997).

Most therapists, neo-shamans, and facilitators of psychedelic sessions believe in one way or another that it is possible to recover previously inaccessible memories and tend to assume the veracity of these memo-ries. They also believe that uncovering these traumas is a necessary step towards healing the symptoms and the disorders theoretically associated with them. Furthermore, they consider that such a discovery is not easy to achieve as many defense mechanisms block the path, so reaching the original traumatic episode is seen as a journey that requires time, anal-ysis, and multiple experiences (Ofshe & Watters, 1994; Spiegel, 1997).

This fits perfectly with the psychedelic paradigm, priming most people to believe in repression theories.

What recent research and meta-analysis seem to have found is that traumatic events are often remembered quite clearly and it is precisely this memory that causes discomfort:

> *Far from forgetting what happened, they were actually troubled by the recurrence of the dramatic memories. Thus, there is substantial evidence that what is often a problem for victims of traumatic childhood experiences is not the lack of memory of those events but the inability to forget them. (Ulatowska & Sawicka, 2017)*

These statements are quite consistent with current theories of post-traumatic stress disorder which, to oversimplify, base the suffering on the inability to block these memories and the continuous reliving of past trauma.

An alternative or complementary explanation, which is much closer to the clinical experience with people who have suffered abuse and have also experienced non-ordinary states (not necessarily with the intention of deepening the knowledge of trauma or healing it), is that of the simultaneous existence of different types of recovered memories, some that are objectively "real" and others that belong to the category of "false memories." Both types of memories can surface spontaneously and during psychedelic experiences.

The first category can be somewhat controversial. While child sexual abuse is an absolutely criminal, deplorable, and savage act, not all victims experience trauma as a result of abusive situations. This greatly depends on the child's stage of psychological development at the time of the abuse, their moral awareness of what is right or wrong, their understanding of what is normal and what is not normal. Therefore, we often find a certain ambivalence when treating people who have suffered early abuse. Many people report that although they did not experience this as traumatic at the time, they knew that something strange or unspeakable was happening to them. This ambivalence, exacerbated when the abuse is perpetrated by someone who is supposed to be a caregiver (such as a friend or member of the family), can be the cause of many later complications and difficulties in overcoming said episode beyond the abusive behaviors themselves. When these people eventually come into contact with the memories in adulthood—memories that may have been forgotten for years—they may realize that these were effectively abusive situations from their current adult perspective. This realization is often followed by difficult emotions, stress, sadness, and the need to reassess past events, sometimes even reviewing whole biographies in light of these "new" memories. Some people may even develop symptoms consistent with PTSD.

In these cases, the memory had not been repressed; it was simply forgotten, as the event was not considered something abnormal or traumatic at the time it happened, or perhaps the memory had been explicitly avoided as a coping mechanism. Many of these people also realize that they actually did have access to the memories of this event at other times in their lives but had forgotten it again. Therefore, the current memory is not new but a re-experiencing of something that had already been present.

According to some authors (McNally & Geraerts, 2009), the difference between these cases and cases rooted in "false memories" can be seen in the way the memory's appearance develops. On the one hand, the people we have described in the previous paragraph tend to recover these memories spontaneously, perhaps after a specific event such as a trip to a house where they used to live as children or the death of the person who abused them. They did not remember having experienced a traumatic situation before this event. On the opposite end of the spectrum, we find people who experience ongoing psychological or emotional difficulties in their daily lives and who are immersed in the process of actively searching for the causes of their suffering; potential childhood abuse is often a central theory in these cases. This hypothesis may be shared by the therapist they have chosen, and therapy can therefore be objectively focused on revealing such trauma. These people tend to recover traumatic memories gradually, through successive exposures to memory recovery techniques, whether they are interpretations, suggestions, dream analysis, or hypnotic inductions, or during experiential therapy sessions. Studies carried out by these authors suggest that the veracity of the memories recovered spontaneously outside of a therapeutic context is usually verifiable to the same extent as normal memories, while those memories recovered through a therapeutic process are not verifiable at all (McNally & Geraerts, 2009). The authors caution that this does not imply that the memories are necessarily false, but rather that they are not verifiable by the methods they used.

It is not the intention of this book to delve into the veracity or falsity of the recovered—or fabricated—memories that emerge in non-ordinary states of consciousness. Abundant literature on the subject exists, and the interested reader will find multiple publications discussing either "false memories" or repressed memories (Shaw, 2016). The intention is to present the theoretical foundations of these situations so that clinicians can form a more educated opinion and simultaneously lay out the difficulties that such situations entail for the integration of a psychedelic experience, while offering effective treatment mechanisms to overcome these difficulties.

Many modern therapists and facilitators like to engage in labyrinthine processes meant to uncover such memories while trying to discern whether or not what their clients are saying is real. In some way, we are experiencing a resurgence of this phenomenon, which already occurred in the 1970s (Ofshe & Watters, 1994), when experiential therapies based on trauma theories appeared. The psychedelic paradigm, particularly among practitioners who are not mental health professionals and do not have actual training in the field, tends to assume that the axioms of the recovery of unknown traumatic memories are true. However, there is abundant evidence pointing to the need to adopt a more cautious position, as strong advocates of these opposing theories coexist, as mentioned earlier. Therefore, it is necessary to offer and articulate a vision from the perspective of psychedelic therapy in relation to the recovery of traumatic memories through the modified states of consciousness.

Psychotherapy's greatest theorists have harbored these same doubts from the very beginning. Freud himself, after "discovering" the traumatic sexual origin of hysteria in case after case, began to doubt his own results (Freud, 1905). Either the rates of sexual abuse in Vienna were much higher than what most people believed or his patients were imagining rather than remembering. The answer, as usual, is probably somewhere in between. The data on the prevalence of sexual abuse is quite dramatic in the supposedly polite and "correct" environment of Western culture and the so-called first world, where approximately one in four girls experiences some form of sexual abuse before reaching adulthood. These abuses are remembered by people who answer these surveys. Thus, the problem responds to a lived reality and has to be approached appropriately, even when it does not bring us any closer to elucidating the veracity of the recovered memories related to unknown abuse.

Moreover, Freud's concern increased after the realization that recovering these memories often did not help relieve the symptoms nor did it cure the person's neurosis and, in addition, these memories seemed to appear too frequently (Freud, 1905, 1932). This called into question both his theory and psychoanalytic praxis in general. Freud was a staunch defender of his own ideas but he was also honest about the aspects of his theories he could not quite prove "yet." Even with all the criticism that Freud has received in recent decades, I believe that Freud's honest attitude should serve as an example for future generations of therapists. As is often the case, his disciples were more Freudian than Freud himself and were not as inclined to revise psychoanalytic theories in the same way that the Viennese pioneer did.

These instances eventually led Freud to doubt the veracity of the memories recovered during the analysis and consider them to be the "false childhood memories of hysteric patients" (Freud, 1905), which he distinguished from the "memory traces" imprinted by events that actually happened. These doubts led to a reformulation of the theory and the general understanding of primary trauma, as well as the concepts of repression and its mechanisms. In most cases, Freud abandoned the theory of "infantile sexual trauma" and replaced it with the concept of "sexual infantilism." According to this view, the etiology of hysteria and its subsequent symptoms did not derive from a traumatic event but from sexual activity during childhood and the child's struggle against these primary sexual instincts. Furthermore, the individual's own reaction to those sexual impulses and reactions became the key factor.

One of the pioneers of psycholytic therapy, R. A. Sandison, encountered similar problems when using LSD with his patients. His conclusion was similar to that of Freud and he stated: "Experience with patients suggests that the earliest memories are a mixture of fact and fantasy, and that they are re-lived with much vivid and colorful detail" (Sandison, 1959).

Cohen, another pioneer of psychedelic therapy, faced a similar dilemma when he encountered the emergence of what appeared to be repressed memories during LSD sessions. "He clearly saw how, as a child of four, he had smothered his baby brother in order to keep him from crying" (Cohen, 1960). After the session, the patient went to the police and confessed to the crime; he was not arrested, however, as there was no evidence. Sometime later, this patient had a psychotic decompensation. Whether their discoveries were "real" or not, we see that the emergence of such content can have devastating effects on a person's mental stability. In my personal experience, I had the opportunity to assist in a similar—and quite moving—case with a patient who participated in a clinical trial with psilocybin.

Steve's case

Steve is an older man with a difficult work life. He had held an important position as an engineer in a large company, but due to the economic crisis and the subsequent staff adjustments, ended up occupying a minor position in a smaller department of the same company. From then on, Steve fell into a deep depression tinted by anxious symptoms and somatizations, which made his daily life very difficult. Despite various pharmacological and therapeutic treatments, he experienced frequent pain.

Steve was able to access a clinical trial of psilocybin for the treatment of major depression and tried the drug twice: a low dose and a high dose. After a few weeks of apparent improvement, Steve's condition deteriorated dramatically. He went back to his previous antidepressant medication with no results. Eighteen months after Steve's experience, the research team contacted me seeking integration therapy since he was experiencing suicidal thoughts, massive anxiety, and very high levels of discomfort.

During his rich and complex psychedelic experience, Steve relived a scene from his childhood: When he was very young, his father had tried to smother him with a pillow. Unlike his relationship with his mother, Steve had always had a good relationship with his father, and consequently this vision left him very upset. If the memory was real, it could provide an explanation for his persistent depression, despite completely changing the way he remembered his father and his childhood. If the memory was not real, Steve would be back at square one. By this point, he felt worse than ever. The revolutionary psilocybin treatment had not worked. He felt left with very few options other than suicide. Furthermore, Steve described his high-dose psilocybin experience as "more real than reality itself."

Steve became obsessed with solving this existential predicament, sinking deeper and deeper into his depression. In his own words, the psilocybin experience had "added another layer" to his depression. In the next chapter, we will see how Steve's case was resolved.

Grof worked extensively with LSD and other psychedelic substances, mapping the effects that these substances could induce. Grof
not only describes the emergence of biographical memories but also
perinatal and transpersonal ones (karmic memories, past lives, and
so on). Due to his eminently clinical disposition, Grof did not debate
the historical veracity of these events; he simply acknowledged their
occurrence in the context of psychedelic sessions and spiritual emergencies. Grof's model incorporates the concept of COEX systems
as the structuring principles that provide the backbone for the content of a psychedelic experience. Grof defines the COEX system in
these terms:

> [A] specific constellation of memories (and associated fanta-
> sies) from different life periods of the individual. The memories
> belonging to a particular COEX system have a similar basic
> theme or contain similar elements, and are accompanied by a
> strong emotional charge of the same quality. The deepest layers
> of this system are represented by vivid and colorful memories
> of experiences from the period of infancy and early childhood
> (Grof, 1975, 1980).

Therefore, these "memories and associated fantasies" constitute a
COEX system, establishing the phenomenology of the psychedelic experience. Grof would later add perinatal and transpersonal dimensions to
his conception of what generates COEX systems. Thus, the primary levels
of a COEX would not be located in childhood but the trauma of birth
and even deeper in karmic tendencies and the archetypes of the collective
unconscious (Grof, 2000).

In psychedelic and Holotropic Breathwork sessions, we often witness
traumatic memories emerge from familiar situations, events that perhaps
were not examined in much detail up until then. It is also common to
find people who are going through difficult physical and emotional experiences that seem devoid of personal meaning. When these experiences

are related to situations of abuse, the event was often already known beforehand, although it had been consciously removed from memory. When dealing with a traumatic situation in a psychedelic psychotherapy context, we usually find an enhanced recognition and better understanding of a previously known situation and the emotional experience of the event itself, and not the recovery of a completely new episode.

Another highly controversial aspect regarding the recovery of traumatic memories has to do with the unusual and extreme nature of some of the memories. The literature on the recovery of traumatic memories abounds with accounts of terrifying abuse, such as ritual and organized killings; satanic cults in which young children are raped and murdered (Ost et al., 2014); alien abductions; intrauterine and perinatal trauma; and traumas in past lives or in the intermediate states or *bardos*. The unusual and eccentric nature of these experiences has sometimes served as an argument to discredit the validity of memory retrieval and, incidentally, the usefulness of these therapeutic models. However, through the prism of the psychedelic experience, these kinds of experiences are not phenomenologically unusual. In particular, all those experiences related to victim and perpetrator dynamics, abusive situations, perverse sexual experiences, dark or satanic magical-religious rituals, all sorts of atrocities and extreme suffering—they all correspond, in Grof's cartography, to the phenomenology of the third perinatal matrix (Grof, 1975, 1980, 2019). These experiences of alien abduction, communications with beings from other worlds or dimensions, contacts with UFOs, and other traumatic contents of a transpersonal nature have also been described as part of the common phenomenology of the psychedelic experience (Grof, 1975, 2002), particularly in experiences with ayahuasca (Shannon, 2003) and DMT (Strassman, 2001; Timmermann, 2018). They have also been described in Jung's (1964) analytical psychology, in psychospiritual crises (Grof & Grof, 2001), and from cognitive perspectives (Newman & Baumeister, 1996). Past life experiences and past life traumas are also themes explored by various authors (Grof, 2002; Stevenson, 1966, 1984,

1987), as are the events that take place in the intermediate spaces between one incarnation and the next (Newton, 2009). Therefore, given what is experientially possible as part of the psychedelic experience (and what can be part of the psychic contents in general), these manifestations could be understood as symbolic aspects of deeply rooted individual and collective dynamics that can emerge in an array of different contexts. Thus, rather than seeking the historical and objective veracity of such manifestations, they must be understood as psychic phenomena that constitute a "subjective reality" for those who experience them.

Building up to this point, research shows that it is possible—and quite simple—to implant false memories in individuals through certain psychological procedures and intentional persuasion (Porter et al., 1999). More worrisome is the possibility of inducing memories of abuse in people who have not been abused (Lindsay & Read, 1994; Spanos, 1996; Porter et al., 1999). Moreover, we now know that memories recovered throughout a therapeutic process are more likely to be false than memories that are recovered spontaneously in a non-therapeutic context (Geraerts et al., 2008). Particularly important is the fact that LSD—and by extension, any other psychedelic substances—increases the suggestibility of those who take it (Carhart-Harris et al., 2014). Suggestibility is an important factor in the outcome of a therapeutic process but it can become a double-edged sword, used in both positive and harmful ways. The final phases of a psychedelic experience are particularly prone to leave lasting imprints, as we saw in Grof's COEX transmodulation theory. Therefore, there may be lasting consequences to an interpretation given by someone with perceived authority (the therapist or the shaman, for example), arguing that whatever happened is a clear sign that the person has suffered repressed abuse.

In Freud's own words, "We don't often succeed in helping the patient recover those repressed memories. Instead, if the analysis is carried out properly, we produce in the patient a certain conviction of the veracity of the narrative, which achieves the same therapeutic result as a recovered memory" (Freud, 1938).

We should therefore be cautious, as therapists, before adopting certain paradigms a priori without having done the research needed to have an informed opinion.

After this theoretical presentation, it is still necessary to explain why someone who has experienced recovered memories may have difficulties during the integration period. Our intention is to understand and empathize with their suffering and to be able to provide the most appropriate and effective therapeutic response.

People who fit into this profile can be divided into two main groups: 1) Those in which the recovered memory has surfaced recently (let us say, in the immediately preceding psychedelic experience), and 2) Those who have been exploring this possibility for some time in their psychedelic experiences.

For people who have just discovered the abuse, the situation seems distressing and is perceived as urgent. On the one hand, there has been a traumatic psychedelic experience (with themes of abuse) and therefore difficult emotions and sensations have been experienced during the session. On the other hand, new information has appeared that clashes with the person's previous experience which now becomes impossible to reconcile with the established biographical narrative.

This situation usually leads to rumination regarding the veracity or falsity of this memory. Each aspect of this conflict is analyzed in detail and every attempt is made to get to the appropriate response. Let us imagine that the memory consists of sexual abuse perpetrated by a parent or grandparent, or any other incestuous situation.

On the one hand, if the memory is true, it means that the person is a victim of abuse. This could clarify certain aspects of their personal and relational challenges, explaining their suffering. However, assuming this reality completely changes the conception of who they are, and an identity crisis can occur. They have become an abused person. At the same time, this activates the need to make decisions in "real" life. Perhaps the person feels that they need to confront the aggressor, speak with the rest of the family, expose the situation, report it to the authorities, or cut all contact with their family. Clearly, choosing this interpretation is neither easy nor acceptable for the person.

On the other hand, if the memory is untrue and a fabrication of their mind, this implies that their mind is capable of conceiving these types of grotesque situations. The question arises as to what kind of person would imagine being abused by their father and project that sort of image of their family. In this situation, the experience adds nothing to the healing and evolution process. It is simply a traumatic experience that shows the person that they are worse off than they previously thought since they can imagine such atrocities (and often simultaneously experience ambivalent emotions and feelings about the situation, such as disgust, fear, and sexual arousal). Accepting this last option turns the person into a monster in their own minds, leaving the feeling that there is no hope for their suffering. This option is also unacceptable.

We see then that the person is caught in a lose-lose situation leading to more rumination. They are desperately trying to decide the right thing to do, and this may entail avoidance of social and family situations that include the possible aggressor. This creates much anxiety while also inducing a sort of paralysis. These people usually come to therapy demanding answers and asking, "Is what I have experienced true? Help me decide."

In the second case, when the person has spent some time exploring the possibility of potential abuse, and their psychedelic experiences indicate that it may be true, the situation is usually different. These people often go to therapy due to worsening symptoms and not because of the explicit content that may have appeared during the session, which can be unclear and undefined. These people experience symptoms that may or may not be related to a potentially abusive situation; however, the main point is a lack of clarity regarding the resurfaced trauma, which inhibits their capacity to overcome the situation. New psychedelic experiences do not usually provide greater clarity, but the opposite: They tend to pile on new information and details that make the situation even more confusing. This profile is similar to what I have termed "repeated experiences without integration," the main difference being the predominantly obsessive pattern related to the search for a primary trauma, the neglect of everyday affairs, and other disabling symptoms, which are now considered to be byproducts of that elusive trauma. What differentiates these cases is the lack of schizotypal symptomatology, nor is there a loss of contact with consensus reality: people tend to remain functional (at least in the initial stages of this situation). Their self-image, however, has been rooted in the obsessive belief in an original trauma that is inevitably determining the course of their lives. Furthermore, this search for the primary trauma, or the belief in a specific trauma, can lead them to make bad personal and interpersonal choices. For example, the belief that two people shared a common trauma in a past life or a past intrauterine experience can lead them to believe that they have to fix the trauma in this lifetime. Therefore, they must leave their respective partners and start a relationship. The longer we continue to live with a potentially false memory—the more it becomes part of our life's narrative—the more difficult it becomes to let go of it, since the thought that our memories were merely symbolic fabrications can suggest even greater insanity.

Jesus' case

Jesus is a well-mannered, agreeable, and intelligent young man who, since his teens, had experienced psychological problems in the form of anxiety, depression, and obsessive tendencies. As part of his therapeutic process, he tried various alternative therapies, including psychedelic substances, transpersonal therapy, attending retreats, and undergoing shamanic diets. While his knowledge of his inner dynamics had increased throughout this process, his symptoms were worse than ever. He suffered from constant obsessive thoughts, which prompted him to perform complex rituals. For example, Jesus could not read continuously because he would often come across "tainted" words, requiring him to write down antonyms to counteract their effects. A similar issue took place when he talked to people or saw numbers that were also contaminated. Furthermore, Jesus had obsessive thoughts about death. As a consequence, his social life was non-existent, and he was unable to maintain any type of job. He lived in total isolation and was financially dependent on his family.

In his psychedelic journeys, Jesus had been scanning his entire biography looking for a trauma that would justify his suffering. Unable to find it, he continued to inquire and explore what he called "past lives" in other times and galaxies. Although Jesus found traumas in those lives, they were never the original trauma, and therefore he had to keep investigating. The more he inquired into those domains, the more acute his obsessive compulsive symptoms became.

During therapy, an approach was taken to reduce the obsessive symptoms, allowing Jesus to live a more normal life. The first interventions reduced the frequency and intensity of the rituals. However, although he recognized that this approach would probably improve his symptoms and quality of life, he was fixated on another type of approach: using psychedelics to deepen his introspection. After I shared my opinion that this would likely not improve his situation and that I could not provide the type of therapy he was looking for, our therapeutic relationship ended by mutual consent. Paradoxically, Jesus chose to follow his own path and managed to leave his house and embark on a journey to the Peruvian jungle, searching for healing through shamanic diets. We remained on good terms, and months later he told me that he was continuing his learning and healing process in a retreat center in Peru. After a year, Jesus contacted me again; the obsessive symptoms had worsened, and he was still searching for an explanation for his suffering. He had now adopted a narrative wherein a shaman had thrown a *"virote"* (a harmful energy dart) at him some years ago. Although Jesus was not successful in curing his obsessive disorder, he had delved deeply into the shamanic path and gained knowledge of the traditional Amazonian system. To this day, Jesus is still on his path and is an example of courage and determination.

Abuse by the Facilitator/Shaman and Interpersonal Difficulties

Harmful interactions between participants and shamans or facilitators are another possible source of integration difficulties. As the interest in ethnobotanical tools increases, particularly the globalization of ayahuasca which has now reached sectors of society traditionally uninterested in these practices, the frequency of these cases also increases. Concurrent with this global expansion, there has been an increased interest in the knowledge and practices of many shamanic traditions and many individuals claim they want to "become shamans" to heal other people. Ayahuasca workshops and ceremonies have multiplied exponentially, both in countries where traditional uses of ayahuasca still exist like Peru, Brazil, Ecuador, and Colombia, and also in places like the United States, Europe, Asia, or Central America. Not all these retreats are managed ethically and professionally, and people who assume the role of facilitator or shaman are not always adequately prepared, nor do they embody the human qualities required to heal or even support other people through this process. The same occurs with the use of psychedelic substances such as MDMA or psilocybin, which have become increasingly popular as alternatives to conventional treatment.

There are different types of potentially problematic interactions between shamans or facilitators and participants. In the first scenario, we have cases in which the person guiding the session lacks the preparation and experience necessary to manage the situations that might unfold during a psychedelic experience. The second scenario is related to expressly abusive and harmful behaviors that the facilitator inflicts on the participant.

Let us look first at those situations that involve unskilled or under-trained facilitators. When the sessions go smoothly, offering psychedelic substances to someone else is relatively straightforward and most people will have positive experiences most of the time. The person might even see the inexperienced guide as being special and possessing outstanding abilities. It is quite easy to gain power and recognition by offering psychedelic experiences and guiding others on their journeys. However, when things go wrong and the experiences become difficult, the actual experience and knowledge of the guide are demonstrated. There are cases in which people attend a ten-day retreat and feel ready to offer sessions to others afterward. Some indeed do offer sessions to others. We have also witnessed certain companies who boasted of training psychedelic facilitators, leading groups without any formal training after having had only a few sessions themselves. Many charlatans have popped up in Amazonian countries, where ayahuasca has become a very profitable business, disguising themselves as healers who conduct sessions for unsuspecting and naïve tourists. Even in formal research contexts, some therapists who assist experimental subjects might lack the therapeutic training and preparation needed to support people in non-ordinary states of consciousness. Becoming a healer requires a long learning process, which includes repeated exposure to non-ordinary states of consciousness and, above all, continuous supervision. The same is true for psychotherapists and psychologists: the designation requires specific and lengthy training, as well as supervised practices.

Therefore, the poor management of a potentially difficult experience is a primary cause of challenging integrations. Facilitators with little experience or inadequate training may react in ineffective or even harmful ways to situations that may be relatively common over the course of psychedelic therapy, such as the activation of aggressive internal dynamics, sexual content, the trauma of abuse, transference, situations of emotional dependence, or experiences of extreme vulnerability related to omission trauma. In such cases, good intentions cannot be a substitute for knowledge, experience, or training.

A more serious situation that is, unfortunately, more common than we would like is explicit abuse by the shaman or the facilitator of the participant. Over the years, I have heard dozens of testimonies from people who have suffered different types of abuse, including physical, emotional, psychological, economic, sexual, and power-related abuse.

Some therapists, shamans, or facilitators may try to get things from their clients: money, recognition, power, followers, or even sex. Hearing about these experiences firsthand reminds us that reality is indeed stranger than fiction. Some internationally recognized and popular shamans carry dozens of cases alleging sexual abuse or abuse of power. Anonymous underground therapists or groups that organize ceremonies with different substances carry out dubious, unprofessional, and certainly unethical practices that can cause psychological problems in their patients and participants.

The difficulty the participant faces in these situations is twofold. Firstly, the person must deal with the challenging experience during the workshop itself. The severity of such an experience can vary considerably, from sexual or emotional abuse to a rude and painful intervention during a group share or integration group to the ongoing poor management of a difficult situation throughout the workshop.

Secondly, there is potential for more significant damage since the person inflicting the harm is responsible for ensuring the safety of a healing experience. The participant has placed total trust in the shaman or facilitator, surrendering to a psychedelic experience under their care, and unwittingly becomes a victim of abuse. In such cases, a fundamental trust crisis takes place, in which the individual who is expected to be the savior becomes the perpetrator.

In these situations, we face symptoms related to the specific content of the experience. However, we also face added difficulty related to feelings of helplessness, shame, and confusion; the struggle to make good judgments about the situation; and a generally disconcerting ambivalence concerning the shaman or facilitator, their practices and actions, and the outcome of the process as a whole. Thus, there is a mixture of symptoms, some of them derived from traumatic events, and some based on relational issues that impact the person's self-esteem and their ability to make objective judgments about the situation.

This can all be exacerbated due to the fact that victims are often met with a negative response from the community or group that follows the teachings of the shaman or facilitator; the victim is often labeled a liar, told that they are exaggerating and are blind to the shaman's true intentions and practices. The person can be effectively gaslit by their community, which shuns or withdraws their support, blaming the person for instigating conflict within the community. This situation, as can be imagined, has implications that go beyond the psychological and overflow into the social lives of the affected persons.

Michaela's case

Michaela is a young woman who has had a difficult life. She has sought relief from her suffering through living in community and working with master plants. She is intense, passionate, and brave, with the ability to travel to all corners of the world to participate in rituals and learn from shamans and facilitators. She has vast experience in all sorts of shamanic practices. Underneath a semblance of strength and independence, Michaela is perceived to be quite a vulnerable woman. Sadly, her trajectory of working with shamans and master plants is full of traumatic experiences. In the recent past, Michaela had a romantic relationship with a high-profile facilitator of *Bufo alvarius* experiences. This facilitator, who has a dubious reputation in the psychedelic world, abused her on a psychological, physical, and sexual level. On one occasion, alone in their room, the supposed shaman gave her a very high dose of this substance. Michaela lost consciousness, and upon waking up she felt that the person in question had abused her.

On another occasion, as Michaela was engaged in a healing and learning process with a famous *ayahuasquero* in the Peruvian Amazon, she suffered another instance of abuse. During an ayahuasca ceremony, the shaman and her assistants performed a "cure," which involved inappropriate touching of her breasts and genitals. This took place repeatedly over a few successive sessions.

While these events were painful and traumatic enough already, the truly devastating part was being questioned and rejected by her community once she shared with them what had happened.

Traumatic Dissociative Experiences

This particular problem involves two different aspects: 1) What happens during the session and 2) The symptoms that appear later, during the integration period.

Although the content of the session is usually very disturbing, both from the point of view of those who experience it and from the point of view of those who witness it, people mostly reach out for integration support based on the symptoms that appear well after the session. We will describe each of these aspects in more detail.

During the Session

Experiences that usually lead to difficulty during the session are extremely intense experiences of difficult negative emotions, particularly fear—which can become true panic—and aggressiveness, which can result in violence.

When analyzing the nature of the fear we experienced, we see that it often comprises paranoid feelings and thoughts. The participant feels they will be attacked, whether by the organizers of the ceremony (who now appear to be leaders of a dark sect), by ghosts, demons, incorporeal entities, spirits, or other non-physical beings (or a combination of both, in which the session leaders or facilitators are joined by evil spirits wanting to cause harm to the participant). Sometimes, we may experience the emergence of fear and paranoia without a specific reason or awareness of what is causing it. The breakdown of trust in the guides, the session, and the process itself may lead to attempts, of greater or lesser intensity, to protect and defend oneself against these attacks, perceived to be external. People may then try to escape, lock themselves in the bathroom, hide, attack, or harm others (including themselves) in a desperate attempt to feel safe.

This manifestation can be described as psychotic: an external projection of an internal experience in which the individual loses touch with the consensual reality shared by the rest of the people present at the ceremony.[34] This projection often involves erratic behaviors such as inappropriate yelling, punching, or intruding into the space of others, among other unpleasant attitudes. In such circumstances, it can be difficult for the people guiding or facilitating the session to remain calm and support the person adequately.

These circumstances tend to become dramatic due to their relative rarity, the number of resources required to deal with them, and the fact that they usually disturb the development of the session as a whole. In many cases, the tension can become such that physical restraint is necessary to avoid greater damage, even when the physical restraint in itself ends up being one of the factors that contributes to the experience being perceived as traumatic for all those involved.

Handling these situations in the best possible way requires extensive resources. Firstly, it requires a team of facilitators or at least enough assistants; that way, at least two to four people can pay attention to the person experiencing the crisis while the others remain in the ceremony or session with the rest of the group. If this occurs in a clinical setting (which is much less common), a minimum of two people are already present (the two therapists), supported by a team of nurses and psychiatrists who can assist if needed. In the context of a group, we also need the proper distance to be able to deal with this situation. As we have written before, these experiences can cause serious disturbances in the dynamics of the rest of the group. Therefore, it is necessary to have an isolated and quiet area designed to help the person feel safe, preferably furnished with mattresses, cushions and blankets, and free of any material perceived as dangerous. Furthermore, the assistants must be trained in non-violent and effective physical containment to protect the person and themselves. Lastly, for all of this to work, a good bond must exist between the participant and the team helping them.

Frequently, the resources we need are not available, the facilitators lack the capacity and experience to react appropriately, or the situation simply overwhelms the team due to its intensity. It is not uncommon for people who go through these episodes to sustain scratches, bruises, and even broken bones. In more severe situations, the person wanders through open spaces beyond the retreat, attempting to escape the threatening situation, with the additional risks and fear that this implies. Sometimes other professionals such as the police, firefighters, or health services may intervene. The situation can vary in intensity, but it almost always results in a profoundly traumatic experience.

It is important to recognize that a psychedelic experience can be retraumatizing or create trauma where there was none before. This should be clear to anyone who is exposed to such experiences and, in particular, to those individuals who offer these experiences. In Chapter 2, we covered the factors that can help minimize the likelihood of these situations: The best way to prevent these challenging episodes is to thoroughly screen participants, properly prepare them for the experience, and be honest about the resources and experience available.

A characteristic aspect of this profile is that the psychotic symptoms manifested during the experience will usually subside as time passes and the substance metabolizes. The person returns to a notable degree of "normality;" the aggression, paranoia, and erratic behavior have all but disappeared. We will observe some situations later in which this symptomatology does not disappear and must be addressed pharmacologically after the experience; however, this pertains to a different profile. In this case, the psychotic break does not last beyond the psychedelic session.

After the Session

Most patients I have attended to have come to me after taking ayahuasca in a neo-shamanic context. Other colleagues who work in this area have reported similar observations: It seems that these reactions happen more frequently with ayahuasca. The reason is not obvious, and there is no way of determining whether it is due to some particularity of the substance or the context, because of the particular type of people who choose to participate in these sessions, or because ayahuasca is the primary substance being used in psychedelic circles (thereby more people are exposed to its effects). I have also encountered similar experiences in recreational settings with the use of high-dose LSD. In these settings, I typically have direct experience with the development of the crisis and its immediate resolution, but not of the medium and long-term consequences, nor do I know whether or not they needed integration psychotherapy.

When I first encountered these cases, I did not have a very clear idea of what could have triggered the crisis, the subsequent symptoms, or how to deal with it. However, I observed that people typically approached me a few days or weeks following a session, not because of what occurred during the session but instead due to the symptoms they developed post-session. These symptoms often included insomnia, feeling startled, distress, intrusive thoughts, the feeling of re-experiencing the effects of the substance (especially when the lights were off or right before falling asleep), flashbacks, feelings of dissociation, depersonalization and derealization, low moods, and avoiding certain situations that may be reminiscent of the experience (leaving the house, being with the lights off). In addition, I often encountered amnesia concerning the events that occurred during the experience or confusion about whether or not the events took place or were imagined.

As we can see, the issues have little to do with the symbolic material of the session but rather with what happens afterward. Most people report "having had a bad trip" and wanting "to be like they were before the experience." That is, there is no express request for integration of the content of the session. The aim is to get rid of the adverse effects that have appeared.

The list of symptoms that people reported matched quite precisely what the DSM-V describes as "acute stress disorder,"[35] a disorder that can occur after experiencing traumatic situations and that can turn into post-traumatic stress disorder if a series of diagnostic conditions are met, including the persistence of these symptoms for more than a whole month.

In this particular case, what we have is a traumatic experience that takes place during a non-ordinary state of consciousness: a trauma induced by a psychedelic experience. As paradoxical as it may sound nowadays, even though psychedelics such as MDMA and ayahuasca can be used to treat trauma, they can also induce it.

Paracelsus famously wrote that *dosis sola facit venenum* ("it is the dose that makes the poison"). Of course, the dose is a decisive factor in this regard, as Hanscarl Leuner pointed out when he spoke of the different courses of a psychedelic experience: the scenic course, which is therapeutic, as opposed to the fragmented-psychotic one, which is not beneficial and can even be counterproductive (Passie, 1996).[36] As per Grof (1985), we could add other important factors in the case of psychedelics such as dose, the personality of the subject, the personality of the therapist, set, setting, preparation, and integration.

Some people have ironically proposed a new diagnostic category: PSSD, or Post-Shamanic Stress Disorder, and it is even the title of a psytrance music album. Although it is a rare experience, it has potentially serious consequences.

Georgina's case

Georgina, a woman in her thirties with extensive experience in therapeutic processes, decided to participate in an ayahuasca retreat as part of her personal growth path. During the experience, she experienced intense fear—she was afraid of disappearing. Georgina traveled through spaces that she interpreted as *bardos* or intermediate spaces, limbos, and hells. After the experience became extremely intense, Georgina got up from the circle and, totally out of control, began to undress, speak loudly and yell at other participants, insult others, pull her own hair, scratch her skin and face, and bite her own arms. The facilitators had to physically restrain Georgina and when she finally came to her senses, she did not remember anything except feeling exhausted, expressing a feeling of peace and relief as the experience ended.

In the days following, Georgina felt a constant sense of unreality and very high anxiety, especially at night. These night terrors overwhelmed her as she experienced intense panic reactions. She moved in with a friend who was able to support her for a couple of weeks until she calmed down.

However, some problems remained. Georgina continued to suffer from a great deal of anxiety and insomnia, fearing that she could lose control again, and sometimes she felt like she could exit her own body. In order to deal with the situation, she avoided any potentially stressful situations and always fell asleep next to someone, as she was terrified of being alone. This caused major disruptions in her day-to-day life, to the point that she needed to leave her job and stop doing most ordinary activities.

Seeking out Repeated Experiences without Proper Integration

The following profile is particularly interesting because of how little attention it has received in the psychedelic and psychotherapy literature. Perhaps one of the reasons is that the number of these cases has traditionally been limited and has only grown in recent years due to the hike in interest, the globalization of psychoactive substances, and an increase in their availability, in particular the use of different ethnobotanical tools such as ayahuasca, *Bufo alvarius*, changa, rapé, and kambó, among others, in neo-shamanic contexts.

This situation is characterized by frequent or very frequent exposure to non-ordinary states of consciousness. There is usually a primary technique or substance—often ayahuasca—used for psychonautical, exploratory, or therapeutic purposes, later combined and interspersed with a diversity of other experiences and substances, almost always with the same therapeutic intention. Although there is often a main group or therapist they attend more frequently, these people tend to alternate between different groups and participate in a multitude of ceremonies in different contexts. These individuals lack continuous monitoring of their progress and it is difficult for the session facilitators to gauge how the participant's process is unfolding, form a clear idea of their "normal" psychological state, and notice any suspicious or worrying changes. In contrast to this shamanic learning process, psychotherapy or other formal techniques provide participants with a reference figure who can support them effectively during the process and maintain a global perception of the participant's development, stages, and evolution.

People who seek out repeated experiences often report an increase in intensity as their sessions go by. After an initial period in which the sessions contain mostly personal elements related to their biography and their search for healing in shamanic practices or non-ordinary states of consciousness, the experiences begin to incorporate mainly transpersonal content, with multiple energetic and spiritual elements that could be described as belonging to the astral dimensions. A characteristic that differentiates these experiences from other well-integrated transpersonal experiences, which happen in stages of psychological and spiritual maturity, is the confusion that appears during and following the experiences. The confusion is shared with the people close to them: relatives, friends, and fellow travelers. If they see a therapist, the practitioner is also often unable to make sense of the experiences shared by the person.

The experiences and the daily life of the person are now packed with unusual phenomena, such as the presence of energies, spirits, entities, beings from other dimensions, synchronicities, and suspicious coincidences that are perceived as highly significant elements. These types of psychic phenomena are characteristic of schizotypal thinking, in which strange psychological and physical experiences and unusual sense-making abound. Another common phenomenon is the tendency to perceive conspiracies of spiritual, alien, or cosmic magnitude. Self-referential ideas are also common: The ongoing feeling that the person is at the center of events, that others are talking about them or are conspiring against them. People may feel like they can read minds or have energetic connections with other people.

Often, another phenomenon is happening in parallel to this growing mental disorganization: the abandonment and neglect of other areas of personal life. These people focus exclusively on their inner experiences and seek repeated access to new psychedelic experiences. Attention is directed only to spiritual phenomena, to the detriment of biographical dimensions, interpersonal relationships, work or financial issues, and sometimes even physical health.

In parallel to these events, annoying and inexplicable symptoms appear, apparently unrelated to the person's inner work, although they are evident to the therapist. Isolation and avoidance behaviors, social anxiety, insomnia, hyper-alertness, fear of the dark, the gradual decrease in daily activities, and episodes of generalized anxiety are quite common. These symptoms are the ones that usually set off the alarm signal and motivate the person to find professional support.

One of the characteristics of these situations is a tendency to seek more experiences in search of the resolution of these confused states. Although the person feels that they are advancing and learning, that their knowledge of non-ordinary realities has increased, and that they can perceive things that they did not perceive before, a feeling of incompleteness is always present, as if there was a puzzle to be solved. Most of the time, the idea is that one more experience can provide the solution. The next experience can always be the definitive one, which will help us understand, integrate, and solve everything that is happening. This, of course, is rarely the case, and approaching a problem like that only makes it worse. As Don Juan said, "Your fault is that you seek suitable explanations, explanations that fit you and your world" (Castaneda, 2018).

This situation can be understood as a combination of the so-called spiritual bypass with a lack of psychological maturity which prevents the person from becoming aware of the true unfolding of the situation. For many people, the seeking process starts because of relatively specific reasons: a certain phobia, social anxiety, or some other precise symptom. However, throughout this process, the initial goal is usually replaced by another goal, often less specific and more difficult-to-resolve issues, such as the spiritual aspects that we pointed out. It is an example of cases where the attempted solution becomes the main problem.

This situation can become potentially serious: As the person's psychic life deteriorates, anxiety levels increase, and the symptoms interfere dramatically with the person's daily life. At the same time, the lack of attention to other areas of personal life begins to cause secondary problems in the workplace, family, and relationships.

Although this phenomenology is not usually described in psychedelic therapy manuals, nor in treatises on psychonautic and explorations of expanded states, we find references to such situations in different spiritual traditions.

Alan Watts compared the use of psychedelics on a spiritual path to the use of the microscope by a scientist: "The biologist does not sit with the eye permanently glued to the microscope, he goes away and works on what he has seen." In the Zen tradition, meditative experiences are understood as *makyo*, meaning illusion or, in its literal translation, the "devil's cave." Clinging to these experiences, however spiritual they may be, is just another form of self-deception that distances us from true spirituality. In view of the current explorations regarding the use of psychedelics, this can even be dangerous and counterproductive (Legget, 1977).

A useful metaphor is that of a group of moths hovering around a bright bulb, smashing into the glass one after the other, unable to let go of the light. The moth either spends its limited life span blinded by the light and unable to see beyond it or dies, burned by the heat emanating from the bulb.

Another similar description can be found in the prologue to Badiner's work (2015), in which Stephen Batchelor writes: "One Theravada monk likened the mind on psychedelics to an image of a tree whose branches are overloaded with low-hanging, very much ripened, heavy fruit. The danger is that the heavy fruit—too full and rich to be digested by the tree all at once—will weigh down the branches and make them snap."

Some iconic figures from psychedelic culture, such as John Lilly, Marcia Moore, and Terence McKenna, went through episodes that could be understood as manifestations of repeated experiences without adequate integration. Despite this, these authors knew how to formalize, systematize, and transmit what they learned in their experiences in a way that has been useful for later generations of psychonauts and researchers, regardless of how many of their ideas and inner journeys can seem pretty strange, even for people in psychedelic circles.

I was surprised to discover descriptions of similar situations in different spiritual traditions. In the Jewish tradition, one of the main spiritual practices is the study of sacred texts. The Hasidic schools distinguish between two types of texts: those that are "רוא" (*Ohr*, light) and those that are "כֵּלִים" (*Kelim*, "vessels"). The *Ohr* texts contain mystical and esoteric teachings, while the *Kelim* contain halachic (law-related) questions of daily application. Excessive study of mystical texts without deep roots in the *Kelim* texts can lead to *ribuy orot*, "a multiplicity of light," which implies an "overabundance of immersion in the mystical rapture and an uprooting and a loss of contact with reality" (Mishor, 2019). The community's Rabbi is the person in charge of helping his students find balance between the *Ohr* and *Kelim* texts.

In Hinduism and the yogic traditions, there are concepts similar to the one we characterized as repeated experiences without integration. Swami Vivekananda, who was studying with Sri Ramakrishna, shared his experience of *siddhis* (supernatural powers, such as clairvoyance, that can manifest during *sadhana* or spiritual practice). Ramakrishna immediately ordered him to stop practicing until these powers disappeared. When he reported back that no visions or non-ordinary states of consciousness appeared in his practice, Sri Ramakrishna replied, "That is fine!" Those who get attached to this type of experience (visions, non-ordinary states— *siddhis*) are called *yoga-brashtas* or "the fallen ones of yoga." These people have confused *visesha-anubhavas* (visions) with *brahma-jnana* (knowledge of oneself, or the ultimate self).

Kornfield (1997) talks about Buddhist views on non-ordinary states of consciousness and the danger posed by non-ordinary experiences such as visions, energetic openings, *kriyas,* and kundalini experiences, among others. On the one hand, they can be profound experiences of ecstasy and physical and emotional release, but on the other hand, they can become an obstacle in our path of psychological healing and spiritual growth when we get attached to them and keep trying to repeat them over and over again. Kornfield says that, "Spiritual experiences in and of themselves are not worth much," and that "they do not bring wisdom." In addition, according to Kornfield, and in a concept similar to the "spiritual emergency" of Stanislav and Christina Grof (Grof & Grof, 1995), excessively intense or sudden openings can create imbalances in our daily lives. The symptomatology described by Kornfield is similar to the casuistry that we describe in this section, although mixed with characteristics of some of the other profiles that I propose in this cartography (unresolved experiences, traumatic experiences, spiritual emergencies). These symptoms include intense agitation, lack of sleep, paranoia, disorientation, loss of boundaries, physical symptoms, and in some cases, psychotic symptoms such as hearing voices, visions, and hallucinations. Kornfield also speaks of "close enemies," described as "qualities that arise in the mind, disguised as authentic spiritual fulfillment, when in fact they are only an imitation that further separates us from our true feelings, rather than helping us communicate with them."

In the *Dhammapada* discourse, Buddha says to his followers: "One who has no longing for this world or another, who is free from craving and aloof from detachment, is one that I call priestly." In other words, without attachment to this world or other worlds. Attachment to non-ordinary states of consciousness and the notion of how things should be can become a factor that derails us from our path of psychological healing and spiritual evolution.

In the previous chapter, we saw how ego inflation can have negative consequences and how it can occur as a result of repeated experiences without integration, even if less intense than what we have described here and with less serious consequences. Jung spoke of ego inflation as an identification of the personal self with aspects alien to it, such as archetypes or numinous contents and the eschatological knowledge of the collective unconscious. The consequences of ego inflation range from a distortion of the ego, as is evident to almost everyone except the affected person, to a dissolution or destruction of the ego. This latter case corresponds more specifically to the description that we are proposing here, although this phenomenon can obviously manifest with different degrees of severity. According to Jung, this phenomenon happens when consciousness absorbs too many unconscious contents without gaining the ability to discriminate which conditions allow consciousness to exist (Schlamm, 2014). Paradoxically, this expansion of consciousness ends up triggering a regression towards unconsciousness.

Previously Existing Mental Disorders

Another situation that can become a source of complication after a psychedelic experience is when the person suffers, or has previously suffered, a serious mental disorder. One of the risks attached to psychedelic substances is the precipitation of symptomatic episodes in people who have previously suffered them (Smart & Bateman, 1967). People diagnosed with a previous mental disorder, or who have suffered manic, psychotic or depressive states before, may experience a reappearance of symptoms during or after the use of psychedelic substances (dos Santos et al., 2017).

My clinical experience in these cases is limited, particularly in relation to the acute stage of these episodes. The symptomatic manifestations are usually so intense that the person or their family members often resort to emergency psychiatric care services where the primary treatment is typically psychiatric and pharmacological. Antipsychotics, mood stabilizers, and benzodiazepines are the most common drugs prescribed. It is relatively rare, although not impossible, for a person going through such a situation to seek psychological care in the first instance. In most of these cases, however, the family members are the first to contact an integration psychologist, as they often lack any knowledge about psychedelic substances and master plants: They do not know what to do, whom to turn to, or what is the most appropriate treatment. After the initial emergency intervention, the family often needs information about what happened, as well as guidance and support as the treatment unfolds.

Integrative psychotherapy should not be limited to the person who is immediately suffering an adverse reaction following a psychedelic experience. If the person reaching out is a family member of the affected person, there are efficient ways to engage in psychotherapeutic and psychoeducational work that is useful for the family. Such an intervention can positively influence how the episode is being addressed and, furthermore, provide support to the caregiver, who is probably the person with the most influence on the psychological state of the affected person.

Gonzalo's case

Gonzalo had reached out to me in the past, and we had met for a single counseling and support session concerning his use of psychoactive substances in recreational contexts. After using substances, he sometimes experienced prolonged episodes of instability, including disconnected and even delusional thoughts, insomnia, and manic tendencies. Gonzalo had been previously admitted to a psychiatric hospital and had taken antipsychotic and anxiolytic medication for a period of time due to an apparent psychotic break. After a period of stability, he stopped taking the medication and led a relatively normal life (although his social context was complex, as he had no job or studies and depended on the financial support of his parents).

Two years later, I received another request from Gonzalo for an integration session and we made an appointment. However, the next day, I started receiving inconsistent emails, calls, and messages from him. He would share strange, delusional thoughts he had, emotional problems, and doubts about his sexual identity. At times, Gonzalo would ask me about plots against him and wanted to verify my involvement in them. In addition, he interspersed insults and inappropriate interpellations. Given the situation, I decided to treat him urgently that same day.

Gonzalo was clearly agitated. Unable to sit still in the room, he lit one cigarette after another while simultaneously saying that he wanted to quit smoking because "they" were killing him with the tobacco and the messages that "they" put on the cigarette packs. Gonzalo kept jumping from one topic to another incessantly, and it was very difficult to understand anything he was saying. During the session, I tried to establish a relationship of trust. Little by little, Gonzalo shared what had happened in more detail. His current state of mind had started after taking ketamine several times, intensifying over time. He had been feeling the situation getting out of hand for over a week, while his partner tried to support him through it. My perception was that a manic episode was unfolding.

I was able to speak with Gonzalo's partner, who confirmed what he shared with me and helped me better understand the situation. I tried to find a psychiatrist who could provide a diagnosis and start drug treatment to prevent the situation from getting worse. Although Gonzalo's condition was worrisome and his psychotic episode was still unfolding, I felt that he was still in touch with reality and timely intervention could keep the situation under control. I thought pharmacological support could help regularize his sleep (Gonzalo had not slept for two days), hopefully normalizing the situation without requiring psychiatrization.

Unfortunately, I could not find a professional who could take care of him on such short notice. His very supportive family members came to pick him up that day and took him home. After a visit to the psychiatrist, Gonzalo's family decided to commit him to a psychiatric hospital. After spending three weeks in the hospital, he returned to a more normal state and was able to begin the recovery process.

Some months later, Gonzalo contacted me again. The experience at the psychiatric hospital had been very traumatic, but luckily his parents moved him to a better hospital where he received good care. After some time on intensive medication, Gonzalo returned home and progressively reduced the dose of antipsychotics which he had initially been prescribed. We scheduled a couple of sessions to deal with some problems related to social-anxiety and decided to stop there, since he was feeling well and was able to take care of his own life.

HIC SUNT LEONES: SPIRITUAL EMERGENCY, PSYCHOSIS, AND INTEGRATION

One of the issues that raises major doubts and fuels ongoing debates in the psychedelic community, particularly amongst facilitators of sessions and ceremonies, is how to differentiate between a spiritual emergency and a psychotic episode. Should the potential complications after a difficult psychedelic experience be understood as a spiritual emergency or as a pathological process that could be diagnosed as psychosis?

The term "spiritual emergency" was coined by Stan and Christina Grof, and refers to both an "emergence" and an "emergency or urgency" situation. The Grofs defined spiritual emergencies as:

Critical and difficult phases of an experience, which entail
a profound psychological transformation that involves the

whole being. They take the form of non-ordinary states of consciousness and involve strong emotions, visions, and other sensory changes, strange thoughts, and various physical manifestations. These episodes sometimes revolve around spiritual themes; they include sequences of psychological death and rebirth, experiences that appear to be memories from other lives, feelings of unity with the universe, encounters with mythological beings and other similar themes (Grof & Grof, 2001, 57).

The Grofs also distinguish between two ways in which these types of experiences are presented. On the one hand, we have an emergent spiritual experience, and on the other hand, the spiritual emergency. While most people in the psychedelic community are familiar with the second term, few are familiar with the first. In the Grofs' original conception, a spiritual emergence is framed in the broader context of an "evolutionary process that leads to a fuller and more mature way of life" (ibid., 60). This process can be slow and gradual, and often even unconscious, for we often only realize it when we look back and see how we have changed over the years. This process often evolves naturally over time, unfolding with different phases and themes, while our life adapts to these changes progressively and fluidly. However, "When the spiritual emergence is very quick and spectacular, what is otherwise a natural process can turn into a crisis; that is, a spiritual emergence or awakening becomes a spiritual emergency" (ibid., 62).

Anyone who has undergone a process of psychological or spiritual evolution is familiar with the ups and downs that the process entails, what Jack Kornfield calls "spiritual roller coasters" (Kornfield, 2001). Phases of expansion and phases of contraction follow one another throughout a process of transformation. Sometimes we experience the joy and happiness inherent to the ecstatic phases of our process, while at other times we must deal with painful emotions. All of this is part of a "spiritual emergence."

The concept of "spiritual emergency" is reserved for much more dramatic situations, which interfere significantly with the person's daily life. Descriptions of the different types of spiritual emergence and Christina Grof's own experience are an example of this (Grof & Grof, 2001; Grof, 2019).

Many people who are in the process of therapeutic or psychological evolution self-diagnose a spiritual emergency when they go through difficult experiences. However, only a minority of these cases would meet the actual criteria established by Grof to define spiritual emergencies; therefore, most of these cases should be understood as complex phases of a spiritual emergence but not an emergency. Thus, we can only diagnose a spiritual emergency when exceptional circumstances dramatically interfere with the person's life.

The diagnostic criteria needed to distinguish between psychosis and a spiritual emergency are described by the Grofs, and include both medical and physiological examinations as well as cognitive evaluations regarding the person's capacity for discernment and the nature of the experience, the person's anamnesis, the content of the experiences, and the presence and quality of coping mechanisms (Grof & Grof, 2001, 307-308).

John E. Nelson (2008) has also described the aspects that must be explored in order to differentiate between a spiritual emergency and a psychosis, practically coinciding with those proposed by the Grofs.

COMMON PROBLEMS IN INTEGRATION: A CARTOGRAPHY OF ADVERSE EFFECTS			
TYPOLOGY	ETIOLOGY/CAUSES	USUAL SYMPTOMATOLOGY	DYSFUNCTIONAL ATTEMPTED SOLUTIONS
1. LACK OF PREPARATION	One or more of the following: • Lack of knowledge about the effects and possible range of experiences. • Lack of knowledge of the context in which the experience takes place. • Interpersonal interactions. • Lack of bonding with the leader of the session.	• Confusion regarding what happened. • Concern and anxiety about the implications of the experience and its possible consequences. • Doubts about one's own psychological state. • Paradigm or worldview crisis.	1. Forcing the spontaneous: • Pretending to react normally in exceptional circumstances. • Minimizing the impact of the experience 2. Postponing that which is feared: • Avoiding talking about the matter. • Trying to fix it on our own, not seeking help.

COMMON PROBLEMS IN INTEGRATION: A CARTOGRAPHY OF ADVERSE EFFECTS			
TYPOLOGY	**ETIOLOGY/CAUSES**	**USUAL SYMPTOMATOLOGY**	**DYSFUNCTIONAL ATTEMPTED SOLUTIONS**
2. DIFFICULT UNRESOLVED EXPERIENCE	• Emergence of psychological material (unconscious or not) of a high emotional intensity that is not processed and resolved adequately during the session. • Lack of "closure." • Negative COEX transmodulation at the end of the session.	• Flashbacks (usually mild-moderate intensity). • Anxiety. • Ongoing and permanent contact with emotions and unresolved content. • Intrusive thoughts, rumination. • High reactivity to situations that remind of the experiential contents.	1. Postponing that which we fear: • Avoidance of experiential confrontation with our present emotions. • Avoidance of places or situations that may increase awareness of what happened. • Avoidance of future non-ordinary experiences. 2. Forcing the spontaneous (trying to eliminate unpleasant emotions): • Attempt to induce relaxation. • Attempt to reduce anxiety. • Distraction and calming-down mechanisms. • Breathing exercises. • Use of alcohol and other drugs.

COMMON PROBLEMS IN INTEGRATION: A CARTOGRAPHY OF ADVERSE EFFECTS			
TYPOLOGY	ETIOLOGY/CAUSES	USUAL SYMPTOMATOLOGY	DYSFUNCTIONAL ATTEMPTED SOLUTIONS
3. EMERGENCE OF PREVIOUSLY UNKNOWN TRAUMATIC MEMORY	• Appearance of an apparently biographical experience of abuse, previously unknown. • Interpretation of the experience by the facilitator or therapist as an indication of actual abuse. • Attribution of difficulties in the present moment and in everyday life to potential unknown abuse or trauma at the biographical, perinatal, or transpersonal levels.	• High anxiety • Intrusive thoughts and ruminations about the event. • Needing to reach a conclusion about the veracity of the fact, which generates anxiety. • Ambivalence about the scenarios that both options imply. • Anxiety related to the need to take action (legal, family, etc.) if the memory is true. • High reactivity to situations that remind of the experiential contents.	1. Forcing the spontaneous: • Trying to decide: forcing a conclusion with insufficient and ambiguous information. • Pretending to solve the situation through rational analysis. • Forcing a simple resolution to a complex issue. • Over-analysis of experience. Request for definitive interpretations from different professionals. 2. Postponing that which we fear: • Avoidance of interpersonal contact with the people involved in the memory (when previously there was contact).

COMMON PROBLEMS IN INTEGRATION: A CARTOGRAPHY OF ADVERSE EFFECTS			
TYPOLOGY	ETIOLOGY/CAUSES	USUAL SYMPTOMATOLOGY	DYSFUNCTIONAL ATTEMPTED SOLUTIONS
4. ABUSE BY FACILITATORS / SHAMAN AND INTERPERSONAL DIFFICULTIES	• Inappropriate interactions between the session guides and the participants. • The guide's lack of experience or ability. • Bad intentions on behalf of the guide. • Power, economic or sexual abuse. • Abuse in an asymmetrical relationship. • Traumatic interpersonal experience in non-ordinary states of consciousness. • Rejection and invalidation by the community.	• Loss of basic trust in care-based relationships. • Variable symptoms depending on the case; usually symptoms compatible with traumatic situations. • Ambivalence towards the perpetrator: Abuser vs. healer. • Shame, guilt, and a sense of isolation. • Intense, difficult emotions: fear, anger, sadness.	1. Forcing the spontaneous: • Trying to eliminate negative emotions. • Doubting who is responsible for what happened. 2. Postponing that which we fear: • Avoiding talking about it, for fear of generating further rejection. • Experiential avoidance with difficult emotions. • Social isolation, silence.

COMMON PROBLEMS IN INTEGRATION: A CARTOGRAPHY OF ADVERSE EFFECTS			
TYPOLOGY	ETIOLOGY/CAUSES	USUAL SYMPTOMATOLOGY	DYSFUNCTIONAL ATTEMPTED SOLUTIONS
5. TRAUMATIC EXPERIENCE WITH DISSOCIATION	• Very intense experiences with the presence of: panic, paranoia, loss of control, erratic behavior, possible aggressiveness, extreme acting out. • Ineffective containment maneuvers by facilitators that can lead to serious interpersonal situations. • Apparently "psychotic" experience (which reverses over time).	• Symptoms similar to acute stress disorder. • Panic attacks, generalized anxiety, distress. • Insomnia, nightmares, flashbacks. • Depersonalization and derealization. • Cognitive difficulties. • Low mood. • Few complaints regarding the content of the session.	1. Postponing that which we fear: • Avoiding experiential confrontation with present emotions. • Avoidance of places or situations that may increase awareness of what happened. • Request for help. • Avoidance of loneliness. Dependence. 2. Forcing the spontaneous (trying to eliminate unpleasant emotions): • Attempt to induce relaxation. • Attempt to reduce anxiety. • Distraction and calming mechanisms. • Breathing exercises. • Use of alcohol and other drugs. (Neither of these mechanisms typically work).

COMMON PROBLEMS IN INTEGRATION: A CARTOGRAPHY OF ADVERSE EFFECTS			
TYPOLOGY	ETIOLOGY/CAUSES	USUAL SYMPTOMATOLOGY	DYSFUNCTIONAL ATTEMPTED SOLUTIONS
6. SEEKING OUT REPEATED EXPERIENCES WITHOUT INTEGRATION	• Too frequent exposure to non-ordinary states of consciousness. • Use of different methods and substances. • Little rooting and grounding in everyday life. • Lack of integration strategies. • Increasing the intensity of sessions. The material that emerges becomes mainly transpersonal and difficult to relate to everyday life.	• Increasing confusion regarding the meaning of experiences. • Abandonment of daily activities. Exclusive focus on non-ordinary states. • Schizotypal phenomenology: synchronicities, delusions, conspiracies, concern for aliens and spirits, ideas of reference. • Psychic disorganization, unstructured understanding of the situation. Disorientation regarding one's own needs. • Seemingly unrelated symptoms: social isolation, increasing anxiety, fear of loneliness or darkness. This is what usually motivates the demand for integration.	1. Forcing the spontaneous: • "More of the same:" trying to solve all problems through "one more experience." • Although they tend to vary in techniques, the principle is always the same: healing through non-ordinary states (ayahuasca, toad venom, MDMA, breathwork, etc.) • Striving for an absolute solution to all problems through a supposed spiritual enlightenment or a definitive experience. 2. Postponing that which we fear: • Avoiding dealing with relevant personal issues (both past biographical events and present situational issues). • Spiritual bypass.

COMMON PROBLEMS IN INTEGRATION: A CARTOGRAPHY OF ADVERSE EFFECTS			
TYPOLOGY	ETIOLOGY/CAUSES	USUAL SYMPTOMATOLOGY	DYSFUNCTIONAL ATTEMPTED SOLUTIONS
7. PREVIOUS MENTAL DISORDER	• Exposure to an experience in non-ordinary states that for some reason causes a destabilization (sudden or progressive) of the psychological state. • There are usually past episodes of emotional instability or a relatively severe psychiatric history. • The use of psychedelic substances is sometimes motivated by a search for greater well-being or healing.	• Severe psychological destabilization. • Exacerbation of symptoms: manic states, delusions, or psychotic outbreaks. • High-intensity and long duration of these symptoms requiring external support, often psychiatric medication and hospital admission.	1. Forcing the spontaneous • There is usually a tendency to try to control the onset of the episode by one's own means, and to avoid the intervention of third parties. • Family and friends can cause a forced internment, which can be a traumatic experience. 2. Postponing that which we fear: • "Trying to control until losing control" (fear of psychiatric admission or medication, therefore help is not requested and the problem escalates).

In clinical practice, it is challenging to establish such clear criteria and there are very few cases where we can affirm without a doubt that we are facing a true spiritual emergency. Most of the time, the episode is not severe enough to be classified as an emergency and, even when the episode is severe, it is difficult to miss aspects that could point to a possible psychosis. Most of the transpersonal therapists I have spoken to agree that, throughout their careers, they have seen very few cases of spiritual emergency as described in the literature. In my limited experience, I have only seen one case that strictly coincided with a spiritual emergency of the "kundalini awakening" type; half a dozen cases that fluctuated between emergence and emergency but could not be classified, based on their phenomenology, as either of the types described by the Grofs; and two cases that combined aspects of a spiritual emergency and psychosis.

Literary examples of turbulent episodes where we cannot be sure whether the protagonist is going through a spiritual emergency or developing some kind of pathology can be found in the novels *The Catcher in the Rye* and *Franny and Zooey* by J. D. Salinger and in the novel *Demian*, by Herman Hesse. These situations effectively describe the ambiguity of such episodes, which often makes it hard to choose the appropriate approach.

However, establishing a diagnosis is of little interest from a clinical and therapeutic perspective. What is genuinely innovative in the Grofs' approach is not so much "spiritual emergency" as a diagnostic category, but the proposed treatment approach for such episodes, which differs from the usual treatment for psychosis. Therefore, the relevant question is not, "Is this a spiritual emergency or a psychosis?" but rather, "Which treatment is going to be more useful for this person: Do we treat this as a spiritual emergency or as a psychosis?"

The main factor to consider when deciding on the best treatment is whether the person is aware or not that what is happening is due to an ongoing internal process and whether they are willing to deal with it. In cases where the person is not able to understand the intra-psychic nature of the conflict and addresses it by projecting outward and blaming others, with a poor understanding of what is going on (for example, the presence of delusions, manic states, paranoia, and a feeling of persecution, etc.), the most useful approach still seems to be the use of psychiatric medication meant to control the symptoms, after which we can continue with a therapeutic process. This criterion is common in both Grof's and Nelson's models, since the establishment of trust is vital for the success of any therapeutic process, particularly if non-ordinary states of consciousness are involved. Of course, we are referring to the period after the session, when the pharmacological effects have worn off and a reasonable time has elapsed which makes it safe to assume that the intensity of the symptoms should have decreased or disappeared. In fact, many manifestations common during a psychedelic experience coincide with the phenomena described in spiritual emergencies, but they do not constitute a spiritual emergency, as the person is still under the influence. This type of experience, if well supported and well resolved, can be profoundly transformative. Neither a psychosis nor a spiritual emergency can ever be diagnosed in the acute phase of the experience.

In cases where people comprehend the experience as the unfolding of an internal process, it is possible to approach the treatment as a spiritual emergency. The context is equally important as, depending on the available resources (space, personnel, time), some cases may be successfully handled and others not. According to Grof's model, if we had a private center at our disposition, sufficiently staffed by people trained in transpersonal psychology who could work shifts around the clock supported by a comprehensive treatment program, we could support much more complex cases than what we are able to offer with a one-hour videoconference session once a week. Thus, beyond the diagnosis, contextual factors and the availability of resources must also be taken into account.

The approach we present in this book is not meant to facilitate a diagnosis of either psychosis or spiritual emergency but rather to provide useful therapeutic answers for the array of complex situations that can arise after a difficult psychedelic experience.

In the terminology used in this chapter, the conditions that can lead to "emergency" situations are mainly those that I have grouped into the "traumatic dissociative experience," "seeking repeated experiences without proper integration," and the "emergence of a previously unknown traumatic memory." These are typically the situations with the most destabilizing implications in the person's daily life and require immediate intervention, and therefore do imply a sort of emergency. However, the emotional, cognitive, and phenomenological manifestations can vary quite a lot from those described in Grof's literature on spiritual emergencies. In general, we can observe common elements such as high anxiety, psychosomatic symptoms, intense emotional states that disturb daily activities, and confused cognitive processes. In my experience, it is difficult to classify these situations under the eleven profiles described by the Grofs.[37] A recent publication, *Breaking Open: Finding a Way Through Spiritual Emergency* (Evans & Rhead, 2020) illustrates the various manifestations of a spiritual emergency differently, and is probably the best example of the types of crises most commonly encountered.

Grof further described an increasingly common situation: the so-called "possession states," where people feel that they have been attacked or possessed by some evil spirit or entity. This phenomenon, which deserves a whole other book, is much more common in the context of the use of ayahuasca, particularly when embedded within Indigenous worldviews such as the Shipibo or the syncretic *Santo Daime* churches. However, it can also be found amongst people who experiment with smoked dimethyltryptamine (DMT). This complex phenomenon has sparked many fierce debates among proponents of the different worldviews. Beyond the debate regarding the ontological reality of such situations, the fact is that these phenomena are becoming the quintessential spiritual emergencies of our time, and they pose a real challenge for clinical practice.

In my experience, these cases are difficult to treat for multiple reasons. They can be understood as a combination of some of the profiles that I have previously described, including repeated experiences without proper integration, the emergence of a memory (in this case, something that happened during an experience: possession), and a potentially traumatic dissociative experience. In a traditional Indigenous context, these situations must be resolved by an experienced shaman who can expel the entities and restore balance. However, the situation is more complex when the affected person is a Westerner who constructs their reality based on Western cultural parameters, and they may or may not partially agree with the animist/spiritist worldview. This means that treatment by shamanic means is often only partially effective and can sometimes even be quite harmful. Frequently, seeking more experiences with ayahuasca or DMT does not improve the problem but instead worsens it (this coincides with the profile of seeking repeated experiences without proper integration). An alternative treatment would typically include elements described in the usual literature (Grof & Grof, 2001; Kornfield, 2001; Nelson, 2008) designed to help the person settle down, as described in the corresponding section. However, the resolution of a possession experience often requires some work under non-ordinary states. In my experience, such cases are best handled in the context of Holotropic Breathwork, where manifestations of demonic possession are not judged, and their expression is supported, whereas in ceremonial contexts these types of experiences can be disruptive and lead to some of the situations we have described in this chapter.

The following two cases describe processes that could be understood from the perspective of spiritual emergency because of the context, how they manifested, and, above all, because of the therapeutic approach used to treat them. The first case describes a process triggered by a romantic break-up in which non-ordinary experiences were the main therapeutic approach. The second case describes an emergency that arose after exposure to various experiences in non-ordinary states of consciousness. Both cases describe elements that traditional psychiatry would diagnose as highly pathological and treat with psychiatric medication. The following cases demonstrate how a broader approach can effectively address the symptoms and facilitate the resolution of the process as a whole.

Katharina's case

Katharina's process was long and complex due to the multitude of symptoms and emotional manifestations that she presented. These included self-destructive behaviors, difficult and conflictive interpersonal relationships, and the emergence of what appeared to be a dissociative disorder (multiple personalities). However, the process was approached primarily as a spiritual emergency, which allowed it to unfold safely under continuous monitoring. While serious situations in Katharina's day-to-day life were difficult to manage, the intervention consisted mainly of intensive supportive psychotherapy and a long series of Holotropic Breathwork experiences. The drawing of mandalas was a crucial tool during her process. The following is Katharina's account in her own words:

The process was triggered by the end of a very dependent relationship that I had to my partner at the time. That relationship had been the center of my life. My friends, my community, my home, my hobbies, and even my job were built around that relationship. So when it was over, I was plunged into a deep life crisis. I felt that I was a burden, that I was not loved by anyone, and that I was not welcome in this world.

I was unable to ask for help and the situation got more and more out of control. At one point, I felt that I was fragmented into different sub-personalities that were in charge of attending to those daily needs that I could no longer manage. There was no connection between those individual pieces and my identity was seriously disorganized. I felt like I was in a process of death and rebirth, and my internal chaos was overwhelming me.

During this process, past experiences of the sexual abuse that I had suffered throughout my life emerged in my consciousness.

I felt hatred towards myself and towards my body. I was distant from everything and I felt that death was more present than life itself.

The beginning of the healing process happened with the establishment of trusting relationships with the Holotropic Breathwork facilitators, throughout many sessions in which I felt like a needy baby. I experienced the trauma of my own birth and what it felt like not being loved by my mother. I came into contact with a deep loneliness and understood that many of my current emotions came from that time. By expressing these intense emotions during the breathwork sessions, coupled with incessant drawing and the experience of feeling seen and cared for by the facilitators, I was able to build, little by little, a new concept of myself. Thus, my healing advanced in baby steps, through confronting my traumatic experiences and connecting with other human beings.

My conflicts related to sexual abuse cropped up over and over again over the years, but the more I dealt with the conflicts of my early childhood, the better I was able to deal with the experiences of abuse. My problems didn't go away, but I found a different way to handle them. I realized that my self-destructive behaviors were a normal response to an abnormal childhood. This allowed me to be more compassionate towards myself, and I stopped judging myself for those behaviors—eventually that became the key to stopping them altogether.

Furthermore, thanks to the care provided by the facilitators and everything that I had learned in the Holotropic Breathwork sessions, I was learning to take better care of myself. When this happened, I no longer had a need for my sub-personalities and they disappeared one by one. I began to develop healthier relationships with other people while being better able to manage my own needs.

As this process deepened over the years, I realized that my problems were not something exclusively personal. I tapped into some energies on a transpersonal level and understood that I was dealing with something collective, even though I had my own biographical experiences related to it. This allowed me to feel more connected to the rest of the world as I went through these experiences.

Seven years after the end of the relationship that had marked the starting point of my process, I felt that somehow I had come to a conclusion. Not everything was perfect in my life, but I had learned that not everything had to be. I am now more loving to myself and I feel more welcome, just the way I am. Nowadays I don't have the need to hold onto others and be part of dependent relationships.

Barbara's case

Barbara is a psychiatrist with extensive experience treating psychotic patients. Towards the end of her four-year psychoanalytic process, she decided to participate in a week-long Holotropic Breathwork module. Her sessions were long and difficult, and it took her considerable time to return to an ordinary state of consciousness. Her behavior was somewhat eccentric, and she spent long nights without sleep, but she managed to recover satisfactorily and came back feeling empowered.

A short time later, a refugee who had been admitted to the mental hospital where Barbara worked hanged himself in her room. She was the first to find him and to ask for help, but attempts to revive him were in vain. The episode had a profound impact on Barbara's emotional state.

A few months later, Barbara had her first experience with MDMA. Although the context was appropriate and she was well cared for, the experience was overwhelming. Barbara had not been able to take time off work and had to rush to a twenty-four hour shift at the hospital immediately following her experience. That shift turned out to be particularly difficult and Barbara had trouble getting back to an ordinary state of consciousness.

During the following weeks, Barbara began to feel progressively more unstable. The circumstances at the hospital did not help either: Four young patients, all diagnosed with psychosis, were found dead in what appeared to be possible suicides. Coincidentally, one of those patients had a twin brother, just like the man who hanged himself in her office. Barbara began to think that the hospital was cursed, and she developed strange fears. For example, fear that she would hurt herself or that she would jump out of the window while she was sleeping.

Barbara decided to take a vacation and participate in another Holotropic Breathwork module, where a full-blown crisis broke out. She experienced intense emotions, strange physical sensations, and severe pain that forced her to make sounds, gestures, and engage in stereotypy. She relived multiple biographical episodes, as well as the recent incidents in the hospital. Barbara remained in a continuous non-ordinary state, needing support at all times, every day. The facilitators and the team took turns making sure that she was safe, nourished, and rested. In order to sleep, Barbara had to resort to benzodiazepines.

Upon returning from the breathwork training, the symptoms persisted, and she had to stay with her mother for a year. A group of facilitators from the Holotropic community provided ongoing support. Barbara continued taking high doses of sedatives, and a psychiatrist familiar with spiritual emergencies prescribed low doses of antipsychotics. During this period, she received intensive psychotherapy.

Barbara's process continued to unfold. For several months, she constantly drew mandalas, many of them. She performed strange rituals, took long walks, and looked for ways to ground herself. Her inner experiences pervaded every dimension of her life. Barbara was overwhelmed by all sorts of memories, ideas, intense emotions, and racing thoughts about future projects.

About seven months later, Barbara was somewhat more stable and she was able to participate in Holotropic Breathwork retreats once again. The most extreme phase of the crisis was followed by a period of depression and frustration during which she progressively regained her independence. Twelve months after the crisis broke, Barbara was living on her own again, working as a psychiatrist in a new job. Despite her challenging processes, she lived a "normal life" in the following years.

To this day, Barbara continues to deepen her understanding of this episode. She finds that "a psychiatrist's emergency" is the term that best describes her experience.

Drawing from a young woman after a challenging MDMA experience, in which she got in touch with deep emotions of sadness and despair related to traumatic childhood events. The hand that comes from the right side represents the support of the facilitator during the difficult moments of the experience, although the contact is not complete. The complex contents that arose did not resolve well during the session and the integration process was difficult and challenging.

Examples of collages made according to Seena Frost's original SoulCollage technique and one using free technique (upper left).

Mandalas illustrating symbolic aspects of perinatal content as well as early experiences of deprivation. These experiences were hard and difficult to integrate as they were closely related to early biographical experiences in which elements of domestic violence were abundant. The ambivalence towards the birth process as well as the difficulty in surrendering to the experience due to the need to maintain control hindered the complete resolution of the sessions and their integration.

In these images, we can recognize contents related to abuse experiences, both at a biographical and transpersonal level. In this case, the experiences were perceived as related to biographical aspects that had really happened, but combined with archetypal and transgenerational elements.

A challenging aspect of the patient's process was the development of a dissociative disorder in which she experienced having different subpersonalities that were related in a complex system. Throughout the period depicted here, the patient was integrating these subpersonalities.

Examples of integrative experiences through connection, in the final stages of the therapeutic process. The patient not only concluded the therapy, she also completed her training as a facilitator and currently organizes her own workshops.

MANDALA 1
THE DIVINE CHILD

Examples of the use of mandalas and creative writing in the process of integration of a spiritual emergency and Holotropic Breathwork sessions. The images and text that follow are by John Ablett. A full report of John's history can be found in *Breaking Open* (Evans & Read, 2020). More mandalas from John's work are also published in *Into the Deep: Integrating Psychedelics and Psychotherapy* (Read & Papaspyrou, 2021).

"These mandala artworks were made approximately three years apart. They represent before and after 'snapshots' of a powerful spiritual emergency in which I believed I was enlightened and travelled as a barefoot guru in my early twenties.

At that time (Mandala 1), I felt transcendent, as if I could do or be anything."

MANDALA 2
THE UNBORN TWIN

"Returning home (Mandala 2), I felt naive and traumatized, rendered spiritually homeless and deceived by my own thought processes.

Holotropic Breathwork experiences in non-ordinary states of consciousness enabled me to reframe my story as a symbolic narrative told in terms of amplified and reimagined biographical experiences."

MANDALA 3
THE NEGOTIATION IS MORE IMPORTANT
THAN THE OUTCOME

"In my session, I 'dream' that I travel to the Lower World (Mandala 3), swept along by the Drums of War. Like a clockwork toy, I find myself unable to stop, until I become a Skeleton Drummer, summoning the armies of the world to fight to the death.

When I cry out: 'Stop! I don't want to fight my father!' there is finally peace between opposites. My unborn twin is there, amongst the Masked Spirits, who ask me to pray for them.

I leave alone through a tiny opening, gathering again amongst the community of the living, where I survey the devastation of a battlefield and we collectively mourn the dead on Armistice Day.

Emotions rooted in transcendent imagery inspire multitudes to go to war when taken literally and projected outwards. I recognized that the passion and energy that drove my spiritual transformation was also the source of the internal conflicts I felt following my spiritual emergency."

**MANDALA 4
THE GOOSE BOY**

"In this session, (Mandala 4), I am frozen in the moment between birth and death, unconsciously 'carrying' my unborn twin inside a series of nested symbols.

My unborn twin became a symbol of every life cut short—the children who died in infancy, the refugees drowned at sea, and the soldiers who died in battle not even knowing that the war was over.

In paying homage to the most embryonic life, I found myself honoring all lives. When unconscious personal experience becomes collective through acceptance and expression it represents a particularly poignant moment of integration."

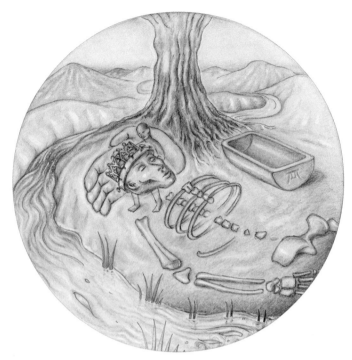

**MANDALA 5
LAYING THE
BONES TO REST**

"In this session (Mandala 5) I'm carefully laying out the bones of an Ancient King. When I finally reassemble them all, they are too large to fit into the child-sized coffin.

In connecting with our own unexpressed stories and telling them, we feel our own share of the world's collective traumas and contribute to the wider work of integrating them into society. In this way, integration is a necessary counterpart to the visionary flight of the Shaman or the Guru. Unlike the heroic inner journey however, the sacred work of integration is slow and unglamorous, often closer to the work of an archaeologist.

Whereas the symbolic unborn twin can travel anywhere or be anything, her returning human counterpart must carefully sweep the battlefield, inch by inch. It is only when the ancestral relics of the psyche are reverently identified and reconstructed that life can truly begin again."

Mandala after Barbara's first Holotropic Breathwork session, which was long and difficult. Following the session, it was difficult for Barbara to distinguish between "being in process" or being in ordinary reality. Her behavior was somewhat eccentric; she would spend long hours drawing mandalas in the middle of the night while remembering traumatic memories from her childhood as well as from recent events.

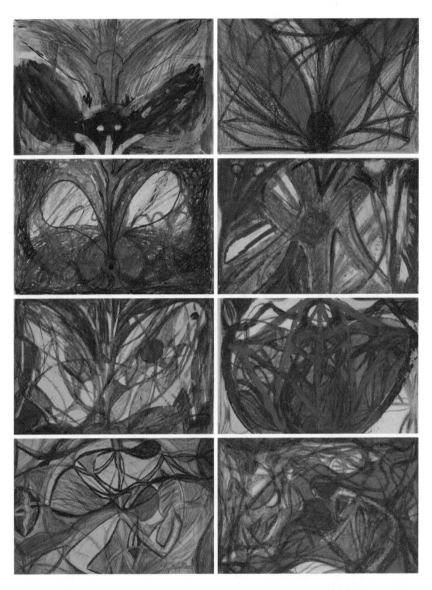

Sequence of mandalas produced during the outbreak of the crisis. Symbolic elements become harder to identify and shapes become more confusing, with fewer borders, as the sequence progresses. These images represent emotions and repressed memories, as well as excruciating pains she constantly felt. The last mandala of the sequence depicts the final loss of control. During this time of the retreat, Barbara needed support 24 hours a day for more than a week.

In the months that followed, Barbara was not able to keep living her usual daily life. She had to take a leave from work and move to her mother's place. She was receiving constant support, intensive psychotherapy, and psychiatric medication. The process kept on evolving in a very intense way. To ground herself, Barbara drew dozens of mandalas, performed strange rituals and picked up objects she found during walks around her house to create symbolic elements she would place in her living room.

After the initial phase that was very active and intense, Barbara entered a depressive state that lasted for several months. She continued to draw many mandalas and was receiving intensive psychotherapeutic support.

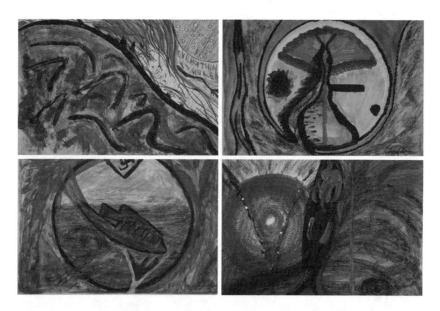

Almost a year after the outbreak of the crisis, Barbara was able to come back to Holotropic Breathwork retreats. Although her experiences were long and intense, she progressively learned to go in and out of the process with more control. We can see how the mandalas progressively contain more defined shapes and symbols, and some of the elements can be better understood.

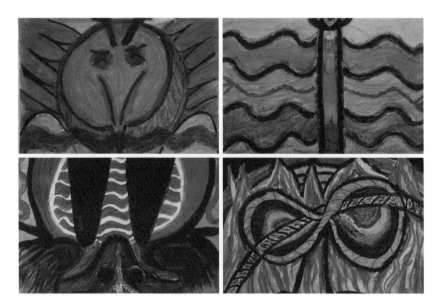

Some of the more recent mandalas Barbara has drawn. Similarities with early mandalas can be appreciated (upper left). Common elements, although with more definition and order, are shared with the post-MDMA experience (upper right), and generally speaking we can see more defined and recognizable shapes.

INTERVENTION
IN INTEGRATION
PSYCHOTHERAPY

6

"Ultimately, man should not ask what the meaning of his life is, but rather he must recognize that it is he who is asked. In a word, each man is questioned by life; and he can only answer to life by answering for his own life; to life he can only respond by being responsible. Thus, logotherapy sees in responsibleness the very essence of human existence."

VIKTOR FRANKL

"Whether a key works well or not does not depend on finding a suitable lock that fits it, but only on facilitating the path to the goal we want to achieve."

ERNST VON GLASERSFELD

CONTEXT IN WHICH THE INTERVENTION
FORMAT WAS DEVELOPED

The intervention format presented in this book has been decisively influenced by the context in which it has been developed. In 2012 I began collaborating with ICEERS, answering the requests and queries we received by email and telephone. Due to the increasing volume of these requests, we decided to create a dedicated section on the website with an associated email. At first, it was labeled the "Help Center," later renamed the "Integration and Support Service." From 2012 to 2018, I was the only person attending to this service: answering emails, receiving phone calls, and offering videoconference sessions. As of 2018, the service began to change and new people joined the project. At the time of writing this book, the service is undergoing a shift, as many more therapists are now offering online integration sessions.

281

The ICEERS integration service has always been free: I worked as a volunteer in the initial years and users have never paid for sessions. However, it later became necessary to look for funding to sustain the service. We currently receive donations from philanthropists and grants from public programs focused on harm reduction, such as the 2015 call for New Approaches in Harm Reduction Policies and Practices (NAHRPP), funded by the European Commission. This setting, where I began my early work with integration, had limited financial and personal resources. Despite the difficulties that this entailed, the context also forced me to develop an intervention methodology that would assess the real needs of users and respond to their challenges in the best possible way.

The users typically came from various western countries, mainly from Europe, the United States, and the United Kingdom. Therefore, the method developed carries a bias in terms of the population to which it has been applied. All sorts of profiles have reached out, from absolute neophytes to very experienced psychonauts with a lot of theoretical knowledge.

In the early years, most interventions were carried out through email exchanges; if the person genuinely required it, videoconferences were also available. Most of the cases I handled required a few email exchanges and a single video conference session. Thus, I have carried out hundreds of single visit interventions. The objective, at that time, was not to solve the problem as much as to provide information and resources for users to find the support they needed in their immediate environment. However, a single session was often successful in significantly reducing the person's suffering, particularly in less severe cases (such as the scenario that I have described as "lack of preparation").

Subsequently, I was able to provide more sustained attention to users who needed it. In these cases, between three and ten sessions were offered. In very few cases, more than ten sessions were required. Therefore, the intervention format that I have developed over the years can be defined as brief. This was primarily motivated by the available resources; however,

I soon realized that this brief format was in fact the most suitable for approaching the integration of experiences in non-ordinary states, particularly those where "adverse effects" and anxiety symptoms were present. Brief interventions focused on the immediate problems experienced by the person seem to reduce difficulties, and instead of creating a dependency on therapy, these interventions promote empowerment so the person can continue their life.

The methodology was defined organically, as was the theoretical paradigm adopted and the type of interventions carried out. It may be of interest to the reader to understand the evolution of the intervention format in more depth, so I will briefly describe it below.

EVOLUTION OF THE THERAPEUTIC METHOD

I conducted the first integration sessions in 2012, and the service was formally established in 2013. At that time, my main training included a degree in Psychology, training in Transpersonal Psychology and Holotropic Breathwork as part of the Grof Transpersonal Training, and various other unregulated psychedelic therapy courses. I had also conducted training in the use of music in expanded states of consciousness, as well as studies on comparative religions. The interventions carried out at that time were based on the principles of active listening, empathic support, psychoeducation, and the dissemination of factual information about different aspects of psychedelic therapy. Above all, the work focused on the person's own story of the experience and its contextualization, offering different possible interpretations based on various models and cartographies of the psyche and the psychedelic experience.

In practice, this translated into sessions where additional information and resources were provided or sessions in which different aspects of the person's experience were discussed, interpreted, and analyzed, in an attempt to elucidate its meaning and help the person get better insight into themselves concerning the lessons received during the journey. These interventions did not follow any particular format; moreover, I must confess that I lacked adequate training to deal with some situations. At the time, I was working in the dark, based solely on the experience of my own personal process and the transpersonal training courses that I had undergone. An important aspect of these sessions was my relationship with the patient: I always tried to maximize the benefit of a good therapeutic relationship, considering this as an intervention in itself. Thus, during this time, my interventions focused mainly on the spiritual and cognitive dimensions of integration.

In 2014, I decided to enroll in a psychotherapy training course and chose an integrative model which combined the systemic and constructivist perspectives, particularly in their narrative aspect. This was helpful for acquiring more knowledge and more tools related to the construction of meanings. Furthermore, it helped me understand the basic principles of the brief interventions. That same year I had the opportunity to participate in the MAPS MDMA-assisted psychotherapy training, which allowed me to understand the therapeutic mechanisms of the experiences facilitated by this entactogen more in-depth, and watch other professionals (in this case, Michael and Annie Mithoefer) lead integration sessions. During this time, I became more effective in the cognitive and emotional dimensions of the interventions, and I began to take into account the importance of the social dimension of integration.[38]

However, it became increasingly clear to me that this type of intervention (cognitive and emotional) was not particularly useful—or, at least, not very efficient in certain cases— especially when adverse effects or anxious and depressive symptoms were present. I began to differentiate between the different scenarios of integration work: maximizing benefits and reducing adverse effects. This crucial point guided the future development of the clinical approach to my work with the ICEERS Integration and Support Service. In 2015, I decided to pursue training in constructivist therapy, according to the model of the Mental Research Institute of Palo Alto, in order to be able to provide effective responses to more complex cases. Constructivist therapy is a flexible and creative cognitive-behavioral approach which I found particularly useful in the brief format of psychedelic integration offered at ICEERS. Consequently, the interventions became more rounded, taking into account the behavioral and physical symptomatic dimensions, in addition to those already mentioned above.

Between 2015 and 2016, I began to classify the different profiles of users who requested help from the support service. Far from being complete, the model presented in this book is a first attempt to map out the therapeutic needs of psychedelic integration, which will continue to develop and unfold in upcoming years.

In 2017 and 2018, I received further training in strategic therapy from the Palo Alto school. My supervisors had no particular experience handling cases related to psychedelic experiences, but they found it interesting that my work tried to integrate seemingly unrelated disciplines.[39] I also tried to develop a greater understanding of how to individualize therapy for different character structures through the study of Claudio Naranjo's enneatypes.

In 2019, I had the opportunity to train in the use of psilocybin for the treatment of resistant depression, and the specific integration technique used, based on the theory of perceptual control and the Method of Levels, proved especially useful for maximizing the benefits of single-session interventions or an ultra-short format.

This academic training, together with my own personal process and ongoing experiences in expanded states, Holotropic Breathwork, psychotherapy, and the study of different spiritual traditions (mainly Zen, yoga, and the Jewish tradition) have helped shape the therapeutic format and the principles of intervention that are presented here.

I have not created most of the principles presented. Instead, they represent a synthesis of different principles common to several schools and specific interventions created by significant figures of philosophy, psychotherapy, and spirituality. I have tried to unite these principles as coherently as possible to structure the transpersonal and spiritual aspects of psychedelic therapy while providing more depth and reach to the cognitive and behavioral psychotherapeutic practices. I have made my best effort to cite all the sources relevant to the concepts presented here so the reader can delve into aspects that are of most interest by referring back to the original works.

BASIC INTERVENTION PRINCIPLES

Regarding Treatment Duration and Number of Sessions

As mentioned previously, the intervention format was brief from the very beginning, at first as a matter of available resources and later as we realized that it was useful and effective.

In this context, the maximum number of sessions offered is ten. In some cases, it is not necessary to use all of them, and in other exceptional cases, it is necessary to do a few more sessions but seldom more than fifteen.

The ten sessions can be distributed over varying lengths of time, with the first four sessions being held weekly and subsequently spaced out. For this reason, an intervention can last for six months but only require ten sessions or less.

This contrasts sharply with the usual therapeutic paradigms, where the process is considered to be open-ended. However, recent statistics from studies in public health services and cognitive-behavioral treatments for PTSD and depression show that most psychotherapy patients carry out fewer sessions than previously thought. The average is between four and eight sessions (O'Donohue & Cucciare, 2008; Connolly-Gibbons et al., 2011), either because the therapeutic goals have been reached, because the therapy has not functioned as expected, or because the patient has decided to terminate the process for other reasons. Other studies have found that, even with eclectic and insight-oriented psychotherapies, the average number of sessions is also low: around eight, with most patients finishing the process after ten sessions and two-thirds of patients before fifteen sessions (Koss, 1979). Most studies agree that only a small part of psychotherapy patients undergo more than fifteen sessions, and very rarely does the process continue beyond twenty-five sessions (Garfield, 1986, 1989; Phillips, 2014). Thus, it is reasonable to expect a tangible change or improvement within this range of sessions. However, it is understandable that most therapists find this to be superficial and unorthodox. While the question of therapeutic depth could be the subject of debate, I merely hope that through these pages, the reader realizes that my approach to integration and therapy is not superficial at all.

Even Freud considered whether unlimited treatment was useful and had doubts regarding the proper length of a therapeutic process. In his essay, "Analysis Terminable and Interminable," he writes:

> *It was a case where the treatment was inhibiting itself; he was on the verge of failure as a result of his partial success. In this situation I used the heroic procedure of setting a time limit for analysis. At the beginning of a year's work I informed the patient that this would be the last of his treatment, whatever the result. At first he didn't believe me, but as soon as he was convinced that I was serious, the desired change appeared. His resistance abated and in the last months he was able to reproduce all the memories and discover all the relationships that seemed necessary to understand his early neurosis and get a hold of the current one. When he left me, in the summer of 1914, without suspecting, like the rest of us, what was going to happen next, I believed that his cure was radical and permanent.[40] (Freud, 1937)*

Brief therapy schools follow the same model of limited sessions—around ten—and our interventions can be considered analogous to this psychotherapeutic idea. In these schools, three phases of treatment are usually defined: phase 1, in which we try to understand the problem and the mechanisms that maintain it, as well as clearly defining the objectives; phase 2, in which we carry out specific interventions designed to unblock the symptoms and start to solve the problem; and phase 3, in which learning is consolidated and therapy is completed. The format proposed here is based on a process of approximately ten sessions, although there may be variations, and the therapist should remain flexible. It is necessary to carry out the minimum possible number of sessions needed for the person to regain their autonomy, but always as many as necessary. The number of sessions indicated in each phase is just a suggestion, meant to give an idea of how the development of the process generally unfolds.

An excellent description of the principles useful for shortening a therapeutic process and understanding it from a broad perspective can be found in the magnificent work, *The Tactics of Change*, by Fisch, Weakland, and Segal (1984). This volume is perhaps one of the best psychotherapy manuals available—it masterfully explains the therapeutic principles outlined here and many others useful for any therapist.

Radical Respect for the Client, their Experience, and Worldview

The group of people who use substances and engage in consciousness-modifying practices is very diverse. It ranges from people with a rigid Western, materialistic worldview to people who adopt diverse Indigenous, spiritual, and shamanic worldviews. There have been many frequent, intense, and often conflicting debates between science and spirituality, between neuroimaging researchers and shamanic practitioners, and, ultimately, between different conceptions, traditions, and uses of psychedelic substances. These debates are understandable since each of the theoretical positions explain, in their own way, the appropriate approach, the operative therapeutic mechanisms, and even the nature and origins of the psychedelic experience itself.

Furthermore, there is no consensus within any of these worldviews either. The various schools of psychotherapy fight about the validity of certain axioms, different shamanic schools consider the practices of others to be aberrant, researchers and psychiatrists disagree about the therapeutic mechanisms of psychedelic substances, and so on. Achieving a consensus that makes everyone happy becomes an impossible task; it is in precisely in this context that the integration therapist has to work.

As we have seen in Chapter 3, psychotherapy deals with second-order realities: interpretations that the patient constructs about things that have happened to them. Suppose the integrative therapist has a rigid perspective regarding certain aspects of the nature of the psychedelic experience, its appropriate uses, or the appropriate interpretation. In that case, the range of patients they can work with will be very narrow since their worldview will often conflict with their patient's worldview.

These oppositional dynamics are not useful when trying to build a good therapeutic relationship, which is one factor that influences a good outcome with optimal results in therapy. Therefore, it is most practical and effective to show radical respect for the patient's worldview. This implies that it is not the patient who has to adapt to the perspective or school of thought of the therapist, but quite the opposite. The therapist must strive to understand how his patient sees and interprets the world as much as possible. We must listen carefully to the concepts the person uses to describe their experience and the type of language they use.

This does not mean that we always have to agree with the patient in everything: Of course, it may be appropriate to offer a different view now and then, but we will always do this with radical respect and using the patient's own worldview and language.

Psychedelic substances have a surprising quality: The same dose of the same substance applied on different occasions can cause vastly different experiences. Psychedelics adapt to our reality, situation and needs, and are, as Grof puts it, "non-specific amplifiers of internal processes." Similarly, the integration therapist must proceed with the same attitude, adapting to the idiosyncrasies, needs, and views of their patients in order to help produce therapeutic results from within that same worldview.

In the Holotropic Breathwork model, we argue that the necessary attitude to adopt when working with someone, whether during a non-ordinary state session or any other encounter, is to meet them where they are.

Martin Wainstein (in Nardone & Watzlawick, 1999) tells us that "The therapeutic work does not consist of seeking the truth or directing therapy towards what is considered 'correct.' It only consists of creating those learning conditions in which something different, that is feasible and appropriate to the client's idiosyncrasy, can replace those symptoms and that suffering."

Furthermore, relying on the client's ability and potential to solve their own difficulties—honoring their "inner wisdom" and the psyche's innate tendency to process unresolved content—can afford us a fresh outlook on the person with whom we are working. The vision we have of our patients is a crucial factor in the development of the process. If we see them as capable people full of potential, it will be easier for us to trust the process, and the end result will reflect that greater efficiency. However, if we see our patients as dependent, vulnerable, disoriented, and in need of our ongoing support, unable to solve their own problems, the end result will be much less satisfactory. The power of a self-fulfilling prophecy is decisive in any interpersonal relationship, especially in asymmetrical ones, whether in educational settings (see the well-known Rosenthal experiment or the "Pygmalion effect"[41]) or in psychotherapy.

A representation of these dynamics can be found in the biography of Sonja Knips, a Viennese aristocrat married to a wealthy industrialist who became interested in art. In her story, Knips recounts how the early days of her marriage were not especially happy. In 1898, the painter Gustav Klimt spent a year in contact with the couple and made his well-known work, *Portrait of Sonja Knips*. If one compares Klimt's portrait of Sonja Knips with the photograph we have of her from that same year, we can see a very remarkable difference. The young woman's appearance in the photograph corresponds to a person much older than twenty-four years of age and her expression is almost gloomy and lifeless. However, Klimt's portrait shows a beautiful young woman who bears little resemblance to the woman in the photograph. When we look at yet another photo—taken ten years later—we are surprised to gaze upon a woman who much resembles the one in Klimt's portrait. We may wonder whether Klimt glimpsed that essence in Sonja Knips and if, through the painter's vision, she was able to evolve and transform into the best version of herself.

If, as therapists, we can embrace that vision, we gift our patients more respect and autonomy. We trust that they have the power to become the best version of themselves, whatever that may be. As Paracelsus said, "Just as man imagines himself, so he will be, and he is what he imagines."

The Need for a Clear Definition of the Problem

As we saw in the second chapter, integration and psychotherapy are not the same. "Integration psychotherapy" pre-supposes an intervention focused on a particular event: the psychedelic experience and its subsequent implications. Therefore, it has a limited objective and does not constitute an open-ended therapeutic process—at least not from the perspective presented in this book.

The aim of the integration therapist is to restore the person's sense of control after their psychedelic experience, allowing them to continue their process of exploration and growth without the crutch of psychotherapy. There is no higher aspiration in psychotherapy than to restore the autonomy of a patient. Psychedelic therapy starts from the assumption that healing and learning reside within us; it is by navigating through our soul that we can resolve inner conflicts and acquire greater knowledge and spiritual awareness.

If wisdom resides within us, the integration therapist's attitude should be to honor that wisdom in their patients, helping them access their own resources, allowing them to move forward with their lives in a satisfactory way. Why would we change the attitude we embody during psychedelic sessions in our therapeutic practice? The most widely accepted interventions during psychedelic sessions respect the natural flow of the person's experience. In fact, the individual is encouraged to indulge in the experience without judgment and trying to control what happens. We usually speak of "non-directive" interventions; however, it seems more accurate to say they are "inner-directive" interventions.

This should be precisely the attitude of the integration therapist: to direct the person towards their own inner guidance. Of course, as therapists, we must intervene and prescribe while always focusing on the patient's innate wisdom and extant resources.

For this to happen, it is vital to establish an adequate definition of our therapeutic objectives, which requires that we clearly define the problem. Patients often come to our clinic with a seemingly unsolvable problem. However, once we start inquiring about it, we realize that the problem is poorly defined, even for the patient. People perceive discomfort and suffering, but their own understanding of the problem usually appears quite limited. During the first sessions, it is up to the therapist to explore the problem in-depth and understand it as much as possible. It is necessary to understand the perceived problem, how and when it takes place, how it affects the person's life, and, above all, how such a situation becomes a problem for the patient.

A deeper understanding of the problem can in itself be a source of surprising insights that might lead to its restructuring or even to its solution. Understanding the problem, in this sense, refers to a knowledge of how it operates in the individual, not to its etiological causes or diagnosis. We seek to understand the mechanisms by which the problem presents itself and lingers, rather than the possible past causes of that problem. The causes of the problem connect to the past, but its solution is found in the present and the future. Therefore, even though integration therapy is considering an experience from the more or less recent past, it presents a clear orientation towards the future.

The therapeutic objectives regarding the problem will be defined by the patient. As therapists, we must know what the person expects of us, what he is asking us to help him with, and the parameters we will use to evaluate whether or not we are making progress. In some circumstances, these objectives will seem utopian, unrealistic, or impossible to achieve,[42] and it is the task of the therapist to redefine them in collaboration with the patient to reach consensual goals that are achievable and assessable. Usually, with a good working definition of the problem and why it is being maintained, the therapeutic objectives can be discerned; both the therapist and the patient can then often recognize the appropriate moment for the therapeutic process to end.

We must strive toward a precise description of the problem at hand. It is not enough to work with a general problem such as, "I have to integrate that experience." This type of problem lacks definition and is therefore difficult to resolve. Consequently, we must continue our investigation by asking questions such as: What aspects of the experience do you think you must integrate? What makes you think that you have not yet integrated the experience? How will things be different once you have finally integrated the experience? We must look for multidimensional descriptions of the problem, including behavioral, cognitive, emotional, and interpersonal aspects. I always ask the patient the following questions in the first session: How will we be able to recognize the end of therapy? How can we know that the problem that brought you here has been solved and that no more sessions are necessary? These questions usually help redefine the problem and the objectives toward the specific aspects causing the greatest discomfort. The next question would typically be: What would be the first indicator that the situation is beginning to improve?

We seek a minimally perceptible change—to generate a situation in which we can celebrate small victories that will allow us, on the one hand, to get closer to the solution of the problem and, more importantly, to generate a feeling of control in the patient: autonomy and confidence in their own resources and ability to face the situation.

The snowball or avalanche effect are metaphors that could properly express this type of approach. We seek to produce a small change, a tiny snowball that begins to descend the slope, growing gradually but continuously. Alternatively, consider the work of loggers in the past. When they sent the logged wood downstream, the logs would occasionally get jammed or become stranded at some bend in the river, halting their advance. A professional would then walk through the tangle of stranded logs, examining them carefully, looking for what is known as a key log. Instead of moving logs around aimlessly, the logger would search for the one log that, once moved, would unravel the whole tangle. This idea can also be exemplified by an ocean liner shifting a few degrees at a time. At first the changes might seem insignificant, but hundreds of miles later the ship is in a completely different place. Several authors have discussed the modalities of change that can take place in a therapeutic process (Watzlawick, Beavin & Jackson, 1981; Watzlawick, Weakland, & Fisch, 1976; Watzlawick & Nardone, 1992; Nardone & Balbi, 2009).

In this approach, the therapist may not get to see the potential results flourish: Surprising changes may take place many months after a well-integrated psychedelic experience and a well-resolved therapeutic process. Often we will simply witness the end of suffering and the beginning of a new stage in which the person walks on their own feet with a newfound agency to change their own course. Once the symptoms are unblocked and the new coping mechanisms are consolidated, the therapy can come to an end.

We somehow re-route a situation, going from "dealing with the adverse effects" to "maximizing the benefits" of the same experience.

Bottom-Up & Top-Down Approaches: Symptoms and Narratives

Many therapeutic modalities underestimate the importance of addressing the symptoms, assuming that these only represent manifestations of a deeper, unconscious problem—the real problem. The approach is turned on its head in other schools: any unconscious influence is disregarded, focusing exclusively on behavioral re-education meant to control the symptoms.

Professionals from the transpersonal, Gestalt, and psychodynamic schools usually approach integration work from a perspective that we could call "top-down," that is, trying to address the "real problem" instead of the symptoms, convinced that once the unconscious conflict is resolved, the symptoms will disappear. They propose mindfulness work, self-discovery, and ongoing internal work, often using experiential therapies to achieve this goal. Symptoms are often barely taken into account, and the patient must learn to endure them for the duration of this introspection process; in many cases, an actual disappearance of these symptoms is not even expected.[43]

Cognitive-behavioral therapists work from the opposite direction. They dismiss the etiological and unconscious aspects of the problem and focus on deactivating symptoms through mechanical and not very individualized procedures. We could call this approach "bottom-up," although in most cases, there is no intention of reaching any greater personal or spiritual knowledge since such dimensions are not taken into account. Symptoms can sometimes be controlled, but people are often left feeling like they have not grown or learned much during the process.

Neither of these models is, in itself, considered good or bad. Different models and schools may be suitable for different people and different times. The patient should assess the available options and find the type of therapy best suited to their understanding of the world and human beings. Not all patients need to leave a therapeutic process feeling like they have grown spiritually, nor do they all intend to get rid of their symptoms immediately and return to their office jobs as soon as possible.

In the intervention format proposed in this work, we assume the importance of each of the dimensions of integration, as we saw in Chapter 2. If we want to conduct genuinely integrative psychotherapy, we must consider all the aspects involved in the manifestation of a problem and stipulate a way to address these dimensions in therapy sessions. For this particular approach to work, the therapy and the therapist must adapt to the patient's needs and not the other way around. Therefore, in the previous section, we underlined the need to understand and properly define the problem as well as objectives of the patient, embodying radical respect for the patient's particular perspective.

A comprehensive and well-rounded approach to psychotherapy, particularly integration therapy, means working in parallel with the bottom-up and top-down strategies—working both from the general to the particular and vice versa. It means performing a therapy that addresses two levels of depth: the layers that some consider to be "superficial" (the symptoms) and the deeper, underlying aspects. Of course, these concepts of superficiality and depth are not absolute, and the only definition that should interest us is the one given by our patients. Our patient must have their own feelings concerning the scenarios they present, and we can contextualize our intervention with them, making sure that we are effectively addressing whatever aspects the patient considers to be important, regardless of whether we think they are deep, superficial, or both.

Integration therapy takes place neither at the superficial nor at the deep level (assuming there is such a difference) but rather in the communication between these two levels. If we manage to relate the symptoms to unconscious conflicts (traumas, values, past experiences), we are accomplishing true integration and, above all, we are helping the person get better control over both dimensions since by intervening in one we are influencing the other. Once we bridge the deep with the superficial, both aspects become one; it does not matter which one of the two dimensions we focus on.

In most cases—especially the most severe ones—it is easier to start by addressing the immediate symptoms rather than elaborating upon the story of what happened. Not surprisingly, the disabling symptoms often make it difficult to construct a useful and adaptive account of the experience. Therefore, it is often more appropriate to reduce symptomatic suffering first, allowing the experience to be seen from another perspective and become a potential source of knowledge and growth, rather than just a traumatic experience that we wish to forget. Orthodox and Hasidic thought is based on a Torah passage that says, *na'asé venishma:* literally, "We will do and we will listen," or, as is sometimes explained, "Action first, understanding later." To really understand something, we need to experience it and for that to happen, we need to act (Mishor, 2019).

As integrative therapists, we can assume that the symptoms and their unconscious correlates are closely related. By definition, the unconscious is unattainable and inaccessible at first, but the manifested symptoms are directly related to these unconscious dimensions.

The great poet Leonard Cohen said it several times: "There is a crack in everything, that's how the light gets in." The symptoms represent the crack through which we can access the interior dimension. Similarly, in the poem that opens this chapter, Cohen proclaims: "Do not decode these cries of mine, they are the road and not the sign" (Cohen, 2007).

Communication between the conscious and the unconscious is typically understood in one direction: from unconsciousness to consciousness. It seems that only the unconscious can communicate with the conscious, and not the other way around. Freud called dreams "the royal road to the unconscious" and in our context, we could say the same about the psychedelic experience. We are not accustomed to the idea that the conscious could influence the unconscious. However, this is a strategy as old as humanity itself: divination, hypnosis, Jodorowsky's concept of *psychomagic,* and many other healing systems are based precisely on this inverse influence, starting from the performance of external acts with a strong symbolic charge, capable of influencing the unconscious and promoting individual transformation. A somewhat less profound example—but with more immediate implications—is that of the love-magic practitioners (*alcahueta*) of Medieval Spain whose job was to make two people fall in love even when these individuals had not shown any romantic interest in one another. The *alcahueta* introduced simple suggestions, such as: "Don't say that I told you and, above all, make sure not to give it away, but if you pay attention you'll realize that the baker's daughter is interested in you. You'll see how she gazes at you mischievously when you're not looking." The complementary message was, of course, repeated to the other party too, creating a dynamic that profoundly influenced both individual's minds.

Unconscious content is often too hidden, too painful, too traumatic, or too difficult to experience. It is as if it were a burning frying pan. The symptoms, in that case, would symbolize the handle of that frying pan: the only visible resource available for the integration therapist to work on the unconscious.

For integration therapists, the symptoms can become the royal road to the unconscious. This multilevel therapy consists in traveling both of the royal pathways: from the bottom up and from the top down. The royal road of psychedelic experiences and the royal road of symptomatic manifestations.

Do Not Rush, "Go Slow"

This principle is primarily described by Fisch, Weakland, and Segal (1984) and has become one of the pillars of the therapeutic intervention that I describe in these pages. Most people who come to an integration session after a psychedelic experience do so with a sense of urgency and the need to overcome the problematic situation as soon as possible. They have typically tried various methods to feel better and have contacted various professionals, friends, and others who might be able to help. However, if they contact us for integration psychotherapy, this usually indicates that these other attempted solutions have not quite worked (and we could probably add that they are rather hindering the natural resolution of the problem).

Nearly everyone who has experimented with modified states of consciousness understands that it is impossible to force the rhythm and development of the experience. The guidelines typically encourage us to "Let go of resistance and flow with the course of the experience," something we often manage to do with relative success. However, when we continue to experience symptoms after a difficult and poorly resolved experience, we have the tendency—and for very good reasons—to want to change the course of events and get rid of our suffering as soon as we can. This resistance, to both the nature of the experience and its normal flow, not only prevents its resolution but intensifies our experience of conflict and anguish.

The prescription not to rush to fix things is paradoxical in many ways. On the one hand, as therapists, we effectively want to eliminate abnormal suffering as soon as possible, but, on the other hand, we do not want to oppose the natural flow of the experience. Some therapists from other schools are also oriented towards proceeding slowly and respecting the rhythm of events. However, they do it from a place of resignation, as if telling the patient that they have no choice but to suffer indefinitely.

Our approach is articulated differently. We do want to encourage a context in which the experience can be resolved "as quickly as possible"; paradoxically, going slow is what is required. We must encourage our patients to proceed slowly and not seek immediate improvements. The situation is complex—they have not managed to solve it on their own yet—most likely because we are facing a complicated problem. As therapists, it would be somewhat pretentious to assume that we know how that person could quickly solve their problems.

On the one hand, this fulfills a strategic intention: The patient, accepting the possibility of their suffering lasting a little longer, lowers their defenses, eliminating dysfunctional attempts at resolution (which usually has an immediate impact on perceived anxiety) and allowing the emotionally loaded contents to surface in their consciousness and be processed. On the other hand, and of equal importance, this type of relaxed attitude by the therapist encourages the same reaction in the patient who is actively preparing to work on an effective resolution. The patient perceives that the therapist is not in a hurry or that they consider the problem to be quite complex and unsolvable in a short time, thereby activating a "healthy resistance" in the patient. The patient now tries to demonstrate to the therapist that they have the resources and the ability to overcome their problem. We want to awaken this attitude in the patient, who stops being a "patient" and becomes an "agent": an active ally of the therapeutic process.

An example that illustrates aspects of this principle of intervention is found in a story by Erickson (in Rosen, 2009). Erickson lived in a small town in the American Midwest, which was mainly inhabited by farmers and ranchers. A group of men were trying to get a horse into the shed, pushing and pulling the reins toward the stable. The horse, however, refused to cooperate, and the more force the men exerted, the more the horse resisted. Erickson was watching from a distance and, once the men gave up, exhausted from the effort, he approached the horse slowly and unhurriedly. Then, Erickson grabbed the horse's tail and pulled hard. The horse, startled, hurried into the shed all on his own.

Paradoxical prescriptions, and the perception that the therapist is somehow slowing down the progress of the therapeutic process, generate a change in the role and attitude of the patient. He shifts from being a victim at the mercy of his problem towards seeking his own resources, feeling that he can do better.

Viktor Frankl began many of his therapeutic processes by telling the new patient: "I understand that if you are here, it is because you have a serious problem. However, tell me: How is it that you have not yet committed suicide?" According to Frankl, this prompted the person to realize everything that made sense and was worthwhile in their lives, reminding them of their own strengths and their innate ability to cope with difficult situations.

Using Language: Suggestive Communication, Reframing, and Paradoxical Prescriptions

As we can see in the following sections, the interventions we propose may seem somewhat paradoxical compared to certain therapeutic approaches. However, we have seen that such interventions are not at odds with the psychotherapeutic foundations of psychedelic therapy and follow the non-ordinary logic of experiences in expanded states of consciousness. Furthermore, they are found in other recognized therapeutic schools, such as logotherapy (Frankl, 1991), strategic therapy (Haley, 2006), family therapy (Minuchin, 1998; de Shazer, 2010), the individual therapy of the Palo Alto school (Watzlawick et al., 1976; Weakland et al., 1984), hypnotherapy (Erickson & Rossi, 2001), and the White and Epson schools of narrative therapy, among others. These types of paradoxical interventions are also found in the ritual prescriptions of shamans and healers, as well as in modern art schools, such as Jodorowsky's *psychomagic* (2004).

These prescriptions are not very challenging in terms of the complexity of their execution since, in most cases, they are extremely simple and do not require any special skill on the part of the patient. However, the real difficulty lies in convincing the person to carry out such tasks, exercises, and games. Non-ordinary and paradoxical logic can intimidate and cause reluctance in many people. Therefore, the therapist should be cautious and prescribe such actions only when a good therapeutic bond exists, and we can be fairly certain that the person will listen to our proposal with an open mind. Furthermore, there are different ways we can approach such suggestions: sometimes directly, other times indirectly, and more or less paradoxically, depending on the type of patient and their attitude during therapy (Watzlawick & Nardone, 1992).

The success of these prescriptions is greatly based on the intentional use of language. Like a psychedelic experience, where any detail can be loaded with meaning and relevance, the words we use during an integration therapy session—and all of our language—can be very useful for promoting adaptive changes.

Communication during a therapy session encompasses the words we use, tone of voice, gestures, looks, silences, volume, and cadence of speech. Non-verbal language is as important (if not more important) than the words themselves and can determine whether our interventions are effective or simply go unnoticed. Through language, we not only prescribe tasks to complete between sessions, but the therapy sessions are a continuous intervention in themselves. As therapists, the main tool available to us during a session is reframing, which can be done through metaphors, images, comic strips, examples, or relevant personal stories. By reframing, proposed through conscious and intentional use of language, we can completely overturn the problematic situation, opening up new possibilities for solutions we had not yet considered.

Often patients remember certain crucial moments of their therapeutic process. They tend to remember the exact words that the therapist said and reflect on them, digest them, and give them their own interpretation and meaning, even months after finishing the therapeutic process. These situations are examples of the power of a successful reframing, which has the power to potentially solve a complex problem in a simple and elegant way.[44]

For a better understanding of the use of language, consult the works of Watzlawick, Weakland, and Fisch (1976); Watzlawick, Beavin, and Jackson (1981); Watzlawick (2002); Jodorowsky (2004); Bandler and Grinder (1980); de Shazer (2010); Erickson (2001); and Rosen (2009), among many others. The principles outlined here emanate from these sources.

Doing therapy in the way that is described in the following sections can seem mechanical and even superficial. However, the mere description of the proposed interventions cannot contain the linguistic nuances that we find during the sessions or the reframing that continuously takes place during therapy through the use of metaphorical and suggestive language. The intervention blueprint and the proposed methodology are quite simple, but difficult for the therapist to apply in many cases. Similarly, it can be challenging to convince a patient to carry out certain prescriptions if we do not use the right language. This book cannot convey the subtleties that take place in the sessions nor the vividness of the magical moments of therapy.

Psychotherapy, under this approach, becomes like a loom in which the patient and the therapist advance towards a common goal, weaving new structures through language and creating experiences through the appropriate use of words. The therapist has to remain attentive to the patient and himself, and each session becomes a unique moment and an exciting event.

Recovering Freud's teachings, "Words and magic were the same thing at the beginning, and even today words retain much of their magical power" (Freud in *Introduction to Psychoanalysis*, 1917).

INTERVENTION IN THE DIFFERENT SCENARIOS

This section will describe the interventions that I have implemented for the different problems with integration that we have seen in the previous chapter. These interventions represent a synthesis of therapeutic techniques from different schools and therefore are not of my creation. I have tried to provide a treatment orientation for the different cases, highlighting the main conflicts and ways to deal with them. I have not attempted to create an intervention manual that must be strictly followed but rather to offer therapists a reflection on the main emergent problems and a possible way of addressing them consistent with psychedelic logic.

The treatments offered for some of these problems are distributed in three phases, following the principles of the MRI school of Palo Alto. I have included the number of sessions in each phase for guidance, although, you must be flexible in real cases since establishing these differences is not always clear. However, this theoretical division can help therapists orient themselves in the process. The distinction between these phases does not depend on the number of sessions but on the type of interventions that are being carried out relative to the development of the process.

In phase 1, our main objective is to establish a good therapeutic relationship, understand the problem, and to define it appropriately in order to articulate a treatment strategy. In this phase, we do not typically seek an immediate change in the symptoms (although it may happen), nor do we offer solutions or interpretations about what is happening. Sometimes this phase can be done in a single session, although we may need up to three in other cases.

Phase 2 is characterized by more directive interventions that help the patient address the core of the problem and provide a possible resolution, often in the form of a "corrective emotional experience" (that is, the person feels something other than what they have been experiencing so far). In this phase, we seek to induce situations that allow the unfinished experience to be resolved and to unblock the symptoms. The main tools in these cases are reframing and paradoxical prescriptions. This phase can take between two and six sessions, depending on the case.

In phase 3, the person has experienced a drastic reduction in their suffering. Still, there is a feeling of instability coupled with the fear of regressing and the problem reemerging again. The objective in this phase is the consolidation of new learning, the "integration" of the therapeutic process. Therefore, a solution-focused approach can be very useful (de Shazer, 2010), as well as the paradoxical prescription of relapses, designed to measure real progress and help overcome the fear of going backwards. The number of sessions in this phase is variable: usually between two and four. At this point, we can progressively space out the frequency of the sessions.

I have included examples of specific techniques and verbal interventions that are constant aspects of my clinical work. Again, I am not trying to define a whole methodology but to offer an overview of my approach to these processes, how I reflect back on what I see happening, and the tools I use during interventions. I hope this can inspire other therapists to reflect deeply about their approach to integration and the "what, why, and how" of their procedures. As an admired teacher of mine, Toni Piera, used to say, "The most important thing is to learn how to think well about therapy." Let us take a look at the proposed interventions for each case.

Lack of Preparation or Context

Although this situation tends to be a part of almost all requests for psychedelic integration, to a lesser or greater extent, it is sometimes the main reason.

Facing a psychedelic experience without adequate preparation can mean that we experience whatever happens during the session as negative, causing confusion, fear, and bewilderment.

Eva's case

Eva was an eighteen-year-old woman with no previous experience with psychedelic substances. She had attended a psychedelic festival where she had her first LSD experience. The effects were more intense than she had anticipated, and the experience unfolded very differently from anything she had previously felt. After an initial phase of fun and infectious laughter, she began to feel the boundaries of her body becoming weaker as the intensity of the effects increased. She decided to turn to the psychological emergency care service. The effects of the drug were so intense that Eva could barely stand and when she closed her eyes it felt like she was disappearing and melting into her surroundings. Eva was terrified, convinced that something bad was about to happen to her—perhaps she was going to die or disappear forever. With the support of the team of volunteers, she was able to feel safe and cared for. The volunteers provided comfort by reassuring her that nothing bad was happening to her and it was simply an internal experience.

The experience reported by Eva seems to contain many of the "ingredients" necessary for an ego dissolution or oceanic experience. Most psychonauts would be delighted to have that kind of experience and would perhaps find it enjoyable. However, the same situation can be met with great anguish if the person has no awareness that such an experience is possible.

After such an intense and overwhelming experience—even if it was adequately resolved—many people can be left feeling puzzled and confused, especially those who have no previous experience in psyche-delic states or with practices of consciousness modification, nor a specific theoretical framework about the nature of the visionary experiences and the phenomena they can encounter during and after the journey. These people often feel that what has happened to them is exceptional and abnormal. They are concerned about whether there is something wrong with their experience or their reaction to it.

Therefore, in these cases, the main intervention is focused on the validation of their emotional state. This includes validating all doubts, surprises, and fears, as well as offering insight about the nature of psy-chedelic experiences and, if appropriate, sharing examples from our own personal experience to normalize the patient's experience. We can ret-roactively provide the context that the person lacked before the experi-ence, allowing them to reframe what happened within a framework that includes their perceptions. If the therapist chooses to share some of their personal experiences, they should be careful to do so only when such information is helpful and therapeutic. The focus of the session and the interventions should remain on the client and their needs. Unnecessarily revealing personal information is a common mistake in these types of sessions and, sometimes, far from helping, it can make things worse.

In cases where a lack of preparation was the main issue, where no additional complications arise, and the person experiences specific acute symptoms, it is usually possible to diminish the anxiety through a single intervention, allowing the person to go on with their daily life and the integration of their experience on their own terms.

If deemed necessary, the therapist can provide additional resources, such as books, articles, movies, or other related material that provides further information. Additionally, it is useful to provide the patient with integration tools that they can use on their own to allow them to keep in touch with the unfolding process. We have addressed some of these tools in Chapter 4; artistic expression and the re-telling of the experience are probably the simplest ones to suggest.

At the end of the session, it is important to remind the person that we remain available for future needs. Very often, no further sessions will be necessary, but to know that they have someone to turn to if they need contributes to their peace of mind and allows the person to feel that their support network is expanding.

Unresolved Difficult Experience

People who come to integration therapy after an unresolved experience often complain about not feeling quite well ever since that particular experience. The peculiarities and degrees of discomfort can vary, but they generally take the form of recurring thoughts about the experience, irrational fears about something that happened within it, or a particular theme that emerged and triggered obsessive processing. Cognitive aspects often go hand in hand with relatively strong unpleasant emotions, particularly anxiety, anguish, and fear. Only in a few cases is the situation so serious as to prevent the person's normal functioning, but the internal state often denotes a feeling of instability, vulnerability, and discomfort.

The seemingly uncontrollable perception of these intrusive thoughts, ruminations, and obsessions, as well as the states of anxiety that go hand in hand with them, provoke a paradoxical dynamic in our attempts to resolve this situation. On the one hand, we might feel it is important to solve the issue cognitively, feeling that something has been "left open" and we have to do something about it. On the other hand, coming into contact with these contents and, above all, the way that they show up at the least opportune moments, motivates the person to make these thoughts disappear by any means possible. When anxiety pops up, we do whatever we can to reduce it, such as breathing exercises, meditation or mindfulness, distractions and, in less functional cases, we resort to avoidance mechanisms such as alcohol, cannabis, and other drugs, or potentially harmful behaviors.

Phase 1: Sessions 1-2

To begin with, the intervention is focused on helping the patient rid themselves of the unpleasant symptoms following their experience. At the same time, we are interested in discovering more about the meaning of what happened. Therefore, psychotherapy must be approached in a multifocal and flexible way, adapting to the top priorities.

In some cases, the symptoms will be more disabling, and ongoing anxiety can mean that creating a narrative of the experience will be postponed. In such cases, one must first eliminate or reduce the symptoms before one can address the phenomenological aspects. However, in most cases, we will have to carry out a mixed intervention that simultaneously reduces the symptoms and advances our exploration of the philosophical aspects of the experience.

Various approaches exist, and their use depends on the individual case and the format of our psychotherapy. For people who can function normally and merely perceive the presence of unpleasant or uncomfortable thoughts or emotions, it may be useful to go through another experience in non-ordinary states of consciousness in order to unblock whatever remains blocked and provide proper closure to the experience.

This approach is based on the previously mentioned COEX transmodulation theory, with the intention of providing another experience that facilitates contact with whatever is happening, and allows us to process it in a safe context that promotes a beneficial closure. Ideally, the person will perform another transmodulation towards a positive COEX.

This way of working produces better results in people with mild levels of affectation and normal functioning without many disruptions. People who are not experiencing very high levels of fear or anxiety, or those whose primary emotions are sadness, anger, or a mild level of anxiety may benefit from another non-ordinary experience.

However, in many cases, the person has no intention of undergoing more experiences since their anxiety is high and the perceived risk of enduring the same experience is too great. The existing fear increases the suspicion that another experience could make things worse; this fear is realistic and justified. Psychedelic experiences can be traumatizing and retraumatizing, and should only be suggested when we can fulfill the principle of, "First, do no harm." Even in cases with a good prognosis, my view is that the most effective approach is a Holotropic Breathwork session in an appropriate group context. Holotropic Breathwork can induce an intense and complex non-ordinary state of consciousness combining cognitive, emotional, and somatic manifestations, therefore allowing catharsis and abreaction to unfold safely. The context allows intense emotional manifestations, such as crying, screaming, and making sounds or intense movements. It is a suitable context for resolving difficult emotional states. My first (and safest) choice would thus be a Holotropic Breathwork experience.

For some people, this option may not be feasible because of the format of the therapy (for example, if it is done by videoconference), because no trained facilitators are available in their area,[45] or because the person simply does not want that experience, which should obviously be respected and accepted as a signal of the therapy's unfolding direction.

In such cases, the therapeutic process must first be oriented towards the development of coping strategies that may allow us to get that closure without the need for another psychedelic experience or Holotropic Breathwork session. This can be difficult, precisely because someone who is unwilling or unable to engage in a new experience might be trying very hard to avoid these unpleasant emotions, even if not very successfully. We have seen that it is precisely the confrontation with this material, and its processing, that allows us to unravel the problematic situation and reduce the discomfort. How then can we get the person to confront the uncomfortable material, while at the same time reducing their symptoms? Cognitive behavioral exposure therapies can work for those who are able to do them but they still suffer from a high dropout rate, and for good reason.

How then could we combine the exposure techniques of cognitive behavioral therapy with the lessons of psychedelic psychotherapy, transpersonal psychology, and spiritual traditions? Firstly, it is important to offer metaphors that explain what we are going to do and why, even if we sometimes engage in something like benevolent, strategic manipulation. We want to get the person to do something that they are not necessarily wanting to do, even when deep down they know it is a necessary step in the direction of the solution.

We find invaluable descriptions of this dynamic in the writings of two great thinkers of the 20th century, Alan Watts and Viktor Frankl, which help us provide a spiritual foundation for our cognitive and psychological interventions. The techniques and the general method presented here are based on the contributions of the Brief Strategic Therapy of Watzlawick, Weakland, Fisch, and Nardone, as well as on the logotherapy of Viktor Frankl, complementing them with a few contributions from diverse spiritual worldviews such as Zen Buddhism, Jewish philosophy, mindfulness, and the philosophical and therapeutic traditions of analytical and transpersonal psychology. Just as Huxley (1945) spoke of a "perennial philosophy," we too look for perennial elements in psychology in relation to the elimination of suffering.

As we have seen, it is important that we define the problem well within the first session. We should not be content with the superficial description of an "unpleasant experience." We must dig deep into the question at hand to find out the source of the current problem and how it evolved to the present situation. Perhaps it is anxiety that prevents the person from sleeping well, or recurring and obsessive thoughts that prevent them from concentrating on other issues. Whatever it is, we have to understand the specific problem currently affecting this person. In most cases, it will be related to the content of the psychedelic session; the problem is not in the session itself, but in how the person relates to it.

In the course of a psychedelic-assisted seeking process, we have to face a multitude of experiences. Many of them will be pleasant and full of valuable lessons and insights, but many others will be difficult, involving the confrontation of painful aspects of our psyche. Emotions of fear, shame, anger, loneliness, or abandonment are all inevitable.

In his book, *The Wisdom of Insecurity,* Watts (1987) offers us psychological explanations of this situation in poetic form. Watts writes: "This is the human problem: there is a price to pay for every increase in consciousness. We cannot be sensitive to pleasure without being more sensitive to pain." This insight can help us validate and normalize the current state of the patient. There is nothing "wrong" with what happened in the psychedelic experience. It was simply something that has not been fully processed because our expanded state of consciousness has also given us access to these painful dimensions of life. In his work, *Escape From Freedom,* Erich Fromm (2004) draws from a sociological perspective to propose a similar vision.

The first thing we must encourage in such situations is a "no change" prescription; we are not trying to fix the problem when it appears. This intervention (and many of those proposed in this treatment) are adaptations of the protocols proposed in the Palo Alto model and the Ericksonian approaches (O'Hanlon, 1993) based on the works of Watzlawick (1976, 1980) and Nardone (2007). The first "no change" prescription is intended to block the dysfunctional attempted solution of avoiding unpleasant emotional states.

It is well known that the worst thing we can do when things get tough in a psychedelic setting is to try to oppose the experience. The basic suggestion is to surrender fully to the experience, "into and through it," in the words of Bill Richards, in order to fully experience and process the emergent contents. Trying to contain or "fight" the experience produces anxiety, fear, exhaustion, the feeling of imminent danger, and a loss of control.

However, this is exactly what we try to do in most situations where we feel anxiety or other unpleasant emotions arise. We try to "force something that can only happen spontaneously" (Watzlawick et al., 1976;

Weakland et al., 1984). This often results in more anxiety, more discomfort, and a perceived lack of control.

One way to encourage the person to stop fighting these difficult emotions is to use suggestive language, such as metaphors that can properly illustrate the dynamics we are trying to prescribe. Depending on the client's own style, we can use military metaphors, such as "a special forces commando on an espionage mission" who must spy on an enemy without detection. The therapist can say something like:

This week, whenever the anxiety appears or the intrusive thoughts pop up, I would like you to behave like a commando on an espionage mission behind enemy lines. Whenever we want to spy on the enemy, we have to prevent it from knowing that we are there. Therefore, just observe and do nothing. See what the enemy's movements are, the type of arsenal it has, how it acts, etc. without being seen. What I'm going to ask from you is that, when the problem arises, you do nothing, and just observe.

Another fitting example can be found in Sun Tzu's *The Art of War*, paraphrased as: Whoever does not know himself or the enemy has already lost the battle. He who knows himself but not his enemy will win only half of the battles. But whoever knows himself *and* the enemy will always succeed. The therapist can say something like, "You have done a great job on your personal path getting to know yourself, so we have completed half the job. Now we need to know the enemy better in order to defeat it. The bad news is that you will continue to experience this anxiety for at least another week. The good news is that we will know much better what we are dealing with and which tactics to apply."

For people who are passionately dedicated to their spiritual path and prefer a more intellectual approach, we can be more direct and use these episodes of anxiety as openings to their unconscious, helping us get more information about what is happening in the deep psyche.

Both examples can be understood as well-intentioned manipulation but the experienced reader will be able to see that, ultimately, they represent the truth. After a deep personal crisis catalyzed by a life of loss and difficulties, Maimonides wrote that the only maneuver that worked to treat his patients was to "cry and awaken the pain until the physical vigor is no longer enough to support the suffering of the soul: this relieves those who mourn, just as those who are happy indulge in jokes and play" (Heschel, 1995).

These prescriptions work both on a rational and suggestive level. On the one hand, we tell the person that they will continue to suffer from their problem for "one more week." We thereby reframe the problem as a good thing, as it provides us with a learning experience. We are also externalizing the problem as an enemy as opposed to something internal to the person that is inherently wrong. We foster curiosity and the expectation that something different will happen, placing it in a broad and transcendental framework.

For people who are particularly anxious, prone to sudden anxiety attacks, or people who are prone to get obsessive and entangled intrusive thoughts with an ongoing struggle to silence them, it may be useful to complement this prescription with a record keeping task, in which they are asked to fill in an extensive table that describes different aspects of the problem each time it occurs.

This table can include the time, the day, the place, the company they were with, the duration, the physical sensations, the thoughts, the emotions, the intensity of the episode and so on. This technique has been used under different names, such as "Logbook" (Nardone 2002). The important thing here is not so much the prescription of the technique but how it is prescribed and the intention behind it. This serves both as an awareness-raising exercise and as a distraction maneuver to ward off the most disabling cases of anxiety.

Lorena's case (continued)

In the first session, we explored the problem and triggering events since the end of the retreat. A good part of the conversation was dedicated to the "spiritual emergency" Lorena experienced and the regret she felt for leaving her husband (who did not want to see her again). In the second session, we came up with a better definition of the problematic situation and the ways it manifested itself in the present. Lorena defined these flashbacks and panic states as the main problems she was dealing with, so we agreed to work on that in order to achieve some closure, a reformulation that Lorena accepted.

She was prescribed the 21-minute task, which consists of imagining the worst that could happen, purposely inducing feelings of madness, fear, and vulnerability. Since Lorena had once been a practitioner of mindfulness (abandoning the practice when she found that it reactivated the process), we defined the task as "reverse mindfulness." Instead of seeking relaxation, we were seeking to increase anxiety. A week later, Lorena shared that she had been very unwell, with frequent anxiety attacks, and that the 21-minute task induced a permeating anxiety throughout the day that was difficult to bear. However, during her 21-minute sessions, she managed to rescue several images and thoughts related to her ayahuasca experiences. She had recovered feelings from her childhood, from the time she was abandoned, and she realized that ayahuasca had brought those memories up to the surface; however, she had not wanted to confront them. Lorena reported, "There is a lot of pain inside of me," and wondered how she could live with it. Although it had been a hard week, she framed the results of the task as a "letting-go" and agreed to continue the task for another week. However, Lorena increased the time of each session to 33 minutes, arguing that there seemed to be much material left to process.

In the next session, Lorena commented that it was easier for her to fulfill the task. The unbearable anxiety was no longer present but she still experienced some spikes of sadness and fear, each lasting about a minute, in which she allowed herself to cry. She also shared that she no longer felt anxiety throughout her day. "My crisis is over," Lorena convincingly stated. She had reengaged with sports and other activities that she had abandoned, and she was no longer afraid to meditate because it no longer activated her anxiety. The prescription was maintained but distributed throughout the day in short intervals. After two more weeks, following another check-up session, Lorena recounted the lessons that she continued to gain in relation to her own process, and she felt prepared to continue her journey without the help of a therapist. The intervention ended after four sessions.

Phase 2: Sessions 2-6

Most people report a marked decrease in anxiety after just one week. They often feel relieved by not having to fight or resist the emotional states or intrusive thoughts. In fact, the emotional states are still present but the constant urge to attempt a solution has been blocked, diminishing the anxiety.

We proceed with more or less direct prescriptions depending on the person's response. It is important, always and in all cases, to put the concept of utilization into practice. That means, if we have completed the task and it worked, great. If we have not completed it and still feel better, that is great too. If we did the task and we have not improved, perfect; it is what we expected since we have not yet intervened. If a genuine confrontation with the emerging emotional materials has taken place, the person may have reached some insights and reduced the problem to a manageable intensity. We should take note of cases where very intense episodes were present as these will serve us for the next phase of the intervention.

During this phase, our intention is to provide a safe structure that is adequate for confrontation with the emerging material and its subsequent processing. Again, the basic idea of how we move forward from here is described by Frankl (1991) as follows: "If architects want to strengthen a decrepit arch, they increase the load which is laid upon it, for thereby the parts are joined more firmly together. So if therapists wish to foster their patients' mental health, they should not be afraid to increase that load through a reorientation toward the meaning of one's life."

After taking note of which symptoms are the most disabling and problematic, we will focus on them. We will prescribe engaging with the worst symptoms on a mandatory basis, that is, "we will increase the load." The manner in which this task is prescribed is similar to that developed by Watzlawick, Weakland, and Fisch (1976); Watzlawick (1980); Watzlawick and Nardone (2003); Weakland et al. (1984); Nardone (2002); and Nardone and Babli (2009), sometimes called "the worst fantasy" or imagining the worst. We can present the prescription using suggestive language, adapting it to the patient's worldview and the context of psychedelic integration since the underlying principle is the same. In this way, the prescription will be much more effective and it will be easier for the patient to carry it out.

The goal of the prescription is for the person to voluntarily induce the most disabling symptoms (anxiety, palpitations, fear of death or going crazy, fear of losing control, sweating and tremors, obsessive thoughts, or catastrophic predictions that their state will remain this way forever). For this prescription to seem acceptable, it must be presented appropriately. Psychedelic users tend to respond quite well when the task is prescribed as if it were a "miniature ayahuasca ceremony" or "short, substance-free psychedelic experiences" since most of them understand that an experience may have difficult moments, but completely seeing it through typically resolves the situation as a whole.

The person is instructed to lock themselves daily in a distraction-free room for a specified amount of time (typically 20-30 minutes) and voluntarily induce the worst symptoms. If the person becomes distracted, they must go back to the worst symptoms. If their mind starts looking for solutions to their problems or possible coping strategies, they have to stop and induce the most uncomfortable symptoms again. If during that time the person needs to cry, scream, or drop to the ground, they are free to do so. Once the alarm has gone off, they have to get up, wash their face, and go about their day. This task must be completed daily without exception until the next visit.

The responses to such a task, if completed precisely as indicated, are usually of two types. Some of the people manage to induce discomfort and experience episodes of crying, worry, anxiety and so on. There is a general worsening of the symptoms during the first few days, which begin to gradually decrease until the person perceives an improvement. In most cases, having a dedicated and specific time to feel these symptoms makes the situation more bearable for the rest of the day, as if the unpleasant symptoms were condensed in a limited time and place. Another possible reaction is an inability to induce discomfort, sometimes even feeling more relaxed and calm, getting insights about other daily tasks that they have to carry out. People would even say, "The more I tried to make things worse, the less the problem arose." This is the expected result of the exercise, based on what Watzlawick calls the "paradox of being spontaneous," that is, trying to explicitly induce something that can only happen spontaneously.

In the first case, the indication is to continue prescribing the same task until the problem gets unblocked and the emotional charge has been thoroughly processed. It is important to validate the person and reframe their suffering as being a necessary part of the process, a metabolization of the unconscious contents that remain undigested. We must acknowledge and recognize the courage that it takes for the person to undergo such an ordeal and encourage them to continue with the process, making visible the fact that the situation has not gotten out of control.

In the second case, we can start to shift the prescription to reveal the underlying mechanism: If we process our emotions as they appear, even if we intentionally seek them and intensify them, they dissipate more quickly and sometimes do not reappear at all. "If you chase the ghosts that haunt you, they will be the ones fleeing from you," or in the words of Watts (1987): "Running away from fear is fear, fighting pain is pain, trying to be brave is being scared."

Other times, however, the person is not able to complete the task for fear of getting worse and uses any excuse to get out of it: "I had too much work" or "I was feeling too bad to do it." What these strategies do is perpetuate the suffering since the person continues to face it by trying to avoid a confrontation with their emotions and to "spontaneously force" a sense of well-being through relaxation techniques, which, given the intensity of the anxiety, are practically useless. Watts (1987) goes on to say: "If the mind is in pain, the mind is pain. The thinker has no other form than his thought."

This can happen due to different factors; however, it is mainly the responsibility of the therapist for having rushed to prescribe this task or for not explaining it in a sufficiently convincing way. The patient should never be held responsible for their failure or be told that they show resistance to the treatment. It is the therapist who is at fault. We could say something like, "I apologize for prescribing this task at a time when you were not ready to do it. Tell me what difficulties you have encountered." Again, we have to show up with radical respect for the unfolding of the patient's process.

Frankl writes:

Logotherapy bases the technique called 'paradoxical intention' on a double principle: on the one hand, fear causes precisely what is feared; on the other, hyper-intention prevents the achievement of the effect we desire. Through the paradoxical intention, the phobic patient is invited to do precisely what he fears, at least for a moment or for one time. [...] The reader will notice that this procedure consists of reversing the patient's attitude: fear is replaced by a paradoxical desire. With this treatment, the wind moves away from the sails of anxiety (Frankl, 1991, 69).

Once symptoms are unlocked and the person becomes aware of this dynamic, the intensity of the emotional content tends to drop to manageable levels, and the person regains a sense of functionality. However, the fear of the situation reoccurring usually persists, so continuous work is necessary to consolidate the objectives.

Subsequent prescriptions are based on the same paradoxical intention to force symptoms; this time, the person is instructed to do so for five minutes, five times a day, wherever they are, without stopping whatever they are currently doing. This can be presented as field training, and a potential script could be: "The thirty minutes were a workout in the gym, but that workout is only valid if we then go out on the field and are able to play. So you are going to induce symptoms five times a day, wherever you are, because that is how problems tend to present themselves: unexpectedly."

This prescription is useful because it normalizes the random appearance of symptoms while simultaneously prescribing them. Thus, if symptoms appear without the person inducing them, they can take advantage of the situation by increasing their intensity during those five minutes. Moreover, if they do not appear spontaneously and we try to induce them, the chances are that we will not be able to induce them and therefore gain a greater sense of control. This same prescription is maintained and reduced to smaller intervals during the next session, such as three times a day for three minutes each. A single five minutes of intensification are prescribed as necessary if uncomfortable symptoms appear afterward.

In this phase of learning consolidation and complete processing of stagnant emotions, we can unveil the dynamics and explain why trying to relax sometimes works, while trying to forcefully induce symptoms is sometimes better. Alan Watts (1987) describes it beautifully when he writes: "We try to adapt to the mysterious present by comparing it to the (remembered) past, naming it and 'identifying' it. There would be no objection to this if we tried to get away from something that we can, in effect, get away from. It is a useful process for knowing when to get into the house and get out of the rain, but it does not tell us how to live with things we cannot get out of." Thus, when we cannot enter the house and get out of things, the best thing to do is to feel and dive fully into the emotions, pursue, and intensify them to metabolize them more quickly. This is the same principle we use in psychedelic therapy: intensifying mental contents and emotions and fully surrendering to them. In Holotropic Breathwork training, Grof teaches that, "We heal by intensifying symptoms." That is we are doing here—in the context of ordinary states, where the person can do it independently.

In the words of Stan Grof and Joan Halifax (1978): "Paradoxically, accepting pain, yielding into it, 'going into it and with it,' can make it possible to move experientially beyond pain altogether. In general, the least useful approach to pain seems to be to let it occupy the center of awareness, while at the same time resisting it and fighting against it."

We see that the underlying principle of these two seemingly unrelated schools of psychotherapy is one and the same: the paradoxical prescription and the full and explicit experience of what we are trying to avoid.

Lilly's Case (continued)

In view of Lilly's high level of functioning, her open disposition, the ease of establishing a good therapeutic relationship with her, and the fact that she explicitly requested to relive her difficult experience, she was prescribed a deep reliving of the experience early in the first session: "It's going to be tough, but it's necessary and I think you can do it." She was given instructions to write, in her own handwriting, a daily recounting of the experience from start to end. Every day she was to write the same trip report, adding new details as they appeared and allowing her emotions to fully manifest. In addition, she was asked to discontinue talking about her emotional state with her partner and friends. If they asked, Lilly was to say that she was working on it without giving more details. We did not want to reinforce her role as a helpless victim who needed the support of others.

After a week, Lilly reported that she felt much better. She had completed her tasks and although the first days were difficult and she cried for quite a long time, things became progressively easier as she went along. Furthermore, she uncovered other pleasant aspects of the experience which she had forgotten. In some of her writing sessions, which sometimes took up to two hours, she felt a sense of absolute acceptance of her life and everything that was happening to her. While in our first session Lilly felt 30% confident that she could overcome this problem, she now felt 60% confident that things would turn out well.

When asked what would make her 70% confident in her success (scaling technique), she replied that to really make peace with her experience, only one scenario was left to explore: the possibility that she would die of a substance overdose and the consequences this would have for her mother. Lilly was prescribed the 21-minute exercise where she must imagine that scenario and induce all the suffering possible. The exercise was presented "as if it were a DMT experience, lasting around the same amount of time."

Within a week, Lilly reported feeling much more confident, less anxious, and less fearful of the possibility of dying from an overdose, while developing much greater empathy for her family and friends. The 21-minute experience was emotionally intense in the first few days, and little by little she had lost interest in it (a common result when the task works and the contents are already mostly processed). She felt that the problem was 73% solved (I usually end the therapeutic process when the person indicates that the problem is 70% solved). I suggested that she keep inducing these thoughts and preoccupations five times every day for about four minutes (we thus normalize the occurrence of intrusive thoughts during the day) and a fourth check-up session was planned in the following weeks. The therapeutic process successfully ended after that fourth session.

Phase 3: Sessions 7-10

Once the unlocking of the symptoms has been achieved, we continue to work on consolidating the learning and its influence on the daily life of the patient. It is useful, during this phase of therapy, to space out the visits more and more to promote the patient's autonomy and allow them to face different situations in their daily life on their own. It is useful during this phase to prescribe relapses, that is, to purposefully "create" days when the person feels worse and where the original problem "reappears." That way, when a difficult day inevitably arises, they can feel as if they created it as part of their recovery process. Most people react with curiosity and some with distrust to this prescription, and so the task of the therapist is to propose it effectively.

Relapses, anxiety, disappointments, sadness, stressful situations, and other problems are undoubtedly going to present themselves at some point or another. That is the nature of life. So, by prescribing such a day, we are again normalizing something that we know has a high probability of happening and reframing it not as a step backwards, but as a test that measures growth and the acquisition of new resources. "We cannot know if you are really cured until one or more difficult situations arise. Then, we can see how you react, and what aspects you have to keep working on."

In this phase, the principles that were learned should be reaffirmed, manifesting the paradoxical prescription as a useful tool when needed, gradually automating the newly acquired coping mechanisms. While in the first phases we act strategically, concealing (with good intentions) the real reasons for some aspects of the prescriptions, once the symptoms have been unblocked and the person is able to experience different, non-pathological, and even positive emotional states, we proceed through a more ordinary logic, explaining the mechanisms of the techniques that we have been carrying out and attributing all the merit and courage to the patient for the work they have done.

Frieda's case

Frieda was a woman in her forties who has had an intense and unusual life, with diagnoses of depression, prescriptions of psychiatric medication, and suicide attempts. After a traumatic separation, she decided to go to an ayahuasca retreat to try to improve her mood. The experience was difficult and very intense, and included elements of death, madness, and loss of control, as well as luminous and spiritual sensations. After the experience, she was left in a state of anguish and fear, culminating in a panic attack after reading about possessions and attacks by evil entities in internet forums. Fear of these entities became unbearable and, from then on, she experienced constant intrusive and obsessive thoughts, leaving her in a state of general anguish.

At the end of our first session, she was given the task of evoking the worst fantasy for 21 minutes a day. She was instructed to try to induce her worst fears, thoughts, and emotions, including physical feelings of fear and loss of control. During the second session she replied that, although she had experienced sporadic episodes of anxiety, she improved after doing the paradoxical exercise. She found that she could not induce anxiety and instead felt relaxed with a greater sense of control. She claimed that she could control her thoughts better, but she continued to fear her emotions (which had not been present). She identified the topics that appeared most frequently during her anxiety episodes and was instructed to increase the time from 21 to 27 minutes a day, focusing on the topics that produced the most anxiety and inducing negative emotions. We also worked with the meaning she had assigned to the ayahuasca session and she realized that the topics that caused the most anxiety were those that had manifested in one way or another during the psychedelic experience. In particular, the fear of death (her own death and her mother's), as well as fear of madness and loneliness.

Throughout the next two sessions, we continued to work mainly on the management of obsessive thoughts and anxiety, building bridges between them and her particular experience with ayahuasca (as well as reading the text posted on the forum between sessions). During the fourth session, she reported that the problem was 70% solved during the day, although the nights were still sometimes difficult. The process advanced one step back and two steps forward, and Frieda was learning to handle states of anxiety while losing the fear of confronting difficult mental content. The fear of death began transforming into a tool in her search for life's meaning and Frieda considered the direction she wanted her life to follow in the next few years. In addition to treating the unresolved fears leftover after the experience, therapy began focusing on the changes that she wanted to make in her life, the best sign that true integration had taken place.

After ten sessions over the course of three months, we concluded the therapeutic process. Despite the fact that Frieda still experienced some difficulties and had yet to make the changes she wanted to see in her life, she felt that the ayahuasca experience was no longer dragging her down and preventing her from moving forward. Instead, she viewed the experience as something that gave her guidance about the kind of life that she wanted to live and helped sort her priorities during this moment in her life.

During this phase, most people feel prepared, albeit somewhat scared, to expose themselves to another experience in a non-ordinary state of consciousness. This step is usually a requirement for a good closure to the therapeutic process. Since the initial trauma originated in a non-ordinary state of consciousness, exposing oneself again to such an experience constitutes the final step in confronting and overcoming fear.

For this, it is especially important that: 1) The experience be carried out in a structured context and given a certain halo of rite of passage; and 2) We can guarantee that the experience will not be harmful. If these postulates are fulfilled, the person can go back to their spiritual journey safely and confidently, while integrating previous experiences as fertile ground for their ongoing development.

My recommendation is to always start with a Holotropic Breathwork experience, carried out according to Grof's format and with the presence of trained and experienced facilitators. In these cases, this technique may be the best way to integrate everything that happened in the previous months, since it provides a safe context and a wide container for any type of experience to develop, be it emotionally intense, turbulent, or ecstatic.

Perhaps a few words from Alan Watts are appropriate to close this section: "When you hold your breath, you lose your breath. By letting your breath go, you find it."

Emergence of an Unknown Traumatic Memory

We have previously described some of the scientific discoveries regarding the recovery of repressed or forgotten memories and the different positions of therapeutic and psychological schools in the face of these facts. In this section we are going to focus, beyond theoretical debates, on how to approach these situations in a therapeutic context.

Firstly, it is essential to understand how this situation becomes a problem, no matter how obvious it may seem. There are two relatively different situations: 1) When the traumatic memory has appeared recently and suddenly in a psychedelic experience, but the person had not considered that hypothesis before; 2) When the person has held that basic hypothesis for a long time, perhaps years, and their psychedelic experiences have led them to delve progressively deeper into it.

In this second case, the emergence of that memory is only a secondary issue, since it already belongs to the permanent belief system of the person (the memory, for practical purposes, is already "real"), so the therapy should be oriented toward the specific objectives that the person presents rather than to trying to evaluate or dismantle this belief (which, by the way, is not the therapist's responsibility). Therefore, I am not going to describe this second case in detail, since at a symptomatic and intervention level it is completely different from the first. In general terms, for an adequate intervention in this second scenario, the therapist must assume this memory is true, however rare and incredible it may seem, since it constitutes the lived reality of the patient. Here we are working in a situation analogous to post-traumatic stress disorder. The therapist has to decide whether it is an integration case or not, and whether they want to accept the case. My specific approach to such situations is to work with the consequences that this traumatic event has in the present. Most of the therapeutic work that people have done in these situations is of discovery and inquiry into the past. Therefore, if we want to do integration work, we must change the strategy. Now we will discuss the first situation, in which a traumatic memory has recently emerged.

When the Traumatic Memory has Recently Emerged

In these cases, the symptomatology that people complain about often includes high levels of anxiety resulting from the discovery of this memory. This anxiety is mainly the result of the person's effort to try to decide whether the memory constitutes something real or symbolic. Usually, psychedelic experiences in which a memory seems to be recovered are unclear in terms of their phenomenology, since the biographical elements coexist with symbolic ones (which also come from the perinatal and transpersonal realms as we discussed earlier). In the same scene, we find very real sensations mixed with ones that are clearly impossible from a "physical" perspective, such as seeing through objects, experiencing a separation of consciousness from the physical body, and so on.

The person's request is usually expressed in the following terms: "Help me decide what to make of this experience. Is it something that really happened, or am I making it up?" Earlier, we saw how both of these options can have dire consequences for the person. Therefore, the patient gets trapped in what is known in psychology as a "double bind" (Bateson, 1972). Of course, the worst thing a therapist can do is encourage one of the two options too hastily. We would be taking the same bait that is holding the patient back.

Phase 1: Sessions 1-2

During the first session we have to be particularly careful and respectful. We do not know the person's history, nor the traumatic ("real") events that may have happened throughout their life. Thus, we must proceed with radical respect for what the patient shares with us.

326

It is important to let the person explain themselves and relate their experience in as much detail as they want. It is not necessary for us to know every last detail to carry out successful therapy. In fact, it is not even necessary to know the experience itself.

Typically, people in this situation need to share the experience with a certain degree of detail, so it should not be surprising if much of the session is spent on it. It is important to allow this expression and accept the emotional manifestations that may take place. However, do not rush to try and fix the situation, offer comfort, or provide more agreeable interpretations. Although the person is often in a hurry to find a quick solution, the therapist should convey a sense of non-urgency. Ulatowska and Sawicka (2017) quote Kolańczyk (1999) in his statement: "Another pattern to remember is the individual need to attain a cognitive closure of ambiguous situations, including those retrieved from memory. This tendency is directly related to lowered tolerance of ambiguous situations that must be resolved immediately using the currently available information, even when the information is insufficient and may turn out to be false." So what we want is not to immediately provide that closure, but rather to increase tolerance for uncertainty until we can better elucidate what happened.

After the account of the experience, patients usually wait for the verdict of the therapist: Is it real or is it symbolic? Here, it is important to remain patient and steer the conversation in other directions. It is essential to know how that experience has become a problem for that person and what the person expects of us. What their goals are and how we can help them reduce their suffering during therapy. The patient usually implies that a verdict could be reached, but we have to go beyond that. Why do we want to reach a verdict? What is going to happen, change, or improve if we get our answer?

We can share from our experience and argue that we do not know if that memory is objectively real or not, and that in psychedelic literature there are stories of all kinds. In addition, we have only known the person for one hour, and therefore it would be irresponsible for us to express any kind of opinion on the matter. We need more information before deciding and therefore we have to continue the exploration. Due to their state of anxiety, it would be a bad idea to draw definitive conclusions or, worse still, try to do something about it (such as going to the police, confronting the alleged aggressor, or assuming certain positions toward oneself). Therefore, we are going to wait a few sessions before making a decision. Doubt, in this case, is a good thing that allows us to delve deeper into this situation. In this type of intervention, we try to block obsessive attempts to reach a conclusion, often the main source of anxiety.

We could ask the person to write a "detailed 'first draft' of their experience." We can add that, "It is likely that through the conscious and detailed account of the experience, new aspects will appear—that perhaps you did not remember—which may help us gather more information about this whole situation." With this intervention, we intend, on the one hand, to expose the person to the memory of the experience in a structured and quasi-ritualized way and, on the other, to create a rich and complex first draft of the story of what happened, allowing the clearest details (and the most confusing) to emerge. In addition, we may encounter patterns in the experience that point towards a broader sense of the specific scene. Reality tends to show that the experience contains many more elements, but the person is only focusing on one particular scene. In this case, the leaves are not letting us see the forest. The use of suggestive language is important. That is why we say "a first draft," implying that there will be other versions of the same experience.

People who are experiencing high levels of anxiety as a result of the traumatic memory itself, and not so much because of the decision they have to make, may not respond as well to this idea. The intrusive memories of that experience are precisely what is bothering them in the first place and what they are trying to avoid. In these cases, we must work first with these most disabling symptoms, since without the ability to confront the memory, a decision cannot be made. We will slow down and proceed in a way similar to the case of an "unresolved difficult experience," although in the case of a traumatic experience we replace the technique of "imagining the worst" with the continuous written account of the difficult experience. Systematized ways of working with such situations can be found in Cagnoni and Milanese (2010). Once the person is able to remember the experience without being overwhelmed by anxiety, we can continue with the intervention that we propose here. This specific protocol is described in the section on a "traumatic dissociative experience."

Phase 2: Sessions 2-6

People often report ups and downs during these weeks. There are moments when they feel like they are coping better with what is happening, interspersed with moments of intense anxiety when thoughts and the rush to make a decision reappear. This can be sustained for a while, although in general, if we continue to block attempts to reach a "yes or no" decision, anxiety will decrease.

Generally speaking, these cases are not solved in the way that we might initially anticipate. That is, the resolution does not come with the final decision regarding the truth of the story. Usually, at the end of therapy, the patient says something like: "I'm not 100% sure if it's true or not. I'm 70% sure that it is a symbolic memory. Anyway, I don't care anymore." To arrive at this conclusion, in the successive sessions we must work with the story that the patient has prepared.

We initially pay attention to the point of conflict and analyze its details (insofar as the person wants to tell them, of course), the ambiguities, the contradictions and so on. In short, we are spreading and displaying on the whiteboard all the factors that are creating the conflict. And, little by little, we are analyzing the two possible scenarios: 1) What would happen if the memories were true? and 2) What if they were not? We explore each implication in depth. By doing so, we are giving voice to both possibilities without taking sides for either of them, and simply letting both express themselves. We proceed as if it were a tennis match, in which we are the referee, who simply intercedes to mark turns. The patient acts as a fickle fan, who cheers for one side and now for the other. Our task is to shift the focus from the players to the ball. That is, we shift the focus from the decision between one option or the other to the "conflict of deciding" in itself. Therefore, we make visible the double bind situation in which the patient finds themself, in order to help them discover on their own that their decision can turn into a dead end or that the remedy can be worse than the disease.

It is also the therapist's job to focus on other aspects of the experience. Many times, we will find clearly symbolic elements related to situations of abuse or suffering. We can even find different "octaves" of the same topic: biographical, perinatal, and transpersonal aspects of the same COEX. We are thus broadening the focus of the experience to expand the initial version of it.

During this process, it is likely that we will have to deal with doubts in the sessions regarding how to act in certain social situations. In particular, if the alleged abuser is still present in the context of that person's life or when close relatives are involved in the situation. In this case, it is necessary to discourage any type of action. We must first resolve the intrapersonal conflict before considering what to do about the interpersonal conflict. We can say it exactly like that to the person. Sometimes we have to recommend taking distance or acting as if nothing is wrong and simply observing the behavior of others.

Through this process, a paradoxical phenomenon takes place: The memory becomes more and more confused and ambiguous but concern about this situation also decreases. This is what commonly happens in many psychedelic experiences. We do not remember the details well, but we do not worry too much about it. The range of possible scenarios for solving this problem is beginning to increase and the situation no longer seems like something of vital urgency demanding a "black or white" decision. Anxiety and intrusive thoughts decrease. Often the person will be able to discern that emotional abuse was indeed experienced in childhood, even though the scene that the person saw in their psychedelic experience did not exist as such.

The attitude and beliefs of the therapist are extremely important elements in these cases. Given the asymmetry of the therapeutic relationship, any interpretation can have a high emotional impact and tip the balance towards one option or another. The psychedelic experience, in this case more than in any other, is the "reality of the first order," which happened objectively. The patient's interpretation and what makes them suffer is the second-order reality. This is what we work with.

Therefore, as therapists, we should therefore not care so much about whether what happened is true or not, but about how the person relates to what happened. Claudio Naranjo, in *The Healing Journey,* uses the expression "objective reality" vs. "subjective reality." The interpretations, both of the psychedelic experience and of the events that took place in our biography, belong to this subjective reality and leave a mark upon us. There may not have been an abusive scene in our childhood but the context in which we lived was oppressive and we subjectively experienced it as abuse. In a psychedelic experience, this can manifest in complex ways, rich in symbolic elements.

The important thing is to understand that the therapist's interpretations can greatly influence the construction of this second-order reality. We must strive for the patient's freedom to build and rebuild their second-order reality as many times as necessary, rather than create a certain second-order reality for them.

Angela's case

Angela was a young woman who followed her path of psychological and spiritual evolution with dedication. She had undergone multiple therapies of different kinds. In a cathartic experience she had through breathwork, she entered difficult spaces of suffocation, pain, suffering, and karmic experiences of violence, abuse, and murder.

In the verbal therapy sessions, which Angela interspersed with her breathwork experiences, she began to talk about an experience of abuse that she suffered in childhood by a family friend. Although she did not remember exactly what happened, she knew that it really happened, since she remembered scenes and visions of certain objects in a room. Although she had not thought about it for a long time and she had never identified herself as a victim of abuse, she realized that the memory had always been there, even if she had not interpreted it that way. Curiously, her experiences during breathwork did not offer her a clear image of the scene and she did not even consciously establish a connection between what was currently happening and her traumatic experience.

Throughout the sessions, Angela felt less oppressed for having been a victim of these experiences and began to talk about it with her family, who initially reacted with surprise, but progressively supported her and verified unique aspects of Angela's version of events. Finally, they ended up doing a ritual burning of an object that had been kept in Angela's memory for years. Afterwards, during our verbal therapy sessions, the focus shifted to other non-traumatic aspects of her experience.

Steve's case (continued)

The therapeutic work with Steve lasted a total of eleven sessions spread over six months. For Steve, therapy was to be considered a success if we were able to suppress the added layer of depression brought about by "trying to decide whether the experience was real or not," as well as improve the symptoms of depression (particularly insomnia) and provide him with some guidance regarding his future steps in life.

In sessions two to five, the focus was on processing the two experiences with psilocybin and working with the narrative of what happened. Doing so, the double bind in which he found himself was revealed and we strived to establish a gradual redefinition of events. At this point, it should be noted that although the discovered memory was real and could explain the reason for his depression, it did not help at all in curing the depression. Therefore, it was not necessary to focus on that path. An important aspect of Steve's treatment was that we were able to watch the recording of his high dose session and analyze the moment when he had the revelation. This gave Steve an outside view of what had happened, which was less dramatic than he remembered. We also worked on childhood memories he had about the difficult family situation in his childhood home, due to his parents' problematic relationship. Little by little, we proceeded to find parallels between his childhood and what happened during the psychedelic experience. In particular, the subject of drowning appeared from the beginning and manifested variously in different forms, including his vision of the attempted drowning, a vision of an alien creature that introduced a tube into its mouth, perinatal scenes of drowning, and elements of birds that symbolized his parents getting inside him. Finally, Steve was offered a reframing of the meaning of his experience, which he reconstructed himself during the session, advancing little by little and obtaining his validation at every step of the way. At this stage it was crucial to use suggestive language, copying the specific expressions that Steve himself used, so that the story we were co-building was based on his own reality and emotional tone and not on those of the therapist.

We also began to focus on the multitude of positive elements that had emerged in his experience and actions related to those positive elements were prescribed, such as buying a flower similar to the one in the session (the catalyst of an ecstatic experience) and taking care of that flower for a few days.

From the sixth session onwards, the recovered traumatic memory was considered symbolic, containing many elements of what had happened in his childhood, but not representing a real scene. We then proceeded with a more solution-oriented approach to address the symptoms and helped guide Steve toward achieving his life goals. The road was not flat or fast, and there were numerous ups and downs, but Steve began to feel that he could sustain the ups and downs of his moods and slowly move toward his goals. In one of the last sessions, Steve told us that during the last few days he had experienced "one of his worst days in twenty years and one of his best days in twenty years."[46]

Phase 3: Sessions 6-10

Once the person has reduced their anxiety and the need for a stable and definitive version of the experience, we can continue to broaden the focus even more and include other aspects of the experience that we have not yet contemplated. There may be positive and even transcendental aspects to the experience, so we must give them the relevance they deserve too.

Thus, we can get a much more complex and richer image of their experience. The story shifts from "I relived an abuse" to "I had an incredible experience with countless scenes, some terrible and others fantastic."

At this stage, we can adopt a more focused, solution-based approach that not only allows us to overcome that decision conflict, but also maximize the potential benefits of the experience, directing the person towards action-based scenarios that improve their present situation. Again, the therapist's attitude should always be limited to acting as a match referee without taking part in deciding what the person should do. We only help them to actualize whatever they decide. As therapists, we try to turn the experience into a source of inspiration that helps improve the life of the individual. However, the intervention can end earlier as well.

In some situations, these interventions can be shortened even more, depending on the initial state of the person and the hypotheses that they hold. If we are already convinced that seventy percent of the vision is symbolic, we may just need some additional context to understand how these types of experiences can take place. The therapist can then provide that context through explanations similar to those that we have given here in the respective sections and solve the situation with a very brief intervention, sometimes just one or two sessions.

Matilde's case

Matilde sought help because, in her experience with ayahuasca, she witnessed a scene that had greatly disturbed her. She saw that her grandfather had touched her inappropriately in a sexual manner. Matilde had no recollection of the event taking place and she was scared to discover that she had lived her entire life being unaware of it. She was suddenly overwhelmed by the possibility of being a victim of childhood abuse.

Examining her experience, we found many physically impossible symbolic elements and phenomena, such as being seen through the eyes of her sister. These phenomena made her doubt the veracity of her recovered memory, but she was not yet convinced that it was entirely symbolic.

As the session progressed, Matilde shared that her sister did in fact suffer being touched by her grandfather and that the family knew of it. Moreover, Matilde had witnessed some of these scenes without being very aware of it. Matilde concluded that what she experienced was an identification with the experience of her sister and a memory (which she already had) of childhood scenes in which her grandfather inappropriately touched her sister.

After observing her experience through this prism, Matilde reaffirmed herself in the decision that the scene she saw was symbolic, but based on real events, which perhaps affected her more than she thought. She felt more compassion and empathy for her sister. The intervention ended after that single session.

Abuse by Facilitators

After an experience involving abuse or malpractice by the shaman or facilitator, the specific intervention in each case will depend on the nature of the events. The severity and consequences of what happened will vary depending on whether it is negligence or unskilled practice; poor session management or group dynamics; or a situation of emotional, physical, or sexual abuse.

The differential factor in this scenario is the perverse combination of: 1) a crisis of confidence, 2) a more or less traumatic experience in an expanded state, and 3) ambivalent feelings about what happened. Furthermore, the person who seeks therapy to integrate this type of experience is being subjected to a situation analogous to the one that caused the problem: seeking a professional for support in their therapeutic process. Therefore, the most important aspect when dealing with these cases is not so much the intervention technique, but the relationship established with the person.

It is extremely important that, during the course of the sessions, the person feels that it is safe to trust the new therapist and that trust in the helping relationship can be gradually restored. For this, the therapist's attitude is very important, since they must offer unconditional acceptance and sincere support, while promoting the client's personal autonomy.

This type of situation does not usually require a particularly long therapy if what happened was negligence or malpractice due to the ineptitude of the facilitator. If the situation has been one of abuse, the therapy can take more time.

Phase 1: Sessions 1-2

During approximately the first two sessions, the person should be allowed to share what has happened at their own pace and with the level of detail that they consider appropriate. The therapist has to be respectful regarding the information that the person decides to share and cultivate an attitude of patience and acceptance. In these situations, a complex dynamic usually exists. On the one hand, the patient is angry with the facilitator and blames them for what happened and on the other hand, has veiled anger toward themself for having allowed abuse to happen, ultimately producing feelings of shame.

The important thing is to listen without judgment, without rushing into questions or interventions, and without trying to correct the situation or dismiss anger or shame in the first place. It is not so much about getting information as it is about cultivating a trusting relationship. It is important to be genuinely curious about what happened but without morbid curiosity, so that the person can allow the story to unfold and name what they feel.

During this phase, you have to constantly validate the person and their suffering. It is not important to work with the specific content of the psychedelic sessions, but with the experience of abuse or malpractice. We must validate the emotions they are experiencing and normalize their reaction in relation to what happened, ensuring that the patient knows there was likely no other way to react to such circumstances—this is a normal reaction to abnormal events. This should be the basic message we, as therapists, strive to get across.

Another necessary intervention during this phase is to make a value judgment that validates the reaction of the person and clearly shows that the responsibility rested entirely with the facilitator. The integrative therapist should clearly state which aspects of the patient's narrative constitute malpractice, offer reasonable explanations as to why this is the case, and describe what ethical conduct would have looked like.

This can be simple when there has been abuse or the facilitator has engaged in unethical behavior. However, it can become more difficult when the problem is that the facilitator has stopped doing something that they should have been doing, such as providing support or clearly marking boundaries (for example, in interactions between helpers and participants, etc.). It can be even more complicated when objective issues of the facilitator's behavior are mixed with subjective aspects of the patient's experience. This can occur in experiences of intense fear tinted with paranoia, in which the person feels that the space is no longer safe or that the facilitator is inexperienced or cannot be trusted.

In either case, the facilitator's responsibility should be clearly underlined, whatever happens. Even in extreme situations, facilitators should have a plan to be able to support that person or at least provide adequate support after the experience to address what happened.

Therefore, in this first phase, the important thing is to cultivate a good therapeutic relationship of trust through empathic listening, validation, normalization, and providing context about the responsibilities that the facilitator of a psychedelic experience takes upon themselves when organizing such an event.

If the situation of abuse has caused anxiety, flashbacks, depersonalization, or other serious symptoms, it must be treated without delay. The first intervention will be the one indicated here (validation and the establishment of a good therapeutic relationship), but later we will have to address the symptoms. The techniques required can be similar to those used for "unresolved experiences" and also for "very traumatic experiences," always paying extra attention to the relational aspects of therapy. In this case, the duration of the process will undoubtedly be prolonged.

Phase 2: Sessions 3-5

After having addressed the previous aspects, two conclusions usually emerge. On the one hand, shame and guilt for allowing the abuse to happen might appear. On the other hand, there may be a need to respond to abuse or malpractice in order to deliver justice, either by confronting the perpetrator or by taking legal action.

Regarding the first aspect, you can proceed in the same way as during phase one. Allow the person to develop their story and reach their own conclusions. Paraphrasing, combined with suggestive questions and prompts, can be used to subtly help dispel this sense of guilt and transform it into something positive, such as courage, the ability to trust, and having a good heart. For example: "In other words, you fully trusted the shaman and gave yourself courageously to the experience. Later, you realized that their intentions were dishonest, contrary to what they had led you to believe. Do you feel you didn't do the right thing?" Or another approach: "Most recognized authors agree that, for psychedelic therapy to work, the most important factor is the relationship of trust that is established between the patient and the therapist. You both have to do your part for that to work. You say that you chose to trust, thinking that the shaman would be as trustworthy as you are. Who was it who caused that therapeutic relationship to fail?"

It is not uncommon for the most serious cases of abuse to reveal a biography full of traumatic events, both in childhood and in other therapeutic relationships. In such cases, proceed in a similar way to phase one.

In some cases, it will be necessary to accept the fact that there is ambivalence in the patient's feelings towards the shaman or facilitator. It may be that this facilitator is widely recognized and helped many other participants, including relatives or acquaintances of the person who has been abused. The patient's mixed feelings may also arise from the fact that the facilitator has even helped them. The healer can also be the one who causes harm. This happens mainly among people who are given power that they can use in many ways. We find countless examples in various spiritual schools (Kornfield, 1997, 2001), and this is often an unavoidable risk on the spiritual and therapeutic path. The important thing is that the patient can recognize this power dynamic and broaden their perspective beyond the binary of good/bad or they have helped me/ they have destroyed me.

One of the secondary potential benefits of this type of therapy involves promoting the empowerment and autonomy of the patient. Abuse usually involves prominent people in whom patients place high hopes, believing they have the ability to heal them (and, therefore, also to harm them). In integrative therapy, the therapist should present as someone with limited abilities (which is true) and without the power to heal patients. We intend to break the dynamic of seeking outside help and replace it with the capacity for self-reliance and empowerment. Thus, the therapist must always be one step behind the patient, allowing them to make their own decisions and reach their own conclusions regarding what they need. This even affects the number of therapy sessions, as well as their frequency; the patient must be the one to decide, session by session, whether to continue with the therapy and when to schedule the sessions. This will be the main factor in phase three of therapy.

In the event that the person wants to take sides in the situation and act with the purpose of restoring justice, they must proceed with great caution. Sometimes, patients will want to go to the authorities and report the facilitator (paradoxically, this rarely happens in very serious cases, such as sexual abuse); write a public letter to discredit them; ask that an organization intercede; confront the facilitator directly; or talk to their followers.

The backbone of therapy in these cases is that whatever decision the person makes is fine, but that it is more appropriate to act when one has processed the emotional turmoil. A useful metaphor is that, "Revenge is a dish best served cold."

The therapist should refrain from actively encouraging or advising against any of the patient's actions. This energy should simply be used to aid the patient in processing the emotions of anger, frustration, guilt, and so on. People often understand that coolheaded responses are much more effective and generally respond well to these suggestions. In cases where individuals rush to make these kinds of decisions, additional problems may appear. For example, there is the possibility of being ignored or discredited by the facilitator and the rest of the community, thus producing a new traumatic situation and a sense of rejection, which can further impact their reliance on their support network.

People often come up with big action plans to put an end to the bad practices of the facilitator once and for all, but it is often the case that these plans are difficult to carry out and unfortunately, in many cases, the accusations are ambiguous or difficult to determine. Therefore, many inept and abusive facilitators continue to work, despite carrying dozens of malpractice cases on their backs.

In integration psychotherapy we are not trying to impart justice (which, on the other hand, would probably be the best cure for the patient), since it is beyond our possibilities. What we want is to help the person overcome the emotional difficulties they are going through in order to regain their capacity for autonomy and be able to move on with their lives, whatever decision they make.

A good strategy for meeting their need for justice might be to proceed in a manner analogous to dominoes or a snowball. We are not looking for big actions, but small, significant actions that can start a chain of events aimed at delivering a certain justice without exposing the patient or risking further harm. A metaphor that many patients respond well to is that of a vaccine. Through an action similar to a vaccine, which consists of an attenuated version of the virus, it is possible to gradually create global immunity. Thus, perhaps people can start by writing an anonymous story that they publish on a certain distribution list or perhaps they talk to someone they trust who can help expand the circle of people informed about malpractice. For those patients who have a particular desire for revenge, this metaphor can be modified and, instead of a vaccine, we can prescribe: "Small and almost invisible interventions, as if you were a virus. Power can also be found in small and invisible agents."

Phase 3: Session 5 Onwards

The third phase of therapy consists of the patient gradually leaving the therapeutic relationship, while feeling that the bond is still alive and that therefore, if necessary, they can always reschedule another session.

To achieve this, we always give the client control over the next session. "When do you want us to meet? In three weeks? One month? How should we do this?" We offer alternatives without having an express preference for any of them. We can always remain at their reach in case something happens: "Okay, see you in a month. But if something happens and you want to send me a message, I want you to know that you can do that. And if you need to schedule a session before that, let me know and we will schedule it." This protocol has three intentions. Firstly, we space the sessions and we finish the formal therapy. Secondly, we give control back to the person. Thirdly, we plant a seed for them to think, "No, I don't need a session before that," fostering a sense of empowerment.

It is not uncommon for patients who have had a longer and more complex process to contact the therapist months after finishing therapy to schedule another session or to simply send an email from time to time. This does not mean that therapy has failed or that it is necessary to start over. Rather it is a testament to the success of the therapeutic relationship: experienced as a non-essential support that can be useful at specific moments.

Very Traumatic Experience with Dissociation

The difficulty in dealing with these situations lies in the particular variability of each case. This type of traumatic experience can happen to anyone, no matter the person's individual biography, pathology or absence of previous pathology, and to people with any personality structure. The prognosis of each case depends, to a large extent, on the degree of that person's general functioning prior to the traumatic experience. Successful and effective interventions can be very difficult when working with people with a serious psychiatric history and the use of psychiatric medication may be unavoidable. A history of anxiety or other psychiatric symptoms, rigid character structures, a diagnosis of borderline personality disorder or other personality disorders, a history of accumulated trauma, or any other disturbing intrapsychic or interpersonal element—all these factors can greatly hinder effective and efficient treatment.

As we have written before, the request for psychotherapy is usually motivated by the symptoms experienced by the person and not by the actual content of the psychedelic experience or the events that took place on the day of the session. This symptomatology largely coincides with what the DSM labels "Acute Stress Disorder," where one or more of the following symptoms may be present:

- Hyper-alertness: insomnia, irritability, startle response, difficulties concentrating on daily tasks.
- Re-experiencing the episode: intrusive thoughts, flashbacks, nightmares.
- Mechanisms for avoiding memories from the event and external triggers: emotional flattening, reduced activity, avoidance of people, activities, or places.
- Dissociative symptoms: depersonalization, derealization, or amnesia.
- Low mood and decreased normal functioning abilities.

What is really important in this type of intervention is to always proceed from the bottom up, that is, to begin by addressing the most disabling symptoms until a certain normality is restored in the person's daily life. Later, we can address the integration of the content of the experience, although in most cases our work will be rather poor in terms of its depth, dealing mostly with general aspects of the personality and character of the person. After recovering a certain sense of normality, people usually do not want to keep investigating the experience, so we do not get to enter that phase of the process. This should not be viewed as avoidance, but rather as the right process for the person. Therefore, it is necessary to be respectful, as in any other type of case, with the patient's decision to terminate the intervention at their own discretion.

The specific type of intervention will depend on the main symptoms that are affecting the person's well-being. Therefore, in these cases it is especially necessary to articulate a good definition of the problem and understand the symptomatology well: what it is, how and when it happens, how it affects them, and how it became so problematic. A humble attitude and seeking small objectives that can provide subsequent successes should constitute the guiding principle for our intervention. Improving the quality of sleep may seem like an unambitious or unimportant goal; however, it can be the piece that unravels the whole process and allows the person to find their own way to regaining normalcy.

In general, we can describe two general profiles: one in which hyper-alertness and re- experiencing responses predominate and another in which avoidance, dissociative symptoms, and a low mood predominate. These profiles tend to depend on the time that has elapsed since the experience. While the first profile is more common immediately after the experience, the second is more common after several weeks or months have passed.

Intervention in States of Hyper-alertness and Re-experimentation

Phase 1: Sessions 1-2

The person usually arrives at their first session feeling quite overwhelmed. Emotions are very intense and the individual may experience great difficulty going through their day to day. Some people have had to stop working and ask for a few days off, others have experienced a permanent state of anxiety or uncontrollable crying. In any case, the emotional manifestations can be intense, so we must provide an adequate container and remain welcoming and serene in the face of the patient's despair.

Allowing their emotional expression is important but overflow should not be encouraged. Thus, we must set some gentle limits to provide structure and containment to the person, while validating their emotional state.

Simultaneously, we will have to explore the problem and the symptoms in sufficient detail to get an idea of: 1) what is going on that makes day-to-day management so difficult and 2) how the person is responding to this situation.

Subsequently, we must offer some context that may help explain the occurrence of these reactions, without attributing them to their genetic or psychological qualities or making the person responsible for what happened. Oftentimes, whether explicitly or implicitly, these patients hold beliefs regarding the occurrence. Some patients may believe that the retreat or ceremony organizers feel that it would be better for them not to come back, or these patients believe that there is something intrinsically wrong with them, such as past traumas, which make them unfit to take ayahuasca, and that perhaps they are "too sick" for this model of therapy. We can provide them with an overview of the set and setting, as well as the factors that influence the outcome of these types of experiences, emphasizing the degree of personal safety needed to participate in a psychedelic session or other techniques for consciousness modification. We must transmit tranquility and hope, reassuring them that this transitory, intense state will subside and the person will regain stability in the near future.

One of the risks inherent to these situations is that, if people do end up going to see a psychiatrist, they may end up with a diagnosis of a drug-induced psychotic break and a prescription for antipsychotic medication and benzodiazepines, in which case the disorder can become chronic and remain unresolved. Psychiatric medication can help alleviate some symptoms but, in many cases, it does not offer a viable medium-term solution.

In some cases, people may already be taking psychiatric medication if they chose to see a doctor before seeking psychotherapy. In this case, we proceed in the same way: validating their decision to take medication, mentioning that it can be a useful tool to increase control and a sense of security while working on the psychological symptoms. If the person has been diagnosed, we can be curious about the person's opinion regarding that diagnosis and begin our work based on their own perception.

It is also important to assess the degree of support available to the person in their immediate context. Before considering any minimally sophisticated psychological intervention, we must make sure that the person has the basic needs covered, such as accommodation, food, good company, a grasp on their work obligations, and so on. If those aspects are not covered, we must work to help the person achieve some basic security first. Maslow's "hierarchy of needs"[47] can be a useful concept to keep in mind. Our priority in these cases is the creation of a safe environment for the person.

The most dramatic cases are usually those in which symptoms of hyper-alertness and re-experiencing predominate. In some situations, the person has a vivid image of a particular aspect of the psychedelic session that they define as the most traumatic. It can be, for example, the fear of death, the fear of being attacked by evil spirits, or the fear of going crazy and losing control. The person often feels as if the episode repeats itself over and over again, particularly when they are trying to relax, such as just before bedtime. In other cases, there are only reactions of anxiety and panic, which are not attached to specific content that is clearly related to the experience.

In these cases, we have a paradoxical task: We must create distance between the experience and the person, so that they feel that they can gain control over it and—at the same time—we have to make it easier for the person to confront that unresolved experience.

If the person harbors a specifically frightening memory or is more or less aware of what happened during the experience, a technique that may be useful is a written account of the trauma or of the particular painful experience (Cagnoni & Milanese, 2010). While recognizing how difficult the task is, the person is asked to write the account of the experience daily, from beginning to end, adding more and more details that they will uncover as the writing goes on. If they feel anxiety or the need to cry during the task, they should allow themselves to feel those emotions normally. We must proceed in this way on a daily basis, for at least a week. Much of the time, this writing manages to displace the symptoms in time and space and the person begins to enjoy some moments of rest. However, the situation is often still difficult after the first session.

If there is no expressed memory of the events, we can suggest that the person write down the specific fears or intrusive thoughts as they appear. We have to proceed in the same way: Every day for a limited time—for example, half an hour—write down all the fears and disastrous projections that overwhelm us.

In addition, we have to clearly prescribe the importance of maintaining an organized schedule of activities. It is important to maintain and keep up with good eating habits, hygiene, rest, going outside or being in contact with nature. In general, these are all recommendations that are given in the psychedelic and spiritual psychotherapy literature for similar situations and states of mind, including a spiritual emergency (Grof & Grof, 2001; Kornfield, 1997, 2001). One resource that many have found helpful is a talk by renowned Buddhist teacher Pema Chödrön entitled *Unconditional Confidence, Part 1* (Chödrön, 2010).

It is also advisable to recommend some intense exercise in one of the modalities that currently abound: Tabata, HIIT, or similar. These are short but intense exercises, which generate a rapid and powerful activation of the body and which can help distract us from our own emotional state as well as generate feelings of well-being and regulate stress hormones. Moderate exercise is also helpful, so any type of physical exercise should be encouraged as a therapeutic task.

Phase 2: Sessions 3-7

People often recognize, after a week or two of performing these tasks, that they are better able to think properly about the situation, but that they continue to have some symptoms. It is not unusual for patients to ask for therapeutic support at this point, and to have managed the first phase with medication or to the best of their ability.

We can continue to provide context, exploring the symptoms as well as the resources the person has to deal with these symptoms. Normally, the symptoms tend to become more specific and we can isolate the most salient one (for example, fear of going crazy or fear of dying). When these fears arise, the patient consequently tries to avoid them at all costs by trying to relax through doing breathing exercises or distracting themselves. Faced with the inability to spontaneously relax, the anxiety usually increases. If much of the narrative related to these fears or the experience itself still remains, we can continue with the structured writing task. If the symptom manifests with less complexity and we only come across the phobic component, then we can approach it with the same "imagining the worst" technique that we have described above.

In these cases, we will find resistance to this exercise, so it is particularly important to have established a good therapeutic relationship, to have stabilized the personal context and physical needs, and to have deactivated the most dramatic manifestations. We have to explain the task well, providing context for the rationale behind it, without anticipating the result. The course of therapy will unfold in much the same way as the "unresolved difficult experience," but it is reasonable to expect that progress will be irregular, that severe crises and relapses will happen, and that the person will feel like they are going backwards. It is important to re-define relapses as "real life" training that is testing new abilities. We can use military similes[48] (training ground vs. live rounds), sports (gym training vs. game), or something similar, depending on the language and personality of the patient.

In particularly serious situations, phase 1 can take longer (perhaps up to four sessions, or a month-long period), and the most acute symptoms can last longer.

Usually, the sense of emergency decreases, and we acquire a certain perception of stability. However, the experiential avoidance mechanisms that we outlined before may begin to establish themselves. Although they help diminish the anxiety, these mechanisms can also turn the problem into a chronic issue, especially as the patient becomes more dependent on them. In these cases, the feeling of being in a precarious balance coexists with the fear that the situation will quickly spiral out of control.

We must be flexible throughout this whole process and attend to other aspects that may arise in the daily life of the patient. However, we must not lose focus on integration, the original intention of the therapy. To measure progress and keep sight of the therapeutic goal on the horizon, the use of the "scaling technique" is very useful in these cases (de Shazer, 2010). This technique consists of asking the person to evaluate themselves on a scale from zero to ten, where zero represents the worst they have been and ten represents the ideal situation, once the problem is completely resolved. Subsequently, the elements that qualify the chosen number are explored and the next numerical stage is examined. For example, if the patient tells us that they are at a four, we can ask them, "How will we know when you are at a five?" So, we explore that five state, cognitively, emotionally, and behaviorally. The answers can be intriguing. For example, they could say: "Whenever I am able to watch that movie without stopping it in the middle, that would be a five." Thus, the patient's own logic defines the next prescriptions for us.[49]

On the one hand, we will continue to prescribe the "worst fantasy" technique, decreasing in frequency week by week and, on the other hand, we will be working through the scale to help decrease avoidance behaviors. The worst fantasy is our "gym training" and progressive exposure to the real world is "the game."

Phase 3: Sessions 7-10

We increasingly space the sessions, allowing relapses to happen and even prescribing them, so we can evaluate the progress and mechanisms learned. We reveal the ins and outs of the "worst fantasy" scenario technique progressively and we encourage the person to find creative ways to apply the things they have learned throughout the therapeutic process.

The unfolding of this phase is similar to the "unresolved difficult experience" scenario, although here we may find more variations in terms of the linearity of the improvement. Depending on the patient's previous history, their personality structure and their biography, the sessions will flow at their own rhythm and we might find more or less difficulty concluding therapy.

These patients tend to show even more reluctance to participate in another experience in modified states of consciousness, since their general profile is often more complex than the profile of those who have simply gone through a difficult experience. Therefore, they usually need to become more confident in their own process and feel that they are making some progress in fulfilling the intentions that prompted them to engage in the psychedelic experience in the first place before exposing themselves again. As I have described before, Holotropic Breathwork can provide a way forward, both for its usefulness and its contextual factors.

Intervention in Cases of Dissociative Symptoms, Avoidance, and Low Mood

Dissociative symptoms are not uncommon in people who have had a very difficult experience. After the more dramatic phases of the post-experience period, unpleasant perceptions of depersonalization (DP) and derealization (DR) may appear or may linger.

Depersonalization is the feeling that one is not oneself. On a logical level, they know who they are, but on a perceptual level it is as if the person remains a few inches away from themselves. It is quite difficult to explain and understand this symptom if one has never experienced it. Perhaps the worst aspects of this experience is the dissonance that is created between what one knows and what one perceives. While the person remains essentially the same as they were before, they do not perceive themself as such.

Everything is the same as before but at the same time there is something wrong. It is not a psychotic state, as there is a perfect adaptation to the consensus reality and an absence of delusions or other strange phenomena, although some psychologists and psychiatrists may get scared and interpret the patient's explanations as manifestations of a psychotic process.

Derealization is a sensation similar to depersonalization, but it is usually related to the environment. Although the person knows that the world is real, they do not perceive it as real. They know that it is not a dream but they have the impression that they are dreaming. It is the same feeling that the protagonists of *The Matrix* (1999) must have, knowing that although what they see and do is real in a certain sense, their perceptions do not correspond to the "real" reality.

There is much literature that has been written on these two disorders, which often appear at the same time; the understanding of the reasons why they occur, however, together with their causes and their treatment is still scarce. It is not my intention to offer absolute answers, only to show the possible attempted treatment of these cases.

These two distortions in the person's self-image tend to cause much anguish and often lead to avoidance behaviors and a depressed emotional state. DPDR is the cause of this discomfort, while avoidance and depression are its most measurable consequences. One dimension of the problem is internal, derived from DPDR, and mainly involves obsessing about whether or not this altered perception is really taking place, therefore generating internal anguish. At another level, an interpersonal problem exists: The person avoids social situations due to obsessive thoughts that other people can see and perceive that they are feeling and behaving "strangely." The person therefore reduces their social activity, isolates, and focuses even more on their perceptions and the unfolding of the disorder. Living in such a way entails giving up a reasonably active and interesting life for this period of time; the depressive state then manifests as a direct consequence of all the mechanisms used to deal with the situation. Thus, we have a problem of: 1) perception, 2) rumination and hyper-attention, and 3) avoidance of internal experiences and external situations.

These disorders are usually treated with medication, which tries to resolve the perceptual problem as a way to prevent the rest of the problems from happening. Our course of action will be precisely the opposite: We will tackle the consequences first, that is, cognition and avoidance.

Phase 1: Sessions 1-2

The most important thing during this phase is for the person to perceive that we really understand their problem. People with DPDR typically feel very misunderstood by medical professionals and wander from place to place in search of a pharmacological or psychological treatment that works. Very often, these people find more understanding among others affected by the same condition and there are many forums on the internet in which users with this problem communicate and share about their progress.

The therapist should try to get as accurate a picture as possible of why this perception becomes a problem. For those who have never experienced it, it may seem like a trivial inconvenience but for those who are there, it can even be a motive for suicide. There are some movies that come close to conveying an idea of this disorder. As I've mentioned, one is *The Matrix* (1999), which deals with this topic from an indirect sci-fi perspective. The other is *Numb* (2007), in which a depersonalization disorder is described after an experience with cannabis. It is important not to trivialize the problem or magnify it by looking for psychotic interpretations of the situation.

In the first session, we should simply focus on understanding the problem and showing empathy. For this we will need to paraphrase and reflect the patient's experience, showing them that we are attuned. Otherwise, it will be very difficult to get the person's cooperation in any therapeutic intervention. After establishing this therapeutic relationship, I have sometimes facilitated surprising re-framings of the disorder using metaphors from spiritual traditions or from works of art and film. The message is that the depersonalized perception that the patient is suffering constitutes a reality described by multiple traditions. We tend to identify with our body, with our ego, while in reality many traditions tell us that we are not only that. Even in the psychedelic tradition, death and the transcendence of the ego are sought-after experiences. In Hinduism the concept of *maya* (illusion, deception, dream) refers to the world that we perceive but which is not real, as well as that of *lila* to refer to the "divine game" that the creator sets in motion in our world.

These re-framings fail to eliminate the suffering or make the problem disappear, but they introduce a new perspective that allows them to see the issue from a completely different place. In addition, something can be added that, in my opinion, is a key factor in all depersonalization disorders. People who have successfully recovered from these disorders often report that perceptions of depersonalization had always been there, even before the psychedelic experience, but they had simply not given too much attention or importance to them. Most of us experience states of depersonalization, but they are not perceived as a problem. In the case of a disorder, a stressful experience has often happened, in which this depersonalization becomes clearly perceived and we become obsessively sensitive to it. From then on, we not only perceive it whenever it happens, but we are constantly looking for it, and therefore it happens more frequently.

As in the spiritual stories and *The Matrix* (1999) movie, we have all lived inside Maya/Matrix without knowing it. However, once we become aware of it, it is impossible to abstract ourselves from that knowledge and its consequences. In the movie, Cypher is willing to do anything to forget reality and return to the Matrix, to such an extent that he ends up betraying his own kin.

In the first session, during the conversation, the therapist needs to get as many details of the problem as possible: the type of thoughts they have, the situations they avoid, the internal dialogue that occurs when they become aware of depersonalization, as well as the emotions and bodily sensations that take place in these moments. The therapist needs to understand not only what happens, but when and how it happens.

To do this, it could be useful to keep a diary of all the problematic situations that take place. The "logbook" is again useful here (Nardone, 2002). A grid is built with some relevant information and the person is asked to fill it in when the problematic experience takes place.

Phase 2: Sessions 2-7

Daily tasks will help us identify and focus on the most problematic situations. These situations may take place more frequently in interpersonal contexts and in these cases, the avoidance component is the most important. However, when the situations happen mainly in the intrapsychic space, the obsessive/anxious component will be the main one.

In either case, we will proceed in parallel, paying more attention to the one that is most disabling, but addressing the other one too.

The technique used is the same we use in other situations: voluntary exposure to this sensation through imagining the worst fantasy. We ask the person to induce feelings of depersonalization accompanied by thoughts, emotions, and physical sensations. Oftentimes, these are worries like: "I'm feeling bad," "This is going to last forever," "I won't be able to leave the house because others will realize that I am weird," "There is no hope for me," "The only solution is suicide," "I want this to go away now," and so on. As mentioned, they will induce half an hour of daily exposure for a week and then reduce and vary the context.

On the other hand, we will explore what happens during interpersonal situations, where avoidance is usually prevalent yet there is no choice but to expose oneself, leading to a hyper-analysis of one's own behavior or facial expressions. They might think: "Do others notice that I'm not as present as I would like to be? That I cannot enjoy a situation that I should be enjoying?" We will gradually ask the person to pay attention to their interactions with other people, looking for signs that other people are detecting something strange in them. We try to divert attention from the intrapsychic to the interpersonal, and we want the person to become aware that they are actually behaving normally (as is usually the case). We prescribe progressive exposures to desired social contexts, not necessarily just to enjoy them, but as a diagnostic tool, as if the person were an anthropologist who is studying the reaction of others. Whether they enjoy the situation or have a good time is secondary. There are both literal and strategic components at play.

As we progress through the treatment, we can propose the strategy of "disclosing instead of hiding" (Fisch et al., 1982), which consists of sharing the problem instead of trying to hide it and solve it. For example, "I apologize if you see that I'm making a strange face today. It's just because I am feeling very nervous, but please continue with the conversation." People usually have a lot of resistance to this idea, so it must be prescribed only once we are sure that the person is ready for it. Furthermore, we must propose it suggestively, thinking clearly about who could be an appropriate person for this strategy (some people might find it easier to do it with people they are close to and other people might find it easier to do it with strangers). Usually, when people do this, the response of others is understanding and reassuring. Furthermore, people often empathize, saying that they did not notice anything strange, or that they themselves also experience similar difficulties.

In successive sessions, we can prescribe the worst fantasy in varying and decreasing intervals, up to five minutes and five times a day, in any and every context: at work, at home, on public transport, and so on. The patient thus normalizes the occurrence of altered perceptions but diminishes the importance of thinking about it too much.

The emotional realization that we, as therapists, eventually want to induce is the following: while the alteration of perception can happen, it does not mean that they need to be anxious about it, wanting it to go away or letting it affect their social life and, ultimately, the possibility of a happy life. Of course, if we say this during the first session, when this has not yet been experienced, it will not have the slightest effect and the person will likely find another therapist.

Phase 3: Session 7 Onwards

During this phase, we continue with the scaling technique to evaluate improvement and find the areas on which we must continue to focus. Normally, it involves being exposed to specific places and situations and the ongoing management of stressful circumstances provoked by the perception of depersonalization. We can thus work on consolidating the learning and lifestyle that the person has been acquiring and begin to cognitively normalize the states of depersonalization with the explanations that we offered previously. This is particularly useful if the person has already experienced something similar and says, for example: "I realize that I've already had this type of sensation sometimes," or "I can feel the depersonalization while continuing to do what I was doing, without getting upset," or "I can't tell you for sure whether I've had episodes of depersonalization or not. Maybe I have but I didn't notice them as much and I didn't feel any anxiety."

The procedure during this phase would be analogous to the other case profiles that we have presented, using the scaling, the prescribed relapses, and eventually the idea of repeating the experience of non-ordinary states through Holotropic Breathwork.

Georgina's case (continued)

A few weeks later, Georgina moved back into her mother's home. She did not experience panic attacks anymore, but she did not dare to live on her own or to sleep by herself (avoidance behavior) as she was afraid that they would reoccur. At this time, we prescribed the use of cognitive coping mechanisms, using the technique of imagining the worst. Of course, Georgina was horrified at the prospect of re-inducing those states that she had worked so hard to keep under control. However, I was able to convince her by suggesting that a controlled relapse now, while still in treatment, was a better choice than a possible uncontrolled relapse in the future. This technique was also presented to her as an opportunity to become stronger and as a path forward towards more insights conducive to her personal growth. In that way, she could use her experience with ayahuasca (which she had no intention of taking again) as a catalyst for her personal development.

Georgina worried about the insomnia quite a lot and she had created a whole ritual to "make sure" that she would get a good night's sleep, with many preliminary preparations (lighting candles, different prayers, going to bed earlier, taking relaxing baths, listening to quiet music, and so on), which eventually ended up adding pressure around her sleep problem. Some prescriptions were given, intended to counteract this pressure.

Georgina did not experience particularly severe episodes afterwards and the mechanisms that were still in place consisted, for the most part, of complex forms of avoidant behavior. Therefore, I suggested that we could do a Holotropic Breathwork session. The session was successful and she felt that it helped her get closure in relation to her ayahuasca experience, arriving at a place of resolution.

This case was resolved in just a few sessions, since Georgina began her sessions after the most dramatic episodes of panic had ceased. Furthermore, she had adequate social support and good personal coping skills.

Repeated Experiences without Integration

So far, we have seen a description of the most significant and common symptoms of this problem, as well as some similar phenomena described in different psychological and spiritual traditions. The clinical manifestations of this situation can vary in their severity, as we have also seen. The clinician, however, will usually encounter these cases once the symptoms are already affecting the life of the patient or their environment significantly.

Among the less severe gradients of this situation, we simply find an abundance of transpersonal material, a certain inattention to everyday dimensions, and an increase in unusual, eccentric, or schizotypal thoughts and behaviors in a way that does not interfere with the daily activity or relationships of the patient. In such cases, it is rare for the affected person to seek professional help or even feel that they need support.

In the most serious situations, schizotypal thoughts and behaviors increase to such an extent that they interfere with the person's ability to relate to their environment and carry on with their daily activities.

This is mainly due to excessive worry, anxiety, and continuous or even obsessive rumination about different aspects of their inner experiences, coupled with multiple synchronicities and external connections that the person perceives. The dissolution of clear boundaries between the inner and the outer contributes to the creation of a global sense of being under threat, whether by entities, spirits, shamans, or spirit guides, or by other ordinary people who may somehow steal or insert unwanted content into one's own psyche. This produces a situation of constant fear and anguish, as well as confusion and internal disorganization, which is clearly perceived by the clinician in their interactions with this patient.

In these cases, a straightforward intervention should be proposed. The person should stop seeking non-ordinary experiences immediately. They must abandon their practice or simply stop taking substances. After dwelling in an ordinary state of consciousness for a while, usually a few months, the contents may gradually settle and, most importantly, the person might manage to reestablish themselves in the personal and ordinary dimensions of their life.

Getting the person to actually do this, however, is another matter altogether. People in such situations tend to believe that the solution to their internal conflict will be found in "one more experience." That the next experience will be the one that finally manages to unravel all the confusion. However, this is not the case and such a strategy only aggravates the problem.

The dysfunctional attempted solution to the perceived problem is to keep journeying into the transpersonal realms, to continue taking ayahuasca or other substances, to keep searching inwards. However, it is precisely this attempted solution that is increasingly distancing the person from everyday reality and their ability to relate to it. Therefore, the only way out of this situation is to stop and reverse the dysfunctional attempted solution.

Convincing a person to stop doing what they have been doing requires, on the one hand, a great deal of respect for their idiosyncrasies.

A person who has ended up in such a situation has not done so voluntarily, nor has it been due to vice or excessive hedonism or carelessness. Quite the contrary. At the beginning, the person was very in touch with their suffering and this led them to seek a solution, probably after having tried a whole range of different therapies. From their perspective, the use of non-ordinary states or psychedelic substances is a legitimate attempt to solve a problem that has been going on for a long time. Therefore, it is necessary to validate the initial suffering of the patient, as well as respect and even admire the tenacity that it takes to continue seeking a way out of their suffering. However the focus has shifted away from the initial suffering towards a symptomatology rarely related to their initial problem and the person is now disconnected from their original conflict, which is the gateway into the patient's psychotherapeutic treatment. It takes a lot of patience and imagination to help a person in this situation. From my perspective, direct confrontations are not useful.

Phase 1: Sessions 1-3

Usually, we start working with whatever the person brings, such as the explicit contents of their psychedelic experiences, which we must listen to in detail and validate. We can offer alternative interpretations, always being careful not to dismiss or contradict the patient's version. We proceed as we would with psychotic patients, attempting to dismantle their delusion from within. Curiosity is an important attitude throughout the treatment, not only as a therapeutic strategy to achieve a good therapeutic bond, but as genuine and real curiosity. These patients may have had plenty of unusual and very interesting experiences. Not surprisingly, they are usually psychonauts who have traversed dimensions that many of us have only read about in books, so genuine curiosity and wonder will be our best allies during therapy.

It can be useful to offer maps and cartographies of the psychedelic experience, providing context for the experiences, framing them as part of a broader process and giving them meaning, marking a direction, and simultaneously doing away with the perception that their experiences are unique and special. It is convenient to offer these maps while citing their sources, in particular if they represent authoritative sources, such as Jung, Grof, Wilber, or Buddhist maps of consciousness. In this way, we are not merely giving our opinion, but sharing something that an expert in the field has said. We thus avoid a direct confrontation, while offering alternative and more rational explanations.

This can serve as an antidote to the frequent personal questions these patients often ask. It may seem important for them to validate that the therapist has had similar experiences, has gone through similar difficulties, or believes what the patient is telling them. It is helpful to be cautious in these situations because if we, as therapists, reveal a lot of our personal experiences, we risk enabling the dysfunctional interpretation of the patient and normalizing an unsatisfactory situation or even being discarded as a therapist because we are seen as lacking the necessary internal experience or disagreeing with the patient's ideas. If one does not reveal anything, they will have greater difficulty establishing a good therapeutic bond and the effectiveness of the treatment will be compromised. It is therefore important to reveal something about our own experience but always from the perspective that it is the patient who has authority over their own experience—that their experiences, supported by the maps drawn by authorities in the field, are the ones relevant for therapy.

Defining objectives for this type of intervention can be a complex task, since the patient is usually significantly confused about the nature of their suffering. They can perceive it but cannot explain it. We should not rush to get a clear definition of the objectives in these cases. In fact, it is useful to simply come to an understanding that we are going to work to integrate these unusual experiences. Some questions that can serve as a compass to help define the objectives are: "What aspects of your experiences do you think we need to integrate?" and "How do you know that you are not integrating your experiences?"—or better still, "With all the experience that you have, why did you choose to reach out to me for help with this?"

As an initial intervention, towards the end of the first session we can offer the patient metaphors that indirectly suggest the ineffectiveness of his solution strategy. For example, after validating their multiple trips, the extent of their knowledge, and the experience that they have amassed, we can say: "I have the image of an astronaut who has observed distant areas of the universe and has witnessed incredible phenomena. They have traveled through wormholes, seen quasars and supernovae, and now they are trying to sit in their lab and develop a theory that integrates everything they have seen." People in this situation usually agree that they have to integrate a lot of material, so you can say this directly to them. Another metaphor could be: "What you are sharing with me evokes the image of someone who, after spending a long time under a bright sun, enters the house again. It will take their eyes some time to get used to it and be able to see normally." Indirect messages like these can convey a first impression of the dynamics that we perceive.

Examples of other, more direct messages could be: "Have you ever seen the moths at night, when they swirl around a light bulb? They flutter constantly and never stop. However, they are blinded by the light and no matter how much they move, they are not getting anywhere. Sometimes they even end up scorched." Confrontational messages like these, however, should be done carefully, perhaps during later sessions once the therapeutic bond is consolidated and the patient becomes aware that continuous exposures to non-ordinary states are perhaps doing them more harm than good. If we have several sessions to work with this person, we are in no rush to share these types of reflections. However, if we are working within the context of a one-time session, perhaps we should take a risk and be more direct in our suggestions. The work context will define our approach as it does in all cases.

Phase 2: Sessions 4-8

The methodology and attitude that we have outlined in phase 1 must be maintained throughout this phase as well. However, effective treatment does not lie solely in these first interventions. The key in this type of process is to create bridges between the patient's transpersonal experiences and their personal life.

Diana's case

During our therapy sessions, Diana shared her psychedelic experiences with great emphasis and detail. She elaborated complex theories about their meaning and the implication that they had for her identity and her conception of reality. She recounted how elements of her experience were repeated in her daily life, where she began to have telepathic connections with strangers on public transport. Diana realized that perhaps she belonged to a race of beings from another planet—the same ones who had visited her during her experiences with ayahuasca—and that there were more of these beings living on Earth, disguised as humans like her, who she was learning to identify.

She then recounted the isolation that this caused her, particularly in relation to her roommates and the fear that she sometimes felt at night. She could not sleep much due to the anguish she felt for being able to access those supernatural dimensions and the anxiety that someone or something would harm her in the astral realms. Terrified of the dark, she left the bedside light on all night and did not leave her room if there was someone else in the house. When asked about her fear and whether this had happened to her before, she often gave evasive answers but was sometimes flooded by emotion, recounting traumatic episodes from her life.

These episodes were totally disconnected from the narrative that she had been providing so far and had no relation to the topics discussed in the session. However, they were highly significant episodes, including situations of childhood abuse, difficulties in school and with her classmates, humiliations from teachers, and a myriad of traumatic episodes that had nothing to do with the content of her psychedelic experiences. Diana would cry intensely for a few seconds, never more than a minute, and then she would come back and say: "Anyway, as I was saying..."

jumping back to the fantastical account of her strange experiences. We will see the resolution of this case in the coming pages.

Creating connections between experiences in non-ordinary states and everyday life allows us to focus on the origin and the reality of their present suffering. Similarly, it gives us the possibility to shift our focus, redirecting it away from the retelling of strange theories that are not very useful for the positive evolution of the case. As this dynamic deepens, narratives of earlier psychedelic experiences rich in personal content may begin to appear, eventually reaching the source: the underlying reason why that person started seeking healing in non-ordinary states of consciousness.

As integration takes place and stagnant emotions surface to be processed, more focus can be placed on the dissonance of their story. We can verbalize our perception that the problem, instead of improving, seems to have worsened through intensive use of substances. Our metaphors can become more explicit and provide some direction. We can try to emphasize how psychedelic experiences reflect personal content, even if it is appearing in a different register (this task is not always easy).

It may happen that, spontaneously, the person begins to question their healing strategy and doubt whether the experiences are even beneficial. My approach in such cases is to respond with a certain ambiguity, something like: "I see how these experiences could be making the situation worse. How else could you deal with this problem?" The answer to this question can be something as concrete and surprising as: "Well, I should quit my job and find another one that allows me to pay my bills with more peace of mind." Through this approach, we try to maximize our own resources, redefine the therapeutic needs, and point towards a solution that is meaningful to the person, as opposed to offering closed and abstract answers that do not generate new possibilities, such as: "Of course you have to stop taking ayahuasca! It is clearly not working for you."

The objective during this treatment phase is to change the focus of the patient's attention from the transpersonal to the personal, emphasizing the practical and mundane aspects of the patient's life. Most likely, the entire period of intensive internal exploration has left other aspects of their lives in a state of neglect: work, intimate relationships, former friends, or family. It is important that these topics pop up more and more during the conversations: "So, after you've been able to integrate all of these experiences, how do you think it will influence your job?" These questions imply a rethinking of the patient's relationship with the multiple dimensions of their daily life.

This phase ends once the person becomes aware that they need to slow down their use of substances, even stopping completely, and instead focus on addressing the aspects of their daily life that are still pending. In some cases, it may be necessary to do some specific work on particularly disabling symptoms, especially anxiety and rumination. However, with the decrease in substance consumption and the shift of focus towards personal issues, these issues tend to disappear spontaneously. However, if they continue to seek these experiences and their difficulty increases, specific therapeutic interventions to treat symptoms are often quite useless.

Thus far, I have approached these situations in the following way: getting down to the personal and working with its contents instead of keeping the focus on the "higher" transpersonal content. After a few years of practice and study, I was comforted to find validation of this approach in multiple spiritual disciplines, such as Buddhism, Hinduism, and Jewish Hasidism.

Kornfield (2001) recounts similar situations that happened during his intensive retreats and their solution, which he calls "finding the brake." This entails stopping meditative practice, doing intense physical exercise, taking hot showers and baths, changing your diet and incorporating meat (even during strict vegetarian retreats), sleeping, engaging in daily physical work (sweeping, working in the temple garden), and receiving social support (breaking the silence and being able to communicate, for example).

364

We also find the same strategy in Jungian theories:

Jung argues that, when dealing with extreme cases of inflation, it is far more necessary to strengthen and consolidate the ego than to understand and assimilate the products of the unconscious (Jung 1934, 1950). The decision on how to proceed must be left to the diagnostic and therapeutic tact of the analyst (Jung 1934,1950 in Schlamm, 2014).

Phase 3: Sessions 8 Onwards

Once the frequency of use has decreased or completely stopped and the strange symptoms are no longer as worrisome, we can shift our working style and start creating a global account of the experience. We can begin to do the most classic integrative work, using mandalas, drawings, narrations of multiple experiences and so on.

The need to continue integrating what has been experienced rather than exposing oneself to new experiences should be reinforced. There is often an agreement in these cases that the person has compiled enough material to last several years and that everything they have experienced has been somehow useful, even if they cannot understand it all yet.

We can reveal here, as a way of providing closure, some examples of similar situations from different traditions (see the section of the previous chapter), including the commonly proposed solution to alter or stop the practice altogether. For the most part, once we have reached this stage the person no longer needs any additional therapy, as they feel that it is a good moment to continue with the integration process on their own.

Some of these people will eventually go back to non-ordinary states of consciousness along their spiritual path and others will find alternative ways.

Diana's case (continued)

A year after completing her therapeutic process, Diana had not taken ayahuasca or any other psychedelic substance again. She had changed jobs and residences and now ran a small business with her new partner. Their relationship was going well, they were living together, and Diana was much more stable than she had been in earlier periods of her life. When asked about it, she recommended the experience of ayahuasca to those who were curious to try it. Her personal process had been challenging and it had marked a "before and after" in her life. She recommended caution and recognized that she still had a lot of material to integrate, something that would probably take a few more years.

Previous Mental Disorder

As we have described, people who have previously suffered from serious psychological difficulties such as psychotic disorders, manic episodes, major depression with psychotic symptoms, or severe panic and anxiety disorders may experience an exacerbation of symptoms or the precipitation of a new episode after a symptom-free period.

In the most severe cases, there is little the therapist can do. Most of these patients are taken to psychiatric emergency services and are routinely given antipsychotic medication to control symptoms. Many of these people have already suffered similar episodes in the past and have required psychiatric medication. In these situations, family members are usually the ones arranging a consultation, mostly seeking an explanation for what happened and trying to understand the role that these substances may have played in the general course of their loved one's episode. There is usually a logical confusion about the situation, since the patient has often communicated their intention to participate in psychedelic therapy or use sacred plants as an attempt to improve their psychological situation. Family members thus tend to think that these substances may be part of the solution, while being witnesses to the fact that the patient's psychological state has worsened after the experience. It is the integration therapist's job to provide the necessary information and educate family members on the basics of assisted therapy with consciousness-modifying substances.

As therapists, we can inform them about the way psychedelic therapy is carried out these days and the promises it holds. At the same time, it is also important to note that we still have very limited knowledge regarding the use of such substances to treat psychotic or bipolar pathologies and that only anecdotal reports are available, both from people who have done well (Mudge, 2019; Blackwell, 2011) and others whose symptoms have worsened. It is important to note that in clinical studies, the conditions are usually very different from those that exist in shamanic retreats or underground therapy settings, partly due to professional care, legal coverage, and most importantly the screening process, which in clinical studies is very strict.

It can also be necessary to validate the patient's intention to heal and grow, explaining to them that plenty of hypotheses indeed suggest that these therapies could be useful for treating serious pathologies. However, it is not so much about whether or not ayahuasca, psilocybin, or MDMA are a good fit for a certain disorder but rather about the conditions and circumstances in which the therapies are carried out. Examples such as Grof's early studies in Prague may be helpful. Grof conducted therapy with some psychotic patients with relatively good results, according to the author. However, they had hospital facilities where patients could remain admitted, there were medical and psychological personnel twenty-four hours a day, and they administered medication to control symptoms if necessary. In addition, these therapies could be prolonged during dozens of psychedelic sessions, in which the symptoms went through different phases, improving and worsening. We do not have resources like these currently, which would be necessary if we were to offer a similar therapy to people with more severe pathologies.

During this phase of psychoeducation it could be useful to recommend specialized literature on the subject. Some of the books that can provide a broad perspective on the treatment of the most extreme modified states are *The Stormy Search for the Self* (Grof & Grof, 2001), *Healing the Split* (Nelson, 2008), and *Breaking Open* (Evans & Read, 2020).

Sometimes we may be contacted by a person who has experienced a psychotic episode after the use of psychedelic substances but is now beyond the acute phase. Symptoms have stabilized and they are in a relatively normal situation. In such cases, it is advisable to carefully evaluate the need presented by the potential patient and the reasons why they seek our counsel. A common question is whether they can use psychedelic substances again, either as a healing method or recreationally. The affected person may be in a state of denial regarding the seriousness of the episodes they have experienced, perceiving them as something unproblematic that the rest of their environment failed to understand. In psychiatric terminology, this is called a lack of "disease awareness." In such cases, we should proceed in a way analogous to that described for family members, highlighting the importance of the set and the setting beyond substance and experience, clearly explaining the potential risks. In most cases, the most responsible thing is to advise against the use of any substance. But our intervention should go beyond this stage. Someone who arrives at our office does so because they perceive that they have a problem, so we must make an effort to understand what that problem is, why they want to take psychedelic substances, what they intend to achieve, and how they think that they will improve their life after a successful experience.

Working with people who have suffered from psychotic disorders or psychotic episodes requires a different kind of work than integrative psychotherapy. Although there are some similarities, we should not get confused. These people tend to naturally and spontaneously access experiences that are unusual for the rest of us. What they need is to learn how to reduce the influence of such experiences, rather than access more non-ordinary states, since their reality is quite unusual as it is. In a sense, doing therapy with people experiencing psychotic disorders consists of a constant integration of the non-ordinary into the ordinary. However, the method and procedure of the therapy are different because the patient often has a poor command of the most basic skills (social, professional, interpersonal, problem solving) despite experiencing a rich and varied internal world.

Eduardo's case

Eduardo was a thirty-year-old young man who arrived at the consultation after being referred by a mutual friend. He explained that he had experienced an unpleasant episode with his family, who decided to commit him to a psychiatric hospital, where they forced him to take medication. He did not understand why his family had such a reaction, since he was simply busy cleaning up the house. In the process, however, he kept removing objects from all the rooms until the whole house was left in a chaotic state, which worsened day by day. At some point Eduardo was taken to a psychiatrist who prescribed some medication, to which Eduardo reacted with aggression (this was only revealed after months of therapy). Finally, he was escorted from his home to the psychiatric hospital by the police.

Eduardo wanted to know if, in the therapist's opinion, he suffered from a psychotic disorder. He was taking antipsychotics, antidepressants, and benzodiazepines to control the symptoms and they were working well. The psychiatrist who treated him had a plan to gradually reduce the antidepressant and anxiolytic medication, while the antipsychotics would be maintained for at least nine months. Eduardo complied with the medication and his behavior became seemingly normal.

At first, it did not seem to be a case related to substance use, although Eduardo had a history of heavy use of psychedelics in recreational contexts, which he had stopped approximately four months ago. Throughout the first few sessions, it did not seem that Eduardo's situation was even a particularly serious psychotic disorder. From the symptoms he described, it appeared to be a manic episode with delusions of limited duration, all well controlled by medication. The patient spoke coherently and explained himself well, although there was clearly a lack of awareness regarding the seriousness of events (if the police had to intervene, the situation was probably more dramatic than what the patient was admitting).

The first therapeutic sessions focused on talking about the episode, trying to gain some awareness of what happened and understand other people's perspectives as to why they considered his behavior so abnormal that he was committed to a psychiatric hospital. Eduardo and I created a good therapeutic bond and the sessions took place in a climate of trust. I positioned myself as an ally, trying not to disapprove of his worldview or take the side of the psychiatrist and Eduardo's family, while at the same time trying to understand his perspective and his own concern in relation to the episode. Techniques were offered for better management of the relationship with his parents with the intention of avoiding the conflicts that were perceived as signs of psychosis by his family.

Progressively, over the next few weeks and months, the situation normalized while new details were revealed. We focused on the promotion of a healthy lifestyle, possibility of good social integration, and supporting Eduardo in the process of finding work and maintaining social contact. When he encountered some professional failures and the ending of an emotional relationship, therapy provided him some comfort and encouragement to continue pursuing new opportunities. We also focused our therapy on providing some guidance in the unusual cognitive and emotional states that Eduardo began to reveal.

At one point, Eduardo revealed that, as a child, he was the victim of sexual abuse by his peers. Furthermore, he was ridiculed and stigmatized for it. As a consequence, some of our therapy sessions focused on working out the consequences of that traumatic experience. Perhaps this was the first time that Eduardo had been able to talk about this honestly. He also revealed a violent episode and a suicide attempt, after an episode of substance use and an interpersonal conflict.

Later, Eduardo began to reveal an obsessive thought pattern with delusional and paranoid components, the most obvious manifestation of which was irrational jealousy. Eduardo maintained a stable romantic relationship, which was going reasonably well, although difficult episodes arose due to this jealousy. The therapy also focused on providing tools for the management of this relationship and avoiding unnecessary conflicts.

It seemed these delusional thought patterns had been around for a long time. However, he only gradually revealed them. Eduardo recounted a previous psychotic episode some years ago during a psychedelic experience, in which he became paranoid, aggressive, and had to go to the psychiatrist and take medication. This was the first time that Eduardo's behavior had been classified as psychotic and required medical intervention, although he had been suffering for a long time.

Over the course of two years, we conducted about twenty psychotherapy sessions. Eduardo continued to make follow-up visits whenever he felt that he needed a consultation about a particular topic. In recent months, the focus of our sessions had revolved around the experiences of sexual abuse suffered in childhood and how this impacted his life in the present moment. As we can see, this is a complex case, only tangentially related to substance use. However, it allows us to describe a case of psychotherapy with a person who has suffered a psychotic disorder and required integration. The course of therapy progressed in a slow and disorganized way, attending to the specific situations as they occured but with our compass always oriented so that Eduardo could meet the goals relating to his current stage in life: to achieve autonomy, to develop the ability to establish intimate and social relationships, and to manage the inevitable emotional ups and downs of life.

SUMMARY AND CONCLUSIONS

In the preceding pages, we have described many of the difficulties and challenges we face in the integration of psychedelic experiences. We have addressed the causes of these difficulties in relation to the specific events that precipitated them, rather than to the person and their character, or to the development of their intrapsychic experiences and their psychodynamics. In particular, we have been interested in understanding why such situations become problematic, to the extent that some people feel that they cannot integrate them on their own. Understanding the symptomatic manifestations that lead someone to seek an integration therapist has been our way to propose therapeutic interventions that allow that person to regain control over their internal life and their personal process.

Some profiles share common patterns in terms of symptoms and difficulties, even though they have different origins. In particular, we see that manifestations of anxiety, fear, somatizations, and perceptual and cognitive changes are quite common after a difficult or unresolved psychedelic experience. Faced with these facts, experiential avoidance and the attempt to control these unpleasant symptoms through unhelpful logical strategies are natural responses. However, this leads to the development of phobic, anxious, and obsessive complexes that perpetuate the problem and prevent the unconscious contents and the material that emerged in the experience from being resolved naturally. The therapeutic practice that we have proposed in these cases may seem paradoxical, cold, and even superficial. However, it simply aims to provide a safe context for the person to surrender to their own process, finding their own resources to take charge of their life and its evolution. In other words, we are trying to apply the same experiential logic of non-ordinary states to the context of verbal psychotherapy in an ordinary state of consciousness. I have tried to combine effective therapeutic mechanisms from therapeutic schools apparently disinclined to psychedelic inquiry with a broad and respectful understanding of human beings, their beliefs, and spiritual needs.

Other profiles present different difficulties, mostly related to the dangers and pitfalls we must negotiate throughout our personal and spiritual evolution, which I have described under the "risks of no integration" and include spiritual bypass, ego-inflation, and attachment to experiences. These dangers are not in themselves inherent to psychedelic substances, but common to the individual's search for meaning and a spiritual life. In an atomizing society, increasingly devoid of meaning and hope, it is normal that a growing number of people will attempt to seek answers to the great dilemmas of life. The nature of our social and developmental systems leads us towards some of the difficulties that emerge in integration: Unbridled consumerism, accumulation, competitiveness, a lack of awareness towards others and the environment, banality—all these are part of our way of life and are reflected in the way we approach psychedelics, as well as in the way we approach healing and spiritual evolution. This leads to narcissism, hopelessness, meaninglessness, a lack of responsibility, and greater separation. As a result—instead of greater peace and well-being—we encounter greater suffering, separated from what really matters.

The last category of problematic situations relates to the damage caused by the mistakes and failures of those who facilitate sessions for other people. Shamans, facilitators, therapists, and other helping professionals constitute one of the key factors in the outcome of psychedelic experiences. And as such, they can also cause serious harm to their patients. A lack of professionalism, negligence, malpractice and abuse are, unfortunately, frequent causes of the difficulties that people experience in the integration of their non-ordinary experiences. Multiple factors can lead to problems after a psychedelic experience; however, in most of the situations that I have attended to in my clinical practice, an element related to the facilitator or the person responsible for the experience has been present, either due to a lack of experience or knowledge, inappropriate care or insufficient resources, an excess of optimism, negligence during the preparation of the participants and the environment, or due to a lack of self-knowledge, honesty, or responsibility in relation to one's own ability to lead a session. Thus, the session guide cannot be ignored as a factor.

The personal responsibility of the therapist is equally crucial during an integration process. Over the years, I have successfully supported many people, just as I have failed to help others. This is my own responsibility, unrelated to the difficulty of the case, or to the patient's character. In any type of therapy, successes should be attributed to the patient and failures to the therapist. Unfortunately, in the context of psychedelic substances and master plants, the opposite happens too often. Therapists must continue training, receiving feedback and supervision to address those aspects of our practice where we can continue to improve.

The principles that have guided—and still guide—my work as a therapist are the service and support that help people regain their autonomy while promoting personal responsibility.

While this book has mostly focused on presenting a method of helping those experiencing difficult situations after psychedelic journeys, the potential benefits of the psychedelic experience are undisputed. Current psychiatry has become fond of psychedelics again and researching their therapeutic capacities is a field of growing interest and prestige. Psychedelics have made their way back into the mainstream again.

On the one hand, this presents unprecedented hope for new approaches to treating some of the most common, widespread, and incapacitating psychological disorders, such as depression, addiction, anxiety, and traumatic stress. In the near future, we will witness new treatments, appearing in forms that we may have never though of: microdosing protocols, non-psychedelic analogues of common psychedelic substances, seasonal psychedelic treatments for depression, dermal psychedelic patches, psychedelic clinics and treatment centers, specific music for psychedelic assisted therapy, and who knows what else.

On the other hand, it is difficult to foresee what the mainstream will do to the traditional use of psychedelics, and how well the psychedelic community will withstand the pressures of a market driven approach to mental health. We are currently witnessing some of the turmoil stirred up by psychedelics becoming a profitable business. This could affect the core values of traditional and therapeutic uses of non-ordinary states in a negative way, by trivializing the human experience as a mere byproduct of biochemistry, and ignoring the human aspects involved in any successful kind of therapy. At the same time, it could prevent malpractice by allowing practitioners to work in the open and receive training from reputed and ethical sources. Who will be able to work in the open, and who is going to decide that, will likely bring aggressive debates in the near future. But the era of psychedelic medicines is here to stay.

I hope this brilliant, almost blinding, future we have ahead of ourselves will be compatible with keeping ethical, compassionate, and fair practices, making the benefits of psychedelics accessible to a wider part of the population, not only for those wealthy enough to afford luxurious high-end psychedelic retreats.

In western societies we tend to understand the past as being behind ourselves, with the future in front of ourselves, as we walk towards it. By contrast, some Indigenous cosmologies of the Americas have a radically different perception of time's development. The past is in front of us, and the future is behind. We can see the past, where we come from, but we are unable to see the future. We are actually walking backwards towards a future we don't know.

It is by looking back at how our ancestors have used psychedelic substances and incorporated them into their worldview and social and healing practices, that we may gain wisdom and aspire to find a coherent way to incorporate them now. The San Pedro cactus has been used for over three thousand years, while psilocybin mushrooms and the peyote cactus may have been part of magical-religious practices for over six thousand years. We humans have a long tradition of using mind-altering substances to enter into non-ordinary states of consciousness for learning and healing. It is in our nature.

Psychedelic experiences can lead us to a higher vision of human potential, making visible all the good that we are capable of and helping us become more confident in ourselves and our species. From Abramson with his "integrative function of the psyche" to Grof and his "inner healing wisdom," all the way to our days of neo-shamanic explorations, psychedelic experiences and traditionally used psychoactive plants help us discover our own wisdom, our innate ability to heal, and our potential for learning. Perhaps we can even tap into the intelligence, wisdom, affection, and harmony of Creation itself.

The healing and wisdom that psychedelics can bring, however, lies not only in the intrapsychic experience—the inner worlds that we go through during our journeys—but also in the interpersonal domain. We cannot heal, learn, and grow as individuals alone. We heal, learn, and grow as individuals within our society.

In the age of communication and social media, we are becoming progressively isolated and lonely. We are losing connection to our neighbors and fellow human beings; decisions are being taken from us by algorithms that choose what we will find interesting or want to buy, or with whom we may want to connect online or even date. Our daily lives are becoming devoid of meaning while we try to make it, pay our bills, and buy the next thing that promises us happiness.

Sharing meaningful experiences is probably the best way that humans have found to find peace and harmony, to stick together, create stable societies, and, in the long term, survive. Because psychedelic experiences can be some of the most meaningful experiences of our lives, being together in non-ordinary states is one of the most profound ways to build deep connections with other humans and create the sense of a time spent meaningfully. From the ancient Eleusinian mysteries to the modern neo-shamanic ceremonies and psytrance events, humans want to gather and share precious hours of contact with the extraordinary.

Our society is currently very far away from making these kinds of practices accessible to everyone and finding time to share such moments with other people has become something revolutionary and rare.

If I try to imagine the future I would like to see for psychedelic substances, I envision a world in which people would have access to these mysterious tools and could use them in a responsible way. A world where people in pain could access pharmacological, psychological, and psychedelic treatments to deal with their suffering and regain control of their lives, despite their financial status, race, or religion. Where people who wanted to use psychedelics for their own philosophical inquiry could go to specific places that would provide a safe container to go through that experience in a respectful, ethical, professional, and compassionate way. A future where the growth and production of psychedelic plants and compounds is sustainable and respectful to the environment and the cultures that traditionally used them. A future where responsible adults could gather together, create appropriate settings, and share deep experiences in the intimacy of their group, just as our ancestors did—to heal, to learn, and to feel reverence towards the mystery of creation. In these scenarios, talking about integration will not be needed anymore. Psychedelic practices will already be integrated in our society and we will have learned how to create the appropriate spaces, hold the experiences, and provide the needed support afterwards.

To get there, some steps need to be taken. Psychologists, psychiatrists, researchers, and policymakers need to be flexible enough to understand the core values that psychedelic experiences show us. That is, that healing, growth, and wisdom come from within ourselves. Psychedelics can bring, to the field of mental health, a renewed and much needed compassion and respect towards those who suffer. Psychedelics also show us that healing and learning are processes, not events, and therefore mental health treatments should be planned accordingly. There is also the need to make sure that, as psychedelic therapy grows larger, there are therapists that can apply it with a deep and embodied understanding. Therapists that are not only professional and proficient in the techniques needed to deliver this kind of treatment, but that have also undergone a personal process themselves that convinces them of the need to be ethically impeccable. Again, learning is a process, and programs designed to train psychedelic therapists should take this into account.

The good news is that many of these steps are already happening. Research is flourishing, therapeutic models are being created, and in a short time MDMA and psilocybin will be prescription medicines. There is a growing interest in these therapeutic modalities and people are becoming more and more empowered to choose what treatment and tools they want to use. There are dozens of trainings for people who want to get started on this path and the idea that healing comes from within—not from an expert healer or clinician—is starting to take hold in some therapeutic schools. The dream of many psychedelic pioneers is coming true.

Will it remain true once we wake up? Will we be capable of integrating this revolution that we are collectively going through and make it a reality for our sons and daughters? Time will tell, but I am optimistic.

Sharing experiences in non-ordinary states helps us remember who we really are, our role in this cosmic game. Finding a therapeutic practice that respects that psychedelic logic, that allows us to root and consolidate these elevated states, while helping us reduce human suffering, seems like an indispensable task and has been the purpose of my work and this book.

I am most grateful to my teachers and the remarkable men and women I have learned from, and hope that they find their wisdom honored in my work. In turn, I hope this work inspires future therapists, facilitators, and psychedelic sitters—all those who come after me.

COMMON PROBLEMS IN INTEGRATION: SPECIFIC INTERVENTION PROTOCOLS		
TYPOLOGY	GENERAL INTERVENTION PRINCIPLES	INTERVENTION IN PHASE 1
1. LACK OF PREPARATION	• Validate emotional state. • Normalization. • Provide context according to client's needs • Usually a single session may be enough.	• Active and attentive listening of what happened. • Validate and normalize. • Provide useful cartographies, examples from similar situations. • Provide appropriate resources (books, movies, articles…).
2. DIFFICULT UNRESOLVED EXPERIENCE	• Validate and normalize. Allowing emotional expression and verbal report. • Encourage processing of unfinished contents through modification of coping strategies. • Reaching "closure."	• Do not rush. Validate and normalize. • "No change" prescriptions to block experiential avoidance attempts. • Using suggestive and metaphorical language. • Observation and insight tasks during challenging emotional situations.
3. EMERGENCE OF PREVIOUSLY UNKNOWN TRAUMATIC MEMORY	• Maintain neutrality about the objective reality of the memory: validate and normalize doubts. • Do not rush questions and inquiry. Ask to understand, not to draw conclusions. • Keep in mind the concept of COEX as "events and associated fantasies."	• Active and detailed listening to the experience and subsequent difficulties. • Give context that the phenomenon is relatively common. • Prescription of "no change." • In cases of controllable anxiety: prescription of ritualized writing of the experience. • If anxiety is too high and disabling, apply the protocols of profiles 2 or 5 as appropriate.

COMMON PROBLEMS IN INTEGRATION: SPECIFIC INTERVENTION PROTOCOLS		
TYPOLOGY	**INTERVENTION IN PHASE 2**	**INTERVENTION IN PHASE 3**
1. **LACK OF** **PREPARATION**		
2. **DIFFICULT** **UNRESOLVED** **EXPERIENCE**	• Modifying coping strategies and facilitating emotional processing, beginning with: Prescription of the "Worst Fantasy" exercise for 21 minutes a day. • In following sessions: "Worst Fantasy" 5x5', 3x3' and finally 5' when needed. • When anxious symptoms decrease, we can progressively start working with the meaning of the experience and more adaptive narratives.	• Progressive revealing of the rationale of the dysfunctional coping strategies and their alternatives. • Paradoxical prescription: relapses. • Allow the continuous unfolding of different narratives. • Promote autonomy and progressive exposure to diverse feared situations. • Potential Holotropic Breathwork experience
3. **EMERGENCE OF** **PREVIOUSLY** **UNKNOWN** **TRAUMATIC** **MEMORY**	• Exploration of the first narrative. • Progressive exploration of the two possible scenarios: 1) if the memory is real, 2) if it is symbolic. • Implicit focus on the "conflict of deciding" rather than on the two alternatives. • Possible presentation of the concept of COEX. • Progressive exploration of other elements present in the experience.	• Progressive expansion of the contents. Address positive aspects of the experience. • Solution-centered approach: How to maximize the potential benefits of the experience.

COMMON PROBLEMS IN INTEGRATION: SPECIFIC INTERVENTION PROTOCOLS		
TYPOLOGY	**GENERAL INTERVENTION PRINCIPLES**	**INTERVENTION IN PHASE 1**
4. ABUSE BY FACILITATORS / SHAMAN AND INTERPERSONAL DIFFICULTIES	• Keep in mind the different levels of communication: content and relationship. • Prioritize building a good therapeutic relationship. • Validate their suffering. • Clearly judge the abuser's malpractice. Openly take the patient's side.	• Allow the person to tell the story at his or her own pace and with the necessary amount of detail. • No pressure. Radical respect. • Constant validation. • Clearly indicate which behaviors constitute malpractice. • Cultivate the therapeutic relationship.

COMMON PROBLEMS IN INTEGRATION: SPECIFIC INTERVENTION PROTOCOLS		
TYPOLOGY	INTERVENTION IN PHASE 2	INTERVENTION IN PHASE 3
4. **ABUSE BY FACILITATORS / SHAMAN AND INTERPERSONAL DIFFICULTIES**	• Address possible ambivalence about what happened and about the role of the abuser. • Dealing with the symptomatology that may have appeared (according to the appropriate protocol). • Transforming shame and guilt into courage. • Mentoring and support about interpersonal decisions that the person may want to make. "Revenge is a dish best served cold."	• Continue mentoring the actions that the person is taking. • Give control of the course of therapy to the patient. • Increase time between sessions.

	COMMON PROBLEMS IN INTEGRATION: SPECIFIC INTERVENTION PROTOCOLS	
TYPOLOGY	**GENERAL INTERVENTION PRINCIPLES**	**INTERVENTION IN PHASE 1**
5. TRAUMATIC EXPERIENCE WITH DISSOCIATION	• Address symptomatology first. Begin with the most disabling symptom. • Re-establish "normality:" schedule, emotional stability, etc. • Identify which symptoms predominate: A) hyper-alertness and re-experiencing, or B) depersonalization and low mood. • Be aware that treatment may have breakthroughs and setbacks.	In case A): • Containment and context. • Assessment of the need for psychiatric medication and possible referral. • Stabilization of schedule and activities. Intense physical exercise. • Prescription of "the trauma story," every day for 30', at least one week or until the material is not so emotionally charged. • In case there is no explicit memory, account of the intrusive thoughts, sensations, and fears. In case B): • Use of metaphorical and suggestive language to restructure symptoms. • Creation of a good bond and understanding of the problem. • Diary of the problematic situations. • "No change," observation.

COMMON PROBLEMS IN INTEGRATION: SPECIFIC INTERVENTION PROTOCOLS		
TYPOLOGY	INTERVENTION IN PHASE 2	INTERVENTION IN PHASE 3
5. TRAUMATIC EXPERIENCE WITH DISSOCIATION	In case A): • Assess which specific symptoms are persisting. Continue with " the trauma story" if helpful or address symptoms with the "worst fantasy." • Check avoidance behaviors, address them gradually with controlled exposures, without expecting complete success. Scaling technique. • We proceed similarly to the "unresolved difficult experience." In case B): • Prescription of the worst fantasy about the most disabling experiences (depersonalization, catastrophic thoughts, etc.) 21' / 5x5'/3x3 successively. • Observation of verbal and non-verbal language of others in their social interactions. "Exposing oneself but not enjoying the encounters." Anthropologist attitude. • Subsequently, begin to disclose their difficulty when there is anxiety. • We proceed similarly to the "unresolved difficult experience."	In case A): • Progressive unveiling and explanation of appropriate and dysfunctional coping strategies. • Paradoxical prescription of relapses. • Allowing continuous evolution of the narrative of the experience. • Encourage autonomy and progressive exposure to diverse situations. • Possible experience with Holotropic Breathwork. • Be flexible with the development of the process and setbacks. In case B): • Work with relapses, normalization. • Rational and cognitive explanations of depersonalization episodes. • Consolidation of non-avoidance. • Same interventions as in case A.

COMMON PROBLEMS IN INTEGRATION: SPECIFIC INTERVENTION PROTOCOLS		
TYPOLOGY	**GENERAL INTERVENTION PRINCIPLES**	**INTERVENTION IN PHASE 1**
6. SEEKING OUT REPEATED EXPERIENCES WITHOUT INTEGRATION	• Encourage grounding in everyday reality. • Decrease or even stop the use of psychedelic substances. • As a therapist, remain focused and not be overwhelmed by the weirdness of symptoms. • Establish a good therapeutic relationship (we must earn the patient's respect so that he/she can accept our suggestions). • Be curious and be amazed by the richness of the experiences.	• Understanding the situation and the problems. • Validate the spiritual path walked so far. • Create a good therapeutic alliance. • Give context to the experiences with reliable maps. • Do not hurry. • Metaphorical and suggestive language related to the need for integration. • Sincere questions about the usefulness of the experiences they are having. • How to get worse?
7. PREVIOUS MENTAL DISORDER	During the acute phase and admission: • Ensure the person's safety. • Try to find the most appropriate support. • Minimize the impact of psychiatric admissions. • Minimize the impact on the family. • Become an ally and support for family members. After admission, if we work with the patient: • Understand that this case is not a regular "integration." • Psychotherapy as a support tool to manage the occasional difficulties that may arise.	During the acute phase and admission: • Remain available. • Activate resources (psychiatrists, friends...). • Give context to the family. After admission, if we work with the patient: • Do not rush, work on the therapeutic relationship. • Define therapy as a support. • Psychoeducation.

COMMON PROBLEMS IN INTEGRATION: SPECIFIC INTERVENTION PROTOCOLS		
TYPOLOGY	INTERVENTION IN PHASE 2	INTERVENTION IN PHASE 3
6. SEEKING OUT REPEATED EXPERIENCES WITHOUT INTEGRATION	• Focusing and defining the problem in the present moment. • Build bridges between the transpersonal and the biographical. • Emphasize the need for integration and make clearer suggestions about stopping the use of psychedelics. • Bring attention to neglected aspects of daily life (family, relationships, work, etc).	• Classical integration work (mandalas, stories, readings, etc.) that the patient can do on his/her own. • Solution-centered approach, How to improve the present life? • Spread out the sessions
7. PREVIOUS MENTAL DISORDER	• Proceed in therapy according to the patient's needs. • It may be necessary to be more directive and advise more actively in phases of increased symptomatology. • Focus on solutions, how to improve the present life. • Promote grounding in the everyday.	• Progressively space out the sessions, without terminating the therapy. The patient should be able to schedule a session when needed. • Solution-oriented approach. • Mentor/counselor role.

EPILOGUE

"The man who comes back through the Door in the Wall will never be quite the same as the man who went out. He will be wiser but less sure, happier but less self-satisfied, humbler in acknowledging his ignorance yet better equipped to understand the relationship of words to things, of systematic reasoning to the unfathomable mystery which it tries, forever vainly, to comprehend"

ALDOUS HUXLEY, THE DOORS OF PERCEPTION, (1954).

I finished writing this book in May 2020, in the midst of the COVID-19 crisis. During these months, my grandmother Maria Antònia died from the virus. She died alone in her residence and we were unable to say goodbye to her the way we would have liked. Moreover, we weren't really able to bury her as a family and, to this day, we still have not been able to get together and mourn her. However, I think that this scenario somehow made it easier for my grandmother, a strong and stoic woman from the countryside, to depart without having to feel the pain of those of us who stayed here. May her memory be a blessing to those of us who knew her. During this time, Tav Sparks—a Holotropic Breathwork teacher, mentor, and friend—also passed. Without them I would not be here or be who I am, nor would this book exist. I hope that my work would have been a source of satisfaction for them, and that it can help remember them.

These circumstances have made me reflect on the things that really matter in our lives, and the limitations we face when we choose reductionist perspectives. Psychotherapy is a commendable task, and helping people reduce their suffering is essential work. However, we cannot help but remember that psychotherapy is just a tool, and not an end in itself.

It is surprising to me that even after decades of psychedelic research and experimentation with different treatment formats, psychedelic substances have yet to be accepted as effective mental health treatments.

Since its inception, it has been difficult to demonstrate the positive effects of psychedelic psychotherapy. This is partly due to the complexity of creating and executing a methodologically sound study design. Moreover, once studies are underway, it is necessary to ensure that the therapeutic interventions are appropriate—a complex task in the case of psychedelic psychotherapy. These interventions need to take into account the extra-pharmacological factors (context, music, the therapeutic relationship, preparation and integration, training and experience of the therapists, and so on.), all of which are crucial to ensure good results. I am confident that, with a more systematic development of best practices around these extra-pharmacological factors, legislators can be convinced of the efficacy of psychedelic therapy, while contributing to the general improvement of mental health services in general and the practice of psychotherapy in particular.

Since the discovery of psychedelic substances, their effects have exceeded our capacity for understanding and comprehension. We have tried to catalog and define them under different prisms: psychological, pharmacological, therapeutic, spiritual, and so on, all of them reductionist. The vision presented in this book is not free from bias even if I have tried to be inclusive and comprehensive, and, therefore, has to be understood as one particular approach to a complex phenomenon, and an attempt to further develop the field of psychotherapy assisted with psychedelic substances.

Experiences in non-ordinary states, whether through psychedelics, Holotropic Breathwork, or any other means, can provide relief and hope for those who are suffering. In addition, they can give us new knowledge about ourselves and the world and help us develop our spiritual life. However, for any of this to make sense, it must be manifested in the world. If the outcome of psychedelic therapy remains exclusively in the intrapsychic spheres, we are missing a great opportunity. The therapeutic potential of experiences in expanded states of consciousness is not only individual, but also interpersonal, social, and collective.

When our inner experiences positively influence our view of the world, our relationships, and the way we behave, knowledge becomes wisdom. Ultimately, for me, that's integration.

I am convinced that experiences in non-ordinary states can be a crucial tool, not only for the psychological healing of individuals, but also for building more loving and fraternal relationships with our fellow human beings and the ecosystem as a whole. A friend once told me: "With psychedelic experience comes knowledge. And with knowledge comes responsibility." In these turbulent times, responsibility is perhaps the best we can offer to others and to the planet. Hopefully we can leave a good future for those who will come after us.

Sitges, May 31, 2020.

APPENDIX I: MEDICAL FORM FOR SCREENING

Medical Form for Participants in Psychedelic Sessions

Full Name:_____

Address:_____

Phone Number:_____ Email:_____

Job: _____ Age:_____

Information about the Session

These sessions are intended to be a personal growth experience and should not be considered a substitute for psychotherapy, but rather a complementary therapeutic device. Working with non-ordinary states can involve intense experiences accompanied by strong emotional and physical releases. It is not recommended for people with cardiovascular problems, serious hypertension, psychiatric conditions, recent fractures or surgery, acute infectious diseases, epilepsy, active spiritual emergencies, those who are pregnant, and other physical conditions.

Prior to deciding whether or not participate in a psychedelic session, it is essential that you consult your doctor and therapist, as well as the organizers of the session.

Personal Information

Please answer all questions as fully as possible. Your answers are intended to help us give better assistance and are strictly confidential.

1. Do you currently suffer from or have
    a family history of these ailments?

      a) Cardiovascular disease, including
    heart attack   YES   NO

      b) High blood pressure   YES   NO

      d) Psychiatric condition   YES   NO

      e) Recent operation   YES   NO

      f) Infectious or contagious diseases   YES   NO

      g) Glaucoma   YES   NO

      h) Displaced retina   YES   NO

      i) Epilepsy   YES   NO

      j) Osteoporosis   YES   NO

      k) Asthma (if yes, make sure your bring
    your inhaler to the session)   YES   NO

2. Are you pregnant?   YES   NO

3. Have you been hospitalized in the last 20 years?   YES   NO

4. Have you ever been hospitalized
    for a psychiatric illness?   YES   NO

5. Is there anyone in your family with a history
    of psychiatric disorders?   YES   NO

6. Are you currently receiving therapy or attending
    any kind of support group?   YES   NO

7. Are you taking any medication?   YES   NO

8. Is there anything else about your physical or
    emotional state we should know about?   YES   NO

9. Have you taken psychedelic substances before? YES NO

   If yes, which and how many times?_____

10. Have you experienced adverse or particularly

    difficult experiences with other psychoactive

    substances that you have found hard to integrate? YES NO

If you have answered "yes" to any of the questions above, it is important to give specific details on the back of this form or on another sheet.

Provide a contact person in case of emergency

Name (and relationship):_____

Phone number:_____

Please read and sign the following statement

I declare having read and understood the information contained in this form. I declare to have answered all questions with honesty and with the sufficient amount of detail, and I have not omitted any information that I consider relevant. As far as I know, my physical and psychological health are good.

Name:_____

Date:_____

Signature:_____

APPENDIX II: ADDITIONAL INTEGRATION RESOURCES

Below are some books, movies, and music that can be used as additional resources to foster integration. These are only examples of my personal choice. Not all are appropriate at all times, so each therapist must exercise good discernment in recommending these and other resources.

Books and novels

Beyond the Narrow Life: A Guide for Psychedelic Integration and Existential Exploration (Kile M. Ortigo Ph.D.). Synergetic Press, 2021.

The Stormy Search for the Self: a Guide to Personal Growth through Transformational Crisis (Christina & Stanislav Grof). Jeremy P.Tarcher, 1992.

Healing the Split: Integrating Spirit into our Understanding of the Mentally ill. (John E. Nelson). St. Univ. of New York Press, 1994.

After the Ecstasy, the Laundry: How Heart Grows Wise on the Spiritual Path (Jack Kornfield). Bantam, 2001.

A Path with Heart: a Guide through the Perils and Promises of Spiritual Life (Jack Kornfield). Rider, 2001.

Demian (Herman Hesse). Martino Fine Books, 2011.

Epopteia, avanzar sin olvidar (Josep M. Fericgla). Ed. La Liebre de Marzo, 2005.

The Red Book (Carl G. Jung). W.W Norton & Co, 2009.

Island (Aldous Huxley). Harper,2009.

Franny and Zooey (J.D. Salinger). Little, Brown and Co., 1991.

The Catcher in the Rye (J.D. Salinger). Little, Brown and Co., 1991.

Soul Collage: an Intuitive Collage Process for Individuals and Groups (Seena Frost). Handford Mead Pub, 2001.

Zig Zag Zen: Buddhism and Psychedelics (Badiner & Grey). Synergetic Press, 2015.

Women Who Run with the Wolves: Myths and Stories of the Wild Woman Archetype (Clarissa Pinkola Estés). Rider, 2008.

Movies and audio recordings

Unconditional Confidence (Audio CD. Pema Chödron)

Blueberry (2004, Jan Kounen)

Lars and the Real Girl (2007, Craig Gillespie)

The Fountain (2006, Darren Aronofsky)

The Salt of the Earth (2014, Julian Ribeiro Salgado)

A Monster Calls (2016, J.A. Bayona)

Waltz with Bashir (2008, Ari Folman)

Yalom's Cure (2014, Sabine Gisiger)

Nebraska (2013, Alexander Payne)

Me, Earl, and the Dying Girl (2015, Alfonso Gomez-Rejon)

Samsara (2011, Ron Fricke)

Baraka (1992, Ron Fricke)

Spring, Summer, Fall, Winter...and Spring. (2003, Ki-duk Kim)

La Tortue Rouge (2016, Michael Dudok de Wit)

Going Home (2017, Ram Dass / Derek Peck)

Ram Dass, Fierce Grace (2001, Mickey Lemle)

Mr. Nobody (2009, Jaco Van Dormael)

Cloud Atlas (2012, Tom Tykwer)

Ashes and Snow (2005, Gregory Colbert)

The Holy Mountain (1973, Alejandro Jodorowsky)

Waking Life (2001, Richard Linklater)

Human (2015 Yann Arthus-Bertrand)

Music

Nanas de Sol (Luis Paniagua)

Monsoon Point (Al Gromer Khan & Amelia Cuni)

The Unfolding (Chequerboard)

The Goldberg Variations (Bach / Glenn Gould)

From Sleep (Max Richter)

Nocturnes (Chopin / Claudio Arrau)

Standing in Silence (Rhian Sheehan)

Yearning (Robert Rich)

Motherland, the score (Sona Jobarteh)

Music for Airports (Brian Eno)

Canyon Trilogy (Peter Nakai)

Karam (Salif Keita)

Moffou (Salif Keita)

Stabat Mater (G. Pergolessi)

Islands (Ludovico Einaudi)

NOTES

1. Anyone interested in these reasons can consult Hofmannn's book, *LSD: My Problem Child*. 2008.
2. A recent review of these studies and others related to the effects of these substances in different aspects related to positive psychology can be found in: Jungaberle, H., Thal, S., Zeuch, A., Rougemont-Bücking, A., von Heyden, M., Aicher, H. and Scheidegger, M. 2018. "Positive Psychology in the Investigation of Psychedelics and Entactogens: A Critical Review." *Neuropharmacology*. 142: 179-199.
3. Gøtzsche, Peter. *Deadly Medicines and Organised Crime: How Big Pharma Has Corrupted Healthcare*. Boca Raton: Taylor and Francis, 2013.
4. Neihardt, John G. *Black Elk Speaks: the Complete Edition*. Bison Books, 2014.
5. Samorini, Giorgio. *Los alucinógenos en el mito: Relatos sobre el origen de las plantas psicoactivas*. Barcelona: Los Libros de la Liebre de Marzo, 2001. (Spanish language)
6. Although I might use masculine pronouns throughout this book, especially when referring to the therapist, this is purely done for comfort and flow in the reading experience, with no gender implication whatsoever. This is also a reflection of this book's direct translation from Spanish.
7. In the psychotherapeutic context, there is an ongoing debate regarding the proper terminology to refer to the person receiving treatment. Depending on the situation, I have used the words patient, client, subject, user, participant, and visitor. Throughout this book I will use the words patient and client interchangeably, and sometimes the word participant or subject when speaking of research contexts. I use these words without a particular connotation or intention, simply to refer to the person who hires, seeks, or requests the services of a therapist.
8. It is not surprising that the trope, "a psychedelic session is like ten years of therapy" has become popular. Certainly, the sheer volume of unconscious material that can be produced during an LSD experience, with a dose between 50 and 150 µg , is incomparably greater than what can be produced in a classical psychoanalysis session, in which the vehicles for accessing the unconscious are free association and dream analysis. Similarly, the therapeutic relationship can become much more intense and intimate in a few hours of psychedelic therapy than in a psychoanalytic process of months. Therefore, the transfer can be much clearer and more intense. In the same way, catharses under the influence of a substance can reach greater depth than in an ordinary state of consciousness. However, it is also important to consider the criticism often directed at psychoanalysis for being ineffective in producing results. Condensing ten years of psychoanalysis into a few hours

is certainly progress, although, following the same logic, it should not be surprising that no significant therapeutic changes occurred.

9. Surprisingly, the phenomenology of the experiences did not pose a challenge to the theoretical paradigm in which these pioneers worked, even when high doses (up to 400 µg) were used and re-birthing experiences occurred. Sandison (1955) states that "most of us who have worked with LSD have seen patients regress all the way back to their own birth. Usually, the patient feels as if it is he himself who is being born and sometimes, in female patients, who are giving birth." He relates "objective reality" to the archetypal rebirth experiences of different spiritual traditions. These experiences of psychospiritual rebirth had been described by R. Scott (1950) even in insulin-like coma treatments. It seems that Jungian schools were able to integrate this type of experience into their theoretical paradigm without stopping to consider the particularities of the perinatal dimensions, as Grof would later do (Grof, 1975).

10. I have kept most of the citations in their original source language. The translations of the quotes are my own, for the original Spanish version, except when the cited source was already in Spanish. Quotations that were originally in Spanish have been translated into English.

11. In his early experience using hypnosis, Freud found that it could produce some fast and surprising relief of symptoms but that they could return as fast and unexpectedly as they disappeared. This inconsistency, according to Freud, is what made him abandon hypnosis in favor of analysis. We can see how Freud's reflection can be akin to what sometimes happens with psychedelics.

12. Al Hubbard was a mysterious character who had a great influence on the development of psychedelic sessions and laid the foundations for the decades that followed. The method defined by Hubbard can be found described in MacLean (1961). It mainly consists of prior preparation, through interviews, the presentation of the effects of LSD, and the writing of an autobiographical piece. The session takes place in an aesthetically beautiful setting, with flowers and "universal symbols" and specially selected music. High doses are used (500-1500 µg) and in case of anxiety, a supplementary dose was administered so that the person could completely surrender to the experience. The patient is accompanied by a group of four therapists who are not under the influence of the substance, thus beginning to define the therapist's role during the sessions, providing respectful support without judgment. Additionally, all therapists go through their own psychedelic experiences, allowing them to empathize more and better support patients. At the end of the session, interviews are held, and the patient can either integrate on his own or with the therapist's help. This method laid the foundations for future substance-assisted psychotherapy, providing the blueprint for the way we work to this day.

13. The tension between clinicians and researchers has been a constant in the past and present history of psychedelic psychotherapy. While researchers

tend to place more emphasis on methodological and pharmacological factors in their studies, clinicians emphasize the importance of how treatment, preparation, and psychotherapy are carried out. Designing a methodology that satisfies both continues to be a main challenge nowadays.

14. For a comprehensive review of the history of psychedelic therapy and research in the United States, see the excellent work "The Trials of Psychedelic Therapy," by Matthew Oram (2018).

15. It is surprising to see that even in the paradigm of psychedelic therapy, where it is understood that only one or a few psychedelic experiences can have a dramatic and healing effect on the patient, it is recommended that the person follows through with a therapeutic or supportive process—Alcoholics Anonymous in this case—to maintain the results of the experience. The experience is understood, it seems, as a catalyst that helps the person make the best out of the subsequent therapy. This is not so different from the psycholytic approaches we have seen previously.

16. This comment by Pahnke has implications that we must consider carefully. According to Pahnke, the preparation phase, in addition to informing the technical details of the session and, above all, creating a good therapeutic alliance, should serve to maximize the placebo effect of the psychedelic session. This is an important contrast to the paradigm that generally understands psychedelic therapy as "non-directive." As we will see later, constructivist approaches in therapy support this idea of Pahnke, and they tell us that as a therapist it is impossible not to be directive. Thus, the key would lie more in knowing how to use that directivity, manipulation if you like, in a conscious, ethical way and focused on the patient's well-being. There are different types of directivity: the one used during the preparation phase, which would be a management of expectations and creating a specific setting, and the inner-directivity, which would be a general intention during the psychedelic session. In this regard, it is particularly important to understand the concept of "utilization" developed by Erickson and elaborated by Watlzawick (2012). Psychedelic therapy involves a high degree of manipulation of the setting, the expectations, and the suggestions to facilitate the occurrence of a mystical experience. Recent studies show the importance of the placebo effect in people that microdose LSD (Szigeti et al., 2021).

17. Multidisciplinary Association for Psychedelic Studies. More information: https://www.maps.org.

18. The document "A Manual for MDMA-Assisted Psychotherapy in the Treatment of Posttraumatic Stress Disorder" can be found online. The link is in the bibliography.

19. We see again the importance that many authors and clinicians give to the disappearance of symptoms, often contrasted to unsupervised and underground psychotherapeutic contexts, neo-shamanic circles, and experiential or purely transpersonal approaches, in which the symptoms are considered secondary and receive little attention since the focus is on the underlying causes and the roots of the problem. Even Freud himself believed that one of

the main objectives of psychoanalysis was to eliminate symptoms. However, attention to symptoms is sometimes underestimated as something typical of cognitive-behavioral therapy, which is considered superficial. The importance of working with symptoms and paying particular attention to them will be a topic of discussion in subsequent chapters.

20. Michael and Annie Mithoefer are the two therapists most experienced in treating post-traumatic stress disorder with MDMA in the framework of the studies carried out by MAPS. In addition, they have been in charge of training the therapists who have continued with this line of work.

21. (Mapping Consciousness with LSD [Podcast]).

22. Bache, Mapping Consciousness with LSD Podcast

23. Grof describes the basic perinatal matrices as four dynamic experiential constellations that frequently appear during experiences in non-ordinary states of consciousness. On one level, they are related to four distinct phases of the biological birth process, and on another level, they represent spiritual and archetypal aspects. In turn, perinatal matrices constitute the gateway to transpersonal experiences (Grof 1975, 2019).

24. We are of course referring to the aspects related to the integration sessions. Grof's model proposes an extremely effective intervention methodology during the experience in non-ordinary states. However, there are times when another psychedelic or Holotropic Breathing session may not be feasible or indicated.

25. See Bache's reference in the "Spiritual Dimension" section at the end of Chapter 2

26. The reader who ponders these distinctions will soon arrive at a paradox most common among young children. "How do we know that the color white that I see is the same as the color white that you see?" Thus, the very existence of a first-order reality is called into question and leads us into the abyss of existential emptiness. We understand that constructivist theory is just a theory, and therefore not an accurate description of the "real" world. We accept these self-imposed game rules, nonetheless, knowing that they are rather arbitrary, and we continue to play.

27. Fisch, Weakland, and Segal (1984) defined five common denominators for the different "attempted solutions" that people usually carry out, based on earlier classifications by Paul Watzlawick (1976). Two of them are intrapsychic in nature and three are interpersonal in nature. They are formulated as such: 1) the attempt to force something that can only happen spontaneously ("forcing what can only happen spontaneously"); 2) the attempt to control an outcome that we fear by postponing it ("postponing what we fear"); 3) the attempt to reach an agreement through an opposition; 4) the attempt to submit through free acceptance; and 5) confirming the accuser's suspicions through self-defense. Most of the problematic situations in the integration of psychedelic experiences that we will see in the fifth chapter have to do mainly with categories 1 and 2, that is, the intrapsychic ones.

28. Here we find another striking synchronicity between the pioneers of psyche-delic therapy and the pioneers of strategic therapy of the Mental Research Institute (MRI) group in Palo Alto. In 1960, a symposium on LSD psychotherapy was held at Napa State Hospital, California. The speakers were James Terrill, Charles Savage and Don D. Jackson; all three were members of MRI. Don D. Jackson was already an influential figure in the MRI group, specializing in family therapy, and he greatly shaped the development of the work of Watzlawick, Weakland and other pioneers of brief therapy. At this symposium, he presented a talk titled "LSD and the New Beginning," in which he reported the astonishing healing of an obsessive patient and pointed to the need for integration: "The new experience under LSD can be reinforced by social experiences and further experience with the therapist. Without this reinforcement, the LSD experience gradually pales and dies away; it becomes a memory, not a personality change."

It seems that the Palo Alto group was also aware of the multiple risks of psychedelic substances and the story of their line of research ended in drama partly because of them. A trip with LSD went awry in 1958 when Al Hubbard did not show up to lead the session and the researchers decided to take 200 ug on their own. The subsequent results were the destruction of all files related to this research, an inappropriate romantic affair with another psychiatrist, and the end of the relationship between Jackson and Savage. (Oram, 2018)

Jackson did not conduct further psychedelic research and died just ten years later in 1968. Charles Savage subsequently published several articles about psychedelic therapy in the treatment of alcoholism (Savage & McCabe, 1973) and worked with Pahnke and Grof (1970) and even discussed the use of peyote among Native Americans in the treatment of alcoholism.

The Palo Alto group were pioneers in psychedelic research. They were contemporaries of Hoffer and Osmond in Canada, all before Leary and Alpert, and the connections between these pioneers of psychedelics and strategic therapy, along with the cryptic figure of Milton Erickson (don Juan?) remain a source of mystery and fascination.

29. We could add that perhaps people who score higher in neuroticism are more likely to have difficult psychedelic experiences, not because the content they experience is more "negative" than that of others, but because their reaction to such content is more rigid.

30. The 'dark triad" is the name given to a grouping of three character traits: Machiavellianism (manipulative personality), narcissism, and psychopathy (Paulhus and Williams, 2002), which cause a particularly offensive but not pathological personality. We could argue that people who are attracted to power and social recognition (psychedelic guides, facilitators and therapists, amongst others) could have a tendency to display some of these traits. This personality type is potentially harmful, particularly if one occupies positions of power and influence. Therefore, it would be a good idea for any therapist and practitioner to analyze their own Machiavellian, narcissistic, and psychopathic tendencies for the sake of their patients.

31. The expression "heart and meaning" (*corazón y sentido*) was coined by anthropologist and shamanism expert Ángeles Arrien, who grew up in the Basque tradition and was a collaborator in the creation of integration dynamics for the Holotropic Breathwork technique. Most HB facilitators currently use this expression in sharing groups.

32. I use the words "problems" and "profiles" to refer to typologies of problems and specific constellations of difficulties that can arise after psychedelic experiences. In the next section, I have defined seven different problematic situations, or "profiles," that I have observed in my clinical work. The characterization of these profiles, typologies or problems has been made based on common factors in terms of symptoms, causes for their appearance and indicated therapeutic intervention.

33. Grof's definition of COEX systems can be found in Chapter 2, in the section dealing with the dimensions of integration, as well as in Chapter 3, when the mechanisms of the "attempted solutions" are explained. The reader unfamiliar with this concept may consult these pages, or refer to Grof's cited sources for a more detailed description (Grof, 1975 and 2005).

34. In this context, we are not going to analyze the possibility that attacks by non-physical entities are "really" taking place, or that the organizers really harbor malicious intentions towards the participants. The issue of demonic possessions or spiritual attacks is a topic that requires separate mention, perhaps to be elaborated in a future work. For the sake of simplicity, we are going to stay with the understanding we presented in Chapter 3: from a constructivist perspective, all explanations, including the psychological and the spiritual, constitute second-order realities. The states of possession and their psychological implications can also be understood as spiritual emergencies and will be briefly addressed in the corresponding section at the end of this chapter.

35. The symptoms that characterize acute stress disorder are: 1) Hyper-alertness (insomnia, irritability, startle response), 2) Re-experiencing (flashbacks, intrusive thoughts, nightmares), 3) Avoidance (emotional flattening), 4) Dissociative symptoms (depersonalization and derealization, amnesia), and 5) Decreased cognitive abilities

36. And yet, it could be said that the therapeutic methods employed by some pioneers of psychedelic therapy assumed that people had to enter these emotionally overwhelming spaces and go through difficult experiences in order to heal. Examples are found in Grof's clinical cases (2005), in which his patients confront biographical, perinatal and transpersonal traumas, or in the methodology of Salvador Roquet's psychosynthesis (Roquet and Favreau, 1981), which sought to induce states of "madness" in their patients to later promote healthier restructuring. Grof writes in this regard: "the problem of whether the emphasis of LSD psychotherapy should be on reliving traumatic memories and conflicts or on transcendental experiences has been one of the most controversial issues [...]. Based on my experience [both aspects]

are important and integral parts of the healing process. Furthermore, [both] seem to be mutually interrelated in a dialectical way "(Grof, 2005, 295-296).

37. The Grofs defined eleven different types of spiritual emergency: 1) episodes of unitary consciousness; 2) kundalini awakening; 3) near death experiences; 4) emergence of memories of "past lives;" 5) psychological renewal through a return to the center; 6) shamanic crisis; 7) awakening of extrasensory perception; 8) communicating with spirit guides and channeling; 9) experiences of encounters with UFOs; 10) states of possession; and 11) addiction as a spiritual emergency (Grof & Grof, 2001).

38. The different dimensions of integration have been described in Chapter 2.

39. I use the world "seemingly," since, in my opinion, the creators of the Palo Alto MRI therapeutic model did have a good understanding of the inherent characteristics of the psychedelic experience. Throughout this book I have included examples and anecdotes related to some of the pioneers of this model, such as Gregory Bateson and Paul Watzlawick, as well as the mysterious figure of Milton Erickson. They all seem to have had knowledge of psychedelic substances and other schools of deep psychology, as well as an extensive understanding of Eastern mystical philosophy. For this reason, I dare to venture that the brief therapy school of Palo Alto, in its origins, was influenced by psychedelic substances and non-ordinary states of consciousness.

40. There are several aspects to analyze in this quote; it is striking how much some of the principles alluded to here by Freud have permeated the contemporary practice of therapy. On the one hand, failure is considered "partial success," a common practice of many current patients and therapists. Furthermore, putting a time limit on therapy is considered a "heroic procedure." Of course, such interventions could be classified as heroic for many therapists, but it would be necessary to consider what the patients think of it. Third, regarding the assumption that the cure was "complete," Freud refers here to the outbreak of the First World War in 1914. The patient appears to have worsened during wartime, much to the disappointment of Freud. It is legitimate to doubt whether therapy failed or whether environmental factors, such as war, may justify the appearance of "neurotic symptoms." Psychoanalysis aims to prevent the appearance of symptoms even in such exceptional periods as a world war. All these ingredients, also present in contemporary psychotherapeutic orientations, as well as in Western conceptions of the spiritual path, lead the therapeutic process to a foreseeable and inevitable failure due to its unrealistic expectations and a lack of understanding of the nature of "real" life.

41. The Pygmalion or Rosenthal effect is known as the influence that teachers' expectations have on the actual development of students. Although it has been criticized, the central idea is that if teachers expect students to do well (because, for example, they have been told that they are capable students), the students often do well. The same occurs in psychiatry: the diagnosis dramatically determines the psychiatrist's perception about their patient,

regardless of the patients' actual behaviors. An example can be found in the aforementioned experiment carried out by Rosenhan and collaborators, "On Being Sane in Insane Places," in which participants pretended to have psychotic symptoms to gain secret admission to psychiatric hospitals. Once the diagnoses were established, they behaved completely "normal." However, medical staff were unable to detect that healthy people had been admitted by mistake (Rosenhan, in Watzlawick et al., 2015).

42. See the chapter entitled "The Utopia Syndrome" in Watzlawick, Weakland, and Fisch (1976), very relevant in the context of psychedelic self-exploration and "healing" circles.

43. A good example is that psychoanalytic joke in which a friend asks another friend if, after years of psychoanalysis, he has managed to get rid of his neurosis, to which the friend replies: "no, but now I can give a two-hour lecture about it." Or, as Viktor Frankl succinctly puts it, "being unable to see the forest of reality because of the trees of symbols and images."

44. Reframing is perhaps the main therapeutic intervention. Watzlawick describes it as "changing one's own conceptual or emotional framework, in which a situation is experienced, and placing it within another structure, which addresses the 'facts' corresponding to the same concrete situation equally or even better, thus completely changing their meaning" (Watzlawick et al., 1976).

45. Visit www.holotropic.com. for a list of certified Holotropic Breathwork facilitators trained in the Principles of Holotropic Breathwork as originally presented by the Grofs.

46. A more extensive presentation on Steve's case can be found on YouTube under the title, "Marc Aixalà: Integration of a Difficult Psilocybin Experience in a Clinical Trial. A Case Study."

47. Abraham Maslow proposed a psychological theory based upon the hierarchy of needs of human beings. Maslow divided these needs into levels of a "pyramid" that contains the following (in ascending order): physiological needs, safety and security, love and belonging, self-esteem, and self-actualization. In general, it is understood that it is difficult to meet the needs of a certain level if those of the lower levels are not met (for example, it is difficult to focus on self-actualization if one is in a situation of poverty and physiological needs are not covered).

48. Arguably, military similes are inconsistent with the human values that are supposed to exist in the transpersonal and spiritual scenes. However, they do bring certain practical advantages: their potential to evoke emotions and their capacity to externalize the problem. Most of us have seen war movies and are familiar with the classic images of the training ground with the smoke bombs, the blank shots and the sergeant screaming as soldiers crawl in the mud under barbed wire. As a spectator, one cannot avoid feeling like we are witnessing a ridiculous scene, since it is a fabrication and does not involve any real danger but, at the same time, we can empathize with the fact that the soldiers feel stressed. In this way, we are sending a subliminal

message to the patient that, while the task can be stressful, it is not really dangerous. In addition, these type of war metaphors fulfill the function of externalizing the problem, seeing it as an external enemy rather than as their own personal traits (which, therefore, would be more difficult to eliminate). In my experience, people with phobic personalities or with aggressive and paranoid tendencies respond well to these types of metaphors. Other people may respond better to more cooperative similes, such as sports training, rehearsing a public speech, and so on. Each therapist must sharpen their creativity and find the metaphors that work best for them.

49. The inconspicuousness of this technique can make us doubt its usefulness and effectiveness. To see examples of masterful uses of the "scaling technique" I recommend referring to Steve de Shazer's book, *Words Were Originally Magic* (2010).

REFERENCES

Abramson, H. (Ed.) (1967). *The Use of LSD in Psychotherapy and Alcoholism.* Indianapolis, Estados Unidos: Bobbs-Merrill.

Abramson, H. (1955). Lysergic acid diethylamide (LSD-25). III – As an adjunct to psychotherapy with elimination of fear of homosexuality. *Journal of Psychology,* 39, 127-155.

Abramson, H. (1956). Lysergic acid diethylamide (LSD-25). XIX – As an adjunct to brief psychotherapy with special reference to ego enhancement. *Journal of Psychology,* 41, 199-229.

Abramson, H. (1956). Lysergic acid diethylamide (LSD-25). XXII – Effect on transference. *Journal of Psychology,* 42, 51-98.

Abramson, H. (1961). Lysergic acid diethylamide (LSD-25). XXXII – Resolution of counter-identification conflict of father during oedipal phase of son. *Journal of Psychology,* 51, 33-87.

Abramson, H. (1966). LSD in psychotherapy and alcoholism. *American Journal of Psychotherapy,* 20(3), 415-438.

Abramson, H. (1973). Lysergic acid diethylamide (LSD-25). XXXXI – The use of LSD as an adjunct to psychotherapy: Fact and fiction. *Journal of Asthma Research,* 10(4), 227-235.

Adamson, S., y Metzner, R. (1988). The nature of the MDMA experience and its role in healing, psychotherapy and spiritual practice. *ReVision: A Journal of Consciousness and Transformation,* 10, 59-72.

Aixalà, M. B. (2018). Claroscuros de la psiquedelia. *Revista Ulises,* 20.

Aixalà, M. B., dos Santos, R. G., Hallak, J. E., y Bouso, J. C. (2018). Psychedelics and personality. *ACS Chemical Neuroscience,* 9(10), 2304-2306.

Aixalà, M. B., Oña, G., Parés, O., y Bouso, J. C. (2019). Patterns of use, desired effects and mental health status of a sample of natural psychoactive drug users. *Drugs: Education, Prevention and Policy,* 27(3), 191-198.

Alighieri, D. (2000). *La Divina Comèdia.* Barcelona, España: Quaderns Crema.

Alnaes, R. (1964). Therapeutic application of the change in consciousness produced by psycholytica (LSD, psilocybin, etc.): the psychedelic experience in the treatment of neurosis. *Psychiatrica Scandinavica,* 40(180), 397-409.

Bache, C. (2019). *LSD and the Mind of the Universe: Diamonds from Heaven.* Rochester, Estados Unidos: Park Street Press.

Badiner, A. (Ed.). (2015). *Zig Zag Zen. Buddhism and Psychedelics.* Santa Fe, Estados Unidos: Synergetic Press.

Baker, E. F. W. (1964). The use of lysergic acid diethylamide (LSD) in psychotherapy. *Canadian Medical Association Journal,* .91, 1200-1203.

Bandler, R., y Grinder, J. (1980). *La estructura de la magia.* Santiago de Chile, Chile: Cuatro Vientos.

Baroni, D. (1931). Gestandnisse im Meskalinrausch. *Psychoanalytische Praxis,* 1, 145-149

Barr, H. L., y Langs, R. J. (1972). *LSD: Personality and Experience.* Nueva York, Estados Unidos: Wiley Interscience.

Barret, F. S., Bradstreet, M. O., Leoutsakos, J. M., Johnson, M. W., y Griffiths, R. R. (2016). The challenging experience questionnaire: characterization of challenging experiences with psilocybin mushrooms. *Journal of Psychopharmacology,* 30(12), 1279-1295.

Barret, F. S., y Griffiths, R. R. (2018). Classic hallucinogens and mystical experiences: phenomenology and neural correlates. *Current Topics in Behavioral Neurosciences,* 36, 393-430.

Barret, F. S., Johnson, M. W., y Griffiths, R. R. (2015). Validation of the revised Mystical Experience Questionnaire in experimental session with psilocybin. *Journal of Psychopharmacology,* 29(11), 1182-1190.

Barret, F. S., Johnson, M. W., y Griffiths, R. R. (2017). Neuroticism is associated with challenging experiences with psilocybin mushrooms. *Personality and Individual Differences,* 117, 155-160.

Barret, F. S., Robbins, H., Smooke, D., Brown, J., y Griffiths, R. R. (2017). Qualitative and quantitative features of music reported to support peak mystical experiences during psychedelic therapy sessions. *Frontiers in Psychology,* 8, 1238.

Barsuglia, J., Davis, A. K., Palmer, R., Lancelotta, R., Windham-Herman, A. M., Peterson, K., Polanco, M., Grant, R., y Griffiths, R. R. (2018). Intensity of mystical experiences occasioned by 5-MeO-DMT and comparison with a prior psilocybin study. *Frontiers in Psychology,* 9, 2459.

Bateson, G. (1967). Cybernetic explanation. *American Behavioral Scientist,* 10, 29-32.

Bentall, R. P. (1990). The illusion of reality: a review and integration of psychological research on hallucinations. *Psychological Bulletin,* 107(1), 82-95.

Blackwell, S. (2011). *Am I Bipolar or Waking Up?* Charleston, Estados Unidos: CreateSpace.

Blasco, S. (2018). *The Power Within: The Practice of Holotropic Breathwork* (Módulo de formación del GTT). Catalunya, España: Grof Transpersonal Training. Comunicación personal.

Blewett D. C., y Chwelos, N. (1959). *Handbook for the Therapeutic Use of Lysergic Acid Diethylamide-25, Individual and Group Procedures.* Regina, Canadá: manuscrito sin publicar. Editado en versión digital por MAPS y Erowid en 2002.

Bogenschutz, M. P. (2013). Studying the effects of classic hallucinogens in the treatment of alcoholism: rationale, methodology and current research with psilocybin. *Current Drug Abuse Reviews,* .6, 17-29.

Bogenschutz, M. P., Forcehimes, A. A., Pommy, J. A., Wilcox, C. E., Barbosa, P. C. R., y Strassman, R. J. (2015). Psilocybin-assisted treatment of alcohol dependence: A proof-of-concept study. *Journal of Psychopharmacology,* 29(3), 1-11.

Bogenschutz, M. P., y Johnson, M. W. (2016). Classic hallucinogens in the treatment of addictions. *Progress in Neuro-Psychopharmacology & Biological Psychiatry,* 64, 250-258.

Bogenschutz, M. P., y Ross, S. (2016). Therapeutic applications of classic hallucinogens. *Current Topics in Behavioral Neurosciences,* 2018(36), 361-391.

Bouso, J. C., Doblin, R., Farré, M., Alcázar, M. A., y Gómez-Jarabo, G. (2008). MDMA-assisted psychotherapy using low doses in a small sample of women with chronic post-traumatic stress disorder. *Journal of Psychoactive Drugs,* 40(3), 225-236.

Bouso, J. C., González, D., Fondevila, S., Cutchet, M., Fernández, X., Barbosa, P. C., Alcázar-Córcoles, M. A., Sena, W., Barbanoj, R. J., Fábregas, J. M., y Riba, J. (2012). Personality, psychopathology, life attitudes and neuropsychological performance among ritual users of ayahuasca: a longitudinal study. *PLoS ONE,* 7(8), e4241.

Bouso, J. C., Palhano-Fontes, F., Rodríguez-Fornells, A., Ribeiro, S., Sanches, R., Crippa, J. A., Hallak, J. E., de Araujo, D. B., y Riba, J. (2015). Long-term use of psychedelic drugs associated with differences in brain structure and personality in humans. *European Neuropsychopharmacology,* 25, 483-492.

Bouso, J. C., dos Santos, R. G., Alcázar-Córcoles, M. A., y Hallack, J. E. C. (2018). Serotonergic psychedelics and personality: a systematic review of contemporary research. *Neuroscience & Biobehavioral Reviews,* 87, 118-132.

Bowen, W. T., Soskin, R. A., y Chotlos, J. W. (1970). Lysergic acid diethylamide as a variable in the hospital treatment of alcoholism. *Journal of Nervous and Mental Disease,* 150(2), 111-118.

Bucay, J. (2008). *Cuentos para pensar.* Barcelona, España: RBA Libros.

Busch A.K y Johnson WC.(1950). L.S.D.-25 as an aid in psychotherapy; preliminary report of a new drug. *Diseases of the Nervous System.* 1950 Aug;11(8):241-3.

Butterworth, A. T. (1962). Some aspects of an office practice utilizing LSD-25. *Psychiatric Quarterly,* 1962(36), 734-753.

Calvino, I. (2005). *Las ciudades invisibles.* Madrid, España: Siruela.

Calvino, I. (2012). *Los amores imposibles.* Madrid, España: Siruela.

Camí, J., Farré, M., Mas, M., Roset, P. N., Poudevida, S., Mas, A., San, L., y de la Torre, R. (2000). Human pharmacology of 3,4-methylenedioxymethamphetamine ("ecstasy"): psychomotor performance and subjective effects. *Journal of Clinical Psychopharmacology,* 20(4), 455-466.

Carbonaro, T. M., Bradstreet, M. P., Barret, F. S., MacLean, K. A., Jesse, R., Johnson, M. W., y Griffiths, R. R. (2016). Survey study of challenging experiences after ingesting psilocybin mushrooms: acute and enduring positive and negative consequences. *Journal of Psychopharmacology,* 30(12), 1268-1278.

Carhart-Harris, R. L., Bolstridge, M., Day, C. M. J., Rucker, J., Watts, R., Erritzoe, D. E., Kaelen, M., Giribaldi, B., Bloomfield, M., Pilling, S., Rickard, J. A., Forbes, B., Fielding, A., Taylor, D., Curran, H. V., y Nutt, D. J. (2017). Psilocybin with psychological support for treatment-resistant depression: six-month follow-up. *Psychopharmacology (Berl),* 235(2), 399-408.

Carhart-Harris, R. L., Bosltridge, M., Rucker, J., Day, C. M., Kaelen, M., Bloomfield, M., Rickard, J. A., Forbes, B., Fielding, A., Taylor, D., Pilling, S., Curran, V. H., y Nutt, D. (2016). Psilocybin with psychological support for treatment-resistant depression: an open-label feasibility study. *Lancet Psychiatry, 3*(7), 619-627.

Carhart-Harris, R. L., Erritzoe, D., Haijen, E., Kaelen, M., y Watts, R. (2017). Psychedelics and connectedness. *Psychopharmacology (Berl), 235*(2), 547-550.

Carhart-Harris, R. L., y Goodwin, G. M. (2017). The therapeutic potential of psychedelic drugs: past, present and future. *Neuropsychopharmacology, 42,* 2105-2113.

Carhart-Harris, R. L., Kaelen, M., Bolstridge, M., Williams, T. M., Underwood, R., Fielding, A., y Nutt, D. (2016). The paradoxical psychological effects of lysergic acid diethylamide (LSD). *Psychological Medicine, 46,* 1379-1390.

Carhart-Harris, R. L., Kaelen, M., Whalley, M. G., Bolstridge, M., Fielding, A., y Nutt, D. J. (2014). LSD enhances suggestibility in healthy volunteers. *Psychopharmacology (Berl), 232*(4), 785-794.

Carhart-Harris, R. L., Leech, R., Hellyer, P. J., Sanahan, M., Fielding, A., Tagliazucchi, E., Chialvo, D. E., y Nutt, D. (2014). The entropic brain: a theory of conscious states informed by neuroimaging research with psychedelic drugs. *Frontiers in Human Neuroscience, 8,* 20.

Carhart-Harris, R. L., Leech, R., Williams, T. M., Erritzoe, D., Abbasi, N., Bargiotas, T., Hobden, P., Sharp, D. J., Evans, J., Fielding, A., Wise, R. G., y Nutt, D. (2012). Implications for psychedelic-assisted psychotherapy: functional magnetic resonance imaging study with psilocybin. *The British Journal of Psychiatry, 200,* 238-244.

Carhart-Harris, R. L., Roseman, L., Bolstridge, M., Dematriou, L., Pannekoek, N. J., Wall, M. B., Tanner, M., Kaelen, M., McGonigle, J., Murphy, K., Leech, R., Curran, H. V., Nutt, D. J. (2017). Psilocybin for treatment-resistant depression: fMRI-measured brain mechanisms. *Scientific Reports, 7,* 1317.

Carhart-Harris, R. L., Roseman, L., Heijen, E., Erritzoe, D., Watts, R., Branchi, I., y Kaelen, M. (2018). Psychedelics and the essential importance of context. *Journal of Psychopharmacology, 32*(7), 725-731.

Carhart-Harris, R. L., Mayberg, H. S., Malizia, A. L., y Nutt, D. (2008). Mourning and melancholia revisited: correspondences between principles of Freudian metapsychology and empirical findings in neuropsychiatry. *Annals of General Psychiatry, 7,* 9.

Carrillo, F., Sigman, M., Fernández-Slezak, D., Ashton, P., Fitzgerald, L., Stroud, J., Nutt, D. J., Carhart-Harris, R. L. (2018). Natural speech algorithm applied to baseline interview data can predict wich patients will respond to psilocybin for treatment-resistant depressions. *Journal of Affective Disorders, 230,* 84-86.

Castaneda, C. (2017). *Las enseñanzas de don Juan.* México DF, México: Fondo de Cultura Económica.

Castaneda, C. (2018). *Viaje a Ixtlán*. México DF, México: Fondo de Cultura Económica.

Chabrol, H., y Raynal, P. (2018). The healthy side of positive schizotypy may reflect positive self-report biases. *The International Journal of Psychology and Psychological Therapy*, 18, 55-64.

Chapman, L. J., Chapman, J. P., Kwapil, T. R., Eckblad, M., y Zinser, M. C. (1994). Putatively psychosis-prone subjects 10 years later. *Journal of Abnormal Psychology*, .103(2), 171-183.

Chwelos N., Blewett D. C., Smith C., y Hoffer, A. (1959). Use of d-lysergic diethylamide in the treatment of alcoholism. *Quarterly Journal of Studies of Alcohol*, 20, 577-590.

Cohen, L. (2006). *Book of Longing*. Ontario, Canadá: McClelland & Stewart.

Cohen, S. (1960). Lysergic acid diethylamide: side effects and complications. *Journal of Nervous and Mental Disease*, 130(1), 30-40.

Cohen, S. (1966). A classification of LSD complications. *Psychosomatics*, 7, 182-186.

Cohen, S. (1985). LSD: The varieties of psychotic experience. *Journal of Psychoactive Drugs*, 17(4), 291-296.

Cohen, S., y Ditman, K. S. (1962). Complications associated with lysergic acid diethylamide (LSD-25). *Journal of the American Medical Association*, 181(2), 161-162.

Cohen, S., y Ditman, K. S. (1963). Prolonged adverse reactions to lysergic acid diethylamide. *Archives of General Psychiatry*, 8, 475-480.

Colectivo Interzona (2006). *LSD*. Madrid, España: Amargord.

Connolly-Gibbons, M. B., Rothbard, A., Farris, K. D., Stirman, S. W., Thompson, S. M., Scott, K., Heintz, L. E., Gallop, E., y Crist-Cristoph, P. (2011). Changes in psychotherapy utilization among consumers of services for major depressive disorder in the community mental health system. *Administration and Policy in Mental Health*, 38(6), 495-503.

Dass, R. (1971). *Remember Be Here Now*. Nueva York, Estados Unidos: Hannuman Foundation.

de Shazer, S. (2010). *En un origen las palabras eran magia*. Barcelona, España: Gedisa.

de la Torre, R., Farré, M., Roset, P. N., Lopez, C. H., Mas, M., Ortuño, J., Menoyo, E., Pizarro, N., Segura, J., y Camí, J. (2000). Psychopharmacology of MDMA in humans. *Annals of the New York Academy of Sciences*, 941, 225-237.

Denson, R., y Sydiaha, D. (1970). A controlled study of LSD treatment in alcoholism and neurosis. *British Journal of Psychiatry*, 115, 443-5.

Denson, R. (1967). Dissociative delirium after treatment with lysergide. *Canadian Medical Association Journal*, 9, 1222-1224.

Doblin, R. (1991). Pahnke's "Good Friday Experiment": a long-term follow-up and methodological critique. *Journal of Transpersonal Psychology*, 2(1), 2-28.

dos Santos, R., Bouso, J. C., y Hallak, J. E. (2017). Ayahuasca, dimethyltrypt-amine, and psychosis: a systematic review of human studies. *Therapeutic Advances in Psychopharmacology,*. 7(4), 141-157.

dos Santos, R. G., Balthazar, F. M., Bouso, J. C., y Hallak, J. E. (2016). The current state of research on ayahuasca: a systematic review of human studies assessing psychiatric symptoms, neuropsychological functioning and neuro-imaging. *Journal of Psychopharmacology,* 30(12), 1230-1247.

dos Santos, R. G., Bouso, J. C. (2019). Translational evidence for ayahuasca as an antidepressant: what's next? *British Journal of Pharmacology,* 41(4), 275-276.

dos Santos, R. G., Bouso, J. C., Alcázar-Córcoles, M. A., y Hallak, J. E. (2018). Efficacy, tolerability, and safety of serotonergic psychedelics for the manage-ment of mood, anxiety, and substance-use disorders: a systematic review of systematic reviews. *Expert Review of Clinical Pharmacology,* 11(9), 898-902.

dos Santos, R. G., Bouso, J. C., y Hallak, J. E. (2019). Serotonergic hallucino-gens/psychedelics could be promising treatments for depressive and anxiety disorders in end-stage cancer. *BMC Psychiatry,* 19, 321.

Dyck, E. (2006). Hitting highs at rock bottom: LSD treatment for alcoholism, 1950-1970. *Social History of Medicine,* 19(2), 313-329.

Dyer, C. (2002). NHS settles claim of patients treated with LSD. *The BMJ,* 324, 501.

Eisner, B. (1997). Set, setting, and Matrix. *Journal of Psychoactive Drugs,* 29(2), 213-216.

Eisner, B. (2002). *Remembrances of LSD Therapy Past.* Santa Mónica, Estados Unidos: manuscrito sin publicar. Disponible en https://erowid.org/culture/characters/eisner_betty/remembrances_lsd_therapy.pdf

Eisner, B., y Cohen, S. (1958). Psychotherapy with lysergic acid diethylamide. *Journal of Nervous and Mental Disease,* 127, 528-539.

Erritzoe, D., Roseman, L., Nour, M. M., MacLean, K., Kaelen, M., Nutt, D. J., y Carhart-Harris, R. L. (2018). Effects of psilocybin therapy on personality structure. *Acta Psychiatrica Scandinavica,* 138(5), 368-378.

Erritzoe, D., Smith, J., Fisher, P. M., Carhart-Harris, R. L., Frokjaer, V. G., y Knudsen, G. M. (2019). Recreational use of psychedelics is associated with elevated personality trait openness: exploration of associations with brain se-rotonin markers. *Journal of Psychopharmacology,* 33(9), 1068-1075.

Eveloff, H. H. (1968). The LSD syndrome, a review. *California Medicine,* 109(5), 368-373.

Fadiman, J. (2001). *The psychedelic explorer's guide: safe, therapeutic and sa-cred journeys.* South Paris, Estados Unidos: Park Street Press.

Fericgla, J. M. (2005). *Epopteia: avanzar sin olvidar.* Barcelona, España: La Liebre de Marzo.

Fisch, R., Weakland, J. H., y Segal, L. (1984). *La táctica del cambio: cómo abre-viar la terapia.* Barcelona, España: Herder.

Fischer, R., Marks, P. A., Hill, R. M., y Rockey, M. A. (1968). Personality structure as the main determinant of drug induced (model) psychoses. *Nature, 218,* 296-298.

Fonseca-Pedrero, E., Lemos-Giráldez, S., Paino, M., Santarén-Rosell, M., Sierra-Baigrie, S., y Ordóñez-Camblor, N. (2011). Instrumentos de medida para la evaluación del fenotipo psicótico. *Papeles del Psicólogo,* 21(1), 129-151.

Frankl, V. E. (1991). *El hombre en busca de sentido.* Barcelona, España: Herder.

Franquesa, A., Sainz-Cort, A., Gandy, S., Soler, J., Alcázar-Córcoles, M. A., y Bouso, J. C. (2018). Psychological variable implied in the therapeutic effect of ayahuasca: a contextual approach. *Psychiatry Research, 264,* 334-339.

Frederking, W. (1955). Intoxicant drugs (mescaline and lysergic acid diethylamide) in psychotherapy. *Journal of Mental and Nervous Disease, 121,* 262-266.

Freud, S. (2001). *Obras completas.* Madrid, España: Biblioteca Nueva.

Fromm, E. (2004). *El miedo a la libertad.* Barcelona, España: Paidós.

Frost, S. B. (2001). S*oul Collage: an intuitive collage process for individuals and groups.* Santa Cruz, Estados Unidos: Hanford Mead Publishers.

Gable, R. S. (2007). Risk assessment of ritual use of oral dimethyltryptamine (DMT) and harmala alkaloids. *Addiction,* 102(1), 24-34.

Garcia-Romeu, A., Griffiths, R. R., y Johnson, M. W. (2015). Psilocybin-occasioned mystical experiences in the treatment of tobacco addiction. *Current Drug Abuse Reviews,* 7(3), 157-164.

Garcia-Romeu, A., y Richards, W. A. (2018). Current perspectives on psychedelic therapy: use of serotonergic hallucinogens in clinical interventions. *International Review of Psychiatry,* 30(4), 291-316.

Garfield, S. L., y Bergin, A. E. (Eds) (1986). *Handbook of Psychotherapy and Behavior Change.* Nueva York, Estados Unidos: Willey & Sons.

Garfield, S. L. (1998). *The Practice of Brief Psychotherapy.* Nueva York, Estados Unidos: Wiley & Sons.

Gasser, P. (1996). Psycholytic therapy with MDMA and LSD in Switzerland. *Newsletter of the Multidisciplinary Association for Psychedelic Studies,* 5(3), 3-7.

Gasser, P., Kirchner, K., y Passie, T. (2014). LSD-assisted psychotherapy for anxiety associated with a life-threatening disease: a qualitative study of acute and sustained subjective effects. *Journal of Psychopharmacology,* 29(1), 57-68.

Geraerts, E., Schooler, J.W., Merckelbach, H., Jelicie, M., Hauer, B. y Ambadar, Z. (2007). The reality of recovered memories. *Psychological Science* 18(7), 564-568.

Geert-Jörgensen, E., Hertz, M., Knudsen, K., y Kristensen, K. (1964). LSD-Treatment experience gained within a three-year-period. *Acta Psychiatrica Scandinavica,* (S180, 373-382.

Ginsberg, N. L. (2019). Can psychedelics play a role in making peace and healing cycles of trauma? Early reflections on interviews with palestinians and israelis drinking ayahuasca together. *MAPS Bulletin,* 29(3).

González, D., Cantillo, J., Pérez, I., Farré, M., Fielding, A., y Bouso, J. C. (2020). Therapeutic potential of ayahuasca in grief: a prospective observational study. *Psychopharmacology,* 237, 1171-1182.

González, D., Carvalho, M. C., Cantillo, J., Aixalà, M. B., y Farré, M. (2019). Potential use of ayahuasca in grief therapy. *Omega,* 79(3), 260-285.

Gouzoulis-Mayfrank, E., Heekeren, K., Thelen, B., Lindenblatt, H., Kovar, A. H., Sass, H., y Geyer, M. A. (1998). Effects of the hallucinogen psilocybin on habituation and prepulse inhibition of startle reflex in humans. *Behavioural Pharmacology,* 9(7), 561-566.

Gouzoulis-Mayfrank, E., Schreckenberger, M., Sabri, O., Arning, C., Thelen, B., Spitzer, M., Kovar, K. A., Hermle, L., Büll, U., y Sass, H. (1999). Neurometabolic effects of psilocybin, 3,4-methylenedioxyethylamphetamine (MDE) and d-methamphetamine in healthy volunteers: a double-blind, placebo-controlled PET study with [18F]FDG. *Neuropsychopharmacology,* 20(6), 565-581.

Greer, G. R., y Tolbert, R. (1998). A method of conducting therapeutic sessions with MDMA. *Journal of Psychoactive Drugs,* 30(4), 371-379.

Griffiths, R. R., Johnson, M. W., Carducci, M. A., Umbricht, A., Richards, W. A., Richards, B. S., Cosimano, M. P., y Klinedinst, M. A. (2016). Psilocybin produces substantial and sustained decreases in depression and anxiety in patients with life-threatening cancer: a randomized double-blind trial. *Journal of Psychopharmachology,* 30(12), 1181-1197.

Griffiths, R. R., Johnson, M. W., Richards, W. A., Richards, B. D., McCann, U., y Jesse, R. (2011). Psilocybin occasioned mystical-type experiences: immediate and persisting dose-related effects. *Psychopharmachology,* 218, 649-665.

Griffiths, R. R., Johsnon, M. W., Richards, W. A., Richards, B. D., Jesse, R., MacLean, K. A., Barret, F. S., Cosimano, M. P., y Klinedinst, M. A. (2017). Psilocybin-occasioned mystical-type experiences in combination with meditation and other spiritual practices produces enduring positive changes in psychological functioning and in trait measures of prosocial attitudes and behaviors. *Journal of Psychopharmacology,* 32(1), 49-69.

Griffiths, R. R., Richards, W. A., Johnson, M. W., McCann, U., y Jesse, R. (2008). Mystical-type experiences occasioned by psilocybin mediate the attribution of personal meaning and spiritual significance 14 months later. *Journal of Psychopharmachology,* 22(6), 621-632.

Griffiths, R. R., Richards, W. A., McCann, U., y Jesse, R. (2006). Psilocybin can occasion mystical-type experiences having substantial and sustained personal meaning and spiritual significance. *Psychopharmachology,* 187, 268-283.

Grimm, J., y Grimm, W. (1997). *Cuentos de siempre.* p.Madrid, España: Susaeta.

Grof, C., y Grof, S. (2001). *La tormentosa búsqueda del ser: una guía para el crecimiento personal a través de la emergencia espiritual.* Barcelona, España: La Liebre de Marzo.

Grof, C., Grof, S. (2010). *Holotropic Breathwork.* Nueva York, Estados Unidos: Excelsior Editions.

Grof, S. (1970). The use of LSD in psychotherapy. *Journal of Psychoactive Drugs*, 3(1), 52-62.

Grof, S. (1975). *Realms of the Human Unconscious*. Nueva York, Estados Unidos: Viking.

Grof, S. (1980). *LSD Psychotherapy*. Pomona, Estados Unidos: Hunter House.

Grof, S. (1985). *Beyond the Brain*. Albany, Estados Unidos: State University of New York.

Grof, S. (2002). *La psicología del futuro. Lecciones de la investigación moderna de la consciencia*. Barcelona, España: La Liebre de Marzo.

Grof, S. (2005). *Psicoterapia con LSD: el potencial curativo de la medicina psiquedélica*. Barcelona, España: La Liebre de Marzo.

Grof, S. (2006). *When the Impossible Happens*. Boulder, Estados Unidos: Sounds True.

Grof, S. (2019). *The Way of the Psychonaut: Encyclopedia for Inner Journeys Volume One*. Santa Cruz, Estados Unidos: MAPS.

Grof, S. (2019). *The Way of the Psychonaut: Encyclopedia for Inner Journeys Volume Two*. Santa Cruz, Estados Unidos: MAPS.

Grof, S. (1998) Ken Wilber's spectrum psychology: observations from clinical consciousness research. En D. Rothberg y S. Kelly (Eds.), *Ken Wilber in Dialogue: Conversations with Leading Transpersonal Thinkers*, (pp. 85-116). Wheaton, Estados Unidos: Quest Books.

Grof, S., Goodman, L. E., Richards, W. A., y Kurland, A. A. (1973). LSD-assisted psychotherapy in patients with terminal cancer. *International Pharmacopsychiatry*, 8, 129-144.

Grof, S., Soskin, R. A., Richards, W. A., y Kurland, A. A. (1973). DPT as an adjunct in psychotherapy of alcoholics. *International Pharmacopsychiatry*, 8, 104-115.

Gudjonsson, G.H. (1997). Accusations by addults of childhood sexual abuse: a survey of the members of the British False Memory Society (BFMS). *Applied Cognitive Psychology*. 11, 3-18.

Gurdjieff., G. I. (2001). *Relatos de Belcebú a su nieto*. Málaga, España: Editorial Sirio.

Haijen, E. C., Kaelen, M., Roseman, L., Timmermann, C., Russ, S., Nutt, S., Daws, R. E., Hampshire, A., Lorenz, R., y Carhart-Harris, R. L. (2018). Predicting responses to psychedelics: a prospective study. *Frontiers in Pharmacology, 9*, 897.

Haley, J. (2006). *Terapia de Ordalía: caminos inusuales para modificar la conducta*. Buenos Aires, Argentina: Amorrortu.

Hartogsohn, I. (2016). Set and setting, psychedelics and the placebo response: an extra-pharmacological perspective on psychopharmacology. *Journal of Psychopharmacology*, 30(12), 1259-1267.

Hartogsohn, I. (2017). Constructing drug effects: a history of set and setting. *Drug Science, Policy and Law*, 3(0), 1-17.

Hausner, M., y Doležal, V. (1966). Follow-up studies in group and individual LSD psychotherapy. *Activitas Nervosa Superior,* 8, 87-95.

Hemsley, D. R., y Ward, E. S. (1985). Individual differences in reaction to the abuse of LSD. *Personality and Individual Differences,*d 6(4), 515-517.

Hendricks, P. S., Johnson, M. W., y Griffiths, R. R. (2015). Psilocybin, psychological distress, and suicidality. *Journal of Psychopharmacology,* 29(9), 1041-1043.

Herbert, F. (1991). *Dune.* Barcelona, España: Acervo.

Heschel, A. J. (1951). *Man Is Not Alone: A Philosophy of Religion.* Nueva York, Estados Unidos: Farrar, Straus and Giroux.

Heschel, A. J. (1955). *God in Search of Man: A Philosophy of Judaism.* Nueva York, Estados Unidos: Farrar, Straus and Giroux.

Heschel, A. J. (1995). *Maimónides.* Barcelona, España: Atajos.

Heschel, A. J. (2005). *The Sabbath.* Nueva York, Estados Unidos: FSG Classics.

Hesse, H. (2016). *Demian.* Madrid, España: Alianza.

Hoffer, A. (1957). A review of the clinical effects of psychotomimetic agents. *Annals of the New York Academy of Sciences,* 66(3), 418-34.

Hoffer, A. (1965). D-lysergic acid diethylamide (LSD): a review of its present status. *Clinical Pharmacology & Therapeutics,* 6(2), 183-255.

Hoffer, A. (1966). Treatment of alcoholism using LSD as the main variable. *Prisma,* n. p.

Hoffer, A. (1967). A program for the treatment of alcoholism: LSD, malvaria and nicotinic acid. En H. Abramson (Ed.), *The Use of LSD in Psychotherapy and Alcoholism* (pp. 343-406). Indianapolis, Estados Unidos: Bobbs-Merrill6.

Hoffer, A. (1970). Treatment of alcoholism with psychedelic therapy. En B. Aaronson, y H. Osmond (Eds.)H, *Psychedelics, the Uses and Implications of Psychedelic Drugs.* Nueva York, Estados Unidos: Doubleday & Company.

Hoffer, A., y Osmond, H. (1967). *The Hallucinogens.* Nueva York, Estados Unidos: Academic Press.

Holzinger, R. (1964). LSD-25, a tool in psychotherapy. *The Journal of General Psychology,* 71(1), 9-20.

Hollister, L., Shelton, J., y Krieger, G. (1969). A controlled comparison of lysergic acid diethylamide (LSD) and dextroamphetamine in alcoholics. *American Journal of Psychiatry,* 125(10), 1352-1357.

Hopkins, J. (2008). Jung's warning against inflation. *Chung-Hwa Buddhist Journal,* 21, 159-174.

Huxley, A. (2007). *La isla.* Barcelona, España: Edhasa.

Huxley, A. (2014). *Las puertas de la percepción. Cielo e infierno.* Barcelona, España: Pocket Edhasa.

Janiger, O., y Dobkin de Rios, M. (1989). LSD and creativity. *Journal of Psychoactive Drugs,* 21(1), 129-134.

Jiménez-Garrido, D. F., Gómez-Sousa, M., Oña, G., dos Santos, R. G., Hallak, J. E., Alcázar-Córcoles, M. A., y Bouso, J. C. (2020). Effects of ayahuasca on mental health and quality of life in naïve users: a longitudinal and cross-sectional study combination. *Scientific Reports,* 10, 4075.

Jodorowsky, A. (2004). *Psicomagia*. Madrid, España: Siruela.

Johnsen, G. (1964). Three years' experience with the use of LSD as an aid in psychotherapy. *Psychiatrica Scandinavica,* 40(S180), 383-388.

Johnson, M. W, y Griffiths, R. R. (2017). Potential therapeutic effects of psilocybin. *Neurotherapeutics,* 14(3), 734-740.

Johnson, M. W., Garcia-Romeu, A., Cosimano, M. P., y Griffiths, R. R. (2014). Pilot study of the 5-HT2AR agonist psilocybin in the treatment of tobacco addiction. *Journal of Psychopharmachology,* 28(11), 983-992.

Johnson, M. W., Garcia-Romeu, A., y Griffiths, R. R. (2016). Long-term follow-up of psilocybin-facilitated smoking cessation. *The American Journal of Drug and Alcohol Abuse,* 43(1), 55-60.

Johnson, M. W., Hendricks, P. S., Barret, F. S., y Griffiths, R. R. (2018). Classic psychedelics: an integrative review of epidemiology, mystical experience, brain network function and therapeutics. *Pharmacology & Therapeutics,* 197, 83-102.

Johnson, M. W., Richards, W. A., y Griffiths, R. R. (2008). Human hallucinogen research: guidelines for safety. *Journal of Psychopharmacology,* 22(6), 603-620.

Johnson, M. W., Sewell, R. A., y Griffiths, R. R. (2012). Psilocybin dose-dependently causes delayed, transient headaches in healthy volunteers. *Drug and Alcohol Dependence,* 123, 123-140.

Jung, C. G. (1990). *Arquetipos e inconsciente colectivo*. Barcelona, España: Paidós.

Jung, C. G. (1995). *El hombre y sus símbolos*. Barcelona, España: Paidós.

Jung, C. G. (2001). *Recuerdos, sueños, pensamientos*. Barcelona, España: Seix Barral.

Jung, C. G. (2009). *Las relaciones entre el yo y el inconsciente*. Barcelona, España: Paidós.

Jung, C. G. (2010). *El libro rojo*. Buenos Aires, Argentina: Malba - Fundación Costantini.

Kaelen, M., Barret, F. S, Roseman, L., Lorenz, R., Family, N., Bolstridge, M., Curran, H. V., Fielding, A., Nutt, D. J., y Carhart-Harris, R. L. (2015). LSD enhances the emotional response to music. *Psychopharmacology,* 232(19), 3607-3614.

Kaelen, M., Giribaldi, B., Raine, J., Evans, L., Timmermann, C., Rodriguez, N., Roseman, L., Fielding, A., Nutt, D., y Carhart-Harris, R. L. (2018). The hidden therapist: evidence for a central role of music in psychedelic therapy. *Psychopharmacology,* 235(2), 505-519.

Kelso, P. (1999, 17 de noviembre). Patients sue over LSD treatment side effects. *The Guardian.* Recuperado de https://www.theguardian.com/uk/1999/nov/17/paulkelso

Kettner, H., Gandy, S., Haijen, E. C., Carhart-Harris, R. L. (2019). From egoism to ecoism: psychedelics increase nature relatedness in a state-mediated and context-dependent manner. *International Journal of Environmental Research and Public Health,* 16, 5147.

Kleber, H. D. (1967). Prolonged adverse reactions from unsupervised use of hallucinogenic drugs. *Journal of Nervous and Mental Disease, .*144(4), 308-319.

Kornfield, J. (1997). *Camino con corazón: una guía a través de los peligros y promesas de la vida espiritual.* Barcelona, España: La Liebre de Marzo.

Kornfield, J. (2001). *Después del éxtasis, la colada: cómo crece la sabiduría del corazón en la vía espiritual.* Barcelona, España: La Liebre de Marzo.

Koss, M. P. (1979). Length of psychotherapy for clients seen in private practice. *Journal of Consulting and Clinical Psychology,* 47(1), 210-212.

Krebs, T. S., y Johansen, P. O. (2012). Lysergic acid diethylamide (LSD) for alcoholism: meta-analysis of randomized controlled trials. *Journal of Psychopharmacology,* 26(7), 994-1002.

Kurland, A. A., Unger, S., Shaffer, J. W., y Savage, C. (1967). Psychedelic therapy utilizing LSD in the treatment of the alcoholic patient: a preliminary report. *American Journal of Psychiatry,* 123(10), 1202-1209.

Kurland, A. A., Grof, S., Pahnke, W. N., y Goodman, L. E. (1973). Psychedelic drug assisted psychotherapy in patients with terminal cancer. En I. K. Goldberg, *et al.* (Eds.), *Psychopharmacological Agents for the Terminally Ill and Bereaved.* Nueva York, Estados Unidos, y Londres, Reino Unido:. Columbia University Press.

Lammers, A. C. (2007). Jung and White and the God of terrible double aspect. *Journal of Analytical Psychology,* 52(3), 253-274.

Leuner, H. (1967). Present state of psycholytic therapy and its possibilities. En H. Abramson (Ed.), *The Use of LSD in Psychotherapy and Alcoholism* (pp. 101-116). Indianapolis, Estados Unidos: Bobbs-Merrill.

Leary, T., Metzner, R., y Alpert, R. (2007). *The Psychedelic Experience: A Manual Based on the Tibetan Book of the Dead.* Nueva York, Estados Unidos: Citadel Press Books.

Lebdev, A. V., Kaelen, M., Lövden, M., Nilsson, J., Fielding, A., Nutt, D. J., y Carhart-Harris, R. L. (2015). LSD-induced entropic brain activity predicts subsequent personality change. *Human Brain Mapping,* 37(9), 3203-3213.

Lebdev, A. V., Lövden, M., Rosenthal, G., Fielding, A., Nutt, D. J., y Carhart-Harris, R. L. (2015). Finding the self by losing the self: neural correlates of ego-dissolution under psilocybin. *Human Brain Mapping,* 36(8), 3137-3153.

Leggett, T. (1977). *The Tiger's Cave: Translation of Japanese Zen Texts.* Londres, Reino Unido: Routledge & Keagan Paul.

Levine, J., y Ludwig, A. (1965). Alterations in consciousness produced by combinations of LSD, hypnosis and psychotherapy. *Psychopharmacologia,* 7, 123-137.

Levine, J., y Ludwig, A. (1966). The hypnodelic treatment technique. *International Journal of Clinical and Experimental Hypnosis,* 14(3), 207-215.

Levine, J., Ludwig, A., y Lyle, W. (1963). The controlled psychedelic state. *American Journal of Clinical Hypnosis,* 6(2), 163-164.

Liechti, M. E., Baumann, A., Gamma, A., y Vollenweider, F. X. (2000). Acute psychological effects of 3,4-methylenedioxymethamphetamine (MDMA, "Ecstasy") are attenuated by the serotonin uptake inhibitor citalopram. *Neuropsychopharmacology, 22*(5), 513-521.

Lienert, G. A., y Netter, P. (1996). LSD response in Eysenckian trait types identified by polypredictive CFA. *Personality and Individual Differences, 21*(6), 845-859.

Ling, T. M., y Buckman, J. (1963). *Lysergic Acid (LSD 25) & Ritalin in the Treatment of Neurosis.* Londres, Reino Unido: The Lambarde Press.

Lovecraft, H. P. (2011). *Los mitos de Cthulhu: narraciones de horror cósmico.* Madrid, España: Anaya.

Ludwig, A., y Levine, J. (1965). A controlled comparison of five brief treatment techniques employing LSD, hypnosis and psychotherapy. *American Journal of Psychiatry, 19,* 417-435.

Ludwig, A., Levine, J., Stark, L., y Lazar, R. (1969). A clinical study of LSD treatment in alcoholism. *American Journal of Psychiatry, 126*(1), 59-69.

Ly, C., Greb, A. C., Cameron, L. P., Wong, J. M, Barragan, E. V., *et al.* (2018). Psychedelics promote structural and functional neural plasticity. *Cell Reports, 23*(11), 3170-3182.

Lyons, T., y Carhart-Harris, R. L. (2018). Increased nature relatedness and decreased authoritarian political views after psilocybin for treatment-resistant depression. *Journal of Psychopharmacology, 32*(7), 811-819.

Lyons, T., y Carhart-Harris, R. L. (2018). More realistic forecasting of future life events after psilocybin for treatment-resistant depression. *Frontiers in Psychology, 9,* 1721.

MacLean, J. R., MacDonald, D. C., Byrne, U. P., y Hubbard, A. M. (1961). The use of LSD-25 in the treatment of alcoholism and other psychiatric problems. *Quarterly Journal of Studies on Alcohol, 22,* 34-45.

MacLean, K. A., Johnson, M. W., y Griffiths, R. R. (2011). Mystical experiences occasioned by the hallucinogen psilocybin lead to increases in the personality domain of openness. *Journal of Psychopharmacology, 25*(11), 1453-1461.

MacLean, K. A., Johnson, M. W., Reissig, C. J., Prisinzano, T. E., y Griffiths, R. R. (2013). Dose-related effects of salvinorin A in humans: dissociative, hallucinogenic, and memory effects. *Psychopharmacology, 226,* 381-392.

Malleson, N. (1971). Acute adverse reactions to LSD in clinical and experimental use in the United Kingdom. *British Journal of Psychiatry, 118,* 229-230.

Mangini, M. (1998). Treatment of alcoholism using psychedelic drugs: a review of the program research. *Journal of Psychoactive Drugs, 30*(4), 381-418.

Martin, A. J. (1964). A case of early paranoiad psychosis treated by lysergic acid diethylamide (LSD). *Acta Psychotherapeutica et Psychosomatica, 12,* 119-130.

Martin, J. (1957). LSD (lysergic acid diethylamide) treatment of chronic psychoneurotic patients under day-hospital conditions. *International Journal of Social Psychiatry, 3*(3), 188-195.

Martin, J. (1964). A case of early paranoid psychosis treated by Lysergic Acid Diethylamide (LSD). *Acta Psychotherapeutica et Psychosomatica*, 12(2), 119-130.

Martínez-Hernáez, A. (2018). *Síntomas y pequeños mundos: un ensayo antropológico sobre el saber psiquiátrico y las aflicciones humanas.* Barcelona, España: Anthropos.

Mas, M., Farré, M., de la Torre, R., Roset, P. N., Ortuño, J., Segura, J., y Camí, J. (1999). Cardiovascular and neuroendocrine effects and pharmacokinetics of 3,4-methylenedioxymethamphetamine in humans. *Journal of Pharmacology and Experimental Therapeutics*, 290(1), 136-145.

Masters, R. A. (2010). *Spiritual Bypassing: When Spirituality Disconnects Us From What Really Matters.* Berkeley, Estados Unidos: North Atlantic Books.

McGlothlin, W., Cohen, S., y McGlothlin, M. S. (1970). Long lasting effects of LSD on normals. *Journal of Psychoactive Drugs*, 3(1), 20-31.

McNally, R. y Geraerts, E. (2009). A new solution to the recovered memory debate. *Perspectives on Psychological Science*. 4(2) 126-134.

Milanese, R., y Cagnoni, F. (2010). *Cambiar el pasado.* Barcelona, España: Herder.

Millière, R., Carhart-Harris, R. L., Roseman, L., Trautwein, F. M., y Berkovich, A. (2018). Psychedelics, meditation and self-consciousness. *Frontiers in Psychology*, 9, 1475.

Minuchin, S., y Fischman, C. (2004). *Técnicas de terapia familiar.* Buenos Aires, Argentina: Paidós.

Mishor, Z. (2016). *Digging the well deep: the Jewish "ultra-orthodox" relationship with the divine explored through the lifeworld of the Breslov Chasidic community in Safed* (Tesis doctoral) id. Universidad de Sydney, Sydney, Australia.

Mithoefer, M. (2013). *A Manual for MDMA-Assisted Psychohterapy in the Treatment of Posttraumatic Stress Disorder.* Santa Cruz (California), Estados Unidos: Multidisciplinary Association for Psychedelic Studies (MAPS). Recuperado de https://maps.org/research-archive/mdma/MDMA-Assisted-Psychotherapy-Treatment-Manual-Version7-19Aug15-FINAL.pdf

Mithoefer, M. C., Feduccia, A. A., Jerome, L., Mithoefer, A., Wagner, M., Walsh, Z., Hamilton, S., Yazar-Klosinski, B., Emerson, A., y Doblin, R. (2019). MDMA-assisted psychotherapy of PTSD: study design and rationale for the phase 3 trials based on pooled analysis of six phase 2 randomized controlled trials. *Psychopharmacology*, 236, 2735-2745.

Mithoefer, M. C., Mithoefer, A. T., Feduccia, A., Jerome, L., Wagner, M., Wymer, J., Holland, J., Hamilton, S., Yazar-Klosinski, B., Emerson, A., y Doblin, R. (2018). 3,4-methylenedioxymethamphetamine (MDMA)-assisted psychotherapy for post-traumatic stress disorder in military veterans, firefighters, and police officers: a randomized, double-blind, dose-response, phase 2 clinical trial. *Lancet Psychiatry*, 5(6), 486-497.

Mithoefer, M. C., Wagner, M. T., Mithoefer, A. T., Jerome, L., y Doblin, R. (2010). The safety and efficacy of ±3,4 methylenedioxymethamphetamine-assisted psychotherapy in subjects with chronic, treatment-resistant posttraumatic stress disorder: the first randomized controlled pilot study. *Journal of Psychopharmacology, 25*(4), 439-452.

Mithoefer, M. C., Wagner, M. T., Mithoefer, A. T., Jerome, L., Martin, S. F., Yazar-Klosinski, B., Michel, Y., Brewerton, T. D., y Doblin, R. (2013). Durability of improvement in post-traumatic stress disorder symptoms and absence of harmful effects or drug dependency after 3,4-methylenedioxyamphetamine-assisted psychotherapy: a prospective long-term follow-up study. *Journal of Psychopharmacology, 27*(1), 28-39.

Mohr, C., y Claridge, G. (2015). Schizotypy: do not worry, it is not all worrisome. *Schizophrenia Bulletin, 41*(2), 436-443.

Moore, M., y Alltounian, H. (1978). *Journeys into the Bright World.* Rockport (Massachusetts), Estados Unidos: Para Research.

Mudge, B. (2019). Investigating ayahuasca ceremonies as a candidate therapy for bipolar disorder. *Breaking Convention Conference.* Conferencia llevada a cabo en el congreson. Breaking Convention, Universidad de Greenwich, Greenwich, Reino Unido.

Naranjo, C. (1974). *The Healing Journey.* Nueva York, Estados Unidos: Pantheon Books.

Naranjo, C. (2016). *Exploraciones psiquedélicas.* Barcelona, España: La Llave.

Nardone, G. (2007). *Miedo, pánico, fobias.* Barcelona, España: Herder.

Nardone, G., y Balbi, E. (2009). *Surcar el mar sin que el cielo lo sepa.* Barcelona, España: Herder.

Nardone, G., Balbi, E., Vallarino, A., y Bartoletti, M. (2019). *Psicoterapia breve a largo plazo.* Barcelona, España: Herder.

Nardone, G., y Watzlawick, P. (Eds). (2003). *Terapia breve: filosofía y arte.* Barcelona, España: Herder.

Nardone, G., y Watzlawick, P. (1992). *El arte del cambio: trastornos fóbicos y obsesivos.* Barcelona, España: Herder.

Nelson, J. E. (2008). *Más allá de la dualidad.* Barcelona, España: La Liebre de Marzo.

Newman, L. S., y Baumeister, R. F. (1996). Toward an explanation of the UFO abduction phenomenon: hypnotic elaboration, extraterrestrial sadomasochism, and spurious memories. *Psychological Inquiry, 7*(2), 99-126.

Newton, M. (2009). *Memories of the Afterlife: A Life Between Lives. Stories of Personal Transformation.* Woodbury (Michigan), Estados Unidos: Llewellyn Worldwide.

Nichols, D. E. (2016). Psychedelics. *Pharmacological Reviews, 68,* 264-355.

Nielson, E. M., May, D. G., Forechimes, A. A., y Bogenschutz, M. P. (2018). The psychedelic debriefing in the alcohol dependence treatment: illustrating key change phenomena through qualitative content analysis of clinical sessions. *Frontiers in Pharmacology, 9*(132).

Noorani, T., Garcia-Romeu, A., Swift, T. C., Griffiths, R. R., y Johnson, M. W. (2018). Psychedelic therapy for smoking cessation: qualitative analysis of participant accounts. *Journal of Psychopharmacology, 32*(7), 756-769.

Nour, M. M., y Carhart-Harris, R. L. (2017). Psychedelics and the science of self-experience. *British Journal of Psychiatry*, 210, 177-179.

Nour, M. M., Evans, L., y Carhart-Harris, R. L. (2017). Psychedelics, personality and political perspectives. *Journal of Psychoactive Drugs*, 49(3), 182-191.

Nour, M. M., Evans, L., Nutt, D. J., y Carhart-Harris, R. L. (2016). Ego-dissolution and psychedelics: validation of the ego-dissolution inventory (EDI). *Frontiers in Human Neuroscience*, 10, 269.

O'Donohue, W. T., y Cucciare, M. A. (2008). *Terminating Psychotherapy: A Clinicians Guide*. Nueva York, Estados Unidos: Routledge.

O'Hanlon, W. H. (1993). *Raíces profundas*. Barcelona, España: Paidós.

Oehen, P., Traber, R., Widmer, V., y Schnyder, U. (2013). A randomized, controlled pilot study of MDMA (±3,4-methylenedioxymethamphetamine)-assisted psychotherapy for treatment of resistant, chronic post-traumatic stress disorder (PTSD). *Journal of Psychopharmacology*, 27(1), 40-52.

Ofshe, R., y Watters, E. (1994). *Making Monsters: False Memories, Psychotherapy and Sexual Hysteria*. Nueva York, Estados Unidos: Charles Scrinber's Sons.

Oña, G., y Bouso, J. C. (2018). Therapeutic potential of natural psychoactive drugs for central nervous system disorders: a perspective from polypharmacology. *Current Medicinal Chemistrym*, 28(1), 53-68.

Oña, G., y Bouso, J. C. (2020). Psychedelic drugs as a long-needed innovation in psychiatry. *Queios*. http://doi.org/10.32388/T3EM5E.2

Otgaar, H., Muris, P., Hoew, M.L. y Merckelbach, H. (2007). What drives false memories in psychopathology? A case for associative activation. *Clinical Psychological Science*. 2017 5(6), 1048-1069.

Oram, M. (2018). *The Trials of Psychedelic Therapy: LSD Psychotherapy in America*. Baltimore (Maryland), Estados Unidos: Johns Hopkins University Press.

Ortigo, K.M. (2021) *Beyond the Narrow Life: A Guide for Psychedelic Integration and Existential Exploration*. Synergetic Press.

Pahnke, W. (1969). The psychedelic mystical experience in the human encounter with death. *Harvard Theological Review*, 62, 1-21.

Pahnke, W., Kurland A., Unger, S., Savage, C., y Grof, S. (1970). The experimental use of psychedelic (LSD) psychotherapy. *JAMA*, 212(11), 1856-1863.

Pahnke, W. N. (1967). LSD and religious experience. En C. Richard et al. (Eds), *LSD, Man & Society*. Middletown (Connecticut), Estados Unidos: Wesleyan University Press.

Pahnke, W. N., Richards, W. A. (1966). Implications of LSD experimental mysticism. *Journal of Religion and Health*, 5, 175-208.

Palhano-Fontes, F., Andrade, K., Tofoli, L. F., Santos, A. A., Crippa, J. A., Hallak, J. E., Ribeiro, S., y de Araujo, D. B. (2015). The psychedelic state induced by ayahuasca modulates the activity and connectivity of the Default Mode Network. *PloS ONE*, 10(2), e0118143.

Passie, T. (1996). Hanscarl Leuner, pioneer of hallucinogen research and psycholytic therapy. *MAPS Newsletter*, 7(1), 46-49.

Passie, T. (1997). *Psycholytic and Psychedelic Therapy Research 1921-1995.* Hannover, Alemania: Laurentious Publishers..

Paulhus, D. L., y Williams, K. M. (2002). The dark triad of personality: narcissism, machiavelism, and psychopathy. *Journal of Research in Personality, 39,* 556-563.

Pinkola-Estés, C. (2008). *Mujeres que corren con lobos.* Barcelona, España: Ediciones B.

Pinkola-Estés, C. (2003). *El jardinero fiel.* Barcelona, España: Ediciones B.

Phillips, E. L. (2014). *Psychotherapy Revised: New Frontiers in Research and Practice.* Nueva York, Estados Unidos: Psychology Press.

Pollan, M. (2018). *How to Change Your Mind.* Nueva York, Estados Unidos: Penguin Press.

Rhead, J. C. (1977). The use of psychedelic drugs in the treatment of severely disturbed children: a review. *Journal of Psychedelic Drugs, 9*(2), 93-101.

Rhead, J. C., Soskin, R. A., Turel, I., Richards, W. A. Yensen, R., Kurland, A. A., y Ota, K. Y. (1977). Psychedelic drug (DPT) assisted psychotherapy with alcoholics: a controlled study. *Journal of Psychoactive Drugs, 9*(4), 287-300.

Richards, W. A. (2015). *Sacred Knowledge: Pyshcedelics and Religious Experiences.* Nueva York, Estados Unidos: Columbia University Press.

Richards, W. A., Rhead, J., Dileo, F., Dileo, F. B., y Kurland, A. A. (1977). The peak experience variable in DPT-assisted psychotherapy with cancer patients. *Journal of Psychoactive Drugs, 9*(1), 1-10.

Richards, W. A., Rhead, J. C., Grof, S., Goodman, L. E., DiLeo, F., y Rush, L. (1979). DPT as an adjunct in brief psychotherapy with cancer patients. *Omega,* 10(1), 9-26.

Rock, A. J., Abbot, G. R., Childargushi, H., y Kiehne, M. L. (2008). The effect of shamanic-like stimulus conditions and the cognitive-perceptual factor of schizotypy on phenomenology. *North American Journal of Psychology,* 10(1), 79-98.

Rojas-Bermúdez, J. G. (1960). Tratamiento combinado de psicoanálisis y LSD 25 en niños psicóticos. *Acta Neuropsiquiátrica Argentina,* 6, 497-500.

Roquet, S., y Favreau, P. (1981). *Los alucinógenos: de la concepción indígena a una nueva psicoterapia.* México D. F., México: Prisma.

Roseman, L., Demetriou, L., Wall, M. B., Nutt, D. J., y Carhart-Harris, R. L. (2017). Increased amygdala responses to emotional faces after psilocybin for treatment-resistant depression. *Neuropharmacology,* 142, 263-269.

Roseman, L., Ginsberg, N. L., y Saca, A. (2019). Palestinians, Israelis, and ayahuasca: can psychedelic medicines promote reconciliation? En ICEERS, *III World Ayahuasca Conference.* 9Conferencia llevada a cabo en Girona, España.

Roseman, L., Nutt, D. J., Carhart-Harris, R. L. (2018). Quality of acute psychedelic experience predicts therapeutic efficacy of psilocybin for treatment-resistant depression. *Frontiers in Pharmacology,* 8, 974.

Rosen, S. (2009). *Mi voz irá contigo: los cuentos didácticos de Milton H. Erickson.* Barcelona, España: Paidós.

Rosenthal, S. H. (1964). Persistent hallucinosis following repeated administration of hallucinogenic drugs. *American Journal of Psychiatry,* 121(3), 238-244.

Roth, G. (1989). *Maps to Ecstasy.* Novato (California), Estados Unidos: New World Library.

Ruse, J. M., Halpern, J. H., Jerome, I., Mithoefer, M., y Doblin, R. (2014). *Treatment Manual for MDMA-Assisted Psychotherapy for Anxiety Disorder Due to a General Medical Condition in Subjects with Advanced-Stage Cancer.* San José (California), Estados Unidos: Multidisciplinary Association for Psychedelic Studies (MAPS).

Salinger, J. D. (2010). *El guardián entre el centeno.* Madrid, España: Alianza Editorial.

Salinger, J. D. (2004). *Franny y Zooey.* Barcelona, España: Edhasa.

Sandison, R. A. (1954). Psychological aspects of the LSD treatment of the neuroses. *Journal of Mental Science,* 100(419), 508-515.

Sandison, R. A. (1956). Clinical uses of lysergic acid diethylamide. En L. Cholden (Ed.), *Lysergic Acid Diethylamide and Mescaline in Experimental Psychiatry.* Nueva York, Estados Unidos, y Londres, Reino Unido: Grune & Stratton.

Sandison, R. A. (1959). The role of psychotropic drugs in group therapy. *Bulletin of the World Health Organization,* 21, 505-515.

Sandison, R.A. 1959. The role of psychotropic drugs in individual therapy. *Bulletin of the World Health Organization.* 21,495-503

Sandison, R. A. (1966). Lysergic acid diethylamide. *British Medical Journal,* 2, 48-49.

Sandison, R. A. (2005). A role for psychedelics in psychiatry? *British Journal of Psychiatry,* 187, 483-484.

Sandison, R. A., Spencer, A. M., y Whitelaw, J. D. (1954). The therapeutic value of lysergic acid diethylamide in mental illness. *British Journal of Psychiatry,* 100, 491-507.

Sandison, R. A., y Whitelaw, J. D. A. (1957). Further studies in the therapeutic value of lysergic acid diethylamide in mental illness. *Journal of Mental Science,* 103(431), 322-343.

Sarret, M., Cheek, F., y Osmond, H. (1966). Reports of wives of alcoholics of effects of LSD-25 treatment of their husbands. *Archives of General Psychiatry,* 14(2), 171-178.

Savage, C. (1957). The resolution and subsequent remobilization of resistance by LSD in psychotherapy. *Journal of Nervous and Mental Disease,* 125(3), 434-437.

Savage, C., y McCabe, L. (1973). Residential psychedelic (LSD) therapy for the narcotic addict. *Archives of General Psychiatry,* 28, 808-814.

Schlamm, L. (2014). Jung's definition of inflation. En D. A. Leeming (Ed.), *Encyclopedia of Psychology and Religion.* Boston (Massachusetts), Estados Unidos: Springer.

Schmid, Y., y Liechti, M. E. (2018). Long-lasting subjective effects of LSD in normal subjects. *Psychopharmacology,* 235, 535-545.

Schofield, K., y Claridge, G. (2007). Paranormal experiences and mental health: schizotypy as an underlying factor. *Personality and Individual Differences,* 43, 1908-1916.

Scott, R. D. (1950). The psychology of insulin coma treatment. *British Journal of Medical Psychology,* 23(1-2), 15-44.

Sessa, B. (2007). From sacred plants to psychotherapy: the history and re-emergence of psychedelics in medicine. European Neuropsychopharmacology., 17.

Sessa, B. (2016). The history of psychedelics in medicine. En M. von Heyden, *et al.* (Eds.), *Handbuch Psychoaktive Substanzen.* Berlín, Alemania: Springer Berlin Heidelberg.

Shannon, B. (2003). *Antipodes of the Mind.* Oxford, Reino Unido: Oxford University Press.

Shaw, J. (2016). *The Memory Illusion: Remembering, Forgetting and the Science of False Memory.* Nueva York, Estados Unidos: Random House.

Sherwood, J. N., Stolaroff, M. J., y Harman, W. W. (1962). The psychedelic experience, a new concept in psychotherapy. *Journal of Neuropsychiatry,* 4, 69-80.

Shick, J. F., y Smith, D. (1970). Analysis of the LSD flashback. *Journal of Psychoactive Drugs,* 3(1), 13-19.

Shulgin, A. (1995). The new psychotherapy: MDMA and the Shadow. *Eleusis,* 3, 3-11.

Smart, R. G., Storm, T., Baker E. F., y Solursh, L. (Eds.). (1969). *Lysergic Acid Diethylamide (LSD) in the Treatment of Alcoholism: An Investigation of its Effects on Drinking Behavior, Personality Structure and Social Functioning.* Toronto, Canadá: University of Toronto Press.

Smart, R. G., Storm, T., Baker, E. F., y Solursh, L. (1966). A controlled trial of lysergide in the treatment of alcoholism: the effects on drinking behaviour. *Quarterly Journal of Studies of Alcohol,* 27, 469-82.

Smart, R. G., y Bateman, K. (1967). Unfavourable reactions to LSD: a review and analysis of the available case reports. *Canadian Medical Association Journal,* 97, 1214-1221.

Smith, C. M. (1959). Some reflections on the possible therapeutic effects of the hallucinogens. With special reference to alcoholism. *Quarterly Journal of Studies on Alcohol,* 20, 292-301.

Soskin, R. A., Grof, S., y Richards, W. A. (1973). Low doses of dipropyltriptamine in psychotherapy. *Archives of General Psychiatry,* 28, 817-821.

Speth, J., Speth, C., Kaelen, M., Schloerscheidt, A. M., Fielding, A., Nutt, D. J., y Carhart-Harris, R. L. (2016). Decreased mental time travel to the past correlates with default-mode network disintegration under lysergic acid diethylamide. *Journal of Psychopharmacology,* 30(4), 344-353.

Steinsaltz, A. (1989). *The Sustaining Utterance: Discourses on Chasidic Thought.* Northvale (Nueva Jersey), Estados Unidos: Jason Aronson.

Stolaroff, M. (1993). Using psychedelics wisely. *Gnosis,* 26.

Stolaroff, M. J. (1999). Are psychedelics useful in the practice of Buddhism? *Journal of Humanistic Psychology,* 39(1), 60-80.

Stolaroff, M. J. (2004). *The Secret Chief Revealed*. Sarasota (Florida), Estados Unidos: MAPS.

Stoll, A. W. (1947). Lysersäure-diäthylamid, ein Phantastikum aus der Mutterkorngruppe. *Schweizer Archiv für Neurologie und Psychiatrie*, 60, 279-323.

Strassman, R. (1984). Adverse reactions to psychedelic drugs. A review of the literature. *The Journal of nervous and mental diseases*. 172, 577-95.

Strassmann, R. (2001). *DMT: The Spirit Molecule: A Doctor's Revolutionary Research Into the Biology of Near-Death and Mystical Experiencess*. Paris (Maine), Estados Unidos: Park Street Press.

Stroud, J. B., Freeman, T. P., Leech, R., Hindocha, C., Lawn, W., Nutt, D. J., Curran, H. V., y Carhart-Harris, R. L. (2017). Psilocybin with psychological support improves emotional face recognition in treatment-resistant depression. *Psychopharmacology*, 235(2), 459-466.

Studerus, E., Gamma, A., Kometer, M., y Vollenweider, F.X. (2012). Prediction of psilocybin response in healthy volunteers. *Journal of Psychopharmacology*, 25(11), 1434-1452.

Studerus, E., Kometer, M., Hasler, F., y Vollenweider, F. X. (2011). Acute, subacute and long-term subjective effects of psilocybin in healthy humans: a pooled analysis of experimental studies. *PLoS ONE*, 7(2), e30800.

Styk, J., y Styk, S. (1999). A review of clinical issues in MDMA-assisted psychotherapy. En MAPS. *Conference on the Clinical Utility of MDMA and MDE*. Conferencia llevada a cabo en Dead Sea, Israel.

Szygeti, B., Kartner, L., Blemings, A., Rosas, F., Fielding, A., Nutt, D., Carhart-Harris y R., Erritzoe, D. (2021). Self-blinding citizen science to explore psychedelic microdosing. *eLife*:10:e52878.

Tagliazicchi, E., Roseman, L., Kaelen, M., *et al.* (2016). Increased global functional connectivity correlates with LSD-induced ego dissolution. *Current Biology*, 26, 1-8.

Terrill, J., Savage, C. y Jackson, D.D. (1960). *LSD, Transcendence, and the New Beginning*. Editado en versión digital por MAPS.

Timmermann, C., Roseman, L., Williams, L., Erritzoe, D., *et al.* (2018). DMT models the near-death experience. *Frontiers in Psychology*, 15(9), 1424.

Tucci, G. (1974). *Teoría y práctica del mandala*. Barcelona, España: Seix Barral.

Ungerleider, J. T., Fischer, D. D., y Fuller, M. (1966). The dangers of LSD. *JAMA*, 197(6), 389-392.

Ungerleider, J. T., Fischer, D. D., Fuller, M., y Caldwell, A. (1968). The "bad trip": etiology of the adverse LSD reaction. *American Journal of Psychiatry*, 124(11), 1483-1490..

Ungerleider, J. T., y Fisher, D. D. (1967). The problems of LSD-25 and emotional disorder. *California Medicine*, 106(1), 49-55.

Van der Kolk, B. (2020). *El cuerpo lleva la cuenta: cerebro, mente y cuerpo en la superación del trauma*. Sitges, España: Eleftheria.

Van Dusen, W. (1961). LSD and the enlightment of zen. *Psychologia*, 4, 11-16.

Vangaard, T. (1964). Indications and counter-indications for LSD treatment: observations at Powick Hospital, England. *Acta Psychiatrica Scandinavica*, 40(4), 427-437.

Vollenweider, F., Scherpenhuyzen-Vollenweider, M. F., Bäbler, A., Vogel, H., y Hell, D. (1998). Psilocybin induces schizophrenia-like psychosis in humans via a serotonin-2 agonist action. *NeuroReport, 9*(17), 3897-3902.

Wagner, A. C., Mithoefer, M. C., Mithoefer, A. T., y Monson, C. M. (2019). Combining cognitive-behavioral cojoint therapy for PTSD with 3,4-methylendioxymethamphetamine (MDMA): a case example. *Journal of Psychoactive Drugs, 51*(2), 166-173.

Wagner, M. T., Mithoefer, M. C., Mithoefer, A. T., MacAulay, R. K., Jerome, L., Yazar-Klosinski, B., y Doblin, R. (2017). Therapeutic effect of increased openness: investigating mechanisms of action in MDMA-assisted psychotherapy. *Journal of Psychopharmacology, 31*(18), 967-974.

Walsh, Z., y Thiessen, M. S. (2018). Psychedelic and the new behaviourism: considering the integration of third-wave behaviour therapies with psychedelic-assisted therapy. *International Review of Psychiatry, 30*(4), 343-349.

Watts, A. (1987). *La sabiduría de la inseguridad*. Barcelona, España: Kairós.

Watzlawick, P. (Ed.). (2015). *La realidad inventada. ¿Cómo sabemos lo que creemos saber?* Barcelona, España: Gedisa.

Watzlawick, P. (1980). *El lenguaje del cambio. Técnica de comunicación terapéutica*. Barcelona, España: Herder.

Watzlawick, P. (1984). *El arte de amargarse la vida*. Barcelona, España: Herder.

Watzlawick, P. (2012). *El lenguaje del cambio: técnica de comunicación terapéutica*. Barcelona, España: Herder.

Watzlawick, P. (2019). *¿Es real la realidad?* Confusión, desinformación, comunicación. Barcelona, España: Herder.

Watzlawick, P., Bavelas, J. B., y Jackson, D. D. (1981). *Teoría de la comunicación humana. Interacciones, patologías y paradojas*. Barcelona, España: Herder.

Watzlawick, P., Weakland, J. H., y Fisch, R. (1976). *Cambio: formación y solución de los problemas humanos*. Barcelona, España: Herder.

Widiger, T. A., y Smith, G. T. (2008). Personality and psychopathology. En O. P. John, R. W. Robins, y L. A. Pervin (Eds.), *Handbook of Personality: Theory and Research* (pp. 743-769). Nueva York, Estados Unidos: Guilford Press.

Wilber, K. (1990). *Psicología integral*. Barcelona, España: Kairós.

Wilber, K. (2008). *El proyecto Atman: una visión transpersonal del desarrollo humano*. Barcelona, España: Kairós.

Woolfe, R., Dryen, W., y Strawridge, S. (2003). *Handbook of Counseling Psychology*. Nueva York, Estados Unidos: SAGE.

Zweig, C., y Abrams, J. (1993). *Encuentro con la sombra*. Barcelona, España: Kairós.

ALPHABETICAL INDEX